1 MONTH OF FREE READING

at
www.ForgottenBooks.com

By purchasing this book you are eligible for one month membership to ForgottenBooks.com, giving you unlimited access to our entire collection of over 700,000 titles via our web site and mobile apps.

To claim your free month visit:
www.forgottenbooks.com/free597908

* Offer is valid for 45 days from date of purchase. Terms and conditions apply.

English
Français
Deutsche
Italiano
Español
Português

www.forgottenbooks.com

Mythology Photography **Fiction** Fishing Christianity **Art** Cooking Essays Buddhism Freemasonry Medicine **Biology** Music **Ancient Egypt** Evolution Carpentry Physics Dance Geology **Mathematics** Fitness Shakespeare **Folklore** Yoga Marketing **Confidence** Immortality Biographies Poetry **Psychology** Witchcraft Electronics Chemistry History **Law** Accounting **Philosophy** Anthropology Alchemy Drama Quantum Mechanics Atheism Sexual Health **Ancient History Entrepreneurship** Languages Sport Paleontology Needlework Islam **Metaphysics** Investment Archaeology Parenting Statistics Criminology **Motivational**

797,885 Books
are available to read at

Forgotten Books

www.ForgottenBooks.com

Forgotten Books' App
Available for mobile, tablet & eReader

ISBN 978-1-333-14652-8
PIBN 10597908

This book is a reproduction of an important historical work. Forgotten Books uses state-of-the-art technology to digitally reconstruct the work, preserving the original format whilst repairing imperfections present in the aged copy. In rare cases, an imperfection in the original, such as a blemish or missing page, may be replicated in our edition. We do, however, repair the vast majority of imperfections successfully; any imperfections that remain are intentionally left to preserve the state of such historical works.

Forgotten Books is a registered trademark of FB &c Ltd.
Copyright © 2015 FB &c Ltd.
FB &c Ltd, Dalton House, 60 Windsor Avenue, London, SW19 2RR.
Company number 08720141. Registered in England and Wales.

For support please visit www.forgottenbooks.com

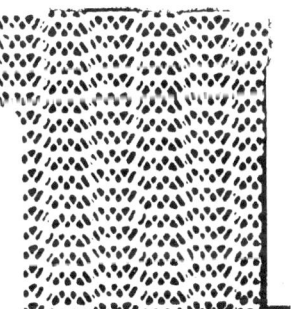

se *and* Fall
of
in Illinois

by

AWLINGS, M. S., M. D.

collaboration with

A. EVANS, M. D., D. P. H.,
D KOEHLER, M. D., and
K. RICHARDSON, A. B.

———

PUBLISHED BY
TMENT OF PUBLIC HEALTH
N OF ITS FIFTIETH ANNIVERSARY
1927

GRAPHS DEVELOPED AND DRAWN
ND WITH PICTURE REPRODUCTIONS
SONS ASSOCIATED IN ONE WAY
THER WITH THE STORY.

SCHNEPP & BARNES, PRINTERS
SPRINGFIELD, ILL.
1927

PREFACE.

Profound changes have taken place during the last one hundred years in all departments of civilization but in none has the transformation been more fundamental nor more nobly crowned with advantage than in the field of health. At the beginning of this period man was little short of a helpless victim to infectious diseases that frequently swept over whole cities and nations in great lethal waves. Today he is able to exercise a marvelous control over the factors involved in health, adding strength to his years and years to his life.

The need for genuine progress in the conquest against disease was essential to the healthy continuity of human life amid the growing complexity of modern existence. Swifter means of communication have brought all men closer together for good or for evil. Disease respects neither wealth nor social rank, becoming a universal hazard when the human carrier of infection may be thrust across a continent between the rising and setting of the sun. When automotive power unites a nation into one great social and commercial commingling, obliterating political boundary lines and increasing enormously the range of individual contact between fellow beings, there can be no compromise with communicable disease. When days have been reduced to hours and hours to minutes in measuring the travel distance between points man has no choice but to conquer or succumb to the agents of epidemic infections. That he has subdued one after another of these ancient enemies is a signal manifestation of man's superiority over all living things and a splendid evidence that humanity is sweeping onward toward that great millennium which has lived in the aspirations of men since the beginning of time.

The story of how man has triumphed over disease in Illinois ought therefore to be of common interest to every person in the State. Life is as dear to the beggar on the street as it is to the lord in the mansion. Factors that tend to preserve or destroy health in the one operate toward like ends in the other. Both may rejoice in the advancements of medical and sanitary science which have made possible the remarkable improvement in health conditions that are described in this volume. Both have inherited a score of years from the wisdom that led sanitarians and doctors to apply their knowledge for the public good.

That the State created, developed and maintains an official agency charged with the duty and responsibility of participating in a movement so pregnant with possibilities for individual and public benefit ought to stimulate pride and confidence in the character of our government.

It is the duty of State officers to record the important features of the public health movement as has been done in this volume. It is the privilege of individuals to read and study these records. Both processes will prove helpful in guiding future activities to even greater triumphs than the past has witnessed over the enemies of human health.

LEN SMALL.

FOREWORD.

The title of this volume expresses a very gratifying actuality with greater approximation to the whole truth than might be surmised at first blush. It may not be universally known that since the coming of white men into Illinois a considerable number of diseases have been kindled, flamed into consuming plagues and were then extinguished altogether or have left only the dying embers of what may soon be transformed into the ashes of history. Cholera, malaria, smallpox, yellow fever, typhoid fever, dysentery and perhaps diphtheria may be included in that group. Tuberculosis, the diarrheal infections and scarlet fever were once far more deadly and widespread than they are now.

These and other diseases were not introduced into Illinois in keeping with some predestined program prescribed by fate to pursue the particular group of people who elected to make the prairies their home. On the contrary they came when conditions created by man himself invited, and they began to disappear when conditions created by man began to be intolerable for them. Most of the conditions which invited disease were in that respect created unconsciously. Nearly all of the factors which have influenced the waning strength of infections were consciously and deliberately employed to improve health conditions.

Thus we have two very definite periods in the health history of Illinois. One embraces the time when communicable diseases played havoc with the public, finding nothing to check them in their gruesome business but the natural limitations of time, space and susceptible material. The other includes the years since the public first began to employ scientific methods of prevention which have played havoc with disease.

Accordingly this volume is divided into two parts. The first relates the story of health conditions from the very earliest times, so far as records permit, down to 1877 when the State began its attack upon disease with the organization of the State Board of Health. The second relates to the fifty year period between 1877 and 1927 during which time a strong public health service developed with telling results.

There was no purpose to make this an exhaustive account of all the factors involved in the field of health improvement. Such an ambitious undertaking would lead into the paths of medicine, bacteriology, chemistry, agriculture, economics, engineering, etc. An effort has been made to trace the history of communicable diseases in broad outline and to describe the origin and development of organizations devoted entirely or in some significant and direct way to the promotion of public health. It is believed that some reference may be found in this volume to all important events bearing upon the subject of public health in the State, thus bringing together in one place many valuable records that were widely scattered before.

It was the original plan to include chapters relating to the organization and development of municipal boards and departments of health in the State. This scheme was abandoned at the last moment, after account had been written of events in several cities and some had been put into type, because of limited time and space. The hope now is that another volume will follow this one, providing space for a fuller story about local public health work than this volume could ever have accommodated.

Aside from the collaborating authors much credit for bringing this material together is due to Miss Clara Breen, whose untiring efforts in searching records, collecting photographs and cross checking source material and to Miss Elin Berg whose services in classifying the source material and managing the stenographic work have made the task easier. Credit is also due to the chiefs of the various divisions of the State Department of Public Health who furnished the records embraced in the account of the divisions and to Dr. Carl Black of Jacksonville who very generously supplied the plates of several photographs that would otherwise have been difficult to secure.

THE EDITOR.

CONTENTS.

PART ONE.

	PAGE
Preface by Governor Small	7
Foreword	9
Introduction	13
General Health History Prior to 1877	15
The Indian	15
The French Regime	22
The British Regime	26
The Spanish Influence	27
The American Regime	27
History of Certain Diseases Prior to 1877	35
Cholera, 43; Consumption, 60; Cynancie, 55; Diarrhoea and Dysentery, 83; Diphtheria, 55; Erysipelas, 50; Gonorrhea, 60; Malaria, 35; Measles, 54; Meningitis, 56; Milk Sickness, 66; Nursing Sore Mouth, 69; Ophthalmia-Epidemic, 57; Pneumonia and Influenza, 62; Puerperal Fever, 65; Scarlet Fever, 53; Smallpox, 49; Snake Bite, 47; Syphilis, 58; Tuberculosis, 60; Typhoid Fever, 69; Typhus Fever, 47; Yellow Fever, 46.	
Infant Mortality	86
Deaths of Children Under Five	88
Seasonal Distribution of Disease	89
Vital Statistics and Mortality from All Causes	96
Health in Some Cities Prior to 1877	101
Chicago	101
Springfield	115
Kaskaskia	116
Shawneetown	118
Vandalia	118

Part Two.

	PAGE
Public Health Administration	127
Genesis of Public Health Law	127
Development of State Health Service	133
State Health Machinery	136
Rauch Regime	139
Egan Regime	159
Drake Regime	174
Rawlings Regime	194
Intra-Departmental Organization	208
Enforcement of Medical Practice Act	273
Auxiliary Health Agencies	287
Health Conditions After 1877	304

    Cerebrospinal Fever, 376; Cholera, 320; Diarrhoeal Diseases, 377; Pneumonia, 382; Poliomyelitis, 380; Scarlet Fever, 348; Smallpox, 307; Tuberculosis, 361; Typhoid Fever, 338; Whooping Cough, 390; Yellow Fever, 327; Infant Mortality, 393.

Summary and Conclusion	396

INTRODUCTION.

According to tradition the first occupants of the Illinois territory were the mound builders.

They were followed by the Indians. Whence they came to the Illinois territory is a matter of surmise.

The rather accepted opinion is that the first Indian occupants of the territory came from the west. Tribes generally accepted as being of western origin occupied the region at the time when the pressure of white men in the country to the westward caused a migration bringing some more easterly tribes of Indians into conflict with the tribes of western origin.

At the time white men began coming into the territory the conflict between the eastern and western tribes had not ended. To the south of Illinois there lay a great hunting ground which served as a barrier against the southern Indians. From Pickett's History of Alabama we learn that one tribe migrated from Mexico north-eastward to the Illinois territory but they did not remain long. They soon moved southward across Kentucky and Tennessee, to come to rest in Alabama, and they never ventured north again.

If the Indians of the south had malaria and other fevers they had little opportunity to spread them in Illinois. If there was any transmission of disease from one Indian tribe to another such transfer was from east to west or west to east.

The first French and French-Canadians came into the territory in 1670. From 1670 to 1763, practically one hundred years, the so-called French period, the territory was occupied by Indians and French and half breeds in varying proportions.

The first French invaders were trappers. These were soon followed by missionaries. Next came the traders and finally the settlers. There was a moderate amount of inter-marriage between the French and the Indians. Most of the half breeds, many of whom remained in the territory after the Indians left, were the results of French and Indian unions.

The sources of information as to health conditions in the French period are few. The missionaries wrote voluminous reports, but they dealt with such subjects as religion, the geography of the countries, the routes of travel, the attitude of the Indians with almost no reference to health. The trappers did not write at all. A few of the traders wrote but they gave scant space to health.

In 1763 the French ceded the territory to the British who retained some control until Clark wrested it from them just prior to 1780. In the British period of less than seventeen years, the governing nation did little more than occupy the garrisoned forts with a few troops and promote intrigue with

INTRODUCTION

the Indians. The population during the British period were Indians, French and mixed breeds, a few American settlers and a few British settlers and a few troops. The British did not mate with the Indians as the French frequently did.

A small Spanish expedition crossed from Missouri to Saint Joseph, Michigan. This incident was too brief and inconsequential to be designated as a Spanish period.

In 1780, after Clark had captured the British fort in the southern end of the territory the American colonists began to settle the State especially the southern part thereof.

The Territorial period beginning in 1784, ran until the State was taken into the Union in 1818.

For the purposes of this history of the State as such, the years between 1810 and 1927, are divided into two periods. 1818 to 1877, fifty nine years, the period of invasion and spread of disease, and 1877—the year of the organization of the State Board of Health to 1927—fifty years—the period of the control of disease.

The first section of the book shows how the settlers and their descendants suffered from the hardships occasioned by disease. To combat this there was no state health department and no local health department capable of coping with situations, except in Chicago, and then not until the decade of the Civil War.

The number of physicians was not large and there were no hospitals outside the cities.

During the period a few diseases declined principally because the land was cleared and drained. Others became worse by reason of the increasing density of population.

The second section deals principally with the development of the State Department of Public Health. There are sections, however, which deal in a more fragmentary way, with some of the extra-governmental health agencies.

Since the State Board of Health licensed physicians and regulated the practice of medicine between 1877 and 1917, the control of medical practice is given some attention.

The second period, 1877 to 1927, is one in which disease has been gradually coming under control. This is particularly true of the diseases which prevail especially in summer, of the diarrheas and dysenteries of adults, the disorders of infancy and early childhood and particularly of the digestive disturbances of babies, the contagious and infectious diseases and a few others. The programs of health departments for the future contemplate control of many disorders now not under control, or even under fire, as well as the promotion of bodily growth and vigor. The title, "period of disease control" does not exactly fit the facts but the discrepancies are not of major importance.

GENERAL HEALTH HISTORY PRIOR TO 1877.

The Mound Builders.

The mound builders whoever they may have been were in Illinois before the Indians. The State abounds in mounds. Even in that day there seemed to have been some separateness between the inhabitants of the north end of the State and those of the south end, between whom there lay the neutral largely unoccupied prairie belt. The mounds of the north are of a different type of construction and had a different purpose. While there are some exceptions the rule is that the mounds of the north end of the State were ceremonial structures not used for burying or for utilitarian purposes, while most of those of the south end of the State were used for the latter purposes.

There is no proof that the mound builders passed on any diseases to the Indians or contributed in any way to the health history of Illinois. However, Zeuch[1] suggests that the mound builders were wiped out by pestilence. If so, the disease seems to have destroyed itself in destroying its host. An allusion to syphilis and the mound builders will be found in the section devoted to syphilis.

The Indians.

The opinion of the times is that the Indians came from Asia arriving on the northwest coast and gradually spreading southward and eastward. In their slow march across latitudes and longitudes, across climates and up and down elevations they acquired habits and customs, religious observances and diseases, disorders, health and ill health, strength and weaknesses that were more or less peculiar to them.

The Indians remained in Illinois for a century and a half after the white man invaded the State. They had their own villages and they did not often remain long in the white man's towns. The rule was that these villages were moved with great frequency though for many years there might be a village at a given location at some time during a part of each year. Seldom did a village remain constantly in one location.

Some white men lived among the Indians as captives and some as squaw men. They were responsible for large numbers of half breeds. The captives and squaw men frequently returned to live with the white men, but

---

[1] Zeuch (History of Medical Practice in Illinois, vol. 1, 1927. Lucius H. Zeuch).

(15)

their Indian wives and their mixed breed progeny did not always follow them in this move. When the Indians moved out of the State they took with them most of these half breeds.

During the more than one hundred years of contact in the district unquestionably the Indian in some measure modified the health of the white man and the white man modified that of the Indian but the influence was surprisingly small.

The Indian constitution was the result of many influences. Because of his lack of thrift, foresight and energy he was subjected to periodic lean years. In consequence of his life he had a capacity for great and sustained effort and an ability to withstand hunger. He had a fine stature on the average and great physical vigor. To those diseases which threatened him in the wild state he had a fine resistance and yet he was short lived. He died at an average early age and there were few children in the average Indian family. It is not easy to understand why so fine a constitution went hand in hand with a short life span and small families with children spaced far apart. History would indicate that wars and famines furnished the explanation.

The history of Indian medicine contributes little to the answer. To begin with the Indians had no literature, medical or other. They had a very elaborate medical machinery, but it was largely religious and political and it was medical in little more than name. Though medical in name, it was magic in fact. Even that part called medical was principally magic.

Beyond a slight knowledge of medical plants and medicinal waters the Indian medicine men had no medical knowledge. They knew almost no sanitary science. The tribe knew enough to move a camp when the soil became badly fouled but there is nothing to show that the medicine men knew any more about this than the others did.

As to sanitary science in general the Indians never knew a tithe of what the Jews did in the time of Moses.

Though they had no books and no written history, they did have legends of outstanding occurrences. Had there been great epidemic disease waves among them some tradition of these must have survived. It is altogether possible that the scanty population, the short life and the small family were qualities for which wars and famines were principally responsible.

This explanation does not undermine our regard for the Indian constitution, but the latter is of small consequence since the Indians removed from the State leaving behind as progenitors of future citizens not very many mixed breeds and still fewer straight bloods.

Dr. Ales Hrdlicka.

Hrdlička[2] says, "The traditions of the Indians, the existence among them of elaborate healing rites of undoubtedly ancient origin, their plant lore in which curative agent's properties are attributed to many vegetable substances and the presence among them of a numerous class of professed healers, honored, feared, and usually well paid would seem to indicate that diseases were not rare, but actual knowledge and even tradition as to their nature are wanting. The condition of the skeletal remains, the testimony of early observers and the present state of some of the tribes in this regard warrant the conclusion that on the whole the Indian race was a comparatively healthy one. It was probably spared at least some of the epidemics and diseases of the old world such as smallpox, rachitis, while other scourges such as tuberculosis, syphilis (pre-Columbian) typhus, cholera, scarlet fever, cancer etc., were rare if occurring at all."

It would be difficult to improve on this statement. It was written by a man who knows well the literature on Indian health written prior to his day and who has had years of opportunity to study the problem at first hand. It is in general accord with all references found in the literature. The statements he makes are a skeleton on which some further comment can be hung.

While the majority of Indians lived in villages, these villages were changed at rather short intervals.

Black Hawk spoke of a village on the Rock River which his tribe was occupying in 1816, saying of it that it was in a good location and had an abundant pure water supply. "Our village was healthy", he said. The point he was making was that they had a village there for fourteen years; therefore, they wanted to be regarded as having ownership and being fixtures in the Rock River Valley. But even at that the population periodically moved in and out of the village returning to it for some part of the time in each year of the fourteen. The Illinois Indians did not have organized community government and town stability as it was known among such southern Indians as the Chickasaws and Mobilians.

This type of Indian village or camp had no organized excreta disposal, the nearby cover speedily became befouled, whereupon the Indians moved their camp to a clean terrain.

---

[2] Hrdlička (Bureau of Ethnology, Bulletin 30, Part 1. p. 540. Ales Hrdlička).

Alexander Ross[a] has a different explanation. He says, "But another cause and perhaps the best that can be assigned for their abandoning their winter domiciles as soon as the warm weather sets in is the immense swarms of fleas that breed in them during that season.'

If there was such a disease as typhoid fever in that day, there is no evidence that the Indians had it. The sparseness of the population (and there were but few Indians) the custom of frequent removal of their villages to new and clean locations would have been some protection against typhoid fever had there been such a disease. Hrdlicka writes that even today typhoid is very rare among Indians.

The Indians had plenty of diarrhoeal troubles. Most of the writers speak of digestive difficulties probably including in the term indigestion due to poor food, constipation and diarrhoea and dysentery. Some go into more details. Ross wrote in 1810 as follows: "The diseases most frequent among these Indians are indigestion, fluxes, asthma, and consumption. Instances of longevity are found, but not often. Babies suckle their mothers until they are old enough to feed themselves (on the Indian diet). The infant is generally robust and healthy but the mother soon becomes an old woman." Alexander Henry (1760-1764) said "The Indians were in general free from disorders and an instance of their being subject to dropsy, gout or stone never came within my knowledge. Inflammations of the lungs are among the most prevalent disorders."

Father Marquette died from a chronic dysentery which had many of the earmarks of amoebic dysentery. It is difficult to see how his disorder could have been other than that.

In Parkman's account of Marquette's illness and death it is stated that on one mission he went far down the Mississippi (as far as the Arkansas) and that somewhere on that trip he contracted dysentery. He and his party turned northward traveling up the Mississippi and Illinois. Somewhere in the Chicago area he became too weak to travel. His companions left him in a cabin and went back to Canada. Father Marquette lived in the vicinity for about three years after he got dysentery, becoming better and almost well at times, but always relapsing. He was able to travel considerably during this period in the territory of Illinois and up on the Wisconsin River and to Green Bay. Finally he had a relapse, became very ill and had hemorrhages. Realizing that his end was near he started around the foot of Lake Michigan and the Michigan shore, dying enroute. If this was a case of amoebic dysentery it would be difficult to think that he did not infect some Indians during these years of illness.

[a] Ross (Adventures of the First Settlers on the Oregon or Columbia River, edited with historical introduction and notes by Milo Milton Quaife.... Chicago, R. R. Donnelley & Sons Company, 1923. Alexander Ross).

That the infant mortality rate among Indians was not exterminating is explained by their custom of keeping the baby at the breast until it was well over one year of age and often for months or even years longer. This custom, however, was in part responsible for their comparatively low birth rate and their stationary population. An Indian woman bore and reared few children as compared with the white woman of the day. The children came far apart.

It is altogether probable that the Indian did not have any form of malarial fever to an extreme degree. There were mosquitoes but they were not infected.

Alexander Henry writing of 1760-1764 said "Mosquitoes and a minute species of black fly abounded on this river. Sickness was unknown." In three places in his reports Henry refers to clouds of mosquitoes, but the mosquitoes could not have been infected. There is no report of malaria or fevers and here is the statement from Henry that sickness was unknown coupled closely with his report on the abundance of mosquitoes.

The Indians lived along the streams and yet the writers do not refer to any disease which could be malaria. Contrast their reports with those of malaria among the colonial settlers who in later years followed the Indian custom of settling along the rivers and in the bottoms. It appears that even today the Indians are fairly immune to malaria.

Hrdlička says that among the Yumas malaria is the most prevalent disease. That the Opatas and Tarahumares have much malaria. A. B. Holder wrote in 1892[1]: "In the Indian territory and among a few tribes elsewhere malaria becomes of greater importance than consumption."

But such reports were not made until the Indian had been long in contact with the white man. How much disease did the Indians contribute to the early history of the State? To what diseases were they subject? What did they pass on to the whites? Let us answer the question as to a few diseases.

Consumption.

Hrdlička says if consumption existed at all among prehistoric Indians it was extremely rare. It was seldom seen up to a century ago. It is gradually becoming more common. When he wrote this he was reporting on the Indians of the southwest (1908), but he knows the Indians elsewhere and their history as well as any man. He also wrote, "Among the uncivilized tribes pneumonia is the worst lung infection, but among the civilized tribes consumption begins to rival it."

However, Drake wrote in 1843, "The most prevalent disease of the Indians is scrofula. It almost annihilated the Peorias." By scrofula he meant

---
[1] New York Medical Record, Aug. 13, 1892.

tuberculosis of the glands, bones and lungs. At the time he referred to the Peorias were at least approaching the class which Hrdlička calls the civilized tribes. It is also to be remembered that the Indians had been in contact with whites since soon after the year 1600. Dr. Esmond R. Long is my authority for the statement that the Puritan fathers suffered heavily from consumption the first years they spent in America. They may have infected some Indians who later carried infection westward. It is not probable that the Indians of the early days in Illinois gave the white man then consumption.

Pneumonia.

Such records as are available, indicate that the Indians had a great deal of pneumonia and pleurisy. Hrdlička referring to the Indians of the southwest twenty years ago says: "Pneumonia has appeared in epidemic form." This disease was epidemic rather frequently among the white settlers in Illinois. If anything saved the Indians from similar epidemics it was the sparseness of the population, the small size of the villages and the open air living.

Diarrhoea and Dysentery.

That digestive disorders including diarrhoeas and dysenteries were prevalent among the Illinois Indians is certain from the records. Next to the rheumatic disorders the diarrhoeas and dysenteries are most frequently alluded to.

Amoebic Dysentery.

Father Marquette contracted what appears to have been amoebic dysentery while going down the Mississippi associating all the time with the Indians. He then returned to the Illinois territory where he remained an infectious case or infective carrier all of the time until his death.

Typhoid.

Hrdlička says, "Contrary to all expectations typhoid is rare." The essay by Louis which established typhoid as a separate disease was not written until eight years before the Indians were moved from Illinois. It was not generally known in Illinois until after the Indians had gone, but the probability is that typhoid was not prevalent among the Illinois Indians. They did not seem very susceptible to fevers of any sort.

Malaria.

Malaria is thought to have pretty well wiped out the Nez Perces. It is very prevalent among some tribes in the southwest, but the writings do not show that Illinois Indians suffered heavily from it if at all.

French flavor and tradition even today. The French-Canadian influence was more enduring in the country than it was in the town.

But there is no evidence that either of these French movements, if the last one can be termed as such, added significantly to the health problem of the Illinois territory. There was some disease; principally venereal disease and consumption in the vicinity of the posts as has elsewhere been indicated. It is more possible that smallpox was introduced to the Indians here and there but there is no record of great pestilential outbreaks of any sort or of definite change in disease type or of any difference in the health and vigor of the people in the wake of this series of intrusions.

However, there is not much health history of the period on which to go. The Indians were not writers—neither were the trappers. The early traders of the period wrote nothing, though later traders were more prolific. The explorers and the missionaries were prolific writers, considering the times, but they wrote about adventures, conflicts, battles, attitude of the natives toward foreigners, geography, topography and religion. In none of the reports of the period is there any reference to the prevalence of malaria or any other disease that is comparable with conditions as they were described by writers who observed from about 1800 onward. Some of the difference may be ascribed to the different interests and viewpoints of the writers, but not all of it can be so interpreted.

It is not believable that conditions such as were described by these later writers could have existed and been overlooked or have gone unrecorded by the Jesuits. The conclusion must be that the health and vigor of the Indians and the traders and trappers, and the French-Canadian settlers between 1680 and 1780 was about the same as that of French-Canadians and Indians in Montreal and along the St. Lawrence in about the same period. Just how different was the picture soon after 1780 will appear in the next chapter.

Malaria.

In the records of the earlier years of the French regime there are few allusions to any disease which can be recognized as malaria. There are some references to endemics and epidemics but these cannot be interpreted as being malaria. In fact, it is difficult to guess what they were.

Zeuch says, "In the year 1730, the settlements in the American Bottoms had, in spite of the stigma that had been placed upon them by sickness, reached the size of a considerable colony." Most of the colony were French. Most of the sickness was malaria.

A French religious order was forced to abandon their home in this region because of malaria. Yet the opinion is general that the French

---
³ Zeuch, Ibid.

St. Martin and of Dr. Beaumont's treatment of him. The first opinion was that St. Martin would die but then as the patient improved Hubbard wrote "about this time the doctor announced that he was treating his patient with a view to experimenting on his stomach being satisfied of his recovery."

There is evidence that French-Canadian trappers, traders and missionaries added very little to the health problems of Illinois. They were almost exclusively young and hardy men. There were no children among the immigrants, no women and no old men. When an immigrant became enfeebled he went back to Canada or tried to do so.

By 1720 out of this movement an off-shoot had grown. Some of these immigrants had founded communities with the intention of remaining. Father Marquette had founded Kaskaskia on the low ground at the junction of the Kaskaskia River with the Mississippi. A few months earlier the same type of settler had founded Cahokia in the American Bottoms about opposite a part of present St. Louis and about 50 miles up the river from Kaskaskia.

The settlers in these villages were some twenty to one hundred French-Canadians. Many of them had married Indians; some had married women from Canada and from the French settlement in Louisiana carried there for the purpose of supplying wives.

These imported indentured women were quickly spoken for when they were reasonably comely but the record shows that when the installment included the lame, the halt, the blind, the prospective benedicts passed them by and took up squaws. The Parisian account of Kaskaskia recites the rapidity with which the cabins of these marrying immigrants "began to swarm with children."

If the Indian women lived in a tent, wandered with her lord, kept her baby at the breast for two or three years and bore but few children and those at long intervals, they were not always emulated by their sisters who married squaw men, took up their residence in houses and brought forth half-breeds. In addition to these settlements there were a number of French-Canadians who settled up and down the Kankakee, along its tributaries, the Illinois and the Mississippi. Most of the half-breed children in time grew up rather more Indian than white. These went with the Indians when they moved out of the State. A few remained.

The distinctly French towns were inhabited by the descendants of the all white marriages and the half-breeds; in mind and manners more white than Indian. In time these towns were abandoned or lost their French flavor. The French system of laying out towns and even farms, the French law, customs and language did not persist. But in some of the rural districts in valleys like the Kankakee and its tributaries there is considerable

plaints and miscarriages would seem to indicate that the Indians did not suffer much from venereal disease, either gonorrhea or syphilis.

The statement that "the Indian withers at the touch of civilization" suggests so far as Illinois is concerned that the white intruders into this territory gave much disease to the Indians there and received but little from them.

Schoolcraft (History of the Indian Tribes of the United States 1857) agrees with the opinion that the low birth rate of the Indians was the reason for their fewness, saying, "It is a well known fact that the Indian tribes do not increase in the ratio of other nations. The average number of children to each family does not exceed two." Other contributing causes given by Schoolcraft were laziness, lack of thrift and prudence, lack of will or even desire to populate, occupy and use the land, and their addiction to alcohol. In his very extensive writings on the subject he refers to no disease as being very harmful to the Indians in a racial way, except smallpox. This disease did at times almost wipe out villages and even tribes. He specifically states that pestilence was of minor importance as compared with low birth rate and alcohol in wiping out the Indian populations

Summary.

Summing it all up it appears that the Indian during his residence in contact with white men in the Illinois territory from the incoming of the white man about 1670 until the departure of the Indian in 1837, contributed but little to the white man's diseases—scarcely more than he contributed to the constitution of the racial stock, composed of several white bloods and a very small infusion of Indian blood.

The French or French-Canadian Regime.

THE FRENCH-CANADIAN TRAPPERS, MISSIONARIES AND TRADERS

Soon after the whites came to America they began to find their way among the Indians. Some of these were captives, some were squaw men and some lived among the Indians because they loved the life.

However, these were of little significance from the social standpoint. They had little influence in the methods of living of the Indians, nor is there any evidence that they altered the health problems of the Indians materially for either the better or worse.

On the other hand, the fairly definite French-Canadian trapper trader missionary movement in Illinois was of social significance. It altered the religious life of the Indians and also their habits and customs in some degree. The biography of Gurdon S. Hubbard contains many allusions to the heavy drinking of the Indians and considerable fighting occasioned thereby. It is interesting to note that Hubbard gives an account of the shooting of Alexis

Venereal Disease.

So far as concerns venereal disease in general the Indians seem to have suffered far more from the white man than the white man did from the Indians. Venereal disease was said to prevail among the drinking, degraded Indians who camped near white men's towns, but not among Indians who kept away therefrom. The tribal regulations were aimed at protection of the Indians against venereal disease among the whites. Their attitude indicated their fixed conviction that the white man was the source of the venereal infections of every kind that the Indian found among his people.

Because of the interest in the discussion of pre-Columbian syphilis a separate heading is given to the history of syphilis of the Indians.

Rheumatism.

It is certain that rheumatism troubled the Indians greatly. It is impossible to say where they got it, who brought it to them, if anybody, where it originated or came from. The Indians seem to have recognized that exposure played a part in causing it. They also seem to have recognized the value of hot baths in curing it. Most of the hot springs enjoying wide vogue today were handed over to the white man from the Indians as health resorts particularly in rheumatic disorders. Wandering a little afield, the fact that the Indians appreciated the value of Sulphur Springs in skin disorders is some proof that they suffered from parasitic skin disorders.

Rheumatism is known to have existed among the Egyptians as proven by the lesions in mummies. Also among the cave dwellers of France and Spain long before the Egyptian period. In fact the skeletons of wild animals found in caves in Europe prove the prevalence of rheumatism among animals in prehistoric times. This is some indication that the Indians had rheumatism before the white man came.

Schoolcraft (History of the Indian Tribes of the United States 1851 and 1857) publishes a letter on the Indians written by Dr. T. S. Williamson of Ohio, after this physician had lived among the Dacotas for many years. The Indian withers at the touch of civilization but not because of fevers or other sickness. Dr. Williamson said: "They know nothing about the proper treatment of fevers." There is no reason to think they had had much experience with malaria or typhoid. "The summer of 1837 is rendered memorable in Indian history by the ravages of smallpox." One reason assigned for the deadly character of this disease among Indians was that it was really a fever and the Indians knew nothing about the treatment of fevers. They were more experienced in treating diarrhoeas and diseases calling for purgation and rheumatic disorders.

He said, "Dacota females are far less subject to what are termed 'female disorders'." Miscarriage was infrequent. The infrequency of female com-

settlers in Illinois did not have malaria and one writer is quoted (elsewhere) as saying the French were immune. This was not true; that the French have no immunity to malaria was shown in Panama.

LaBlanc said to de Lesseps in 1881, "If you try to build this canal (Panama) there will not be trees enough on the Isthmus to make crosses for the graves of your laborers." In 1888, a journalist wrote "Death is constantly gathering its harvest about me. Since the advent of de Lesseps on February 28, 1881, thousands upon thousands have been buried here." Gorgas estimated that the French lost a total of one third of all their white employees. "We estimated deaths at 20,000. A very large part of these deaths were from malaria."

The reasons for the low malaria rate in the French regime in Illinois were several. The early settlers came from a non-malarial country and brought in no infection, the country was sparsely occupied, there were mosquitoes but they were not infected. As immigrants increased in number and in source toward the latter part of the regime malaria increased. By the time the British took charge, the mosquitoes had become rather generally infected.

Other Diseases.

The French-Canadians in Illinois had pneumonia, rheumatism, diarrhoea and dysentery. Of these diseases they had an abundance. It is probable that they had smallpox, whooping cough and other forms of contagion. However, these did not abound because most of the population were adults and hardy, vigorous, resistant adults at that. In addition, the towns, forts and garrisons were small and not crowded. Communication was infrequent. Such other disorders and diseases as prevailed among adults in Canada along the St. Lawrence and the Lakes in the period were brought to the Illinois territory. However, the French made no great contribution to the problems of health in Illinois.

When the British took over the government, many of them moved away. Later when the colonists took charge others departed. Then came the great waves of settlers from other states. Whereupon most of the French departed and those who remained herded to themselves in rather small colonies.

Since they did not marry much with the invaders they made but little contribution to the constitution of the people. They left behind them no outstanding diseases of French importation.

The tendency to inbreed and in that way to fix certain dysgenic qualities which is thought to be marked among the French descendants in Illinois at the present day, was not in evidence during the French regime. In so far as it has been a contribution to Illinois' health or lack of health it is chargeable to the French, though only indirectly to the French of the French regime.

The British Regime.

The British became politically responsible for Illinois in 1763. By 1776 the colonies were in a war to dispossess them. By 1780 British control of the region was ended. Therefore, they can be held responsible for only seventeen years of the history of the Illinois region. During that time they did little more than occupy a few garrisons with small bodies of soldiers. But the diseases and especially the malaria which had been rolling up during the latter part of the French regime continued to mount while the British were in charge.

The following quotations relating to sickness in the Illinois district during the British regime are from *Zeuch's History of Medical Practice in Illinois, Vol. I.*

"Between 1763 and 1778, almost all of the journals of several British officers give harrowing accounts of the battle with their old enemy, malarial fever."

Morgan's Journal (1768) says: "Ague and fever has been remarkably prevalent in so much that few of the garrison and inhabitants of Fort Chartres and Kaskaskia have escaped. He told me that no native there was fifty years of age and few were forty. Neither has any French native been known to have lived to an old age."

The Indians complained that smallpox was transmitted to them by the English saying "They gave us smallpox which made all our children die."

Colonel Wilkins wrote in 1768, "Every officer and private is violently ill with fever." Later Morgan reported "Fifty men are now fit for duty and the disorder has greatly abated."

Adjutant Butterick reported, "Three officers, twenty-four men, twelve women and fifteen children were sent to their graves since September 29. and many more are in a dangerous way though I am in hopes the cold weather will soon help us."

In 1789, Major Hamtramck wrote to General J. Harmon, "The garrison at Fort Knox is very sickly and disease had caused more havoc than the savages. Forty-nine men are ill with intermittent fever."

Zeuch quotes Crogman[6], as writing—"All in the garrison are ill, including myself. Out of fifty men there are not above three officers fit for duty."

Morgan[7] wrote of Fort Chartres 1768 "Every officer and private is violently ill with fever." Buttrick[8] "Three officers, twenty-five men, twelve women and fifteen children were sent to their graves since September 29 and many more are in a dangerous way"

---

[6] Croghan (Illinois Historical Collection, Alvord-Carter, Vol. XI).
[7] Trade and Politics, 1767-1769, Illinois Historical Collection, Alvord-Carter, vol. XVI.
[8] Alvord-Carter, Ibid.

At that the British left the people and the country about as they found them. Just then a gradual increase in disease as is to be expected when nothing is done to prevent it.

Since the British of the period did not settle and did not intermarry with the Indians they made no contribution to the character of the racial stock.

The Spanish Influence.

The Spanish made a moderately effective effort to capture and hold the west bank of the Mississippi in the region of St. Louis. In 1780 they sent a company of sixty men to St. Joseph, Michigan, across the southern end of what is now Illinois. But neither they nor any other Spaniards remained long enough in the territory to alter health conditions for better or worse.

Zeuch[9], quotes the following from the minutes of the Court of Quarter Sessions held at Cahokia in 1799, "In order to keep off the plague of the smallpox that now rages on the Spanish side no one was allowed to cross the river and goods brought from the Spanish side were to be confiscated."

The American Regime.

PERIOD 1780 TO 1877.

There had been some immigration into Illinois territory from the other states prior to 1780, but it was not until Clark occupied southern Illinois in that year that the American colonists began to dominate the picture. By 1800 the population, which had immigrated from other states, though few in number and widely scattered, were numerous enough to control the social life, the customs, habits and religion and to shape such political policy as there was. They shaped the disease history even more markedly.

Between 1800 and 1810, the population increased in numbers but the increase was gradual. After 1816 it was more rapid. There were two great gateways through which the population entered. The north end of the State was settled by people, the great majority of whom came through Chicago. Many of these settled in the immediate Chicago area; many others radiated northward, northwestward and westward. Very few went south of the Kankakee and the Illinois rivers and a line running westward from where the latter river turned southward. In the earlier years, the great majority of those who entered the State through the Chicago gateway came from New England, New York and the states west thereof. Few came from those states that bordered the Mason-Dixon line on the north thereof and fewer still from south of that line. There was little European immigration.

---
[9] Zeuch, Ibid.

The southern gateway was less a portal in a physical way. It included the Wabash basin south from Vincennes and the Ohio valley. Those who crossed these borders pushed across the State, going westward, to the brink of the French settlements along the Mississippi and north and northwestward until they reached the great prairies.

Between the irregular fringe-like north boundary of this immigration wave and the similar vague south boundary of the Chicago immigration, there was a broad neutral belt—a no man's land. The wet, stiff-soil prairies made here a natural geographic barrier.

The waterways were the great arteries of transportation and the lodestones of settlements. It was along the valleys that the people settled almost altogether in the south, and to a large extent in the north. In the prairie section there were no large rivers and no great valleys. Besides the immigrants were a people who knew the soil of valleys and who did not know how to judge nor how to break or to cultivate prairie land. The bearing of all this on health will appear shortly.

There were few foreign born among those who came in through this gateway. The Poles who participated in the Revolutionary war were given large land grants in Indiana toward the north end of this sweep of invasion, but they did not come into Illinois. Among the colonists who crossed the Wabash were some English groups who formed settlements concerning which some references will be made. With few exceptions there were no social or religious or communistic colonies from foreign lands in this southern Illinois territory.

The majority of those who came through this portal were from the Ohio valley states to the east; Pennsylvania and Virginia beyond the Ohio valley and Kentucky on its south. But not all were from these states. They brought with them malaria and some other diseases of the states from which they came to add to the stock of malaria and dysentery with which the country was already provided.

The Colonial period had a health history that is even more distressing than that of the latter end of the French regime and of the British regime. In the writings of those who knew Illinois after 1780 and particularly after 1800, the allusions to health or rather ill health are frequent and illuminating. Health or lack of it was prominent in the public and private mind.

The territory became a State in 1818, but the newly organized State did nothing for the health of the people. The political change in 1818 made no change in health conditions. Therefore, the health story will be told without particular notice of the political change which occurred in 1818. It will be covered in the main by separate treatment of several of the more important diseases.

With the exception of a few Germans along the Ohio and Mississippi rivers, some French who were already here and some Indians who had remained, the population of the State prior to the latter part of the thirties decade were almost exclusively English, Welsh, Scotch and North Irish stock. Almost all were born in the states to the east and southeast.

Toward the latter part of the decade, the first great South of Ireland wave began to roll in. In the forties decade the first great German wave was in evidence. The Swedes and Norwegians began with settlements in Cook, Henry and Vermilion Counties. Their first great wave began to arrive in the middle of the seventies decade. The Poles first tried some settlements in Cook County and along the Illinois Central road well to the south and in Ogle County, but their great waves of immigration did not start until well after the close of this so-called pre-health department period prior to 1877.

These incoming people may have brought with them some of the diseases of the countries from which they came but there is no evidence that they brought anything new in that line. The peculiarities of physical vigor and weakness, of strength and of what is termed constitution, were much the same as those of the people of the British Islands and of the northwest fringe of Europe, the sources from which the Illinois of that day was indirectly populated.

General Unhealthfulness.

During the French-Canadian regime, the Illinois territory did not have a reputation for unhealthfulness. Prospective settlers were deterred from settling by the reputation of the country for danger from Indians and for hardships due to extreme cold and lack of conveniences but they were not held back by the rumors of disease in the land.

By the year 1800 the story was different. Disease had come to be regarded as more of a menace than the Indians, and the reputation of the country for unhealthfulness was both widespread and justified. The settlers of this period included the women and children as well as the men of the family.

The birth rate was high but the death rate approached the same level. The Indian had a low birth rate and a high death rate and no immigration. In consequence he increased very slowly in numbers, if at all. Certain tribes grew, others waned but there were never enough Indians to occupy the country. The white settlers had a high birth rate, a high death rate and a great immigration rate.

The increase of population due to excess of births over deaths was not great. In fact, had these two population factors operated alone the white man would have had considerable difficulty in holding his own in combat or even in competition with the Indian. But the enormous immigration rate made it possible for him to drive out the Indian, to occupy the land, to clear it, drain it, improve it, to develop the resources and finally make the State healthy and prosperous.

The heavy death rate was due to malaria, diarrhoea and other diseases of infancy and childhood, diarrhoeas and dysenteries of adults, pneumonia and a few other diseases.

Malaria so completely dominated the health picture and its effects were so apparent that most of the earlier writings referred to malaria as being synonomous with ill health. Therefore, the quotations of opinion and observation found in this section will occasionally be found to say something about malaria, and in the section on malaria the writers quoted will speak often of the bad general health conditions.

Boggess[10], wrote,

"One who settled in Illinois at that period (1790 to 1809) came through danger to danger for Indians lurked in the woods and malaria waited in the lowlands. In 1780 the garrison was sick and starving and the abandonment of the post seemed imminent. One of the earliest visitors to Illinois to record his impressions was an Englishman named Birkbeck. He wrote, 'Buried in the depth of a boundless forest, the breeze of health never reaches these poor wanderers. * * * The man, his wife, his son and three daughters. * * * They are tall and pale-like vegetables that grow in a vault pining for light; a squalling tribe of dirty brats that are of one pale yellow, without the slightest hint of a healthful bloom. The blood, I fancy, is not supplied with its proper dose of oxygen from their gloomy atmosphere, crowded with vegetables growing almost in the dark, or decomposing, and in either case, abstracting from the air this vital principle.'"

Blane[11], wrote,

"The settlement has shared the fate of all the neighborhood with regard to sickness; two of the immigrants having died and several others being very ill. I rode to Palmyra. This most miserably dirty little village was once the county seat of Edwards County, an honor which it lost in consequence of the superior healthfulness of Albion. Albion is not at all times free from the prevalent autumnal disease of ague accompanied with fever. * * * Wherever else I traveled the people complained of illness. * * * But the great objection is the general unhealthfulness of the neighboring country for if Illinois were as healthy as England it would soon equal all that Mr. Birkbeck has written in its favor."

Speaking of St. Louis, located immediately across from the American Bottoms, he said:

"St. Louis was once the great emporium of all the fur trade but of late years it has declined both in prosperity and population partly owing to the dreadful sickness."

Blane, speaking of the American Bottoms, eight miles before coming to the Mississippi River, said:

"This fertile district is rendered almost uninhabitable by its unhealthiness and will require a great deal of draining before many persons will settle upon it. * * * The French are by no means so liable to be attacked by fevers as the

[10] Boggess (The Settlement of Illinois, 1778-1830. Arthur Clinton Boggess, ... Chicago, 1908. Chicago Historical Society Collection, vol. V).

[11] Quaife (Pictures of Illinois One-Hundred Years Ago. Edited by Milo Milton Quaife. Part 2—"A Tour in Southern Illinois in 1822," from William Blane. R. R. Donnelley & Sons Company, Chicago, 1918).

English or Americans. This is attributed to their very different and much more temperate mode of living. * * * I am persuaded that no people on the face of the earth consume so much animal food as the Anglo-Americans; for at breakfast, dinner and supper, hot meat is always eaten, even by the poorest class. * * * Even during the burning months of summer and autumn they continue to eat the same immense quantity of meat and grease, which last article is a favorite in their cookery."

Henry R. Schoolcraft[12], said:

"The appearance of the inhabitants has corresponded with the opinion before expressed of the unhealthiness of the country. Pale and emaciated countenances; females shivering with ague, or burning with intermittent fever, unable to minister to their children, and sometimes, every member of a numerous family suffering from the prevalent malady at the same time. * * * In this country life is at least fifty per cent below par in the months of August and September. I have often thought that I ran as great a risk every season which I spent here as I would in an ordinary battle. I really believe it seldom happens that a greater proportion of an army falls victims to the sword during a campaign, than there has of the inhabitants of Illinois to disease, during a season that I have been here. That time and cultivation will remove the causes of unhealthiness is a prevalent opinion.

"There are two months of the year when the inhabitants are exposed to fevers and agues which render life irksome."

Mrs. Sarah M. Worthington[13], said:

"By the first of September there was scarcely a well family to be heard of, and in many cases not one individual able to assist another. * * * A few became discouraged and sought refuge in timbered localities."

Tillson[14]:

"A great responsibility which rested upon the women was care of the family in time of illness. An illness native in the prairie country was fever and ague. There was a burning fever following chills which left the patient so weak he could not work. It came with perfect regularity."

By Haines[15], reference is made to central Illinois during the time following the Black Hawk War:

"Time had but little softened grief for those slain by Indians when the cholera spread a funereal pall over the same territory lately stricken by war. The swift flying messengers on horseback in pursuit wherever to be found dotted the prairies with omens of dread. For when the fell disease struck its victim no time could be lost before remedies were applied. Death was the quick result if potent relief was not found within the early hours of attack. In my family four were fatally stricken in as many days. Many who were not at once attacked fled their homes, only to meet death a little later in the lonely prairie or unsettled forest. Bereavement and sorrow was widespread, almost universal over a great part of the West. Typhoid and other fevers followed this dreadful visitation, swelling the death list generally from those who escaped the cholera. Indeed, the 'cholera year' as it was long referred to, was a period of gloom from which memory turns in horror. From this period may be dated most of our country graveyards, being then set apart for burial of our first dead."

---

[12] Quaife, Ibid. Part 3—"A Journey Up the Illinois River in 1821" from Schoolcraft.

[13] Worthington (Original Letter of Sarah M. Worthington of Sterling, Illinois, in a collection of Stories of Pioneer Mothers in Illinois, dated April 24, 1893. In State Historical Library, Springfield, Illinois).

[14] Tillson (Reminiscences of a Pioneer Woman.)

[15] Haines (Social Life and Scenes in the Early Settlement of Central Illinois, p. 35. Publication number 10 of the Historical Library, Illinois, 1905. James Haines).

GENERAL HEALTH HISTORY PRIOR TO 1877

Governor John Reynolds[16] says, "In 1800 to 1805 the idea prevailed that Illinois was a grave yard. This retarded its settlement. The Trappist Monks abandoned their first location in the American Bottoms in 1812 because it was near some lakes and they had bad health."

The History of Medical Practice in Illinois, Vol. 1, compiled and written by Dr. Lucius H. Zeuch, and published by the Illinois Medical Society, has, as its major objective, the biographies of medical men and the history of the practice of medicine. However, it may be fairly said to have the telling of the story of the health of the people as one of its purposes. Volume 1 brings the history down to 1850.

The general unhealthfulness of the regime and the effect of such a reputation on the development of the country in the early days is indicated by the following quotations taken from Volume 1 of this History, as follows:

Thwaite's Jesuit Relations: "A plague broke out among the Indians near Cairo. Half the tribe died and the survivors fled in every direction."

In *American Notes* (1842) Dickens describes Cairo as a detestable morass. The following is quoted from Martin Chuzzlewitt (Dickens). "A native of Cairo (or Eden) when asked to help Mark Tapley and Martin Chuzzlewitt with their luggage replied, 'My eldest son would do it if he could but today he has his chill upon him and is lying wrapped up in blankets. My youngest son died last week. * * * We buried most of 'em here, the rest have gone away. * * * The night air aint quite wholesome. Its deadly poison.'"

Zeuch[17] says, "There were two reasons why colonization took place in the Kaskaskia and Cahokia regions rather than in the more healthy Starved Rock region. An epidemic had seized the denizens of the mission. The frosts did not arrest the progress of the contagious malady, but just the opposite happened." (The reference is to an epidemic of unknown nature in the 17th century.)

In 1819, Flagg wrote from Edwardsville, "The principal objection to this country is its unhealthfulness." In 1820, Flagg wrote from the same section, "Several towns have been very sickly this season especially those situated contiguous to rivers or mill ponds."

On the other hand Fordham wrote about the same time and from the same section that the country was about as healthy as England. "Consumptives are almost unknown. Bilious fevers are rather prevalent but not dangerous when attended to early."

The following references to disease in Illinois are taken from Zeuch's History.

---
[16] Reynolds (My Own Times, embracing also the history of my life. John Reynolds, 1789-1865, Belleville, Illinois. B. H. Perryman and H. L. Davison, printers, 1855).
[17] Zeuch, Ibid.

ss was fastened upon this region." *(The 19.)*
region taxed these valiant Knights of
reference was to Bond County in 1844.)
in Pike and Calhoun Counties, the nature

Dr. Frances Drude said, "There was an
icians due to their exposure to contagious

made concerning the state of health in the
n great economic loss in immigration and
have withstood the ravages of malaria."
:.)
suffered as much from sickness as did St.
ane County.)
the sick year for so much illness was prev-
that few could be induced to locate any-
to Fulton County.)
ry County was reputed as distressingly

f Washington County, Ohio, says: "Since
1788, many of the diseases have changed
ling to Hildreth from 1788 to 1807 most
old, hunger and fatigue. The prevailing
leurisies, pneumonias, scarlet fever and
etimes epidemic. In 1797 to 1807 pallor
l. Since 1815, when typhoid-pneumonia
been increasing.

pneumonia, ophthalmia and malaria; 1807
o 1813 the fevers were mostly typhoid. In
This typhus, I expect, was the same disease
e. So general was the sickness that in the
of a possible 1200 to 1400 votes were cast,
at intervals of eight to ten years. Scarlet
ree years."

ve to our sister state lying in the same
a general way.
Medical Association in 1867 on the epi-
wrote, "The testimony borne by the early
but flattering its (Illinois) character for

al Science, 1829, Dr. S. P. Hildreth).

In 1819 the Illinois legislature passed an act authorizing a lottery to raise funds for the purpose of "draining ponds and lakes in the American Bottoms and of improving the health thereof." In its introduction, this law says, "these ponds and lakes stagnate and annoy the health of the inhabitant of said bottom by producing autumnal fever." It appears that no drawing were held under this law until 1838. It was planned to hold the first drawing on July 1 of that year, "but the sickness of the contractor and the general ill health of the whole country, etc., have caused this unlooked for detention and delay." The first drawing took place November 17, 1839 at Harrisonville. There was a weekly drawing thereafter for some time. The eighth took place at Alton, January 5, 1839, and the tenth at Harrisonville, January 19, 1839.

The lottery did not prosper. Professor George W. Smith[19], wrote "Little was accomplished by the lottery system."

In October 1839, J. A. Townsend, Manager of the American Bottoms Improvement Association asked the owners of land to pay a voluntary tax of $1.00 an acre to pay for drainage. In April 21, 1838 W. C. Greenup, President, Board of Managers, sent a communication to Congress asking that the Board be given the vacant land in the American Bottoms to be used to raise money to pay for the contemplated drainage. The following extracts are taken from that communication—

"It is believed that in the year 1812 the population of the American Bottom was greater than it now is. This is attributed to bad health arising from the stagnant ponds and lakes. The once flourishing villages of Fort Chartres, St. Philips and Prairie du Pont are only known by the ruins and the inscriptions over the dead. Cahokia, Town of Illinois, Harrisonville and Prairie du Roche are in great dilapidation; Kaskaskia seems not to advance although it is reputed to be the most healthful of any other place in the bottom."

---

[19] Smith (History of Illinois and Her People, vol. ? 1927. Prof. George W. Smith).

HISTORY OF CERTAIN DISEASES PRIOR TO 1877

MALARIA.

The dominant disease as early as 1780 in the Illinois territory and for about seventy years thereafter was some form of malaria. It went by many different names such as the "ague", the "shakes", the "chills", "bilious fever", "intermittent or remittent typhoid and typhus", "autumnal fever", and various combinations of these names. As early as 1816 Drake is found adding the term "typhus" to several of the malaria terms. He used the word typhus sometimes alone though usually in combination. He did not mean typhus as the term is used now and probably not typhoid in the modern sense of the word, but he did mean a slow form of malarial fever with oftentimes a collateral typhoid infection that probably was about what Woodward popularized as "typho-malarial fever" sixty years later.

In the main, malaria was brought into the state through the southern gateway and by immigrants from the southern and border states. Whether it came to them from Africa as a result of the slave traffic as some say is not a direct part of this story. Some came in through the Northern gateway brought by immigrants from elsewhere than the south, but most of it was brought in as stated through the Southern gateway. How it was carried north and south in the state as well as east and west will be referred to presently. Once it entered, malaria found conditions fit for its spread. The country was undrained, much of it was heavily wooded, and mosquitoes were plentiful.

In 1829 John MacCulloch wrote a book on malaria. There is no proof that he had Illinois in mind, but what he wrote of the region along the Mississippi river in the south and possibly north would apply to this State. He said:

"In many places in the southern States malaria has been rapidly increasing as almost to threaten the abandonment of the land. And in the newly settled or uncleared lands along the Mississippi and its endless tributary streams the same plague is found to prevail very widely to the surprise and serious grievance of the settlers. What the fate of this new country may be ultimately in this respect is difficult to foresee. It is to be suspected that no changes and no cultivation will ever bring it into a state of salubrity."

Mrs. Tillson, writing of Pike County in Illinois in 1821, said:

"Your father had a shake of the ague. * * * Feeling that he was in fer a smart grip of agy he rode seven miles toward Edwardsville where he stayed to have another shake. The next day being intermediate day he rode twenty-five miles to Mr. Hoxie's where he waited over there fer another shake which Mrs. Hoxie said 'beat all the shakes she ever see. He shuk the hull cabin.'"

In *Pioneer Health Conditions* by the Norwegian-American History Society is found the following statement:

"Everywhere in the West the ague attacked the settlers more or less severely during the first development of the country. * * * Wherever new land was broken in swampy regions the ague harried the people with the most disastrous results. * * * Malarial fever prevailed in the Rock River valley to the Mississippi River in Illinois. At this time (1839) malaria ravaged Chicago very severely and especially many of the poor hard working immigrants who were poorly fed and lived in miserable huts, fell victims to the disease. When fall came only a few were alive. Most of them had succumbed to the unhealthy climate. * * *"

Sandburg[20] says:

"Fall came with miasma rising from the prairie, and chills, fever, ague, for Tom Lincoln and Sally Bush; and many doses of 'Barks,' a Peruvian bark and whiskey tonic mixture, bought at Renshaw's general store in Decatur, was administered."

By long odds the best informed man of his day in the health of the people of the Mississippi Valley was Dr. Daniel Drake of Cincinnati. In 1837 he wrote that in 1825, 1827, 1828 and 1830 malignant fevers were unusually prevalent in the Western territory. Dr. Drake gathered his information through travel, through correspondence and through articles sent his journal. There is no proof that he had visited Illinois so early as 1825 to 1830. He had one regular correspondent in the State, Dr. J. F. Henry of Bloomington.

Through Drake's travels and his correspondence he gathered the following reports on malaria in different sections of Illinois, particularly however, in the basin of the Illinois River.

In 1835-36 Drake made a trip to St. Louis, writing of the American Bottoms opposite St. Louis, he said:

"It is among the most fertile spots in the whole earth, but at present it is infested with mosquitoes and intermittent fevers, the latter followed by enlarged viscera and dropsical infiltrations."

"*Bloomington*—Autumnal fever prevails annually. One of the citizens informed me that he had resided where I found him three years before a member of his family was seized with that fever. Such instances are not uncommon though difficult to explain. Drs. Colburn and Henry were convinced that an extensive plowing up of the soil of the prairies for the first time had been followed by fever especially in those who resided on the northern or leeward side of such tracts. They had rarely seen malignant cases.

"*Adams County*—We have here in autumn bilious diseases more or less for instance the ague, the intermitting and bilious fever. In very rare cases do these diseases prove dangerous. Fifteen or twenty years ago the hepatical diseases, hypohondriasis and jaundice held such a formidable sway that they spared but very few, especially of the immigrants.

"*Woodford County*—In summer miasmatical fevers prevail. In moist springs the inhabitants of the prairie suffer from them. In fall and winter the abdominal typhus fever sometimes occurs, but never real typhus.

"*Pekin*—Intermitting fevers reappear after the lapse of some two, three or four weeks. The best remedy is acid sulphuric Peruvian bark in doses of from 2 to 4 grains at intervals until 10, 15 or 20 grains are taken. Tuberculosis (consumption) is very rare. Acute inflammations of lungs occur in winter. * * *

[20] Sandburg, (Life of Lincoln, Carl Sandburg, Vol. 1, p. 106).

Daniel Drake, M.D.

"*Peru*—In some cases of chills and fever * * * a few outward applications of soap and water no doubt would have relieved the patient. * * * People drink surface water.

"*Tazewell County*—They plowed up the prairie near their residences and in the following autumn experienced a decided invasion of remittent fever, while the surrounding population remained healthy. At length a colony arrived and establishing themselves near each other enjoyed excellent health the first year; but the next spring they broke up a large extent of prairie near their dwellings and suffered severely in autumn from fever, while the country around remained comparatively healthy. Dr. Frye has remarked what has been noticed elsewhere that in low and wet timbered spots the intermittent form of fever is more prevalent than the remittent—also that in some autumns every kind of locality is affected, while in others some places suffer and escape."

Speaking of the especial prevalence of the disease in the valleys of the Wabash Dr. Drake said:

"Between these wet, marshy prairies which will be made dry by cultivation and the bottoms the whole of this extensive and fertile portion of the Wabash basin is infested with autumnal fever, of which many cases assume a malignant and fatal character. The people who live in the hills are healthier and live longer.

"From what can be collected of the travels of Lewis and Clark, Pike Long, Catlin Freemont and dGregg not less than from fur traders and Santa Fe merchants malaria is almost unknown at a distance of more than 300 miles from the west boundary of Missouri and Iowa and above the 37th parallel. To the north it does not prevail as an epidemic beyond the 44th parallel and it ceases to occur even sporadically at the 47th parallel. It came in from the south and it pushed up the valleys to the north."

Daniel Drake[21] writing of his observations on the distribution of malaria along the Illinois river and points not far therefrom in the period between 1840 and 1845 made the following statements:

Kaskaskia—"Such a surface must of necessity give rise to severe autumnal fevers which are known to prevail throughout the whole Kaskaskia basin."

Lower Illinois Valley around Meredosia—"It seems almost superfluous to say that the population along such a valley are subject to grave autumnal fevers."

Jacksonville and Morgan County—"From Doctor Jones I learned that all the forms of autumnal fevers occur at this place. Dr. Prosser informed me the prevalence of these fevers is much less than formerly. Dr. Smith thought them not more frequent or more fatal than he had seen them in the basin of the Ohio River in Keutucky. Dr. English had found them more malignant than in the lower valley of the Great Kanawha in Virginia."

Springfield and Sangamon County—"Doctors Todd, Henry, Merriman and Jayne all of Springfield assured me of the presence of malaria and they afforded me an opportunity of seeing intermittents as malignant as those on the banks of the Tuscaloosa and Pearl Rivers (Alabama and Mississippi)."

Mackinaw—"Dr. Burns told me that there was autumnal fever here and there."

Peoria—"In 1833 the Anglo-American town of Peoria contained not more than twenty-five families. But it was the site of an old French mission and in 1779 it began to be a village of Indian traders, voyagers and hunters.

"Although so old a settlement its autumnal diseases are substantially the same as those of the more recently settled territory. From Doctors Dickinson, Rouse and Frye, I learned that in and around the town intermittent and remittents prevail every year."

---

[21] Drake (A Systematic Treatise, Historical, Etiological and Practical on the Principal Diseases of the Interior Valley of North America as they appear in the Caucasian, African, Indian and Esquimaux Varieties of its Population. Cincinnati, 1850. Daniel Drake, M. D. Winthrop B. Smith & Co., pub.).

Peru and LaSalle—"Dr. Whitehead said in a residence of eight years he had seen epidemics of autumnal fever in only two years and then chiefly in immigrants from the north and in Irish laborers on the Canal.

Ottawa—"From Doctors Howland, Schermerhorn and Hurlbert I learned that autumnal fever is common in this locality. The Irish laborers on the Canal had suffered greatly."

Ottawa to Joliet—"From the best information I could obtain malarial fever is both rare and mild."

Joliet—"Doctors Schoolfield and Bowen told me that Joliet is annually invaded by autumnal fever but it is neither widespread nor of a fatal character."

In 1883 Dr. J. Murphy of Peoria wrote

"When I first settled in Peoria some thirty-five years ago (about 1848) the entire prairie was saturated with malaria. In fact, the entire area of central Illinois was a gigantic emporium of malaria."

In 1842 Dr. Snuce[22] of Darwin, Illinois, Clark County, wrote:

"We have more or less of every grade of fever from the simplest intermittent to the most remittent every year."

In 1843 Dr. R. Robson[23], New Harmony, Indiana, wrote of the fevers of White County, Illinois, and Posey County, Indiana:

"When I commenced practising in 1830-31 the country (except the town of New Harmony) was infested with fevers of almost every grade. During the summer of 1834 very few families escaped a visitation of fever and many of the most respected citizens were carried off."

In 1843 and 1844 Dr. Drake visited Illinois, including Chicago and the north part of the State, a considerable part of Wisconsin and the lower Missouri in his itinerary. After he had left St. Louis and gone up the Mississippi to Alton, Illinois, and some distance up the Missouri, he wrote of the autumn fevers, "which prevail not only on its banks (Missouri) but far and wide in all directions from them."

"I can hear of no spot high or low, wet or dry, wood or prairie, village, town or city socalled that is not invaded. To find a single family some member of which has not had a chill or two, would be a curiosity. In one village every inhabitant except one negro boy had had the disease."

Of Galena and vicinity he said:

"The people on the Fever River are as free from fever as their neighbors; meaning that they had as much malaria, but no more. He discusses three possible origins of the name of this river; one was that it got its name from a Sac word meaning smallpox; another that it came from the name of a local French trader LaFevre and the third was that it was derived from the French word "feve" meaning bean. He did not state his opinion, but he did say 'the name is not undeserved.'"

In 1850 the Illinois Medical Society was formed. In the constitution of this society there was provision for a standing committee on "practical medicine to report annually on the prevalence of epidemics and other matters of interest." The committee reported the experiences of their members in their practices, the answers from correspondents, about disease prevalence.

---

[22] Snuce (Western Medical and Physical Journal, 1842).
[23] Robson (Western Medical and Physical Journal, 1843, R. Robson).

and what they could learn from reports before medical societies and medical journals.

In the committee report for 1857 occurred the following statement: "The fevers of our alluvial formation, intermittent and remittent with their various relatives claim the precedence." They especially referred to articles on the congestive fevers which appeared in the St. Louis Medical and Surgical Journal, January, 1849, and January, 1850. In the 1851 report are found eight references to the several types of malaria. In the 1852 report written by N. S. Davis and L. Hall, there are four references to forms of malaria, and one "Isthmian Fever."

In 1854 Dr. N. S. Davis reported to Chicago Medical Society on conditions in Cook County: "The attacks of ordinary intermittent and remittent fevers were more frequent during September than for several years past." He also wrote that around Ottawa malaria outranked other diseases in importance. In 1855 Dr. Thompson's report on practical medicine had eight references to the prevalence of malaria. The report from Vandalia furnished by Dr. Haller read: "The Okaw river bottom is two miles wide and it is subject to inundation. In consequence bilious, remittent, intermittent and congestive fevers prevail."

Dr. N. S. Davis.

Dr. H. R. Payne of Marshall reporting for Clarke County said: "Every family was attacked last year."

The 1858 report said "Since the completion of the Illinois and Michigan canal in 1847 the health of the Des Plaines valley has been annually improving, by reason of the better drainage. This is especially true in Joliet."

The 1860 report by Dr. Goodbrake contains four references to malaria. In 1867 malaria is referred to by three physicians in the *Report on Practical Medicine*. In the 1869 report there are seven reports of malaria

Dr. Goodbrake.

After that year the subject was not often referred to. Such discussion of malaria as persisted shifted to new battlefields—to wit: is there a typho-malarial fever, and, the relation of typhoid to malaria?

In the 1864 report appear the following statements for which Doctors J. S. Jewell and N. S. Davis appear to divide responsibility: "From 1855 to 1857 there was little of disease except malaria. After 1857 a transition from the periodic to the continued type of fever occurred. In two or three years continued fever almost entirely supplanted the autumnal type." Just how much of the continued fevers referred to was typhoid it is not easy to guess.

In 1850 Dr. Gerhard wrote an immigrant's compendium of information entitled *"Illinois as It Is."* One chapter was devoted to health. He did his best to answer adverse criticism of Illinois such as "When people speak of Illinois in the eastern states they will often express their fears in regard to the fever and ague said to prevail there." He said: "Everybody knows that of all diseases the ague occurs most frequently in Illinois * * * that it depends very much upon the particular plan of abode or manner of living whether the fever is to visit a family or not. Whosoever resides in the Bottoms or close by swamps or in districts where the water cannot rapidly flow off, will be more exposed to the fever. * * * One-half of those who are down with fever have to ascribe this to nothing but their own imprudence and the use of improper food. Causes— drinking stagnant water; too immoderate use of fruits, lard, eggs or fish. Nobody should expose himself needlessly to night air."

Dr. J. S. Jewell.

He had some ground to talk since unquestionably there was less malaria in 1856 than there had been thirty years before that date. He quoted from laymen who were very enthusiastic as to the healthfulness of the State. The six physicians quoted were more reserved. Dr. Daniel Stahl of Adams County said, "There is some malaria but not as much as formerly. Diarrhoea in adults prevailed somewhat." Dr. J. G. Liller of Woodford County said the people of that county had some malaria in the summer and some typhoid in the autumn. Dr. T. A. Hoffman of Beardstown, Cass County, said they had some malaria but not as much as formerly. Dr. F. Borendel of Peoria County said that county had some malaria and typhoid and the last epidemic of cholera affected them. They had very little consumption. Dr. F. Wenzel of Belleville, St. Clair County, said, "The time in which southern Illinois was denounced as the fever country had long since passed by. Dr. C. Hoffman of Pekin said that they had some malaria but it was not bad. They were almost free from consumption.

Zeuch[24] gives the following references to the prevalence of malaria in many of the counties in Illinois. The citations give the year in which the presence of the disease was alluded to in the original sources of the material. In some instances brief comments are quoted.

Shelby County in 1830; Moultrie and Edgar Counties "in the early days"; Sangamon County "prior to 1850."

Vermilion County, "It sought out and attacked every new comer for twenty-five years in the form of fevers, fever and ague and bowel complaints.

"A colony of Norwegians on Beaver Creek was stricken with the prevailing illness of the lowlands and fifty of them perished. The survivors abandoned the settlement.

McLean, Kankakee, Tazewell, Will Counties; "The building of the Illinois Michigan Canal was stopped at times because of the inroads the disease (malaria) had made on the laborers at work upon it.

Kane County, "Intermittent and remittent bilious fevers sorely afflicted the pioneers." Putnam and Marshall Counties, "particularly in 1838 and in 1849. Stark County, "In 1846 Doctors Hall and Chamberlain treated 1500 cases of fever and ague." "Up and down the Rock River," 1839. DeKalb County 1839.

Carroll County, 1837, "The pioneer of early Illinois had to suffer much from malaria before he learned the lessons of elevation and of restraint of the rampant waters."

Dr. Victor C. Vaughan[25] gives a graphic description of malaria as he and his family encountered it in Montgomery County Illinois in the summer of 1865.

"In 1865 every man, woman and child in southern Illinois, at least within my range, shook with ague every other day. * * * That summer I saw enough of a people held in bondage by malaria to make a lasting impression upon a boy's mind."

Dr. Vaughan describes a family named Trelawney as representing the abyss of degeneracy and general incompetence which he inferred was the result of chronic malaria. Continuing the theme he wrote

"How much the present dwellers in southern Illinois owe to the open eyed and keen witted Jesuit who penetrated the interior of Peru and to his patroness the Princess Chincon I will not attempt to estimate, but if quinine has clothed and regenerated the recent generations of Trelawneys I am willing to pronounce it a gift from Heaven."

Dr. C. B. Johnson[26] writing of Bond County and other regions in central Illinois said:

"1866 yielded abundant crops of all kinds including malaria in all its forms." Of the last great endemic wave of malaria in Illinois he wrote: "Toward the close of the summer of 1872 came the last general extensive epidemic of malarial fever in central Illinois. The epidemic lasted from the last days of July till the coming of a killing frost and within the bounds of my practice I think almost no one escaped an attack. All suffered sooner or later from the infant at the breast to the old man tottering to his grave."

[24] Zeuch, Ibid.
[25] Vaughan (A Doctor's Memories).
[26] Johnson (Sixty Years in Medical Harness; or, The Story of a Long Medical Life 1865-1925. Charles Beneulyn Johnson).

Clark Carr,[27] writing of northern Illinois in 1850 and thereabouts gives at least one reason why the fevers of southern Illinois were spread to northern Illinois.

"Large numbers of inhabitants of southern Illinois went to the Galena district to work in the mines after they had made their crops and then returned home for the next crop. The roads in Henry and Knox County were filled with people emigrating, every day movers passed our house."

This was a period of active building of railroads and canals and doubtless a great deal of malaria, dysentery and typhoid was spread through labor camps.

Before leaving this subject the following two references from Bartlett's "Classical Work on Fevers" as to the malarial fevers and particularly the element of periodicity therein are referred to. He writes: "What reason is there to believe or hope that the thick darkness which has ever wrapped and which still wraps this fever so full of mystery and wonder will ever be dispelled." In less than forty years thereafter all of the mystery had been cleared up; in eighty years after Bartlett wrote, malaria had been banished from all but twelve counties in Illinois and it should be easy to banish it from those. He also reports that Dr. Oliver Wendell Holmes once wrote a prize essay on the disappearance of malaria from New England.

CHOLERA.

Hirsch[28] gives the dates of the pandemics of cholera as follows: first, 1817 to 1823; second, 1826 to 1837; third, 1846 to 1863; fourth, 1865 to 1875. The first pandemic is not supposed to have reached America. The second pandemic reached Illinois.

In 1832 there were no vital statistics, but a *Chicago Health Department Report* says that forty-eight soldiers and several citizens died of cholera.

In 1834 Daniel Drake wrote of the cholera epidemic: "Illinois has suffered but little. The Eastern portion of the State has suffered most. Some villages have been scourged."

The following in regard to Central Illinois, following the Black Hawk War, is quoted from the Social Life—Early Settlement of Illinois, Haines:

"Time had but little softened grief for those slain by Indians when the cholera spread a funereal pall over the same territory lately stricken by war. The swift flying messengers on horseback in pursuit wherever to be found dotted the prairies with omens of dread, for when the dread disease struck its victims no time could be lost before active remedies were applied. Death was the quick result if potent relief was not found within the early hours of attack. In my family four were fatally stricken in as many days. Many who were not at once attacked fled their homes, only to meet death a little later in the lonely prairie

---

[27] Carr (The Illini, a Story of the Prairies. Clark E. Carr. Chicago, A. C. McClurg & Co. 1904).
[28] Hirsch (Handbook of Geographic and Historical Pathology).

or unsettled forest. Bereavement and sorrow were widespread, almost universal over a great part of the West. Typhoid and other fevers followed this dreadful visitation, swelling the death list generally from those who escaped the cholera. Indeed, the 'cholera year' as it was long referred to, was a period of gloom from which memory turns in horror. From this period may be dated most of our country graveyards, being then set apart for burial of our first dead."

Parrish[30], writing of the Black Hawk War, 1838, said:

"Cholera which had appeared among General Winfield Scott's troops had detained them at Detroit, Chicago and Rock Island. * * * Nearly one-fourth of his entire detachment of one thousand men having died of the pestilence. * * * Beyond this the entire American loss in the war was probably not in excess of two hundred and fifty."

Parrish, writing of the Swedish Colony at Bishop Hill, Henry County, in Illinois said:

"During the cholera scourge of 1849-52 men would go to work in the morning in good health and be dead before sundown."

From 1837 (or 1838) until 1846 Hirsch says: "Europe, Africa and America were completely free from cholera."

In the third pandemic the disease was widely prevalent and highly fatal in Illinois. It is mentioned in the *Reports on Practical Medicine* in 1851, 1852, 1853, 1854, and 1855. In some one of these reports Jerseyville is quoted as congratulating itself in escaping the epidemic, attributing it to having appointed a local board of health and to the excellent work done by the board. Chicago also appointed a new board of health whenever cholera was seen coming down the road (or down the lake or up the river), but it was not so fortunate as Jerseyville.

The *Transactions of the Illinois Medical Society* reported cholera in 1866-1867 and 1868. It was also present in 1873. By somewhere toward the end of 1865 the fourth pandemic was at hand and cholera was again in Illinois.

The Committee on Practical Medicine reported its wide prevalence in 1866 and 1867. Dr. P. M. Cook, reporting in 1868 said, there were 1582 cases, 970 deaths in Chicago in 1867; 1082 cases were reported in October. October 10th, 175 cases were reported. The population of that city in that year was given as 200,330. In 1868 the disease still prevailed.

Zeuch[31] gives the following instances of epidemics in several counties:

White County, in 1832, 1848, 1856, 1866 and 1873.
St. Clair County, 1832. Governor Edwards died of the disease in this epidemic in Belleville.
Sangamon County, 1849.
Morgan County, 1833. "The little village of Jacksonville received a set back when cholera took a toll of fifty-three deaths."
Greene County, 1844. "An epidemic of cholera destroyed fifty of the struggling colony (Carrollton)"

[30] Parrish (Historic Illinois, The romance of the earlier days. Randall Parrish. Chicago, A. C. McClurg & Co. 1905).
[31] Zeuch, Ibid.

Adams County, 1849, 1850-1851.
Vermilion County, 1834.
Fulton County, 1849.
Henderson County, 1849.
Tazewell County, 1834, 1844, 1849.
Will County, 1844 to 1854. "The epidemic left in its wake a case mortality of 60 per cent.
Kane County, 1849, "The Colony of Swedes at St. Charles was almost decimated by it."
Putnam and Marshall Counties in 1849. "Cholera killed 143 in the Swedish colony at Bishop's Hill."
"In 1832 cholera was mostly in the cities, but by 1834 it had reached the rural populations."

Short's History of Morgan County reported an epidemic of cholera lasting six weeks in Jacksonville in the summer of 1833. "In 1851 cholera visited Morgan County; the path of the scourge was a narrow strip southward as far as Belleville."

The *Springfield Journal* published a letter May 26, 1852, from Cairo which said "Cholera has been prevailing here for the past two weeks principally among recent German immigrants. Ten or twelve have died." June 14th the same paper printed a letter from Walnut Grove which said, "There had been some fatal cases of cholera in Woodford County."

The *Bloomington Intelligencer* corroborated this report of the death from cholera in that city of a man who had recently returned from a visit east and on the river. June 19th cholera was reported in LaSalle, Illinois, but reputed as under control.

June 22nd the *Monmouth Atlas* reported that cholera which had been under control in Warren County had reappeared. Dr. Wright who had been attending the cholera cases was one of those who died of the disease.

The *Springfield Journal* on May 18th reported cholera at Cairo and at Peoria.

The *Egyptian Republican* (June 13, 1927) writing of Williamson County said:

"Cholera made its first appearance in July, 1849, but caused only a few deaths. It reappeared in 1866 and lasted for six weeks during which over twenty-five persons were taken away and the city of Marion vacated. Among the deceased were the three beautiful Ferguson girls, ladies without parallel in all the area for beauty and refinement."

In 1867 the Illinois Medical Society had a red hot debate on the eating of fruit during an epidemic of cholera. Those who participated in the debate were Doctors J. Adams Allen, who introduced the motion, David Prince, W. S. Edgar, E. Ingals, T. F. Worrell, D. W. Young, H. A. Johnson and N. S. Davis. The resolution was aimed at the authorities of St. Louis who had tried to stop the eating of fruit during the prevalence of cholera. The resolution which finally carried, read as follows: "The moderate use of ripe but not stale or decayed fruit, taken at the ordinary meals, is not objectionable as tending to produce cholera, but rather is conducive to the preservation of health during the hot season.

L. T. Hewins of Loda (Committee of Practical Medicine) reported cholera present in 1866 in Alexander, Coles, Champaign, Cook, Iroquois, and probably other counties.

YELLOW FEVER.

The mosquitoes which act as vectors of yellow fever are found in the southern end of the State, yet there are only two records of epidemic of yellow fever in the State. In August, September and October 1878 yellow fever prevailed in Cairo, Illinois. In all there were eighty cases of the disease with sixty-two fatalities. In that year an extensive and highly fatal epidemic prevailed in the lower Mississippi River Valley. The nearest point to Cairo reached by the disease prior to its appearance in Cairo was Hickman, Kentucky. By a strange irony it appeared first in the household of the Cairo *Bulletin* whose editor had been active in stimulating the authorities to clean up Cairo and simultaneously in trying to calm their fears.

So far as the record shows the disease prevailed solely among residents of the city of Cairo and it did not spread to any nearby city nor to the surrounding country. Just who brought it into the city was never known. The first case was the father of the publisher of the *Bulletin* and he died in the *Bulletin* office. Later the editor and two printers of the *Bulletin* died with it. The disease abated in September and the schools opened, but it reappeared in October and lasted until the frost came in the latter part of the month. On October 6th there were six deaths from it.

Perhaps this epidemic was sent as a baptism of fire for the infant State Board of Health.

On several occasions cases of yellow fever have developed among refugees in Chicago. There have never been any secondary cases.

An account of a small outbreak at Centralia is found elsewhere in this volume.

DENGUE.

In 1828 there was almost a pandemic of dengue called by some the Spanish fever. It travelled a long distance up the Mississippi River but there is no evidence that it went north of the 34th parallel, and Illinois probably escaped. There is no record that the people of Illinois ever suffered from dengue. Since the mosquito which spreads this disease is closely related to the variety which spreads yellow fever and since this type of mosquito is only found in the southern most part of the State, dengue should never menace Illinois.

Snake Bite.

In the early Illinois days snake bite was frequent. Many fatalities resulted.

In the *Reports of the Committee on Practical Medicine* snake bite was reported on in 1852. In 1854 Dr. Daniel Brainard made snake bite the subject of his presidential address before the State Medical Society. He did a great deal of scientific research work on the subject. He said Indians used rattle snake venom on their poisoned arrows. He showed that the whiskey cure was worse than useless. He advocated local treatment with iodine.

Snake bite figured in other discussions before the medical societies. As the country became more densely settled and the land better cleared snake bite as a menace to health and life disappeared. The favorite remedy for it, whiskey, remained as a menace for a long time afterward though its use (as a remedy for snake bite) is about to become legendary.

Typhus Fever.

Hirsch[32] makes the statement that he never found a single reference to typhus fever in the Mississippi Valley. It is probably true that European typhus never invaded Illinois. In about 1916 there were a few cases among Mexican laborers along the Santa Fe railroad within the State but the authorities prevented it from spreading. It is also true that cases of Brill's disease or modified typhus have been reported from Illinois but it is a statement of essential fact to say that in the period of Illinois history, now under consideration, typhus was never present.

Drake[33] says that Indians were infected with typhus from a ship at Nantucket in 1763, but no evidence is found showing that typhus ever reached the Indians of the Illinois region. Drake writes about Irish immigrant fever, but mentions no cases in Illinois and Indiana. And yet the disease is rather frequently referred to in the writings of physicians and even in the reports from the Chicago Health Department. It must be remembered that Louis did not differentiate typhoid fever from typhus until 1829, and his views were not generally known in Illinois until at least ten years later. Some of the references to typhus in these earlier reports referred to typhoid and some of the low delirium stages of malarial fevers and other diseases.

[32] Hirsch, Ibid.
[33] Drake, Ibid.

Daniel Brainard.

First health officer of Chicago, appointed in 1837. He was probably the first municipal health officer regularly appointed by a board of health in Illinois.

When the controversy over typhoid was warm, Dr. E. P. Cook of Mendota said he had seen typhus in Ireland and what he saw in this country that was called typhus was not the disease he saw under that name in Ireland.

Hirsch probably overlooked the definite reports of typhus given in some instances by street location found in the *Reports of the Chicago Health Department* in 1867, 1868 and 1869. The diagnosis in these cases was probably erroneous but Hirsch had no way of knowing that.

One sometimes wonders how Hirsch failed to read the so-called Rauch *Report of the Chicago Health Department* made in 1870 or 1871. Hirsch's Handbook is encyclopedic. He seems to have had access to nearly all the literature of the world, yet somehow he seems to have missed this Rauch report and in spite of some of the mistakes found in it we know of no American report of the period which compares with it.

Dr. E. P. Cook.

SMALLPOX.

Smallpox was a disease of the Indians. It was brought to them by white men, but just when is not known. It may have been among the Illinois Indians at the time of the French-Canadian occupation, but there is no proof of the fact. It was elsewhere and it is not easy to understand why the Illinois Indians escaped if they did.

Drake[34] wrote:

"Smallpox has penetrated far into the wilderness and proved extremely mortal among the Indian tribes. Ross tells us the chief remedy used by the Indians for smallpox was to pour cold water over the patient. It was a period in which smallpox was very prevalent and highly fatal among the Illinois population. It came in periodic epidemics and most of these were due to a violent virus. Vaccination was not general."

Catlin[35] says:

"Trade and Smallpox were the principal destroyers of the Indian tribes."

Hrdlička, writes of the Southwest Indians of our times what has been true of Indians for a hundred years or more. "Smallpox is the most dangerous contagious disease." This disease has plagued the white man ever since he landed in America and for that matter long before.

[34] Drake, ibid.
[35] Catlin (North American Indians. George Catlin. 1903). Pub.

Hirsch[36], speaking of smallpox in America says to whatever places the European immigrant came and settled, everywhere they carried the disease with them and gave it to the natives. But a still more terrible source for America was the importation of negro slaves. Every fresh outbreak of smallpox could be traced to importation from Africa.

Table 1.

DEATHS FROM SMALLPOX—CITY OF CHICAGO.
Rates Per 100,000 Population.
1867-1926.

Year	Deaths	Rate	Year	Deaths	Rate
1867	123	55.	1901	4	0.2
1868	146	58.	1902	5	0.3
1869	17	7.	1903	47	3.
1870	15	5.	1904	29	2.
			1905	61	3.
1871	73	22.			
1872	655	176.	1906	......	......
1873	517	138.	1907	1	0.05
1874	90	23.	1908	......	......
1875	10	3.	1909	......	......
			1910	1	0.05
1876	29	8.			
1877	43	10.	1911	3	0.1
1878	21	5.	1912	7	0.3
1879	1	0.2	1913	1	0.04
1880	43	9.	1914	1	0.04
			1915	......	......
1881	1180	220.			
1882	1292	230.	1916	......	......
1883	46	8.	1917	2	0.07
1884	2	0.3	1918	4	
1885	8	2.	1919	......	......
			1920	1	0.04
1886	2	0.3			
1887	2	0.3	1921		0.14
1888	......	......	1922	......	......
1889	2	0.2	1923	......	......
1890	......	......	1924	......	......
			1925	......	......
1891	......	......			
1892	2	0.2	1926	......	......
1893	23	2.			
1894	1033	78.			
1895	157	11.			
1896	......	......			
1897	2	0.1			
1898	......	......			
1899	1	0.1			
1900	2	0.1			

Wherever it came from and whatever the source of reinforcement smallpox was present somewhere in the State practically all the time after 1840 and it was epidemic somewhere in many of the years.

The *Reports of the Committee on Practical Medicine* refer to the disease in 1852, 1855-1857, 1858, 1869, 1872, and 1875, as being epidemic in one or more counties in the State.

---
[36] Hirsch, ibid.

The *Annual Reports of the Chicago Health Department* shows that the disease was prevalent in that city in every year between 1867 and 1888 (See Table No. 1.) It was present in epidemic proportions in many years prior to 1867.

Among the reports of smallpox epidemics in Illinois found in Zeuch's History of the Practice of Medicine are:

Henderson County in 1854 and 1855 and Kankakee County in 1837-38. The account says: "Smallpox ravished the settlements during the winter of 1837-38." A history of Williamson County *(Egyptian Republican June 15, 1927)* says, "The smallpox has visited the county on several occasions but never resulting in many deaths until 1873 when a good many died in the south side of the county."

Erysipelas.

The student who considers the prevalence of the different diseases in Illinois in the first seventy-five years of the nineteenth century is struck by an apparent relationship of a group of diseases now known to be due or in some instances suspected of being due to members of the streptococcus group. The diseases referred to are erysipelas, scarlet fever, puerperal fever, septicemia and rheumatism. In the early days these diseases were very prevalent. In many cases they swept over communities in epidemic proportions. Furthermore, their case fatality rates were higher than in the present day. One of the significant improvements in the last half century is the lessened prevalence and the lowered virulence of most members of this group.

In May, 1927, R. M. Atwater[37], writing of the relationship of this group of infective disorders, said:

"When rheumatic fever is compared with scarlet fever, chorea, erysipelas, septicemia and puerperal fever, it is seen that the trends, as well as the yearly oscillations of these diseases, are alike. Acute rheumatic fever appears to be related to the family of streptococcal infections. There is a community of relationship between these diseases. This correspondence appears in the United States, as well as in the English records where it may be traced back as far as seventy-five years."

In the early history of the State erysipelas was both frequent and fatal. At times it swept over the country in well marked epidemics. In spite of the fact that the sick were generally cared for in their homes and hospitalization was rare, the disease was regarded as contagious at least in certain epidemic outbreaks. Some relations to puerperal fever and hospital gangrene and perhaps other infections were guessed at here and there and at intervals.

A study of epidemic erysipelas made by Dr. Edmund Andrews in Chicago in 1868 will be found in the section dealing with Chicago. He made

---
[37] Atwater (American Journal of Hygiene).

spot maps of the disease and tried to show its relation to the very foul stretches of the Chicago River and to badly sewered sections of the city.

In 1843 and 1844 there was a great epidemic of erysipelas which was reported by Doctors J. F. Henry, and Colburn[2] of Bloomington. They reported that the disease came from the East and that the epidemic extended far beyond the boundaries of the State.

One of the names by which erysipelas went in that early day was "black tongue". Dr. Meeker[3] of Rush Medical College wrote a paper in May, 1846, on black tongue or epidemic erysipelas, as it appeared in LaPorte County, Indiana. He said the epidemic first appeared in Canada. During the winter of 1842 notice appeared in the public papers of an epidemic prevailing along the Illinois River called the black tongue. It was extensive and highly fatal in LaPorte County in 1845. In 1846 Dr. Fitch[4], reported the prevalence of the same epidemic in Logansport, Indiana.

In Drake's[5] writings erysipelas is frequently reported under the name "Black tongue".

In 1861 Dr. N. S. Davis, in reporting for the committee on practical medicine said: "Those epidemic diseases chiefly worthy of mention are erysipelas and cerebrospinal meningitis. Coincidently with the presence of erysipelas, typhoid and typhoid-pneumonia were unusually prevalent. There was a wide-spread epidemic influence of a typhus type." At that date Dr. Davis could not get away from the use of the word typhoid in describing conditions of low vitality regardless of the disease which caused them. He more or less connected together all diseases in which delirium and other symptoms of that class were present.

In the *Report of the Committee on Practical Medicine* of the Illinois Medical Society there are reports on erysipelas in 1854, 1855, 1860, 1863, 1864, 1869 and 1876.

The 1863 report treated especially of hospital erysipelas in connection with gangrene and suppuration and other effects of crowding in war hospitals.

Dr. Samuel Thompson *(Committee on Practical Medicine 1854)* said "Erysipelas the fatal malady made its appearance in Edwards and neighboring counties in 1844-45".

---
[2] Colburn (Western Medical and Physical Journal).
[3] Dr. Meeker (Ill. and Ind. Medical and Surgical Journal).
[4] Fitch (Ill. and Ind. Medical and Surgical Journal).
[5] Drake, Ibid.

Dr. Nance of Lafayette said an epidemic of erysipelas prevailed in his town in 1859.

Dr. Wm. Massie of Grand View, Edgar County *(Committee on Practical Medicine 1876)* quoted Dr. J. S. Whitmore of Metamora, Woodford County, as saying erysipelas and puerperal fever go hand in hand. With this he agreed.

Zeich[42] quotes a physician as saying of Kane County when it was first settled, "Erysipelas was more malignant than it was in 1878."

In 1867 Dr. Hamill told the American Medical Association about two great epidemics of erysipelas in Illinois. One was the great Chicago epidemic of 1863 reported by Dr. E. Andrews and referred to elsewhere, the other was a report by Dr. McVey of an epidemic in Morgan County in 1864 of which McVey said, "Erysipelatous fever which has far exceeded in fatality even cholera itself."

Dr. Wm. Massie.

SCARLET FEVER.

Drake[43] says:

"Between 1791 and 1793 scarlet fever invaded the settlers in Kentucky and Ohio. It was called 'putrid sore throat'. From 1793 to 1808 I do not know that any form of scarlet fever appeared in the Ohio Valley. Since 1821 for twenty to twenty-five years at no time has evidence of scarlet fever been absent from the Valley of the Mississippi and the Lakes. The epidemics in the north are more frequent and more fatal than those of the south."

Parrish[44] quotes *Davidson and Struves History* as saying:

"In the year 1797 a colony of 125 persons, the largest which had yet arrived, was fatally stricken with disease at New Design, (Monroe County, near Burksville). A putrid and malignant fever broke out among the new comers attended by such fatality as to sweep one-half of them into the grave before the coming of winter. No such fatal disease ever appeared before or since in this country."

It is doubtful whether this was scarlet fever. In the quotation preceding this one scarlet fever is called "putrid fever." However, the term "putrid fever" is generally used as a synonym for diphtheria. In all probability this fearfully fatal epidemic was either diphtheria or scarlet fever.

Hrdlička[45] says, "The Indians of the Southwest now have very little scarlet fever. However, scarlet fever in that section is comparatively rare among the whites." It seems probable that scarlet fever was found at times among the Indians and whites in the French regime.

[42] Bruch, Ibid.
[43] Drake, Ibid.
[44] Parrish, Ibid.
[45] Hrdlička (Bureau of Ethnology, Bulletin 34, 1908).

In the early part of this century when the other streptococcic diseases namely, erysipelas, puerperal fever, fatal suppurations in compound wounds and perhaps pneumonia and meningitis were so prevalent, fatal scarlet fever must have prevailed extensively. Even fifty years ago the case fatality rate of scarlet fever was far higher than it is today

Scarlet fever is found reported in the *Transactions of the Illinois Medical Society* in 1851, 1852, 1857, 1858, 1860, 1869, 1870, 1875, 1876, 1877 and 1888.

The Decennial Census Reports for Illinois for 1860 to 1880 show the scarlet fever death rates as follows:

1860	1870	1880	1890
98.7	85.1	44.4	11.5

Rates per 100,000 population.

The Chicago Health Department Reports show the death rates from scarlet fever during the census years as follows:

1851	1860	1870	1880	1890
50.	114.7	99.5	67.4	16.1

Rates per 100,000 population.

MEASLES.

Drake[46] says: "Measles was brought in by the immigrants. It affected white, black and red population in an equal degree. The people of that day recognized the need of isolation as a method of controlling measles."

Measles was reported present in the State in the *Transactions of the State Medical Society* for 1851, 1852, 1855, 1857, 1869, 1872 and 1876.

Zeuch[47] refers to measles as being epidemic in Hardin County in 1818 and in Henry County (Prophetstown) in 1835.

Measles then, as now, was accepted as inevitable. It was probably endemic at all times in the State, though it was only reported on at intervals Probably there was nothing out of the ordinary for the reporter to say

The following statistics show the trend of the disease:

DEATH RATE PER 100,000 POPULATION.

	1851	1860	1870	1880	1890
Illinois		6.3	27.6	19.5	8.2
Chicago	6.	13.7	30.9	25.6	5.5

[46] Drake, Ibid.
[47] Zeuch, Ibid.

Diphtheria.

Hirsch[18] thinks the honor of first describing diphtheria belongs to "Areteus the forgotten" one of the distinguished physicians of the later Greek period. However, he credits Bretonneau with naming the disease and really establishing it, in 1835. However, in 1858 and even much later great confusion prevailed relative to it. Hirsch calls attention to the fact that diphtheria was confounded with scarlet fever in the United States in the beginning of the Nineteenth Century. Elsewhere attention is called to the possibility that epidemics of so-called putrid sore throat among early Illinois immigrants may have been either diphtheria or scarlet fever.

Hrdlička says that among the Indians of the Southwest epidemics of diphtheria have been known to prevail at times. There is nothing on the subject in the literature as to either whites or Indians in the French Canadian regime. In the *Transactions of the Illinois Medical Society* diphtheria was late in making its appearance. It was reported in 1857, 1860, 1867, 1872, 1876, 1878.

The trend of the disease once it became recognized is shown by the following mortality rates per 100,000:

	1860	1870	1880	1890
Illinois	70.0	59.0	122.9	93
Chicago	140.9	53.4	184.8	72.8

Dr. C. B. Johnson[19] recounting some of his trying experiences with diphtheria in Central Illinois in the early days quotes Henry Ward Beecher as saying "When a case of diphtheria occurs the family is apt to attribute it to a visitation of Providence. A dispensation of Providence! Why, it is nothing in the world but rotten cabbage and turnips in the cellar!"

Zeuch[50] says of Kane County: "After 1856 diphtheria displaced typhoid fever. Diphtheria made many a household desolate."

Cynanche.

The death of General George Washington was caused by cynanche in the opinion of the physicians in attendance. This was in 1799. For three quarters of a century thereafter Washington was not the subject of critical inquiry. About that time the habit of inquiring into everything and everybody was developed. Then the almost sacred traditions and myths about Washington came under the microscope. Somewhere in the same general

---
[48] Hirsch, Ibid.
[49] Johnson, Ibid.
[50] Zeuch, Ibid.

period bleeding as a treatment for disease having been abandoned was in for some condemnation. This meant a battle of the pros and cons. The cons alleged among other things that George Washington had been bled to death. This opened the subject of George Washington's last illness. Post mortem and quite belated diagnoses of diphtheria, pneumonia and other diseases were made.

One reason for the uncertainty as the nature of General Washington's last illness lay in the cause of death as given by the attending physicians. It was cynancie. The disputants had never heard of cynancie. They could not find it in the books. The way was cleared for attributing death to whatever the contenders might claim.

In 1926, Dr. Walter A. Wells of Washington reviewed the evidence and proved that George Washington was not bled to death nor was there any kind of malpractice. He agreed that the ex-President did not die from diphtheria or pneumonia. His death resulted from an inflammatory oedema of the larynx due to some unknown infection and the accepted name for the disorder in that day was cynancie.

Whether the name cynancie was coined by the Edinburgh School of Medicine or not does not appear, but the great medical lights of that city wrote much about the disorder calling it cynancie. Cynancie might be called a creation of Edinburgh. In that day Edinburgh was the fountain head of medical lore. Two of Washington's three physicians were ardent students of the Edinburgh school.

The diagnosis of cynancie was a proper one in that day. There are a few reports on it by physicians of the upper Mississippi Valley in the medical journals of the early day.

The 1869 *Report of the Chicago Health Department* which carried vital statistics by causes of deaths for each year after 1851, contained reports of deaths due to this disease yearly from 1852 to 1867, inclusive, except in 1856 and 1865.

Presumably death certificates giving cynancie as the cause of death were being filed elsewhere in the State as late as 1865.

It may be that cynancie has ceased to trouble the people of the state, or it may be that the disorder still exists but that it goes by other names.

MENINGITIS.

Hirsch[51] says: "The earliest information on epidemic meningitis dates from 1805 in which year the disease was prevalent in Geneva, Switzerland."

In the United States the disease appeared first in New Hampshire and Massachusetts in about 1807. By 1816 it had spread to the western and

---
[51] Hirsch (Handbook of Geographic and Historical Pathology, vol. III).

southern States. It seemed to spread from centers. That first epidemic in the United States came to an end in about 1816.

In 1846 Gray reported an epidemic in Jefferson County, Illinois, and elsewhere in southern Illinois occurring in 1845.

Hirsch says that from 1857 to 1874 the United States was again the chief seat of epidemic meningitis. Scarcely a year passed without its being seen over a larger or a smaller area, its diffusion from first to last covering the whole of the country.

In 1863-64 it was epidemic in the southern and central parts of Illinois. Hirsch quotes from Davis[52] and McVey[53], "But in the winter of 1865 it broke out anew in various parts of Illinois. In 1872[54] it was epidemic at Edwardsville, Crawford and other parts of Southern Illinois."

Hirsch says from 1805 to 1830 the disease was in isolated epidemics at various places in Europe but was more general in the United States. From 1854 to 1875 the malady reached its widest diffusion throughout most of Europe and the United States. In Illinois under the names of spotted fever, meningeal fever and meningitis, cerebro-spinal meningitis prevailed with considerable frequency. At times definite epidemics were recognized. Oftentimes meningitis was confused with other diseases in spite of the fact that the disease loomed large in the minds of the physicians of the State. It is referred to in the *Reports of the Committee on Practical Medicine* of the State Medical Society in 1852, 1855, 1864, 1870, 1873, 1874, 1876 and 1878.

In the report for 1864 Dr. N. S. Davis as chairman wrote "Those epidemic diseases chiefly worthy of mention are erysipelas and cerebro-spinal meningitis." The report for 1873 said "Meningeal fever rapidly extended over the valley of the Wabash."

Zeuch's History of the Practice of Medicine refers to an epidemic of it in Kane County in 1856.

Epidemic Ophthalmia.

In 1835-36 according to Drake, a widespread epidemic of ophthalmia prevailed in the territory in which Illinois is embraced. Drake wrote "It would be interesting to discover its cause." In the same paper he wrote "Neuralgias, dyspepsia and chronic hepatites are common."

In 1864 in the *Report of the Committee on Practical Medicine*, N. S. Davis wrote "From 1852 to 1855 erisipelatous ophthalmia prevailed."

The references to ophthalmia in the literature of the period were many.

---
[52] Davis (Transactions, Ill. Med. Soc., 1867).
[53] McVey (Transactions, Ill. Med. Soc., 1867).
[54] Southern Illinois. (Philadelphia Med. & Surgical Rpts. May, 1872; Mar. 29, 1873.)

We of this day would like to broaden the query of Drake and say "It would be interesting to learn what was this ophthalmia which so plagued the people of that early day, what was its cause and why has it disappeared."

SYPHILIS.

The venereal diseases were recognized as of public health importance in the early medical history of Illinois in spite of the fact that the population was largely rural. The *Transactions of the State Medical Society* for the year prior to 1877 contain a small number of papers on the subject. Some of these papers proposed laws and other community action for their control in view of their social and pathologic importance. However, action was delayed for many years.

Syphilis is of especial interest in this health history of Illinois because the early settlers were in contact with the Indians for a long time. There is a wide belief that syphilis was of Indian origin and that the Spanish sailors on the expeditions of Columbus contracted the disease and carried it to Europe where they spread it somewhat. Europe according to this theory was syphilized by invading armies from the Mediterranean district, these armies having themselves been syphilized by people infected by Columbus' sailors. The current seems now to be running away from that theory. The present trend of opinion is that the Europeans brought syphilis to America rather than that they carried it in the other direction. Since syphilis had a tendency to cause bone lesions this disease lends itself unusually well to speculation of this character.

On this point Hrdlička[55] says:"Syphilis exists in the Indians as it does in the whites, therefore, if syphilis existed before the Spaniards reached this country signs of it should be at least occasionally discovered in the ancient burials. But the bones of the old burial places are as a rule free from any sign of the disease and this is true of the bones from ancient graves in California, the northwest coast and other localities exclusive of some mounds. It is difficult to see if the disease existed before the whites came, how, with the well known wide intercourse among the Indians whole regions could escape it. It may be remarked that it is also absent in the older burials in Peru and other localities in South America."

With this Joseph Jones[56] who investigated the skeletons of mound builders in the Ohio Valley principally in Kentucky, Tennessee and the states to the north of the river, does not agree.

He found evidence of syphilis in the bones of the mound builders. Based on this finding he expressed the opinion that syphilis was one of the

[55] Hrdlička (Journal. Am. Medical Assn., Mar. 10, 1906).
[56] Joseph Jones (N. O. Med. & Surgical Journal, June, 1878).

pestilences which destroyed vast numbers of the aborigines. It is not certain from the reading of the text whether he meant to say that syphilis among Indians was a pestilence prior to the coming of the white man, but it is certain that he was sure that the bones he examined showed that the mound builders had syphilis of the bones prior to the discovery of America. His report supported the Columbian theory of the origin of syphilis.

Joseph Jones was an able scientist and a learned pathologist for his day but he could easily have been in error. It will be recalled that at one time the bone lesions found in the Egyptian mummies were thought to be syphilitic and this was given as proof that the Columbian theory was wrong. It was not until a very capable modern British pathologist, Ruffier examined these Egyptian mummies that it was proven and accepted that the lesions were not syhilitic. Probably a review of the evidence in the case of the mound builder's bones might lead to a reversal of Joseph Jones' opinion as it did in the case of the Egyptian specimens.

Dr. Michel Gandolphe[37] says the origin of syphilis is one of the most controverted points in medical history. The epidemic of the disease which prevailed so widely in Europe about 1900 acts like a curtain in shutting out all the history of syphilis which preceded that conflagration. He says the research in the literature made by Notthaft of Munich exhausted all the possible ties of solution on the literary side and came to no conclusion. Therefore, he advocated trying to solve it by study of the bones of ancients.

Lortel found what he thought was evidence of syphilis in the skull of an Egyptian mummy. Gandolphe examined this specimen and disagreed with Lortel.

But in 1911 Raymond sent Gandolphe two bones from a skeleton found in a cave in the Marne region in France. These bones were from people who lived before the days of Christopher Columbus. Gandolphe and also Raymond thought these bones were syphilitic.

Whether or not the Indians infected the whites with syphilis originally, or vice versa, it is nevertheless true that this disease was moderately prevalent among the whites during the period covered by this history. They doubtless brought some of the infection into the State with them. The several army posts located in the area must have contributed to its spread. However, the great majority of the people were males. They lived isolated lives. Syphilis was not a major health problem.

Kramer holds that the Indians had syphilis in the pre-Columbian period. He bases his opinion on the relative freedom of the Indian from general paresis. This he thinks is because they went through that phase in the evolution of the disease prior to 1500. The white European became subject

---

[37] Gandolphe (Lyon Medical, Aug. 4, 1912. Dr. Michel Gandolphe).

to it about 1500. About 1700 he began to develop nerve syphilis. Since 1900 he has been passing out of the stage of nerve syphilis. The black man is following in his footsteps about two hundred years behind the white man just as the red man preceded him.

There are many accounts of the presence of syphilis and other venereal diseases among the Indians at later periods. Ross names the venereal diseases as being among the more common complaints of the Indians in the eighteenth and nineteenth century.

Hrdlička[58], speaking of modern Indians says "Venereal diseases, while predominant among the more degraded Indians, are more or less effectually guarded against by others. The Indians tried hard to prevent the whites from infecting their people with venereal diseases

I. W. Hunter[59] who lived a captive among the Indians from 1796 to 1816 reports "They had no syphilis until they contracted it from the whites." So far as it is possible to conclude from so little evidence the conclusion is that syphilis was in France long before Columbus sailed from America.

Gonorrhea.

Gonococcal infections are supposed to be far older than syphilis. They are mentioned in the Bible in several places. For all that is known they were present in Egypt before the Hebrews were there. When these infections came into Illinois is not known, nor where. Armies of some sort and army posts were always in evidence in the State. There were French, Spaniards and British to be fought and the Indians were a constant menace. All in all there were enough sources of infection.

Fortunately the people were hard-working and they lived in rural communities in the main. Gonococcal infections never constituted a major health problem.

Consumption and Other Forms of Tuberculosis.

In 1843 Daniel Drake[60] wrote "The most prevalent disease of the Indians is scrofula. It almost annihilated the Peorias." His description of scrofula shows that he includes tuberculosis of the lungs and bones with tuberculosis of the glands and lungs. But this opinion was not the general opinion. It may have been true of the Peorias as Drake had heard but if so it was for some special reason. Although the Indians of the period had tuberculosis the general opinion coincides with that of Hrdlička that Indians living under primitive conditions are not wiped out by consumption. To

[58] Hrdlička, Ibid.
[59] Hunter (New York Med. & Physical Journal, 1882, 1-174. I. W. Hunter).
[60] Drake, Ibid.

add to the improbability that Drake's opinion held for all Indians the physicians of the State at that time did not regard consumption as very prevalent among patrons.

In 1844 Drake travelled across the State to St. Louis and up the rivers to Chicago westward to Galena and south down the river. He wrote in his journal "The physicians from Jacksonville to Joliet tell me that consumption is one of the rarest diseases in Illinois." He recommended that the State be investigated as to its advantages as a tuberculosis resort. As late as 1873 Dr. Harrison Noble included in his *Report on Practical Medicine* to the Medical Society this statement "I have never seen a case of consumption in Illinois that could not be traced to New England soil."

In 1859 Dr. G. W. Phillips of Dixon wrote: "It is a fact that consumption is rare in the prairie State of Illinois."

Gerhard[61] said that the consumption death rate in Illinois was only 136 per 100,000. That rate was the lowest in a list of consumption death rates in twelve states given by the writer.

The only references to consumption found in the *Reports of the Committee on Practical Medicine* were found in the reports of 1852, 1855, 1859, 1869, 1873, 1874 and 1875.

In his *Report on Practical Medicine* to the American Medical Association in 1867, Dr. R. C. Hamill wrote "The opinion is entertained by some of the oldest practitioners that consumptives emigrating from the New England States have found length of days by residence in our broad prairies". But he did not accept their opinion for he wrote: "Consumption leads the list of diseases that consign to early graves the youth and promise of our Country."

In a second report on epidemics in Illinois made to the same association in 1870, Dr. Hamill quotes Dr. Haller of Vandalia as writing "Pulmonary consumption is increasing here at a fearful ratio. Nearly all the land in the county is drained". There were many who

Dr. Haller.

thought malaria due indirectly to poor drainage protected against consumption.

The general trend of these references was that the disease was of small consequence in the State. Occasional articles were devoted to the explanations of and reasons for the comparatively small amount of consumption in

---

[61] Gerhard (Illinois As It Is, 1856) (Illinois As It Is: Its History, Geography, Statistics, Constitution, Laws, Government, etc. Frederick Gerhard, Chicago, Ill.).

Illinois. The death rates from the disease as given by the Census Office were per 100,000 population:

1850	1860	1870	1880	1890
	114.5	145.6	131.4	148.9

The death rates in Chicago as shown by the *Chicago Health Department Report* were:

1851	1860	1870	1880	1890
123.5	252.8	176.8	169.5	163.2

The figures do not substantiate the opinions of the physicians of the time. It is not necessary to discuss the reason for their error. It is enough to say the error is a common one. Everywhere in the period when the general opinion is that consumption is a rare disease it is found that the death rate from it is around 280 per 100,000. As attention is directed to it, the consumption death rate commonly declines. The limits of this decline is about 140 per 100,000.

During this period the causes indirectly responsible for the decline are certain changes in customs and attitudes. The cases are recognized and some effort is made to prevent them from spreading infection. Carelessness in spitting gives way to some degree of care. Sleeping with consumptives becomes less general. Ventilation is improved. Wages go up. Standards of living are raised, food is more abundant and of better quality. Profound fatigue is less general. These are illustrations of the kind of change in custom, habit and attitude which reduces the consumption death rate from about 280, the level of no information of facts nor interest in them, to about 140, the level at which specific work against the disease is generally added to the program. These added features called specific work against the disease, consist in such procedures as reporting cases of the disease, building and operating tuberculosis hospitals, sanitaria and dispensaries, maintaining centers and nurses, enforcing spitting regulations and other ordinances and laws.

The decline in this period of systematic control is from about 140 to about 70. This epoch was entered in Chicago in 1907 and in the remainder of the State about five to ten years later.

PNEUMONIA AND INFLUENZA.

In the history of disease in Illinois, it is impossible to separate the pneumonias from influenza at all times and with certainty. The former were always present and probably always will be. The Indians were unquestionably subject to the pneumonias and so were the French-Canadian settlers during their regime. In the earlier writings the disease was often called pleurisy. Still other names were employed.

Dr. L. C. Taylor, late president of the State Board of Medical Examiners and of the State Medical Society, was accustomed to tell of an epidemic of pneumonia which prevailed about fifty years ago near Williamsville in the northern end of Sangamon County. He described it as sweeping as an epidemic wave through the community and presenting some evidence of being contagious. It was his opinion that the disease was ordinary endemic pneumonia which had become epidemic.

Many of the older physicians were of the opinion that ordinary endemic pneumonia at times became epidemic. In the light of the present-day opinion it seems probable that the epidemic waves reported in the literature were really epidemics of influenza. On this account no sustained effort will be made to keep the diseases separate.

The year by year reports as found in the *Reports of the Committee on Practical Medicine* probably refer in the main to endemic pneumonia; the reports of epidemics refer in the main to outbreaks of influenza.

The *Transactions* of the society for the following years contain references to pneumonia: 1851, 1852, 1855, 1857, 1858, 1860, 1869, 1870, 1872, 1874, 1875, 1878.

Hirsch[62] says that the year 1807 witnessed a great pandemic of influenza. "In October of that year it was in the Western States (that is the upper Mississippi and the Ohio Valleys) but we have found no record that the sparse population of the Illinois territory suffered from it." However, they probably did.

In 1815-16 it was again pandemic. It was generally diffused over North America. However, there are no specific reports of it in the Illinois territory. In 1833 Silas Reed[63] wrote of the Western Reserve region saying "Typhoid pneumonia prevailed in 1813-14 in the Western Reserve." The probability is that the Illinois territory also suffered from it.

In 1817 the *Medical Repository of Original Essays, Vol. III*, ran a series of fourteen articles from eminent clinicians on the great epidemic of winter pneumonia which ran through several years from say 1812 to 1816. Of the fourteen clinicians, at least three regarded the disease as influenza. The clearest thinking in this series of papers was that of Dr. Singleton of Virginia. He recognized the disease as influenza and referred to epidemics of it in America in 1733, 1775, and 1770. At the conclusion of his paper he propounded the inquiry "Could the disease have been brought to this country by the British soldiers?"

---
[62] Hirsch, Ibid.
[63] Reed (Western Medical & Physical Journal).

No one can read the symposium without concluding that a high general sickness rate went with the epidemics of influenza and pneumonia. Certain of the sickness and maybe of the epidemics were cerebrospinal meningitis, then a newly described but but poorly recognized disease.

Capt. I. D. Edgar[64] says: "In December, 1812, and January and February, 1813, a very severe and fatal epidemic of pneumonia appeared in both the army and the civilian population." He refers to the epidemic at French Mills in which 47 per cent of the command were sick. Of the sick 52 per cent had dysentery, 24 per cent pneumonia, 8 per cent typhoid, while 16 per cent had ergot paralysis attributed to bread made from flour which contained fungus material.

"An epidemic of influenza prevailed in Shawneetown in the very early days."

Hirsch says influenza was again in pandemic proportions in 1824-26. It was generally present in North America and was reported from the west. An account of a limited epidemic in the Wabash Valley found in Drake's magazine[65] refers to a part of this epidemic. In 1843 he reported another pandemic in North America. In this epidemic influenza was reported from Illinois.

Drake wrote, "Influenza prevailed in 1843 in New Orleans and St. Louis and in all the intervening towns."

In 1849 a report on pneumonia in Illinois credited the gaseous emanations from the school stove as a cause of the prevailing disorder. The theory that carbon monoxide from stoves is a contributing cause of pneumonia is being revived today. In 1855 Dr. Crothers of Bloomington reported an epidemic of pneumonia in McLean County. Dr. Spalding reported a similar epidemic in the same year from Galesburg.

In 1852 Dr. Thomas Hall of Stark County wrote: "Last winter Dr. Chamberlain and I treated 70 cases of pneumonia

Dr. C. B. Johnson of Champaign writing of his practice in Chatham, Sangamon County about 1868 to 1870, said "During the two and a half years that I practiced in this locality I saw more cases of pneumonia (lung fever) than I have seen in so many years of practice since."

Dr. Forry, the Surgeon General of the Army, and Dr. Coolidge gave very good accounts of epidemics of pneumonia particularly in the army, in the *New York Journal of Medicine* and in the *Army Statistical Reports.*

The pandemic of 1873 was said to have been "universal in America." It was highly fatal in Illinois. It was peculiar in that it was shortly followed if not accompanied by a pandemic of epizootic among horses. The great pandemics of 1889-91 and 1918-20 are matters of more recent history

[64] Edgar (Military Surgeon, March, 1927).
[65] Drake (Western Medical & Physical Journal).

HISTORY OF CERTAIN DISEASES PRIOR TO 1877

Some statistics as to the prevalence of pneumonia are taken from the census reports for Illinois in 1850 and 1860, 1870 and 1880. These are presented in Tables 4 to 8. No others for the State outside of Chicago are available. In addition there are given in Table 16 the mortality rates for pneumonia in Chicago from 1851 on. In these figures pneumonia, bronchopneumonia, bronchitis and influenza are combined.

PUERPERAL FEVER.

In the second volume of Hirsch's Handbook, these statements are found:

"Under the title of infective traumatic diseases we may place together three nosological forms—erysipelas, puerperal fever and hospital gangrene which have this much in common that they bear the characteristics of an infective process and are in their origin dependent on the existence of some breach of continuity in the external or internal surfaces of the body."

He quotes Leasure[66] as saying that when malignant erysipelas was prevalent in New Castle, Pennsylvania, in 1852 all the maternity cases in his own and another physician's practice got puerperal fever. He refers to similar reports by Holsten, Galbreith, Ridley and other American practitioners of the period of the great erysipelas epidemic.

The discoveries in bacteriology since Hirsch wrote have furnished further proof of what in his time was largely speculation. Hirsch especially stresses hospitals in the history of puerperal fever, saying that its position of importance was not assumed until the development of hospitals and hospitalization.

Hirsch quotes Leasure[67] as saying, "In this country we have fortunately but little experience of the alarmingly fatal epidemics that have spread their devastating influence over different sections of Great Britain." The article by Hildreth[68] elsewhere referred to says, "Puerperal fevers are much less common than in more populous places."

The opportunities for the spread of puerperal fever are better in hospitals, but even in the rural districts this infection has always found a way to travel from household to household and from patient to patient at times, while some of it is due to the presence in households and persons of the causative bacteria. A parallel is seen in tetanus infections.

Some of the above quoted literature refers to puerperal fever and even epidemics of it in rural districts.

The reports in the Transactions of the Illinois Medical Society have frequent reference to the prevalence of the disease in the rural communi-

---
[66] Leasure (American Journal Medical Sciences, 1856).
[67] Leasure (American Medical Journal, 1835).
[68] Hildreth (American Journal Medical Sciences, 1830).

ties and towns of the State. In the *Practical Medicine Report* for 1853, Dr. Hamill the chairman, wrote, "Puerperal fever was rife and I think it was invariably fatal."

In Dr. R. C. Hamill's *Report on Practical Medicine* made to the American Medical Association there is an account of an epidemic of puerperal fever in County Hospital which began in June, 1868, reported by Doctors H. W. Jones and W. E. Quine, the latter an interne was later President of the State Board of Health. Doctors Jones and Quine clearly connected the prevalence of the disease with two sources of infection.

The obstetrician of the hospital doubled as pathologist there. He alternated jobs between the obstetric wards and the autopsy table. The internes, students and physicians were allowed to examine parturient women almost without limitation.

Dr. Robert C. Hamill.

In 1843, Dr. Oliver Wendell Holmes wrote, "The disease known as puerperal fever is so far contagious as to be frequently carried from patient to patient by physicians and nurses." He had in mind childbed fever as it was in hospitals, but there is proof that the disease was sometimes conveyed by persons who have no hospital contacts

It is the custom now to say that there is no decrease in the mortality rate from puerperal fever. The statement may be true when the present day is compared with say twenty to twenty-five years ago. But it is not true when the present day is compared with the period between fifty to one hundred years ago.

In spite of the distance between homes and the almost total absence of hospitals for maternity cases in that earlier period puerperal fever prevailed.

MILK SICKNESS.

In the *Report on Practical Medicine* made to the Illinois Medical Society in 1851, this statement is found "It seems singular that a disease specially belonging to one soil, the fear of which has turned back many an immigrant from settling in our State should have found so few historians."

Milk sickness, while not specially belonging to the soil of Illinois was very prevalent in the State in the early days and may have prevented many prospective settlers from entering or remaining in the State.

Drake wrote of milk sickness under the name "Indian trembles". He says "Hennepin first wrote of the trembles according to this version. The Indians know of it and suffered from it. It is difficult to understand how they could have escaped it. They may not have had any cow's milk but they ate the flesh of animals which doubtless suffered from 'trembles'."

Drake says, "To escape it whole communities broke up before they had well acquired a firm footing. Many fruitful tracts of country stood long unoccupied on account of it."

John Reynolds, in a Pioneer History of Illinois, writing of conditions prior to 1833, said:

"The stock of Col. Judy was injured by the mysterious disease known as the milk sickness. It made its appearance in early times in his stock and remains to exist, there is no doubt. The human family, as well as animals, are destroyed by it. I had a sister whose death it was supposed was caused by it. It is known that the disease is a poison. Dogs and other animals die with the poison when they eat the dead bodies. The victims of this disease, the human beings who die by the disease, derive it from the milk, butter or meat of the animal infected with the poison. The name of the disease arises from the milk the victims eat. This much is ascertained; but what is the poison is not so well known. It is the general approved opinion that the poison is emited from some poisonous mineral substance in the earth. It rises in a gaseous state, falls back on the vegetation, is infused in the water and in the morning before the dew is evaporated the animals eat the poison with the vegetation and thereby die. The disease only appears in the fall of the year and in shady, damp localities. A vegetable cannot cause the disease because it would have been discovered, and in some cases animals that are kept up and eat no green food die by the use of the water impregnated with the poison. It makes its ravages on stock in many parts of the West. Sometimes for many years it almost disappears and afterwards returns and assumes its former virulence."

Another reason other than its prevalence which draws attention to milk sickness is the fact that a number of people connected with men of prominence died of it. Among these was Nancy Hanks Lincoln the mother of Abraham Lincoln. A sister of Abraham Lincoln and several members of the Hanks family died of it. It caused the death of the mother of Governor Chase Osborne of Michigan. It caused the deaths of several members of the family of Dr. A. J. Clay who for many years was a local health officer of Hoopeston. Dr. Clay was stimulated by his family and personal experiences to study the cause of milk sickness. No one did more than he did to establish the fact that eating white snake root was the cause of the disorder.

A considerable part of the interest in milk sickness grew out of the difficulty in deciding what caused it, the various theories about it, the discussion of those theories and a certain amount of mystery which attached to the disease and its cause.

In 1841 Dr. Daniel Drake wrote that the first good description of the disease was that of Dr. Thos. Barbee who saw it in Bourbon County, Ohio in 1809.

In 1838 John Rowe a farmer announced the theory that milk sickness in animals was due to their having eaten a plant eupatorium ageratoides. Soon afterwards Dr. McGarragh advocated the Rowe theory before the Highland Medical Society.

In 1840 Dr. Barbee of Marshall, Edgar County, Illinois, (possibly a relative of the Thos. Barbee of Ohio) reported several cases of milk sickness that he had treated in Edgar County where the disease was very prevalent. He gave it as his opinion that the disease was caused by animals eating a plant eurpatorium ageratoides. However, instead of crediting John Rowe and Dr. McGarragh with the discovery, he gave the credit to Dr. Dale Owen, state geologist of Indiana. Dr. Barbee says Dr. Owen made a decoction from the plant and gave it to a calf, causing the disease. Dr. Barbee was of the opinion that milk sickness in cattle may be caused by their eating any one of several plants. Human beings were poisoned by drinking milk or eating meat from affected animals.

In 1841 Dr. Daniel Drake made a trip to the vicinity of Washington, Ohio, to study the disease. He accepted the general opinion of the day that the disease was related in some way to the type of soil, the trees and the plant life. His reports on all of these are exhaustive and thorough. He investigated various types of plants including eupatorium and came to the conclusion that milk sickness was a form of food poisoning that several plants could cause; that runs was the most important, that many different animals including man, cows, hogs, dogs and buzzards could contract it and that carniverous animals such as men, dogs and buzzards got it from drinking milk or eating meat from poisoned animals.

It was not until very recent times that milk sickness in Illinois was proven to be caused by animals eating white snake root. For this discovery Dr. Clay of Hoopeston was largely responsible. Other plants can cause it and in other sections of the country they are the principal cause of it. Rowe and other farmers, Barbee, Drake, McGarragh and other physicians were not far wrong in their speculations and experiments made between 1838 and 1858. Had they and their successors stuck to their lead the cause of the trouble should have been discovered at least a quarter of a century earlier than it was.

The following quotations are from Zeuch's *History of the Practice of Medicine:*

"Even as late as 1855 much distress was created by the appearance of milk sickness near Albion."

"Dr. Joseph Gates of Marine was called all over the State to treat milk sickness which had an extensive prevalence. This was in 1830 and for several years thereafter."

"Many people died from this worse than the plague." (The reference was to milk sickness in Crawford and Clark Counties.)

"The milk sickness lay in wait for man and beast along nearly all streams throughout the county and often proved as fatal as the horrible malarial." (This is quoted from some pioneer as being descriptive of conditions that were rather wide-spread in the State.)

"Milk sickness was frequently reported from Edgar County."

The disease, if it can be properly called such, began to diminish in importance early in the history of the State. In 1851 the *Report on Practical Medicine* contains one reference to milk sickness. That of 1855, devoted considerable space to the subject and quoted a fair amount of literature dealing with it. That of 1858 discussed milk sickness extensively. After 1858 it was seldom alluded to at meetings of the State Society. Of all the prominent diseases of the early days of Illinois history milk sickness was one of the first to diminish in importance.

Nursing Sore Mouth—(Possibly Scurvy)

Somewhere about 1856 a peculiar malady prevailed. It was called nursing sore mouth. It affected mothers who were nursing babies and some of the reports refer to nursing babies having the same malady.

Nursing sore mouth is found covered in the *Practical Medicine Reports* for 1857. It may have been that this sore mouth was scurvy. In 1858 Baily devoted much of the *Report on Practical Medicine* to a discussion of scurvy as a source of illness in Illinois. Among other things he held that it was a factor in the prevailing sore mouth of nursing mothers.

The literature does not record the acceptance of Dr. Baily's opinion that scurvy underlay many of the ills of the people of the State. Dr. E. P. Cook of Mendota, in an earlier *Report of the Committee on Practical Medicine*, had referred to scurvy as being in part responsible for the continued fevers of the period.

Dr. J. H. Hollister reported on the prevalence of nursing sore mouth in Illinois in 1859.

Typhoid Fever.

The travellers, historians and other lay writers who wrote incidentally or otherwise of health in Illinois in the first half of the nineteenth century or prior thereto, made no mention of typhoid fever.

The medical men who wrote in the same period wrote rather frequently of continued fevers of one sort and another calling them by different names. When they began to refer specifically to typhoid fever by that name, about 1850 and for several years thereafter, they spoke of the disease as having rather definitely invaded the State though they do not state by what means nor from where.

In 1854 Dr. N. S. Davis told the Chicago Medical Society: "Typhoid fever first became epidemic in 1848, and was highly fatal. Since then it has been milder."

In 1850, Dr. Roe of Bloomington wrote: "Typhoid fever is now first in importance. Perhaps not even cholera exceeds in the number of its victims this fell disease. It is almost as yesterday this disease made its first appearance among us."

In 1851 the *Report of the Committee on Practical Medicine* of the Illinois Medical Society, contained this statement: "Much has been written on the extension westward of typhoid fever."

In 1863, Dr. Noble told the State Medical Society: "Typhoid first came to McLean County in 1846 and 1847."

In 1864, Dr. J. S. Jewell wrote: "In two or three years after 1857 the continued fevers almost entirely supplanted the autumnal fevers."

Dr. J. E. Reeves[69] gives an account of the first appearance of typhoid fever in Virginia in 1843. "It seemed to have suddenly appeared in that year." By 1845 it was one of the major epidemic diseases."

I think it is a fair assumption that the general opinion about 1860 was that typhoid came into Illinois about 1845.

History of Steps in the Establishment of Typhoid Fever as a Specific Disease.

Physicians everywhere had such great difficulty in recognizing typhoid as an entity that it is interesting to trace the steps by which this disease emerged from the fog which obscured the entire field in the first quarter of the nineteenth century.

To travel this path properly it will be necessary to begin far away from Illinois and prior to the date of Illinois statehood. However, the place of Illinois physicians in the world wide controversy will be established before the story has been completed.

It seems probable that typhoid fever has always existed, though the disease was not clearly established as an entity until the study by Louis appeared in 1829.

Dawson[70] says: "The low fevers of Hippocrates and Galen may have been typhoid."

Dr. C. G. Gumston[71] thinks typhoid fever a very old disease. He quotes Thucydides' description of a fever which prevailed in the Greek army in the Peloponesian wars and gives his opinion that the disease was typhoid. He says: "Petechial fever—what we now suppose was typhoid—ravished the

[69] Reeves (Practical Treatise on Enteric Fever, 1859).
[70] Dawson (Western Medical Medical and Physical Journal, 1844).
[71] Gumston (N. Y. Medical Journal and Record, Feb. 16, 1927).

island of Cyprus at the end of the fifteenth century, and Italy in 1501 during the expedition of Louis XII against Naples. Hence it appears to me that typhoid fever was not a new disease appearing at the end of the 15th century."

Murchison[72] says: "Some of the descriptions of the Greek writers probably referred to enteric fever." He quotes from the writings of Hippocrates and Galen. Spigelius speaks of this fever as common in various parts of Italy. With this statement, however, Hirsch[73] disagrees, saying: "I do not agree with Murchison that Spigelius wrote of typhoid fever in the 17th Century." However, Hirsch says: "In the writings of the 16th and 17th centuries there are accounts of certain forms of sickness which can hardly be interpreted than as referring to typhoid.

Among those who wrote of what Hirsch said was typhoid were: Sydenham (1661); Welles (1682) which description Hirsch pronounces "the first clear description of typhoid"; Lancise (1718); Hoffman (1728); Strothers (1729); Gilcrist (1735); Chirac (1742); Morgagnini (1761) and Huxham (1784).

He also gives a large number of citations from the French, German and Italian, all of which show that a considerable amount of accurate knowledge of typhoid fever was known to Europeans prior to 1800. In most instances the literature cited by Murchison is the same as that cited by Hirsch.

Bartlett says that the first good description of the pathology of typhoid fever was that of Prost (1804). Murchison quotes Prost as having made post mortems on 200 cases of typhoid.

In this connection the year 1804 should be kept in mind. It will be referred to in discussing the American doctrine of the unity of fevers as put forth by Benjamin Rush.

Hirsch says: "Petit and Serres (1814) gave an accurate account of typhoid fever." Murchison says of Petit and Serres (1813): "They were the first to regard typhoid as specific."

These are a few citations of the literature prior to that of 1829. In that year Louis wrote the treatise which fixed the name "typhoid" and secured general recognition of the disease as an entity. In the period prior to 1829 typhoid was frequently confused, especially with typhus. Lois' pupils, drawn from all over the world, returned to their homes carrying the teachings of the master.

It was Gerhard of Philadelphia, an almost yearly visitor to European hospitals during this period, who brought back to America definite ideas as to typhoid and spread them over the country, but particularly along the Atlantic seaboard.

---
[72] (Continued Fevers, 1862).
[73] Hirsch (Handbook of Hist. & Geog. Path., 1881).

Subsequent to the year 1829 most of the continental writers of prominence ranged themselves behind Louis. On the other hand the British were very much disposed to hold that typhus and typhoid, and other forms of continued fever, were due to the same group of causes. Their scientists, Sydenham, Huxham, Welles, Strothers and Erasmus had contributed valuable information sustaining the position ultimately taken by Louis, but this they seem to have disregarded. In adopting what might have been called the British doctrine of the unity of fevers, they may have been under the influence of patriotism growing out of the Napoleonic wars. Who knows?

It was not until Sir W. Jenner wrote in 1849 to 1851 that the British finally abandoned this position—the doctrine of the unity of fevers.

In 1804 Benjamin Rush was an outstanding figure politically and in American medicine. He had signed the Declaration of Independence, meaning American independence of Great Britain, but in his views on the continued fevers he was anything but independent of British contemporary opinion. It was in that year, or 1805, that he wrote his views on fevers as follows:

"The usual forms of the disease produced by the miasmata from the sources of them which have been enumerated are:
1. Malignant, or bilious yellow fever.
2. Inflammatory bilious fever.
3. Mild remittent.
4. Mild intermittent.
5. Chronic, or what is called nervous fever.
6. Febriculi.
7. Dysentery.
8. Colic.
9. Cholera morbus.
10. Diarrhoea (morbus)."

Dr. Benjamin Rush had just passed through a great epidemic of yellow fever in Philadelphia, and some part of this opinion was founded on his experience there and then. But much of it was due to his reading of British medical literature. Thereafter, as will be seen, this doctrine became known as the American doctrine of the unity of fevers. Perhaps one statement by Rush in the paper quoted is enough to absolve him for the harm he did by advocating this theory. It is: "I look for the time when our courts of law shall punish cities and villages for permitting any of the sources of bilious and malignant fevers to exist within their jurisdiction."

About this time (1799) Noah Webster contributed to the same grave error of a common meteorologic and miasmatic origin of contagion in his otherwise great work, "A Brief History of Epidemic and Pestilential Diseases.

But not even the name of Webster could displace that of Rush. The doctrine of the unity of fevers travelled under the mantle of fame of Rush until it reached the Northwest Territory embracing Illinois and the contiguous states. In the East, Nathan Smith, Jackson, Gerhard and Hale, and probably Oliver Wendell Holmes were doing their best to spread the facts about typhoid, but they were not wholly equal to the task of overcoming the influence of the views of the signer of the Declaration of Independence.

J. W. Monette of Mississippi attacked the theory that yellow fever was caused by the cause of malaria in a series of articles, most of which appeared in the *Western Medical and Physical Journal*, and the *American Journal of the Medical Sciences*. Dr. Monette's papers were masterpieces and left Rush with nothing to stand on.

In these early days the principal discussion was over the separateness of typhus and typhoid. In 1842 Bartlett published his magnificent, clear-cut study entitled *"A History of Continued Fevers"*. After that the opinion of Rush as regards the oneness of typhus and typhoid was without foundation. The same may be said of the oneness of typhoid and malaria though it was more than two decades before the notion that these two diseases or groups of diseases were related some way or other came to an end.

And now, let us move from the Atlantic seaboard to Ohio, Indiana and Illinois.

The outstanding medical-man of influence in this region from about 1815 to about 1850, was Daniel Drake of Ohio. He lectured in Cincinnati and Lexington, he wrote a textbook, he conducted the first medical journal in the region, and he carried on an extensive correspondence with physicians in all parts of the Mississippi Valley. There was scarcely a section that he did not visit. His acquaintance was wide and his influence was great.

Drake was very much under the influence of Rush. Both he and his correspondents believed in miasmata and telluric influences as being able to cause malaria and other fevers, perhaps typhus. He showed a marked tendency to hold that the typhoid state, or a fever of the type of typhoid could be the outcome of these miasmas.

If Drake had read any of the contributions which paved the way for Louis in that year, there is no evidence that they changed his views; nor is it certain that he read Louis or Gerhard anywhere soon after 1829.

Early in the 19th century the physicians of the upper Mississippi Valley seemed to have accepted the opinion that the slow fever in that region was not typhus. After about 1830 the difficulty in this region on this question seemed to be limited to differentiating between the low fevers caused by malaria and those caused by typhoid.

In following the difficulties in distinguishing between these various diseases at this time, the limitations of the equipment of the physicians of the period, must be taken into consideration. They had no Widal examinations, no bacteriologic examinations of the blood, no microscopic examinations for malaria. In fact, it was not known that there were either bacteria or plasmodia. They had no clinical thermometers, no nurses, no hospitals, and no autopsies, or almost none.

There were no medical societies. The Aesculapian Society of the Wabash Valley was not established until 1846; the Illinois Medical Society was not organized until 1850. For a long time Drake's journal was alone in the field. Sending journals through the mails was expensive.

Oliver Wendell Holmes once wrote to Dr. William Osler: "I am pleased to remember that I took my ground on the existing evidence before the little army of microbes was marched up to support my contention." He had reference to his article on the contagiousness of puerperal fever, written in 1843, but the men who mapped out typhoid from typhus and malaria could pride themselves on a similar accomplishment.

From about 1850 for about forty years the most influential member of the Illinois profession was Dr. N. S. Davis. In 1855 Dr. C. N. Andrews of Rockford spoke to the Illinois Medical Society as follows: "Several articles on fever written by Prof. N. S. Davis have appeared in the *Northwestern Medical and Surgical Journal.* He advocated the American doctrine of the unity of fevers, which doctrine I regard as truthful as nature itself. It has been advanced and supported by the most able and distinguished of American physicians and, above all, Dr. Benjamin Rush."

Here comes this doctrine of the unity of fevers again. It was of British ancestry. Then the signer of the Declaration of Independence made it American. His name almost became a part of its name. And, at last, we find it here in the Northwestern Territory almost become the Illinois doctrine of the unity of fevers, and even the Davis of Illinois doctrine of the unity of fevers.

Dr. N. S. Davis said: "I do not think that all typhoid is caused by a specific cause. The disease can be caused by any one of many causes."

In a discussion of fever before the Illinois Medical Society in 1874, Dr Crawford said: "The whole family of the continued fevers are from the same cause. The cause is miasmatic."

But Dr. Cook of Mendota said he differed from Dr. Crawford: "We are all in error in considering these fevers as a unity. I have seen typhus fever in Ireland. I never saw a case here."

In 1844 one of the ablest physicians in Illinois moved to Jacksonville, Morgan County. This was Dr. David Prince. In November, 1846, Dr. Prince read a paper on the fevers of Morgan County[74]. He named four kinds of malarial fever as prevailing in that county. The third of the series of four was called typhoid fever. He said the fevers of one type tend to run into another type. There had been some change in the fevers of Morgan County since 1837. Those of 1837 to 1840 were more sthenic and stood bleeding better. Those of 1841 to 1846 inclusive, and especially 1844 to 1846, tended to be of a lower type with more tendency to typhoid, stood bleeding and active treatment less well, and called for supportive treatment.

Dr. David Prince.

Dr. John Wright of Clinton said:

"Typhoid is not caused by the same cause as ordinary malarial fever. There are those who believe they have one common origin and cause but the evidence to my mind is not convincing."

In the report on the diseases of Iowa and Missouri made by Reyburn[75] this statement is made:

"The term typhoid is used (in this region) to designate an autumnal epidemic fever of a periodic type which is ultimately lost in the continued febrile movements. An exact distinction is not made in this part of the country between those different types of fever, so far as the terms used to designate are concerned."

The authorities which have been quoted show that the paper by Louis was a consummation of a trend of opinion that had been forming for some time.

Dr. John Wright.

[74] Prince, (Illinois and Indiana Medical and Surgical Journal, April, 1847).
[75] Reyburn (Trans. A. M. A., 1856).

Anders[76] says: "Although typhoid fever was known beyond the reach of tradition, it was not until 1829 that typhoid fever was clearly distinguished from typhus fever. . . . . . The decade from 1840 to 1850 witnessed the overthrow of the erroneous notions concerning the similarity of typhoid and typhus."

In 1842 Elisha Bartlett's wonderfully clear cut text on fevers appeared. While an eastern work, it had some western circulation, and it made the picture clear. After it appeared, the only job that remained was to get the physicians to read, observe and think.

In 1843 Carroll[77] reported what seemed clearly to have been a definite outbreak of epidemic typhoid fever in Lane Theological Seminary, Cincinnati.

However, the old Rush influence, particularly as regards malaria and typhoid, was not entirely ready to die, particularly in Illinois and Indiana. The great leader of medical opinion in Illinois was Dr. N. S. Davis. The yearly transactions of the Illinois Medical Society show that he was a believer in the theory that the same basic cause, modified one way, caused malaria; modified another, caused typhoid.

Up to the middle of the decade of 1850-1860 this was the prevailing opinion of the physicians of the State, though the minority who thought otherwise was increasing year after year. By 1860 the majority seems to have swung the other way. Dr. Davis himself changed his views gradually, though still holding to some part of his basic belief. We find him stating his adherence to some part of this basic belief as late as the year 1874. Dr. Davis said: "I do not think that all typhoid is caused by a specific cause. The disease could be caused by any one of many causes."

In the *Transactions* we find him reporting cases of typhoid in the fifties. In 1864 he reported having treated 113 cases of "definite typhoid fever." 50 in his private practice and 63 in the wards of nearby hospitals in the previous six months.

At the 1874 meeting of the Illinois Medical Society, Dr. E. P. Cook of Mendota said: "Typhoid is not caused by the same cause as ordinary malarial fever. There are those who believe they have one common origin, and that one can be converted into the other. But the arguments have never satisfied me." At the same meeting, Dr. Crawford said: "The whole family of the continued fevers are from the same cause. The cause is miasmatic."

In 1875 Dr. Cook again reporting for the Committee on Practical Medicine, of the State Medical Society, said that typhoid was a specific disease. He predicted "we will yet find a specific living virus for typhoid fever."

---
[76] Anders (Practice of Medicine).
[77] Carroll (Western Medical and Physical Journal).

Some of the physicians of Illinois began to recognize typhoid fever when they saw it as early as 1845. By 1850 the number of these men able to diagnose typhoid in spite of their limited equipment was fairly large. By 1860 almost every physician in the State recognized the typical cases at least. However when the possibility of malaria was great, definite diagnosis was difficult or impossible. In fact it was not until the Widal test for typhoid and the microscopic test for malaria came into general use that accurate differentiation between these diseases became the rule. This was not until later than 1880. The confusion in the minds of the medical profession relative to typhoid and malaria was the result of several factors. In the first place it was not an easy matter to differentiate the one from the other prior to the general use of laboratory methods although the popularization of the clinical thermometer was a great aid.

The therapeutic test for malaria, namely the use of quinine, was of great value in the diagnosis of intermittent fevers but these were not confused with typhoid after the clinical thermometer came into use. In remittent fevers and particularly in the more continued types of malaria quinine lost much of its value as a diagnostic agent. When the diagnostic laboratory procedures came into general use this factor in causing confusion became unimportant.

Other factors which contributed greatly to the confusion were the various speculations as to the relationship between the diseases.

One of these speculations was that typhoid evolved out of malaria. Some believed that cases started in as malaria and ended as typhoid. Some believed that typhoid was a disease evolved out of malaria.

Another speculation or hypothesis was that there was antagonism between the two diseases. One idea was that the antagonism related to agents which directly caused them, the other was that it related to the environmental influences which indirectly caused them. And finally there was a theory that the two diseases could and did exist simultaneously in the same patient each influencing the other. It is not to be wondered at; that under the influence of so much speculation and hypothesis unchecked by procedures for exact determination confusion arose and continued general for nearly four decades.

In Bartlett[78] appears this statement: "Typhoid is probably less common in those portions of the U. S. which are visited by the various forms of intermittent and remittent fever, though further observations are necessary to settle this point." The view that there was some antagonism between these diseases was rather general, even as late as the middle nineties of the last century. Physicians were reading papers in medical societies, principally

---
[78] Bartlett, ibid.

in the southern states, denying the existence of typhoid in malarial sections as late as 1900. No longer ago than 1910, there was discussion in the medical journals of the question whether typhoid exists in the tropics. It took routine Widal tests and the routine blood examination to establish the question in the affirmative.

The theory that there was an antagonism between typhoid and malaria Hirsch says was first proposed by Boudin. In 1847 the *Illinois and Indiana Medical and Surgical Journal* quoted an article by Dr. Boudin from the Lancet of 1846. In this, Boudin had argued there was an antagonism between typhoid fever and malarial fevers. This view was advocated by many authorities. In fact, it was the accepted opinion of the times. Austin Flint[79] supported it, as did Daniel Drake in the same year and for many years. Drake showed that as malaria waned typhoid increased.

There was and is a great deal of opinion to the effect that a change in environment was responsible for the subsidence of malaria and the development of typhoid. An early traveller in Illinois wrote: "As the country was cleared up the trees were cut away and the air could circulate, malaria lessened and typhoid appeared."

J. A. Egan[80], Secretary, State Board of Health, Illinois, said: "The people of the early day were compelled to meet chills and fever, cholera, smallpox and other scourges as best they could. At first there were the diseases of the wilderness, plasmodial diseases, cholera, dysentery and other ailments which gradually disappeared with the cultivation of the prairies and the destruction of the forests. But in the place of these came the sanitary problems of denser population."

Hirsch wrote: "That the prominence of typhoid as malaria wanes is because the population grows crowded in proportion as the sources of malaria disappeared from the soil by drainage and cultivation." There is no statement that better expresses the relation of environment to the two diseases.

The theory that typhoid grew out of malaria was also popular toward the middle of the nineteenth century.

Dr. W. L. Felder[81], described a fever which he said was originally intermittent and lapsed into typhoid. Mettauer[82], writing of the fevers of Virginia, 1816 to 1829, described a continued fever which was of malarial origin. Of this fever there were three varieties: synochia, or ordinary malaria, typhoid and typhus.

[79] Flint (Buffalo Medical Journal, 1847.)
[80] Egan (Military Tract Medical Society, 1906).
[81] Felder (Trans. A. M. A., 1852).
[82] Mettauer (Amer. Jour. Med. Sc., 1843).

S. H. Dickson[83] says: "In the long protracted cases of ordinary remittent fever of the malarious region, there is a tendency of the fever to continuousness, the whole appearance is that met with in continued fever—simple, nervous or typhoid. In common professional parlance, such cases take on the 'typhoid character.'"

W. P. Veatch[84] wrote: "In Sangamon County, Illinois, there are three classes of typho-malarial fever, two of which are probably malarial and one, typhoid."

Typho-Malarial Fever.

It was in 1876 that Dr. Woodward of the United States Army read a paper before the International Medical Congress on the subject of typho-malarial fever. This paper served to fix "typho-malarial fever" in the literature. It also served to precipitate a great volume of discussion on several phases of both the malarial question and the typhoid question. The view of Dr. Woodward met with a mixed reception from the Army Medical Corps. Dr. Charles Smart[85] says: "Before the introduction of the term the association of typhoid symptoms with malarial fever and of malarial symptoms with typhoid fever was well recognized."

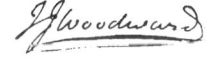

If it be contended that Woodward's paper was a piece of special pleading for typho-malarial fever, it can be answered that Smart's discussion in the *Medical and Surgical History of the War of the Rebellion* is special pleading against it.

Vaughan[86] says: "Early in our Civil War medical officers reported fevers which, in their opinion, differed from typhoid fever as seen in the north. The first board appointed (1861) to investigate the matter reported the fever prevalent among the soldiers was bilious remittent fever (malaria), which not having been controlled in its primary stage, has assumed that adynamic type which is present in enteric fever. The second board was convened (1862) for the purpose of revising the sick report. Major Woodward, the chief of this staff insisted that the prevailing fevers of the Army of the Potomac were hybrid forms resulting from the combined influences of

---
[83] Dickson (Trans. A. M. A., 1852).
[84] Veatch (Chicago Medical Examiner, 1866).
[85] Smart (Medical and Surgical History of the War of the Rebellion)
[86] Vaughan (Epidemiology and Public Health, Vol. II).

malarial poisoning and the causes of typhoid fever; and he insisted they should be reported as typho-malarial fever. This designation became official July 1, 1862, and from that time until June 20, 1866, 57,400 cases with 5,360 deaths were reported under this name."

The action taken by the Army Board in 1862 under the influence of Woodward, produced a great amount of discussion, some of which was acrimonious. It was asserted that the adoption of the term "typho-malarial fever" was a recurrence to the badly discredited and well nigh abandoned doctrine of the unity of fevers. Some said it provided a way down for some men of eminence who had allowed themselves to become stranded on that dead limb, the unity of fevers. It is said that there is a way out for those who had denied the existence of typhoid fever. Also that it furnished a new way for men who wanted to cover up and hide the prevalence of typhoid fever in their regions and communities.

The same statement was made in the reverse, namely, that the term was used as a camouflage for malaria.

It was said that its use led to sloppy diagnoses, lack of care in sanitation and hygiene, and to wrong treatment of the patient. It was said to be unscientific, as well as incorrect.

The fire and heat was so intense that the term fell into disuse. To this doubtless the decrease in malaria contributed. In time the theory that there may be simultaneous infection with a bacillus and a plasmodium will be revived, though there may never be a great, impelling reason for reintroducing the term typho-malarial fever into the popular vocabulary.

There is no reason why an individual may not be simultaneously infected with the protozoan of malaria and the bacillus of typhoid. The two organisms can exist side by side in the same individual either with active symptoms of each, or with one or both latent, or in the latent or passive carrier state.

Dr. C. B. Johnson[87] who began practice in Illinois soon after 1865, and who has practiced widely since in central Illinois, expresses the opinion which was almost universal among the rank and file of practitioners of the period. It was that there is a fever which should be called (and was so-called) typho-malarial fever—"the result of a double infection."

Dr. Breed of Princeton held that typho-malarial fever was due to three causes operating simultaneously in the same patient. These were the cause of malaria, the cause of typhoid and the cause of scurvy—typho-malarial fever was a combination of typhoid fever, malarial fever and scurvy—all three of these diseases abounded in Illinois in the same general period in the early day.

---
[87] Johnson, Ibid.

The *Transactions of the Illinois Medical Society* for 1875 show that in that year typho-malarial fever was both attacked and defended. Dr. E. P. Cook of Mendota said: "I think there is no doubt but what the malarial poison and the typhoid fever poison can and do affect the system at the same time, giving typho-malarial fever."

Food Poisoning as a Source of Confusion.

Some confusion as relates to typhoid has always existed because of speculation as to some forms of food poisoning as a cause of this fever.

A knowledge of bacteriology has lent something to the confusion. There are cases which are clinically typhoid but which do not give the serologic or bacteriologic tests for typhoid. These are called cases of para-typhoid.

Recent research work by Savage and White[88] tend to show that the typhoid bacillus is a member of the great Salmonella family. Some of the members of this family produce food poisoning, some typhoid and some other disorders. Largely as a matter of speculation they suggest that the typhoid bacillus may evolve into other members of the group and possibly that typhoid fever may have a similar relationship to food poisoning and the allied disorders.

If these theories are correct then typhoid may have evolved. And it may have done so in Illinois. In fact, it may have done so in 1845 and it may be doing so now. On the other hand typhoid bacilli may be evolving back into the Salmonella group, to produce food poisoning, or even harmless bacilli right now and every day, and here.

If somewhere between one and three per cent of all convalescents from typhoid become chronic carriers, or intermittent carriers, and remain so for life, what becomes of all the carriers? Why are they spreading so little typhoid? If practically the entire mature population of thirty years ago had had typhoid, if ninety-two per cent of those who had the disease recovered, and 2 per cent of those became chronic carriers, the carrier population of the country must have mounted to more than a million. Why is it they infected so few people? Could their typhoid bacilli have lost the special qualities of the bacillus typhosus? These are questions to which there can be no answer now. In the investigation of typhoid among troops in the Spanish-American War, the typhoid commission found, among other conclusions, two that have a bearing on this discussion.

One was that typhoid was often inaugurated by a diarrhoea which developed during the incubation period of the disease. The other was that of the troops who had diarrhoea some weeks prior to the onset of the epidemic of typhoid, very few subsequently developed typhoid and, conversely, ninety per cent of the men who developed typhoid had no preceding intestinal disorder.

---

[88] Savage and White (British Research Council 1926 Special Reports 91, 92, 103).

The bacterial cause of these diarrhoeas was not determined. Therefore what they show either for or against the Savage and White theory is purely speculative.

Conclusions as to Typhoid in Illinois prior to 1877.

A reasonable interpretation of the evidence with due regard to what is known of the habits and customs of the people and making use of what is now known about malaria and typhoid leads to the following conclusions as to typhoid fever in Illinois prior to 1877:

1. Typhoid was brought to Illinois by people who were carriers, and at times, by a typical and incubatory case.
2. In the early days the sparsity of the population operated against great prevalence of the disease.
3. Its presence was obscured by the overwhelming prevalence of malaria.
4. Much of it was unrecognized because of the meagre facilities for diagnosis.
5. With the increase in density of population the disease became more prevalent.
6. With the decline of malaria and the improvement in the methods of diagnosis recognition became easier and more certain.
7. It is possible that some typhoid evolved out of the diarrhoeas and food poisonings which were so much in evidence among the early settlers. It is possible that such evolution, backwards and forwards, is going on all the time but that fact is not proven. It is purely speculative.

Increase in Typhoid.

In the early days, according to all authorities, the conditions were right for the increase of typhoid once it found entrance. Flies abounded; water was poor and frequently polluted; toilet facilities were meagre. The salvation of the people was then isolation. By the decade 1840-1850 there was a tendency towards the building of cities.

Railroads were being built and canals dug. There was travel. Some congestion was in evidence and isolation no longer dominated the picture. Typhoid fever began to be recognized as a menace.

Dr. C. B. Johnson[89] said: "In most instances when a case of typhoid occurred in a family where there were young people, all would be apt to become infected before the disease had spent its force."

Prevalence of Typhoid Fever After 1850.

The earlier decennial reports of the U. S. Bureau of Census did not include mortality reports. The first to include such data was that for 1850.

---
[89] Johnson, ibid.

in that year, according to the census report, Illinois had a population of 851,470. The number of deaths reported as due to typhoid fever was 615. This corresponded to a rate of 71.7 per 100,000.

In 1860 the census report gave the number of deaths in Illinois as due to typoid and probable typhoid as 1182 or a rate of 69.5 per 100,000. In 1870 as 1888 or a rate of 75.5. In 1880 in Illinois outside Chicago as 1487 or a rate of 49.5. As the third decade of the 20th century draws to a close this rate is close to 4.

Typhoid Fever in Chicago.

The Chicago record began in 1852. The yearly death rates per 100,000 population by years are as given in Table 12.

The record is so incomplete that deducing from it is risky. Acknowledging this it is found that the typhoid rate for both Illinois and Chicago about 1850-1852 was somewhere about 70 to 100. It would seem that even at that date the disease was so widespread as to suggest that it had been in the area for some time. Between 1860 and 1870 what was being done by the communities to protect themselves against typhoid was about an offset to the natural tendency for it to increase as population increased. The country outside the city did a little better than the city in the decade 1870-1879, though a portion of the good showing of the country is more apparent than real.

However, neither the county nor the city was making well considered effort to bring the disease under control.

In another part of this volume is shown how Chicago began its mastering fight against typhoid soon after 1890, and the results of that fight and how the State followed a few years later, and how it in turn succeeded in conquering the disease.

Diarrhoeas and Dysenteries.

There is no question but that diarrhoeas and dysenteries were prominent in the disease history of Illinois. The writers are agreed that this was true of the Indian regime. Their food habits and their water supplies both contributed to the diarrhoeal diseases. They affected both adults and children. The same was true of the French-Canadians, during their regime. Father Marquette suffered from a chronic form of diarrhoea and finally died from it. The literature of the period makes it plain that diarrhoea and dysentery of both adults and children were prevalent.

The literature of the American period deals largely with the diarrhoeas and dysenteries of adults. All information is that the death rate among babies was very high. The importance of the high infant mortality rate came to be recognized very early. The very first mortality reports from

Chicago had deaths of children under five years of age as its only division except that by months. However, the physicians of the period did not separate of diarrhoeas of children under separate headings. Their reports did not analyze this heavy child death rate with its contributory causes.

Diarrhoea and Dysentery in Adults.

The Zeuch's *History of the Practice of Medicine* makes the following references:

In Union County, 1850. There was "an epidemic of diarrhoeal diseases which proved fatal to many."

In Jo Daviess County, 1827. "An epidemic of dysentery prevailed to an alarming extent. Many deaths occurred."

Dysentery was epidemic in Sangamon County and Springfield, 1849.

In Stark County in 1840. "Dysentery of a very fatal type prevailed."

In Kane County. "Dysentery was more malignant and fatal among the early settlers."

In the Medical and Surgical History of the War of the Rebellion Woodward tabulates and analyzes 259,000 cases of acute dysentery and diarrhoea and 28,000 cases of chronic dysentery and diarrhoea and yet in the two volumes of *Drake's Principal Diseases of the Interior Valley of North America (1850 and 1854)* neither dysentery nor diarrhoea are treated except as incidental symptoms of three disorders.

What is the reason for these apparent contradictions? It is rather easily understood.

Diarrhoea and dysentery were very common disorders. In most cases they were treated by domestic medicines and by refraining from eating. When a physician was called he generally treated the disorder symptomatically. Not much was known about either diarrhoea or dysentery. Most cases got well with simple treatment. In order to account for the serious cases the doctor frequently attributed the disorder to some other malady. Malaria was the generally ascribed cause. In 1852 Dr. Thomas Hall of Toulon, Stark County in the *Report of the Committee on Practical Medicine* said physicians all accepted the view that:

"The dysentery is the very fever itself, with the particularity that it is turned inwards upon the intestines and discharges itself that way." Dr. Hall was correct. Physicians either accepted diarrhoea and dysenteries as incidents of the day's work and gave them no special thought or else they ascribed them to malaria and wrote of what they regarded as the basic disease.

In 1851 Dr. Samuel Thompson, Chairman of the Committee on Practical Medicine, Illinois Medical Society expresses it as his opinion that diarrhoea, dysentery, typhus fever, cholera and milk sickness were modifications of the same disease. But whatever may have been their opinions of the cause, from time to time the malady would be so widespread and so fatal that the physicians writing papers would mention it one way or another.

Dr. S. H. Shoemaker of Columbia, Monroe County, wrote in the *St. Louis Medical Journal, March, 1850:* "Almost every physician in the course of his practice in 1848 and 1849 must have remarked a great proclivity in almost every disease to diarrhoea."

In 1852 Dr. N. S. Davis in the *Report on Practical Medicine,* Illinois Medical Society, says Dr. S. H. Shoemaker of Columbia reports an epidemic of dysentery of a very severe type in southern Illinois. Dr. J. T. Stewart of Peoria wrote Dr. Davis, "The most prevalent disease in this locality was diarrhoea. It showed a tendency to run into cholera." Dr. Thomas Hall of Stark County wrote, "Early in August diarrhoea was prevalent in some localities. On September 9th dysentery broke out."

In 1853 Dr. Thomas Hall of Toulon reported to the State Medical Society an epidemic of dysentery which followed one of diarrhoea and which was followed by an epidemic of typhoid.

In 1857, Dr. C. N. Andrews of Rockford reporting for the Committee on Practical Medicine told of an epidemic of "spasmodic cholera" near Rockford in September and October.

In 1858 Dr. F. K. Baily of Joliet reporting for this Committee wrote of an epidemic of dysentery in his practice. He described one case—a lady who came from "a place where a severe and fatal form of dysentery appeared about the time she was taken sick."

In 1860 Dr. C. Goodbrake of Clinton, Chairman of the Committee quoted Dr. R. G. McLaughlin of Heyworth as saying dysentery was one of the most prevalent diseases. Dysentery was quite prevalent during August and September.

Dr. J. W. Coleman of LeRoy, McLean County, reported an epidemic of dysentery which appeared in August. "No class, age or sex were exempt. About one patient died out of each fifteen sick but five miles from LeRoy on the Bloomington road twenty cases developed of whom six died."

In 1876 Dr. W. H. Veatch reported an epidemic of dysentery at Roodhouse, Greene County. It appeared suddenly July 1, 1875, and lasted sixty days. There were 300 cases and many deaths. Few families escaped.

In 1889 Dr. H. W. Chapman reported an epidemic of dysentery at White Hall. "It started in June, 1889. By the middle of the month the epidemic was on. It lasted until the last of October. There were 59 deaths from dysentery. My death rate was 1 in 11."

In discussing Dr. Chapman's paper Dr. J. P. Matthews of Carlinville said he had seen two such epidemics. One was near Corinth, Mississippi, in the army in 1863. The other was in Bird eight miles west of Carlinville in 1864. In that epidemic 25 died in a radius of five miles.

Dr. W. J. Chenoweth reported that in an earlier day he had been in a similar epidemic in Decatur in which one tenth of the cases died.

Dr. W. L. Goodell of Effingham reported an epidemic between 1850 and 1860 in which he saw 27 cases. Dr. Stahl of Grandville said fluxes were very prevalent in his section. Dr. E. P. Cook of Mendota reported an epidemic in which he had served in 1864.

In 1867 Dr. L. T. Hewins of Loda *(Committee on Practical Medicine)* reported "Dysentery in an epidemic form has not prevailed in the eastern and southern parts of the State except in Edgar County and some parts of Coles County." However, Dr. George Ringland reported an epidemic that year in a town of 600 inhabitants. The first case appeared June 28 and the last in September. There were about 100 cases and 13 deaths.

Silas Reed[80] wrote that typhoid dysenteries were especially prevalent in the Western Reserve in 1824, 1826 and 1828. In those years Illinois was drawing heavily on the Western Reserve for accessions to its population. The annual reports of the Committee on Practical Medicine of the Illinois Medical Society (there were years in which no reports were made) contained reports on the prevalence of diarrhoeas and dysenteries in 1852, 1853, 1855, 1857, 1858, 1860, 1867, 1869, 1872 and 1876. Some of these referred to diarrhoea in children, some to the disease in adults. Some referred to epidemics of diarrhoea and dysentery though in most of them the disease is reported as endemic.

Infant Mortality.
(Especially that due to diarrhoeal diseases.)

Every person who wrote of health conditions during this period placed especial stress on the sickness rate and especially on the diarrhoeal disease rate among babies.

If there was confusion as to the causes of the different kinds of diarrhoea among adults there was more of it as to the same symptom or disease among babies.

Diarrhoea, summer complaint, cholera morbus, cholera infantum and dysentery were terms used more or less interchangeably.

In 1858 Dr. F. K. Baily of Joliet proposed that the term cholera infantum americana be used since the disease was so prevalent in America. He said that it was often confounded with ordinary diarrhoea. He said one of the questions which he had asked related to cholera infantum. Nobody replied to that question but he knew the disease was prevalent because he had seen much of it in his practice in Joliet for four or five years.

---
[80] Reed, ibid.

In 1871 Dr. D. W. Young of Aurora quoted Dr. A. Jacobi as saying that cholera infantum was the result of paralysis of the nervous system caused by heat.

In 1883 Dr. L. H. Corr of Carlinville said cholera infantum was a neurosis. Many writers thought it a manifestation of malaria. Dr. J. Murphy of Peoria told of his success in preventing it by giving prophylactic doses of quinine in the summer time.

In 1857 Dr. C. N. Andrews of Rockford *(Committee on Practical Medicine)* reported diarrhoea and cholera morbus were also somewhat prevalent particularly among the children.

In 1858 Dr. Hiram Mance of Lafayette wrote "Cholera infantum prevails every summer in this vicinity." In 1859 Dr. J. O. Harris of Ottawa wrote "During the summer months diarrhoea among children was extremely prevalent." In 1871 Dr. D. W. Young gave this opinion: "it is generally conceded that more children die annually from cholera infantum than from any other disease."

Dr. L. H. Corr.

In 1879 Dr. L. H. Corr of Carlinville said "Nearly one half the children born die before reaching 5 years of age and nearly one half of these deaths are from bowel troubles commonly called cholera infantum or summer complaint."

In the *Transactions of the State Medical Society* either through papers or through references in the report of the Committee on Practical Medicine, cholera infantum was covered in 1858, 1860, 1869, 1871, 1876 and 1878.

Diarrhoea and dysentery usually referring to these diseases in children were covered in 1852, 1853, 1855, 1857, 1858, 1860, 1867, 1869, 1872 and 1876.

For twenty-seven years 1843 to 1869 inclusive the *Chicago Health Department Annual Reports* carried a table in which was shown the total number of deaths at all ages and the total number occurring in children five years of age and younger. Table 2 shows the percentages of the total deaths in each year which were in children as aforesaid.

Twice in the period the number of deaths of children was less than 30 per cent of the whole. Six times it was between 30 and 40 per cent of the whole. Six times between 40 and 50 per cent. Eleven times it was between 50 and 60 per cent. Twice it was over 60 per cent. It seems almost inconceivable that in any year the deaths of young children should more than equal, should even approximate two thirds the total deaths at all ages. And yet that happened in Chicago and probably also in those other portions of the State in which no record was kept. In those years the total death rate was high, making the child death rate very high.

In *The History of the Practice of Medicine* Zeuch says: "By 1878 the death rate from infantile diarrhoeas had fallen to one-fourth the number in 1845."

The graphs shown in Figures 1 to 7 showing the high mortality in the summer months in the early years also point to a high child death rate in that period. The great part of the death rate of babies was due to digestive disorders.

Deaths of Children Under Age Five in Relation to Deaths at All Ages.

In view of the fact that the Chicago vital statistics tables had shown since 1843 the relation between deaths under 5 and all deaths Dr. N. S. Davis was interested in that subject. In 1873 he told the Illinois Medical Society that in Norway the deaths of children under five years of age were only 15 per cent of the total deaths; in Massachusetts 20 per cent; in Bavaria 50 per cent. It would be interesting to know whether Illinois was in the class with Norway or with that of Bavaria—or was somewhere in between. In all probability it was nearer Bavaria than Norway but there is no way of knowing for certain since Illinois was not keeping books in terms of vital statistics at that time.

But Chicago was and the figures are available for comparison. While the death rate of children under 5 years of age down-state was not quite equal to that of Chicago the difference was not great. Table 2 shows the proportion of deaths of children under five years of age to total deaths in Chicago from 1843 to 1877 inclusive and for purposes of comparison the proportion for 1925, a typical year in the present period is also shown. This table shows that 1871 had the worst record with a percentage of 70.7. In 1873, the year in which Dr. Davis made the slighting reference to Bavaria, the proportion in Chicago was 59.3, in Bavaria 50. The average for all the years 1843 to 1877 was 49.4, the average for the ten years 1864 to 1873 inclusive was 54.5. Compare this with Chicago's present day proportion 17.8 and Norway's 15.

In 1879 Dr. L. H. Corr of Carlinville said one half the children born in Illinois died before reaching five years of age.

In the U. S. Registration Area in 1925, the number of deaths among children under five years of age per 1000 total deaths was 187.5. The number in persons over five years of age was 812.5, or a ratio of 23 per cent.

Seasonal Distribution of Disease.

As early as 1867 there were physicians who found the menace of respiratory diseases in winter almost as much as that of digestive diseases in summer. In 1867 Dr. Hamill told the American Medical Association that in Illinois three-fifths of all the deaths from lung diseases occurred in March, April and November. The least mortality occurred in July and August.

Table 9 and Figures 1 to 7 show the radical change in the monthly distribution of disease which has occurred in Chicago since 1843. It is reasonably certain that a similar change has occurred elsewhere in the State though the statistical data to establish the fact are not available. The figures given and used as a basis for the charts are ten-year averages and therefore temporary epidemic influences are eliminated.

The exceptions to the statement that the figures show ten-year averages are the charts made by Dr. Michael Mannheimer for Chicago in 1867 and 1868, the chart for 1922 and the one for 1843-49. The charts made by Dr. Mannheimer are included because they show the seasonal distribution of fatalities in that day and also because they were pioneer productions and of superior excellence. It was nearly thirty years after 1869 before the Chicago Health Department resumed the plan of charting disease.

Dr. Michael Mannheimer.

Table 2.
RATIO OF DEATHS AMONG CHILDREN LESS THAN FIVE TO ALL DEATHS.
CHICAGO 1843-1877 AND 1925.

Year	Ratio	Year	Ratio
1843	28.5	1862	55.
1844	41.6	1863	50.7
1845	40.	1864	51.4
1846	33.3	1865	52.7
1847	37.	1866	48.8
1848	41.6	1867	57.5
1849	26.3	1868	42.2
1850	36.7	1869	54.4
1851	42.7	1870	62.3
1852	33.9	1871	70.7
1853	48.5	1872	45.2
1854	32.9	1873	59.3
1855	44.5	1874	61.
1856	52.7	1875	61.2
1857	58.5	1876	57.
1858	57.3	1877	56.2
1859	56.6		
1860	55.7		
1861	54.8	1925	17.8

The single year 1922 is charted as a sample year in the present unexpired decade. The chart for the forties represents an incomplete decade because the figures for 1840-41 and 42 are not available.

The charts illustrate total deaths rather than rates and in consequence the scale has had to be changed. In order to prevent visual misconception as to the relative summer rise in 1843 to 1849 Fig. 7 is inserted. In this chart the scale is different from that used for 1843-1849 in the chart shown in Fig. 3.

The striking features disclosed by these charts are the summer peaks in the earlier charts and the winter peaks in the later one.

The summer peak which was the outstanding feature of the sickness rates prior to 1880 gradually declined thereafter. Some slight tendency to decline was noticed several years before 1880 in Chicago where the health department began to be somewhat efficient in the latter part of the decade 1860-1869. By 1920 this peak had wholly disappeared. The disappearance of this peak is due to the disappearance of malaria, the near disappearance of typhoid and

Table 3.
AVERAGE DEATHS IN CHICAGO—BY MONTHS—DECADES.

Decade ending.	Jan.	Feb.	Mar.	Apr.	May.	June.	July.	Aug.	Sept.	Oct.	Nov.	Dec.
1849*	26	27	26.3	27.1	49.9	42.6	92	80	64	44	38	29
1859	92.6	84.4	93.6	95.6	96.6	117.9	272.5	386.7	273.5	156	107.4	102.2
1869	279.3	263.9	274.4	253.8	240.5	224.9	499.8	583.3	454.5	405.3	296.9	302.4
1915	2938.6	2836.2	3158.	2934.	2893.7	2362.4	2527.5	2686.	2539.6	2457.0	2483.7	2964.4
1925	3254.9	3263.4	3436.5	3125.7	2926.1	2459.1	2417.8	2475.9	2413.3	3290.6	2673.1	3343.3

* 7 years only.

the great decrease in the diarrhoeal diseases and other causes more or less related to the work of health departments and physicians. The winter peak began to appear in the decade 1870-79. It was fairly in evidence in 1880-89. Since 1890 it has been the striking feature of the picture. Its eminence is in part due to the recession of the summer peak. However, that does not tell the whole story.

During a part of the time the sickness rate of this peak period has been absolutely higher as well as relatively higher than it was during the prewinter peak period. The contribution of the pneumonias and influenza to this result has been elsewhere discussed. In order to draw conclusions from statistics of the acute lung infections which shall not be very misleading it is necessary to combine lobar and broncho pneumonia, bronchitis and endemic influenza (either actual or so-called). It may be possible to separate influenza in great epidemic years without radical statistical error but not at other times. This has been referred to in the section dealing with pneumonia and influenza.

Scale of
Monthly
Mortality
700

650

600

550

500

450

400

350

300

250

200

150

100

50

0
RAIN
E.WIND
W.WIND
CLEAR DAYS
CLOUDY DAYS

FOLDOUT BLANK

FIG. 2. Second Mannheimer chart.

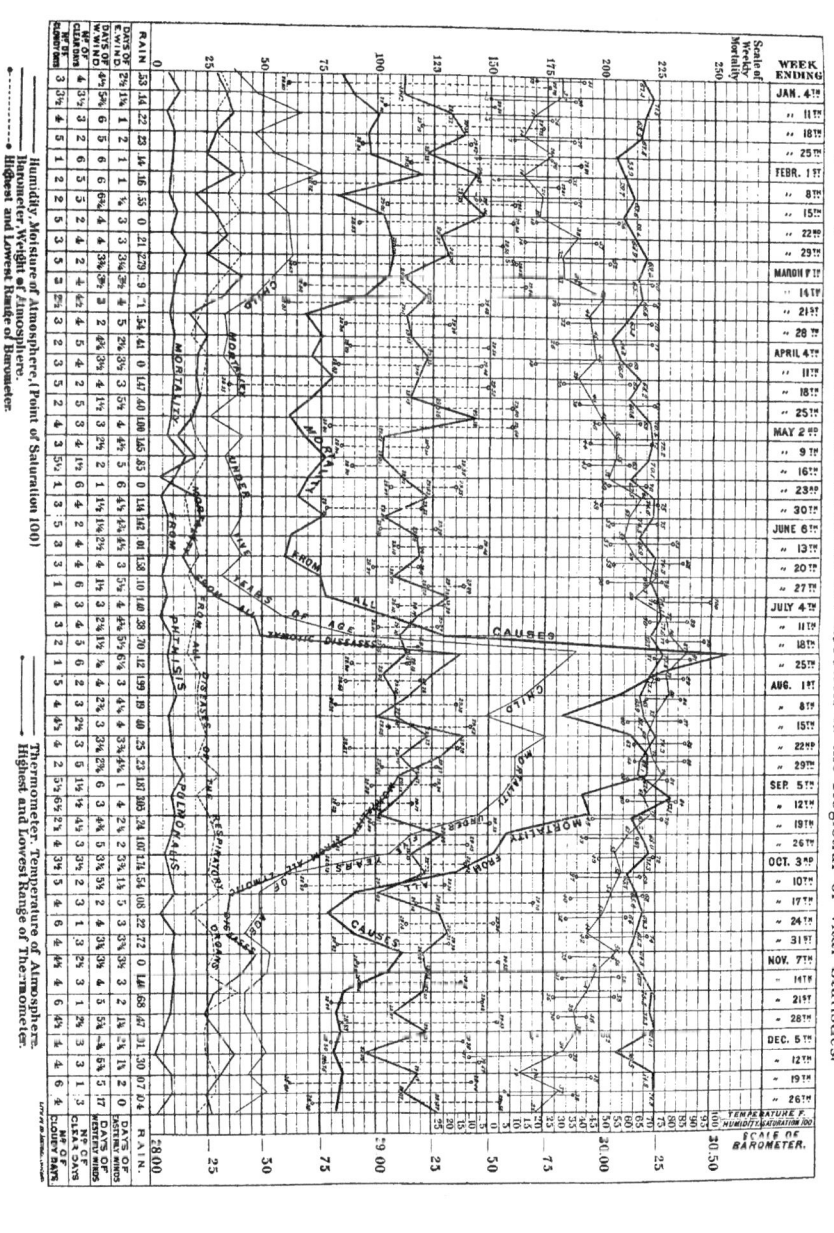

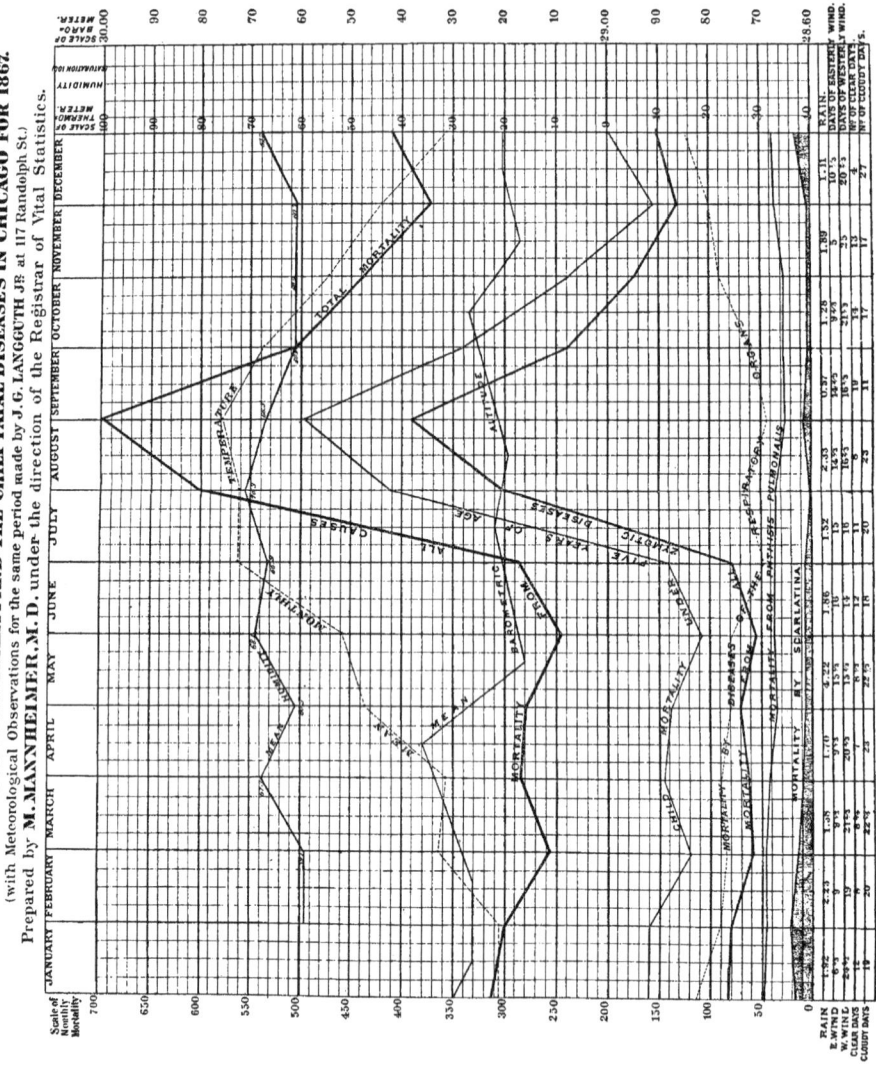

Fig. 1. First Mannheimer chart.

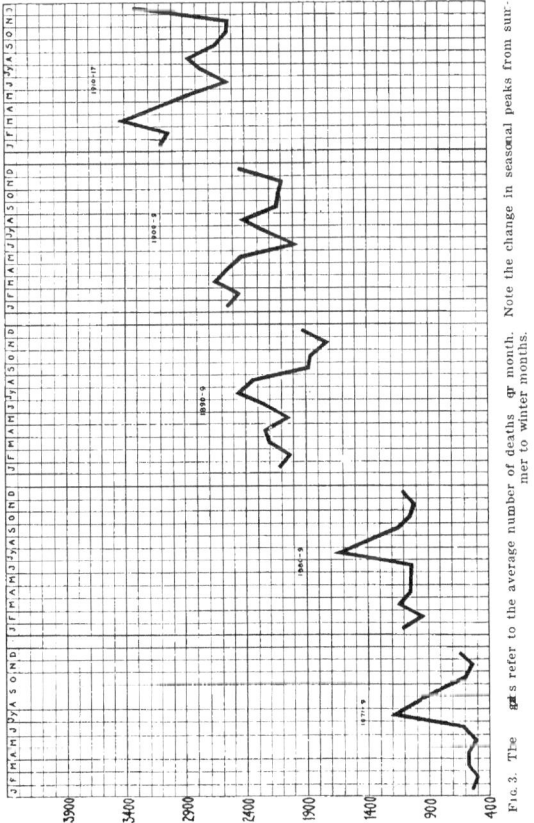

Fig. 3. The figures refer to the average number of deaths per month. Note the change in seasonal peaks from summer to winter months.

92   HISTORY OF CERTAIN DISEASES PRIOR TO 1877

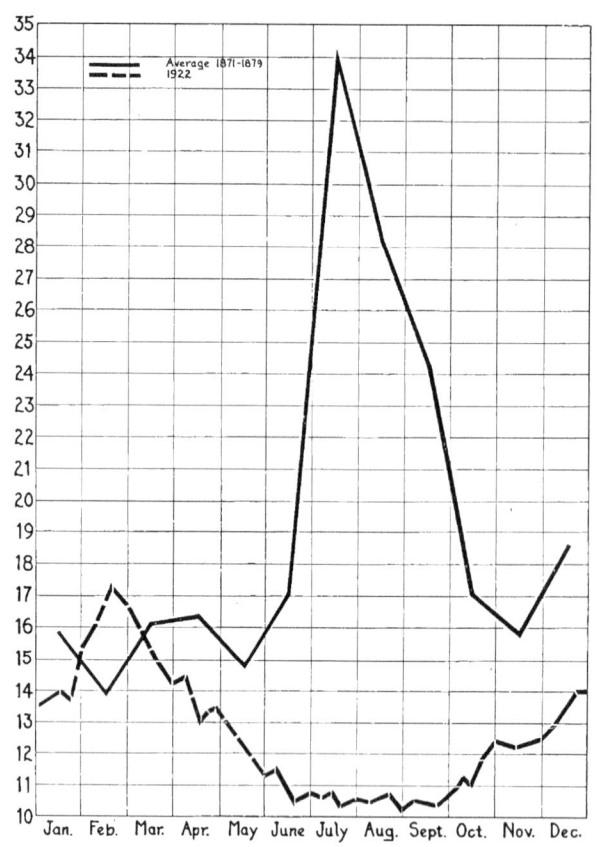

FIG. 4. Monthly mortality rates in Chicago showing the change fifty years have wrought in seasonal distribution.

Chicago Mortality Rate for Acute Respiratory Diseases by Decades

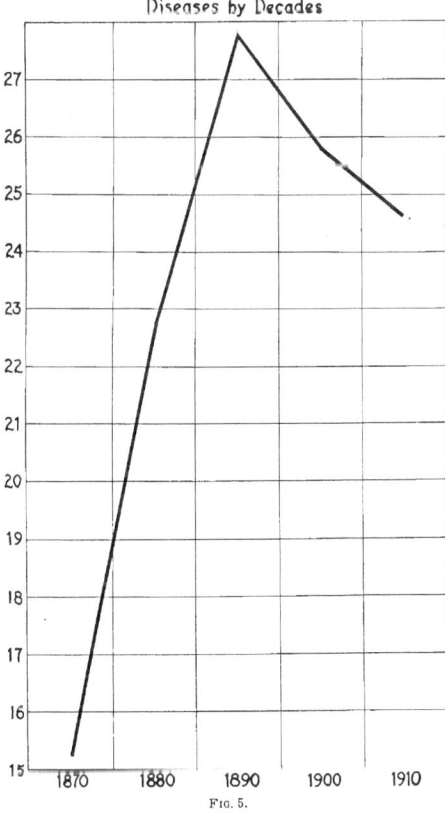

Fig. 5.

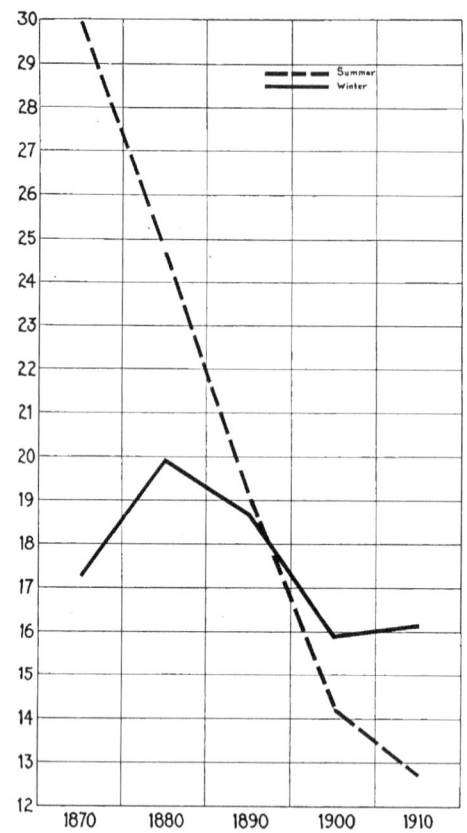

Fig. 6. Showing decennial mortality rates from all causes in Chicago for January, February and March contrasted with that for July, August and September.

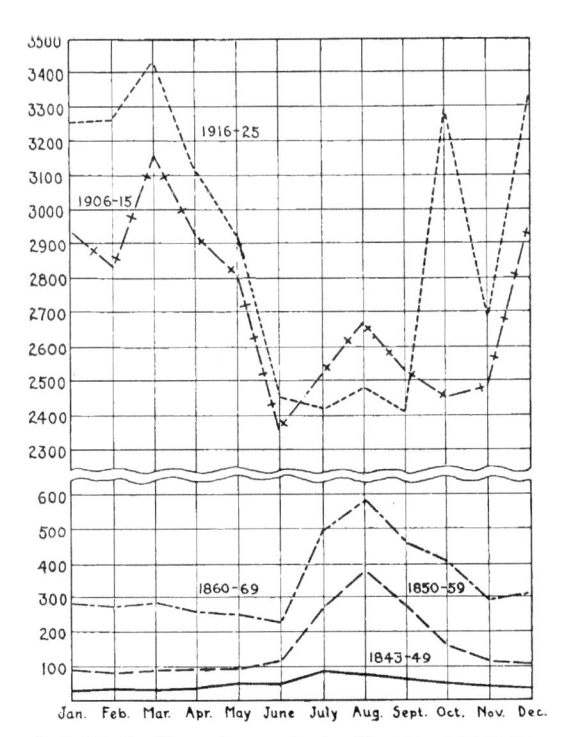

FIG. 7. Note the difference in seasonal peaks. The autumnal rise in the 1916-1925 decade was due to the influenza pandemic of 1918.

But in addition to influenza and the pneumonias the winter peak is made up of contributions of other diseases less easily related to respiratory infections. The death rates from smallpox, measles, scarlet fever and diphtheria —all important diseases of the winter peak period—have declined without any decided or certainly without a pari passu decline of the winter peak. Some of the few health students who have studied the development of this winter peak have attributed it to the great influenza wave which prevailed in Illinois during a period which began about December, 1890. But the tables and the charts show that whatever was operating to change bacteria or people or environment or several of these combined was in operation prior to 1890.

The solution of this problem is bequeathed to the Illinois Department of Public Health during the next few years. The solution will require their best thought. It will require research, planning and strategy because it is possible that the people may need to change many of their social methods and customs before they can enjoy good health and low death rates during the winter and early spring.

Vital Statistics and Mortality Rates From All Causes

The Seventh Census, that of 1850 was the first to give any vital statistics and what it gave was limited to population gain, to population figures and gross death and birth rates.

The introduction to the report of this census contains the following statements:

"The tables of the census which undertake to give the total number of births, marriages and deaths in the year preceding the first of June, 1850, can be said to have very little value"—"Upon the subject of deaths no one can be deceived by the figures of the census since any attempt to reason from them would demonstrate a degree of vitality and healthfulness of the United States unparalleled in the annals of mankind and would overthrow the best established principles of statisticians and contradict all science and experience. The truth is but a part of the deaths have been recorded varying for sections from a very small to a very large part of the whole"—"In the form in which these deaths are published they are of no value, yet in the opinion of medical gentlemen in different parts of the Union of high reputation who have been consulted and whose testimony is now on file in the census office and in the opinion of the National Medical Convention (American Medical Association) who are equally aware of the precise character of the data, the publication of the names of the diseases for each of the counties of the United States, the period of sickness, the age, birth-place and occupation of the deceased, the exact time of death, defective in many respects though the returns maybe, would essentially subserve the interests of the medical profession of the country and tend to the promotion of public health."

The death rate as given by this census for Illinois was 13.6—this is the death rate that was esteemed impossible because it "would demonstrate a degree of vitality and healthfulness unparalleled in the annals of mankind and would overthrow the best established principles of statisticians and contradict all science and experience." The statement was true in 1850 but by 1910 the death rate had fallen below 13.6 and it has been below that figure every year since except in the influenza epidemic period. What was thought to be impossible in 1850 is now more than achieved and being achieved is accepted as a matter of fact and almost without comment to say nothing of praise.

By 1860 most of the standards referred to in the introduction to the report in the Seventh Census had been adopted. Nevertheless, the actual returns of death were far from satisfying as the Superintendent of the Seventh Census had warned. In the introduction to the report of the Eighth Census are found the following statements:

It is manifest that neither in 1850 nor in 1860 was the entire mortality of any state ascertained and reported nor was even such an approximation obtained as will permit any reliable calculation to be made of the rate of mortality. The same holds true of the deaths reported as due to the several causes of death such as consumption."

In Tables 4 to 10 are presented some excerpts from the U. S. Census reports of 1850-1880 relating to mortality in Illinois and the population of the State.

Table 4.

DEATHS FROM ALL CAUSES AND CERTAIN DISEASES IN ILLINOIS—DECENNIAL YEARS 1850-1880—FROM U. S. CENSUS REPORTS.

Illinois.	1850.	1860.	1870.	1880.
Deaths	11,819	19,300	33,672	45,017
Death rates	13.6	11.2	13.2	14.6
Death rates under 1 yr. per 1,000 births				
Deaths under 5 (percent of total)		51.4	50.3	43.4
Bronchitis				
Pneumonia		87.	123.8	168.2
Influenza				
Pleurisy				
Cholera		4.1	1.2	0
Consumption		113.7	145.6	150.9
Diarrhoea				
Dysentery				
Enteritis				
Cholera—infantum		128.8	188.3	148.
Cholera—morbus				
Teething				
Bowels, disease of				
Diphtheria and Croup		70.	59.	122.9
Malaria				
Intermittent		66.9	35.5	36.1
Remittent				
Measles		6.3	27.6	19.5
Typhoid and Typhus		65.7	70.3	53.6
Meningitis				
Cephalitis				
Cerebro Spinal		41.2	77.3	18.5
Meningitis				
Encephalitis				
Scarlet Fever		98.7	85.1	44.4
Smallpox		.4	6.7	1.4
Whooping Cough		22.3	23.2	15.8
Erysipelas		10.6	10.5	10.7
Yellow Fever		1.	2.	3.
Typhus Fever			5.1	.7

HISTORY OF CERTAIN DISEASES PRIOR TO 1877

Table 5.

POPULATION AND NUMBER OF DEATHS—ILLINOIS

U. S. CENSUS REPORT 1850.

Total Population 851,470
White 846,034
Free Colored 5,436
Number died during year... 11,619

Table 6.

NUMBER OF DEATHS FROM CERTAIN DISEASES—ILLINOIS

U. S. CENSUS REPORT 1860.

Population 1,711,951.

Deaths	19,300	Fever typhoid	1,183
Bowels, disease of	26	Infantile	373
Bronchitis	75	Influenza	14
Cephalitis	701	Measles	109
Cholera	70	Pleurisy	46
Cholera infantum	315	Pneumonia	1,357
Consumption	1,948	Scarlet fever	1,698
Croup	1,158	Smallpox	8
Diarrhoea	607	Teething	198
Diphtheria	41	Deaths under 1 year	4,407
Dysentery	845	Deaths under 5 years	9,928
Enteritis	329	Whooping cough	382
Fever intermittent	464	Yellow fever	1
Fever remittent	682		

Table 7.

NUMBER OF DEATHS FROM CERTAIN CAUSES—ILLINOIS

U. S. CENSUS REPORT 1870.

Population 2,539,891.

Deaths all causes	33,672	Typhus	131
Cholera infantum	1,869	Meningitis	1,932
Croup	886	Diarrhoea	1,284
Whooping cough	640	Dysentery	664
Measles	762	Enteritis	603
Pneumonia	2,882	Bronchitis	219
Smallpox	170	Under 1 year, Total	9,215
Diphtheria	603	Under 1 year, Females—4,149	
Scarlet fever	2,162	Under 1 year, Males —5,066	
Malaria	888	Under 5 years, Total	16,953
Meningitis	43	Under 5 years, Females—7,836	
Typhoid	1,758	Under 5 years, Males —9,117	
Typhomalaria	17		

Table 7—Continued.

ILLINOIS—1870—DEATHS.

Disease.	Male.	Female.	Total.
Yellow Fever	2	0	2
Cholera	19	13	32
Typhomalarial	12	5	17
Influenza	2	3	5
Erysipelas	139	125	264
Encephalitis	688	522	1210
Croup	472	414	886
Pleurisy	28	12	40
Teething	131	157	288

Table 8.

NUMBER OF DEATHS FROM CERTAIN CAUSES—ILLINOIS AND CHICAGO

U. S. CENSUS REPORT 1880.

Population 3,077,871.

Number deaths	45,017	Typhus fever	23
Bronchitis	109	Yellow fever	5
Cholera infantum	1,884	Whooping cough	488
Cholera morbus	169	Measles	603
Consumption	4,645	Meningitis	594
Diarrhoea	770	Pneumonia	4,378
Diphtheria	2,403	Smallpox	45
Dysentery	698	Erysipelas	334
Enteritis	988	Yellow fever, group 2	2
Fever	77	Yellow fever, group 3	3
Meningitis	278	Bowels	111
Enteric fever	1,652	Croup	1,370
Malarial fever	1,114	Pleurisy	91
Scarlet fever	1,369		

Table 8—Continued.

CENSUS—1880—ILLINOIS.

Living 1 yr. of age	87,859	Deaths under 5	19,667
Death per 1000 births (males)	94.1	Percent of total deaths (males)	44.8
Death per 1000 births (females)	75.8	Percent of total deaths (females)	41.9
Total deaths under 1 yr.	10,968		

DEATHS—CHICAGO—CERTAIN CAUSES—UNDER 1 YEAR.

Per 1,000 births (males)	166.7	Under 5 years	5,871
Per 1,000 births (females)	122.4	Percent of total deaths (males)	57.3
Total under 1 year	3,533	Percent of total deaths (females)	54.8

Table 9.

POPULATION OF ILLINOIS—CENSUS YEARS FROM U. S. CENSUS REPORTS 1810-1888.

Year.	Population.	Increase. Per cent.	Increase. Numerical.
1810	11,282		
1820	55,211	349.52	32,929
1830	155,455	185.16	100,244
1840	476,183	202.44	320,728
1850	851,470	78.81	375,287
1860	1,711,951	112.8	860,481
1870	2,539,891	48.36	827,940
1880	3,077,871	21.18	537,980

Table 10.

INCREASE OF POPULATION BY CENSUS YEARS FROM U. S. CENSUS REPORTS 1810-1850.

Year.	Whites.	Increase.	Free Colored.	Increase.	Slaves.	Increase.	Total.	Percent.
1810	11,501		613		168		12,282	
1820	53,788	367.68	457	20.44	917	445.83	55,211	349.52
1830	155,061	188.28	1,637	258.2	747	18.53*	155,445	185.16
1840	472,254	204.56	3,598	119.79	331	55.68*	476,183	202.44
1850	846,034	79.14	3,436	57.08			851,470	78.81

* Decrease.

HEALTH HISTORY PRIOR TO 1877 OF SOME OF THE CITIES, IN ILLINOIS.

Chicago.

In a health history of Illinois, Chicago and the Chicago area deserves especial consideration. It was the portal of entry for that great part of the population which now dominates the State and which has been prominent in the State since 1840 at least. They or their parents or grandparents entered Illinois at Chicago and remained there or somewhere else north of the center of the State. This population has been a health factor differing somewhat from that of other parts of the State.

Chicago is the largest center of population in the State. It had a health department many years before the State organized one and this example helped the medical profession to get a state health department. At times it has contributed diseases to other parts of the State and at times other parts of the State have contributed disease to Chicago.

The great Irish wave of immigration of the thirties and forties, the great German wave of a little later period, the great Scandinavian wave of the seventies and the lesser immigration waves from other lands, all these great masses of people influenced the health of the population among whom they settled.

The immigration into the State from other states which came through this portal, speaking in a general way, came from different states than that which settled in the prairies and to the south thereof.

The great aggregation of people, several millions in number near the Chicago River, by their very congestion, created health problems that differed in quantity and to a degree in quality from those of the other parts of the State.

The location of Chicago did not presage good health. There were no currents in Lake Michigan by which sewerage and soil pollution could be kept away from the water supply and the city was near the lake head where these forces are most potent for harm. The country was flat and drainage was not possible. Mosquitoes abounded. Long John Wentworth makes the statement that there were no mosquitoes in the Chicago area prior to the opening of the Illinois-Michigan Canal but in this he was mistaken. This statement is found in his address on the early days in Chicago made in his later life long after the opening of the canal. Doubtless his recollection of things political and economic was correct but he forgot the mosquitoes. He is contradicted by a number of witnesses who wrote when the matter was fresh in their minds.

(101)

Gordon Salstenstill Hubbard writing of his first portage through Mud Lake, Chicago, in October, 1818, says, "The lake was full of these abominable black plagues (leeches or blood suckers) and they stuck so tight to the skin that they broke in pieces if force was used to remove them. The use of tobacco to remove them was resorted to with good success. Having rid ourselves of the blood suckers we were assailed by myriads of mosquitoes which rendered sleep hopeless."

In spite of all this the indications are that up to 1803 or thereabouts the people of the Chicago area had rather better than average health. There is no record of great departure from normal health among the Indians of the area or among the French-Canadians nor among the other inhabitants prior to the beginning of immigration from the other states. The travellers of the period who visited Chicago generally referred to the lake water as healthy though one statement to the contrary was found.

In 1804 Surgeon General Forry of the U. S. Army wrote of the Chicago Region—"This position is one of our most salubrious stations." But right at this point the story changes. Quaife[91] says, "Soon after the arrival of troops (1803) they suffered much from bilious fever."

Whistler reported "that in one year after Fort Dearborn was occupied more than one-half the men had been ill."

In 1820 Dr. Alexander Wolcott came to the fort as an Indian agent. He wrote, "The fevers of that season were unusually rapid, malignant and unmanageable." The reports of this period indicate that malaria was very prevalent. Excerpts from records and writings of the period as chronicled by Rauch[92] and Koehler[93] are here presented to show the major facts relating to the health and sanitation of Chicago from 1829 to 1876:

```
1829.  Fort Dearborn troops.
       Man strength of the garrison.................................... 91
       Diseases, intermittent fever.................................... 17
       Respiratory organs ............................................. 11
       Digestive organs ............................................... 30
1830.  Man strength of the garrison.................................... 90
       Deaths from remittent fever..................................... 15
```

However, in that year the Canal commissioners wrote, "The inhabitants say the site is decidedly healthy."

1832. In this year cholera attacked General Scott's troops en route to the Black Hawk War. The rate was 200 per 1000. There were forty-eight deaths. Because of the epidemic these troops never got to the front.

1833. The first sanitary ordinance was passed.

---
[91] Quaife (Chicago and the Old Northwest).
[92] Rauch (Sanitary History of Chicago, Chicago, 1871).
[93] Koehler (Annals of Health and Sanitation Octennial Report of Department of Health, Chicago, years 1911-18, Chicago, 1919).

1834. A temporary board of health was formed and also a cholera vigilance committee. These activities were inaugurated in order to fight cholera which threatened. When cholera did not appear all this lapsed.

1835. Another board of health was appointed consisting of seven members.

1837. Chicago was incorporated and a board of health was appointed. They appointed a health officer.

1838. Nearly all who resided along the line of the canal excavation had malaria as did the laborers digging the canal. "A very deadly and strange epidemic appeared; it was called the canal cholera."

1840. City got a water supply from the lake.

1841. "An ordinance requiring reports of deaths was passed but was not enforced for several years."

1843. One hundred and twenty-nine deaths were located by means of inquiries of undertakers. (This was Chicago's first mortality record.)

1844. "Inquiry among undertakers discovered 306 deaths. A violent epidemic of scarlet fever was responsible for many of these."

1845. Scarlet fever still prevailed. Board of health practically defunct for several years.

1848. Chicago had a smallpox scare.

1849. In April forty-five district health officers were appointed. Cholera appeared in that month. In that year there were 687 deaths due to cholera. In one month there were 1000 cases and 314 deaths. Great activity in sewer building. Smallpox also prevailed.

1850. Cholera again appeared. In one month 416 persons died from the disease. Smallpox still prevalent.

1851. A new city charter gave much larger powers in health matters to the city council. A committee of the Chicago Medical Society reported the mortality rates 1846 to 1850. That of 1850 was 46.6 per 1000. Smallpox and cholera present.

1852. Cholera was present. The number of deaths caused by it was 630. From 1849 to 1852 inclusive, 1944 died from cholera which represents one death per each 64 of the population. Smallpox prevailed. The Marine Hospital was opened. During the first three months the hospital treated 20 cases of malaria. The city health officer's salary was $500 per year.

1853. Smallpox more prevalent.

1854. There were 1424 deaths from smallpox. Cholera present. Cholera and smallpox hospitals were maintained.

1854 and 1855. There were 1571 deaths from cholera or one for each 99 of the population.

1855. Deaths from smallpox 30; from cholera 147.

1856. General health better. No deaths from cholera but typhoid was on the increase. Typhoid very prevalent in September.

1857. Board of health went out of existence. Malaria death rate was 53.6 per 100,000, the highest rate shown by the records. Also an epidemic of dysentery which was very fatal.

1858. Scarlet fever still prevailed and dysentery was very prevalent in children during the summer months. Tuberculosis death rate was 392.2 per 100,000, highest in the history of the city.

1859. Scarlet fever still prevalent. The death rate from scarlet higher than that from any other disease. Many sewers built.

1860. Board of health abolished. Raising of the city grade completed. The term typhus fever disappears from the mortality records this year.

1862. Policeman Perry appointed acting health officer. Diphtheria and smallpox prevalent. Increase in deaths from all causes. Typhoid and scarlet fever increased especially. Bridgeport sewerage pumps started.

1863. Death rate increased. There were 947 cases of smallpox. Epidemic of erysipelas present. This outbreak was studied by Dr. Edmund Andrews who showed how the disease prevailed along the filthy Chicago River and in the unsewered parts of the city.

1864. The result of the almost total neglect of sanitary laws during the past five years in addition to the fact that the construction of sewers did not keep pace with the increase of population is apparent from the great mortality of this year. Compared with 1863 there was a great increase of cholera infantum and cholera morbus. Erysipelas and the low grades of fevers almost doubled and smallpox trebled. There was a great increase in diarrhoea and dysentery. There were nearly five times as many deaths from measles and a great many more from pneumonia.

Another remarkable fact is that only 164 more died in the last six months than in the first. Erysipelas continued to be epidemic until July. This year witnessed the first great increase in pneumonia and the first tendency to a change in the seasonal distribution of fatal disease from a summer to a winter peak. The tendency was scarcely perceptible for several years.

1865. The high pneumonia rate continued. The effect of the heat and sudden change increased the mortality particularly among the children. Fear of cholera stimulated owners of property to make sewer connections. Cholera was reported on its way and Dr. T. B. Bridges was appointed health officer

1866. A total of 1,581 cases of cholera occurred. Health officer was given 32 assistants. The death rate was 32.55 per 100,000. The death rate of children under 5 was high. "The heavy rainfall from July to October in connection with the localities in which cholera occurred goes far toward corroborating the ground water theory of Pettenkofer", says Dr. Rauch.

1867. Chicago organized a board of health which followed the lines of the Metropolitan Board of Health of New York of which Dr. Stephen Smith was the moving spirit. The Chicago board made Dr. Hosmer A. Johnson president and Dr. J. H. Rauch, a former surgeon in the Civil War, as its executive officer with the title sanitary superintendent. Dr. Rauch was an unusual health officer for his day. Dr. Arthur R. Reynolds, formerly commissioner of health of Chicago, has written a good short sketch of the life of Dr. Rauch. (Three Chicago and Illinois Public Health officers, J. H. Rauch, Oscar C. Dewolf, F. W. Reilly, Bulletin Society Medical History of Chicago, August 1912.)

The only diseases which prompted municipal action were smallpox and cholera. Little attention was paid to health ordinances until 1849, when the city was threatened with cholera.

Drainage was inaugurated after the great cholera epidemic of 1854. Sewer building lagged from 1856 to 1866 when cholera again started sewer building. The agitation against privy vaults began.

An epidemic map by Dr. Mannheimer in the report of the department for this year shows the distribution of an epidemic of erysipelas in 1863 and one of cholera in 1866. Erysipelas followed the river and bad sanitation, poverty and congestion more closely than cholera did.

1868. Dr. Mannheimer's second chart appeared; showed the seasonal distribution of disease and correlated the weather changes with the death rate. The report contains an elaborate study of Texas tick fever. Smallpox continued, with 1,286 cases and 150 deaths.

1869. "Owing to the low, wet and level plain upon which Chicago is situated its proper drainage is one of the sanitary problems of the age. When the population was sparse and the winds had free access to every portion of the city the general health was good, but as the population grew dense with its necessary concomittants of filth and offal and buildings covered the ground and the wind was cut off, the city became unhealthy. It was not until the cholera visitations of 1849 to 1855 that the citizens began to realize that without better drainage they would be constantly liable to epidemics. Public meetings called in 1854 passed good resolutions but it was not until after suffering six successive epidemics, five of cholera and one of dysentery, that this conclusion was arrived at", says the annual report for this year.

The report also gave the number of sewers built each year from 1856 to 1869, inclusive. A study was made between the death rate of the different wards and the proportion of sewer main and sewered homes in each.

The years of great scarlet fever epidemics were given as 1844-45; 1857-1858 and 1868-1869.

"From the results of drainage and other sanitary measures it may be inferred that the judicious expenditure of money for sanitary purposes is a sound maxim of municipal economy. From past experience I am satisfied that the mean annual death rate can be reduced to 17 by continuing the present sanitary and drainage regulations and thereby making Chicago one of the healthiest cities in the world." This prophecy by Dr. J. H. Rauch, was made in 1869. The rate fell below 17 many years ago.

1870. High mortality among children; 916 died from cholera infantum; 62.8 percent of all deaths in children under 5 years of age.

1871. This is the year of the fire. Records of the health department burned. Smallpox present. Death rate high. In this year appeared an extraordinarily good report from the Chicago health department, most of the copies of which were burnt in the fire.

1872. Death rate 27.64. 2,382 cases of smallpox. General death rate 27.64. Death rate of children under 5 high. 1,150 horses died of epizootic.

1873. Cholera appeared. 48 deaths, 1,766 cases of smallpox. Dr. Rauch resigned as sanitary superintendent on August 5, and was succeeded by Dr. Ben S. Miller.

1874. Smallpox present.

1875. City chartered under Cities and Villages Act. This provided for a board of health.

1876. Department of health with a commissioner superseded the board of health. Greatest scarlet fever epidemic in the history of the city occurred this year.

The health history of Chicago as set forth in the annual reports of the health department show the rather rapid development of great health problems. The seriousness of the situation was appreciated rather early. The raising of the data to make drainage possible was begun. This work was undertaken because it was thought to be necessary for health. A desire for health was one urge though not the principal one behind the digging of the Illinois and Michigan Canal. Almost from the beginning Chicago had some sort of a board of health. In times of great fear of cholera or smallpox the board was supported; at other times it was neglected. This board was not of great importance so far as prevention or even sustained study of health problems was concerned until the organization of a real health department in 1867.

The report of the board of health 1867, 1868 and 1869 is a very valuable document. It indicated that during those years sustained study of health problems was made.

This report gives the total number of deaths all ages and ages under 5 and 5 to 10 years, each year from 1843 to 1851. These statistics were gathered from undertakers' and sextons' reports and from clippings from newspapers and medical journals. Dr. Rauch supplied corrective factors which when applied made these figures approximately accurate.

Annual Death Rates

From July, 1851 to 1869 the vital statistics are given with increasing detail and are probably increasingly accurate. A study of these figures supplies the following data:

Table 11.

ANNUAL DEATH RATES PER 1,000 POPULATION—CHICAGO, 1843-1877.

Year.	General death rate.	Year.	General death rate.	Year.	General death rate.
1843	18.60	1855	27.26	1867	21.21
1844	33.04	1856	24.8	1868	23.74
1845	28.46	1857	27.56	1869	23.17
1846	27.81	1858	25.06	1870	23.88
1847	33.93	1859	21.59	1871	20.87
1848	31.86	1860	20.73	1872	27.64
1849	73.80	1861	18.99	1873	25.15
1850	48.96	1862	20.52	1874	20.30
1851	27.26	1863	25.83	1875	19.72
1852	46.70	1864	26.26	1876	21.03
1853	22.41	1865	22.57	1877	18.67
1854	64.02	1866	32.55		

While recognizing the inaccuracy of the figures they are sufficiently complete to show a general picture of the health conditions at the time. Taking out certain years for reasons presently to be stated, the average death rate for what is left of 1843-49 inclusive, is found to be 31.02 per 1,000 population. For 1850-59 inclusive, it is 24.03; 1860-69 inclusive it is 22.56; for 1870-79 inclusive it is 19.87; 1843 is withheld because it is obviously inaccurate; 1849 is reported as having a death rate of 73.80, more than twice that of any preceding year. It is withheld because it is freakish. One of the outstanding causes of the great death rate of that year was the prevalence of cholera. In the next decade, 1850 with a rate of 48.96 and 1852 with one of 46.70 are withheld. 1850 was a cholera year. 1854 was a cholera year. 1866 is held out as being abnormal. It will be noted however that 1866 had a death rate that was only a fraction higher than the prevailing rate in 1843 to 1849. 1866 was a cholera year. In the decade 1870-79, 1872 and 1873 with rates of 27.64 and 25.15 are held as being abnormal. The great influenza pandemic was the principal cause of the abnormality though both cholera and smallpox prevailed.

This study shows a fairly satisfactory decrease in the average death rate between 1843 and 1880 but the decrease was occasionally interrupted by great epidemic waves. The increase in efforts to promote health more than equalled the increasing tendency toward bad health due to poor drainage, water pollution, sewerage, contamination, crowding, poor housing and rapid immigration.

Typhoid Mortality.

An interesting item of the general health picture is the yearly death rate from typhoid fever. It was as shown in Table 12.

Table 12.

ANNUAL DEATH RATES FROM TYPHOID FEVER PER 100,000 POPULATION—CHICAGO, 1852-1879.

Year.	Typhoid death rate.	Year.	Typhoid death rate.	Year.	Typhoid death rate.
1852	132	1862	61	1872	142.6
1853	59	1863	99	1873	71.6
1854	164	1864	128	1874	53.4
1855	62	1865	106	1875	51.7
1856	109	1866	106	1876	41.2
1857	120	1867	73.3	1877	37.
1858	61	1868	79.3	1878	33.4
1859	61	1869	65.3	1879	42.3
1860	44	1870	87.4		
1861	61	1871	61		

In the eight years 1852-59 inclusive the typhoid death rate per 100,000 population was 98.5. However, in this period there were at least two years 1852 and 1854 that were much above the average. They were abnormal for some reason.

Table 13.

ANNUAL DEATH RATES FROM DIPHTHERIA PER 100,000 POPULATION—
CHICAGO, 1852-1879.

Year.	Diphtheria death rate	Year.	Diphtheria death rate.	Year.	Diphtheria death rate.
1852	78	1862	133	1872	97.2
1853	57	1863	203	1873	62.1
1854	82	1864	150	1874	44.
1855	62	1865	230	1875	67.2
1856	35	1866	115	1876	184.5
1857	172	1867	79.1	1877	135.8
1858	195	1868	77.4	1878	120.2
1859	168	1869	91.8	1879	196.9
1860	269	1870	139.3		
1861	220	1871	73.6		

Scarlet Fever Mortality.

The average annual mortality rate from scarlet fever of five years between 1852 and 1859 was 61.8 per 100,000 population; of seven years between 1860-1869 was 61.6; of seven years 1870-77 was 44.3. 1855 was withheld because the rate was abnormally low. 1858-59-62-63-69-76 and 77 because they were abnormally high. The disease increased in the late fifties and in the early sixties. It is probable that the decrease in scarlet fever began in 1870 but the very bad epidemic of 1876-1877 must not be lost sight of. It is proper to say of scarlet fever that the efforts put forth to control the disease just about balanced the tendency of the disease to spread and grow worse with increasing population. The great waves of the disease generally lasted two years. There were many years when scarlet fever was responsible for a higher death rate than that of typhoid fever.

Table 14.

ANNUAL DEATH RATES FROM SCARLET FEVER PER 100,000 POPULATION—
CHICAGO, 1852-1879.

Year.	Scarlet Fever death rate.	Year.	Scarlet Fever death rate.	Year.	Scarlet Fever death rate.
1852	117	1862	294	1872	31.8
1853	59	1863	260	1873	30.3
1854	38	1864	43	1874	26.6
1855	6.2	1865	52	1875	51.4
1856	13	1866	63	1876	198.9
1857	82	1867	44.9	1877	190.5
1858	245	1868	72.2	1878	30.5
1859	262	1869	204.6	1879	79.1
1860	113	1870	99.5		
1861	40	1871	37.1		

Pneumonias.

Under this head are grouped all the deaths reported as due to pneumonia, pleurisy, bronchitis and broncho-pneumonia and influenza although the last term was just coming into use at the end of the period.

Table 15.

ANNUAL DEATH RATES FROM ACUTE RESPIRATORY DISEASES PER 100,000 POPULATION—CHICAGO, 1852-1879.

Year.	Rate.	Year.	Rate.	Year.	Rate.
1852	87	1862	67	1872	174
1853	51	1863	125	1873	171
1854	63	1864	135	1874	134
1855	70	1865	99	1875	172
1856	62	1866	119	1876	137
1857	71	1867	86	1877	122
1858	95	1868	165	1878	152
1859	64	1869	134	1879	140
1860	49	1870	143		
1861	54	1871	146		

The death rates from acute respiratory diseases from 1852 to 1879 are shown in Table 15.

In the 1852-59 decade the worst year was 1858—95; the best 1853—51; the average was 70. In the next decade the worst year was 1868—165; the best 1860—49; the average was 103. The acute respiratory disorders were getting worse. No explanation was found for the great upward jump in 1863 and a similar jump in 1868. In the next decade the worst year was 1872—174; the best was 1877—122; the average was 149. The fatal acute respiratory infections were rapidly increasing. In less than thirty years the average for a ten year period had more than doubled. The increase continued until the early part of the twentieth century since which time there has been a slight decrease except in the years of the great 1918 influenza pandemic and its recurrence in 1920. The high rates of 1872 and 1873 were due to the pandemic of influenza which prevailed in those years.

Consumption

The death rate from consumption by years is shown in Table 16.

In spite of the repeated statement that there was no consumption in Illinois, or but little, the rate the first year the record was begun in Chicago was 299 per 100,000 population. It is now in the vicinity of 75. The worst record in Chicago's history was 370 in 1858. The average for the decade was 298. The worst year in the next decade was 1869, 269, the best 1865, 187. The average was 234.5. Consumption appeared to be on the decline.

In the next decade the worst year was 1870 with 281; the best 1879, 173; the average was 228, a further decline though a small one. This decline showed a disposition to stop in the early part of the twentieth century.

Under the impetus of a new type of activity in control it began again. At the time of writing (in 1927) it has again come to a stop. There has been no decline for several years.

Table 16.

ANNUAL DEATH RATES FROM CONSUMPTION PER 100,000 POPULATION—
CHICAGO, 1853-1880.

Year.	Death rate.	Year.	Death rate.	Year.	Death rate.
1853	299	1863	188	1873	244
1854	324	1864	242	1874	218
1855	201	1865	187	1875	219
1856	311	1866	203	1876	217
1857	288	1867	210	1877	212
1858	370	1868	248	1878	196
1859	274	1869	269	1879	173
1860	251	1870	281	1880	195
1861	263	1871	248		
1862	247	1872	274		

Smallpox Mortality.

The years 1852-9 had an average smallpox death rate of 36.1; 1860-69 an average of 52.66; 1870-79 an average of 43.17. In 1857 there was a bad smallpox outbreak and it extended into 1859. But 1859 was the only year in the early history of Chicago after 1852 that did not record a death from the disease. 1863 and 1864 were years of bad epidemic conditions but there was a low rate 6.1 in 1869; 1872 and 1873 were bad epidemic years. 1879 had a rate of only .2. The disease was more than holding its own against society until 1869. From that time on it lost ground though, in 1872 and 1873 it again more than held its own. The epidemic waves were farther apart and in the low years the disease was near the vanishing point.

Table 17.

ANNUAL DEATH RATES FROM SMALLPOX PER 100,000 POPULATION—
CHICAGO, 1852-1879.

Year.	Death rate.	Year.	Death rate.	Year.	Death rate.
1852	23	1862	36	1872	178.3
1853	32.1	1863	76.6	1873	136.1
1854	18.2	1864	166.6	1874	22.8
1855	37.5	1865	317.	1875	2.5
1856	19.	1866	45.	1876	7.1
1857	114.	1867	54.7	1877	10.
1858	55.	1868	57.9	1878	4.8
1859	0.	1869	6.1	1879	.2
1860	27.	1870	4.9		
1861	25	1871	21.8		

Measles Mortality.

Between 1852 and 1859 the yearly average death rate from measles was 33 per 100,000 population. 1860-69 it was 37.5; 1870-79 it was 18.44. 1853 1854 and 1857 were bad measles years whereas 1859 had a low death rate of 10.7. In the next decade 1864 and 1866 were bad measles years. 1865 was low with 11. The rate in 1866 was the highest Chicago ever knew. 1871 had an epidemic but scarcely comparable with that of 1866, 1874, 1876 and 1878 had rates well under 10. The records show that until 1876 measles was winning its fight against society. Since then society has been gaining the upper hand but backslides occur occasionally.

Table 18.

ANNUAL DEATH RATE FROM MEASLES PER 100,000 POPULATION—
CHICAGO, 1852-1879.

Year.	Death rate.	Year.	Death rate.	Year.	Death rate.
1852	34.6	1862	28.5	1872	10.1
1853	32.1	1863	18.6	1873	27.6
1854	69.	1864	78.3	1874	3.8
1855	11.5	1865	11.	1875	29.2
1856	19.	1866	83	1876	3.7
1857	43.	1867	39.1	1877	13.7
1858	24.2	1868	42.5	1878	8.2
1859	10.7	1869	38.9	1879	10.4
1860	13.6	1870	31.		
1861	21.6	1871	46.7		

Whooping Cough Mortality.

The average annual mortality from whooping cough for 1852 to 1859 was 23.7 per 100,000 population. 1860-69 was 33.5; 1870-1879 was 29.19. The years 1854, 1863, 1866, 1869 and 1878 were bad whooping cough years. There is no evidence that Chicago was gaining in the control of this disease prior to 1880.

Table 19.

ANNUAL DEATH RATES FROM WHOOPING COUGH PER 100,000 POPULATION—
CHICAGO, 1852-1879.

Year.	Death rate.	Year.	Death rate.	Year.	Death rate.
1852	18	1862	21	1872	33.8
1853	29	1863	62	1873	40.8
1854	52	1864	11	1874	27.1
1855	24	1865	8	1875	26.5
1856	11	1866	92	1876	32.6
1857	22.5	1867	27.6	1877	12.1
1858	20.5	1868	25	1878	53.8
1859	12.5	1869	46.8	1879	6.7
1860	21.6	1870	29.7		
1861	20.	1871	18.8		

Malaria Mortality.

The average malaria annual death rate 1852-9 was 51.1 per 100,000 population; 1860-69 it was 20.8; 1870-79 it was still falling. It was not until 1909 that malaria disappeared from the causes of death in Chicago but it was plain by 1880 that the disease was coming under control and would eventually disappear.

Table 20.

ANNUAL DEATH RATES FROM MALARIA, CONGESTION, INTERMITTENT AND REMITTENT FEVERS PER 100,000 POPULATION—CHICAGO, 1852-1879.

Year	Death rate	Year	Death rate	Year	Death rate
1852	102	1862	15.5	1872	15.5
1853	57	1863	18.	1873	16.5
1854	10.5	1864	18.	1874	7.8
1855	37.5	1865	17.	1875	11.
1856	26.5	1866	37.	1876	15.3
1857	55.	1867	19.	1877	4.8
1858	16.	1868	22.	1878	13.5
1859	10.	1869	27.	1879	9.0
1860	22.	1870	15.9		
1861	12.5	1871	10.4		

Baby Death Rates.

It would be interesting to show what has been the improvement in the health of babies as shown by the infant mortality rate since 1833. But this will prove impossible, because in some years there were no vital statistics, while in other years the groupings were not uniform.

Beginning in 1843 such statistics as are available show that the health authorities understood the relation of the health of the children to the welfare of the community. In that year there is a record of 129 deaths all ages of whom 37 were of children under 5 years of age and 10 of children 5 to 10 years of age. No other data are given. This is the classification that was followed until 1854. In that year a group "above 70 years" is added. This was the age grouping made use of for many years. The present classification into deaths from all causes of babies under 1 and deaths from diarrhoeal diseases in children under 2 was not employed for many years. Finally the number of births as a basis for determining baby death rate was not available in Chicago until very recent times. There is a mass of testimony from health officers and physicians that the infant mortality in these early years was excessively high but there is no statistical data from which the exact facts can be adduced.

The earlier records do not separate deaths from diarrhoeal diseases into deaths of children and deaths of adults. It is shown from health officers and physicians that in the early days the death rates of adults from diarrhoea and dysentery were heavy. These have disappeared as a cause of death of adults, but there are no statistics on the subject.

Table 21.

ANNUAL DEATH RATE FROM ERYSIPELAS PER 100,000 POPULATION—
CHICAGO, 1852-1869.

Year.	Death rate.	Year.	Death rate.	Year.	Death rate.
1852	13	1858	4.4	1864	20.5
1853	17	1859	4.3	1865	11.
1854	10.5	1860	3.6	1866	10.5
1855	4.	1861	2.5	1867	7.
1856	1.2	1862	3.6	1868	10.
1857	6.8	1863	12.	1869	11.

Erysipelas Mortality.

The average annual death rate from erysipelas 1852-9 was 7.7 per 100,000 population. 1860-9 was 9.17. Prior to 1870 this disease was gaining.

The earlier health authorities of Chicago were very much under the influence of the Pettenkofer doctrines. They devoted most of their attention to raising the city datum and building sewers, the suppression of yard privies, removal of slaughter houses and other nuisances—cleaning the streets and private premises, improving the filthy condition of the Chicago River and the water supplies.

In times of great epidemics they became interested in reporting and quarantining but at all other times they were working at sanitation, the improvement of environment. Of course this was before the days of the germ theory and the doctrines of Pettenkofer were paramount everywhere. The work they did along these lines educated the people and established a sanitary conscience as well as a sanitary intelligence, which contributed to the control of disease. Sanitation also contributes greatly to such control. It is necessary ground work for such control, but knowing what is known now, one can well understand why disease did not come under control as rapidly in those old Pettenkofer days as men hoped for.

The records show that further improvement followed the application of methods based on the germ theory of disease.

Springfield.

The first settlement on the present site of Springfield was made in 1818, the year Illinois entered in Union. The town was not regularly surveyed and laid out until 1823, in which year Elijah Iles and Pascal P. Enos performed the necessary service. At first it was called "Calhoun," in honor of the great nullifier of South Carolina, but the name proved to be unpopular and few people used it. They preferred the name Springfield, which was the name given the postoffice in the embryo city of Calhoun.

Early in the career of Springfield, born Calhoun, the municipality began acquiring political honors, a habit which it shows no tendency to forsake. In 1821, two years before it was officially laid out, it acquired the title of county seat of Sangamon County. This was in spite of the fact that it was not incorporated until 1832.

In 1837, as the result of a rather strenuous political contest, it became the State capital, and the first session of the legislature to meet there assembled in 1839. Abraham Lincoln, as a member of the long-nine, had much to do with the removal of the State capital from Vandalia to Springfield. Among the many rumors of reasons for removing the capitol from Vandalia to Springfield were two that relate to health.

One was that the legislature had grown tired of the preponderance of venison, wild turkey, wild duck and other game meats supplied them at Vandalia, and they moved the capital to Springfield where they could get more pork and beef.

Another is that the Kaskaskia bottoms around Vandalia made the location so highly malarial that the legislature wanted a healthier site for the State capital.

Sangamon County was so near the geographical and population center of the State that it was a popular prospective location for the Capitol as soon as the people began thinking in terms of the State as a whole. There is a story that the plan was to place the Capitol at Illiopolis, a town in Sangamon County, about ten miles to the east of Springfield. The name was cut to fit. So were the plans, but dame rumor, or is it scandal, says, some parties high in power bought up the land around Illiopolis, whereupon the indignant many not in on the deal "kicked the fat into the fire" and threw the Capitol into the willing lap of Springfield.

Among the books and papers of the late Dr. A. W. French, DDS.,[95] of Springfield, was found an old black book, the binder's title on the back of which is "Minutes of Springfield, Illinois, 1832-1840." On the fly leaf of the book is written: "Minutes of Board of Trustees of the Village of

---

[95] French (Journal Illinois Historical Society, Vol. 2).

Springfield, Illinois, of its meetings from April 1832 (first meeting) to the organizing of a city in 1839."

On July 19, 1832, at an extra meeting of the board, the following preamble and some resolutions were read and passed: "Whereas, we have information that the Asiatic cholera is now prevailing in Chicago, and whereas, it becomes the duty of the trustees to guard the town from infection from that source,", etc. The usual orders were then made as to the cleaning of the town. On November 14, orders were given out that the court house be fitted up as a hospital in case it was needed for the cholera patients. Some indication of the improvement in the health of Springfield is indicated by Table 22.

Table 22.

ANNUAL DEATH RATES FROM ALL CAUSES AND CERTAIN OTHER DISEASES—
SPRINGFIELD, ILL., 1875-78 AND 1923-1926.
PER 100,000 POPULATION.

	1875	1876	1877	1878	1923	1924	1925	1926
Population	18,553	18,791	19,074	19,357	61,833	62,718	63,923	64,700
Death rate all causes, per 1,000 population					15.3	14.5	17.5	16.9
Death rate per 100,000 population—								
Typhoid Fever	26.5	26.6	78.	56.1	4.8	6.3	6.2	6.
Scarlet Fever		74.2	88.4	30.6		1.5	4.8	1.5
Whooping Cough	5.3	26.6	36.4	10.3	6.4	4.7	3.1	16.5
Diphtheria	164.3	85.1	26	102.	12.8	14.2	4.8	4.6
Tuberculosis	275.6	190.8	239.2	265.2	92.1	57.4	89.6	80.3
Diarrhoea and Enteritis	153.7	127.2	72.5	56.1	41.6			
Malaria	15.9	26.6	10.4	15.3				
Infant Deaths Under 1 Year Age		339.2	332.6	285.6	174.6	156.2	186.1	75.2

Springfield's bad year for typhoid since the keeping of records began was 1881, with a rate of 171.5 per 100,000 population; for scarlet fever, 1879; with a rate of 230; whooping cough, 1877 with a rate of 36.4; diphtheria, 1875, rate 164.3; tuberculosis, 1881, rate 303.8; infantile diarrhoeas 1875, rate 153.7; baby death rate, all causes, 1880, rate 433.5; malaria, 1881, rate 29.4.

Kaskaskia.

This town located at the point of junction of the Kaskaskia or Okaw River with the Mississippi, was founded by Marquette in 1672. The earlier French settlers married Indians or girls brought to Kaskaskia for wives from Canada and Louisiana. These earlier French half-breeds and Indians enjoyed good health in spite of the location of their town. The English took possession in 1765. Settlers began to come in from the South in 1770; Clark was there in 1778 and 1779 to about 1783. A military garrison there

Father Marquette.

suffered severely from disease during some of this time. There was a United States land office there in 1804. In 1809 the Territorial Capitol was located in Kaskaskia and there it remained until the State was organized in 1818, whereupon Vandalia became the capital city.

Although in the later years of its existence the health of the people of Kaskaskia was poor that was not the reason for the removal of the capital. Overflows and the caving banks of the adjoining rivers brought that about. However, had Kaskaskia retained a large population between 1818 and 1877, it would inevitably have become a hotbed of malaria, typhoid, dysentery and pestilence generally.

Shawneetown.

The principal reason for writing especially of Shawneetown is the fact that it was the seat of one of the land offices through which the colonists of other states who located in the south end of the State secured their lands.

In his article on a Pioneer Medical School Dr. C. E. Black[96] of Jacksonville, says:

"When Illinois became a state in 1818 most of its inhabitants were south of the mouth of the Illinois River."

All of those who owned land in this section had entered their land through the Shawneetown office. Many of them had been there in person taking their diseases with them and swapping diseases while there.

Dr. C. E. Black.

In "Pictures of Illinois, One Hundred Years ago"—(Lakeside Classics, 1918) we read:

"Shawneetown enjoyed something of a real estate boom in 1814, but due to the annual inundation of the Ohio River and to the general unhealthfulness of the place the boom speedily collapsed."

Vandalia.

Vandalia became the State capital in 1818 and retained this honor until some date between 1837 and 1839. It is located on the banks of the Kaskaskia River, which river was sometimes called the Okah. Elsewhere in this narrative are accounts of malaria and other forms of disease at Vandalia. Most of the reports were taken from communications from Dr. F. Haller. While the low ground of the Kaskaskia bottoms made Vandalia a malarial

[96] Black (Ill. Historical Library, Publication No. 10, 1905).

location in the early days that disease does not appear to have influenced the legislature to remove the capital. One account says the change was made because the only meat available in Vandalia was turkey and venison, of which the members of the legislature had grown tired. They preferred hog meat and they moved the capital to Springfield where this luxury was available.

Vandalia is a prosperous city having withstood the loss of the capital better than other cities have done. The eradication of malaria from the Okah bottom has greatly increased the health futures. It is in the midst of the belt in which white snake root grows and therefore milk sickness long remained a menace.

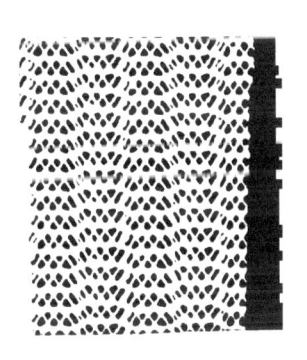

TWO

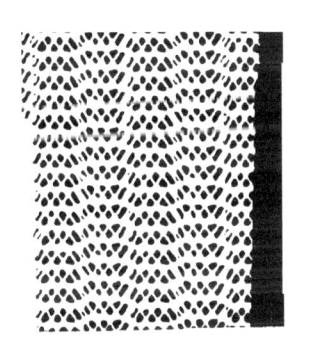

Administration.

ractice Act.

alth Agencies.

ions After 1877.

d Conclusion.

MEMBERS APPOINTED
Newly Created Illinois State Board of Health

Newton Bateman, LL.D.
1877 – 1891

Reuben Ludlam, M.D.
1877 – 1892

Anson L. Clark, M.D.
1877 – 1893

Wm. M. Chambers, M.D.
1877 – 1881

J. M. Gregory, LL.D.
1877 – 1883

John H. Rauch, M.D.
1877 – 1891

Horace Wardner, M.D.
1877 – 1881

The first Board of Health in Illinois, organized July 12, 1877.

Newton Bateman LL. D.

NEWTON BATEMAN, Galesburg; was born July 27, 1822, Fairfield, New Jersey. Taken by parents to Illinois in 1833. Graduated from Illinois College at Jacksonville in 1843 and studied the following year at Lane Theological Seminary. Became a teacher in 1846 and held a number of responsible positions in public and private schools until 1858, when he was elected to the office of State Superintendent of Public Instruction, a position he held for fourteen years. President of Knox College, Galesburg, 1875-1893. Member State Board of Health, 1877-1891. Author of numerous historical books and publications. Died in Galesburg, October 21, 1897.

Reuben Ludlam, M. D.

REUBEN LUDLAM, Chicago; born October 7, 1831, Camden, New Jersey. Graduated from the medical college of the University of Pennsylvania, 1852 and went to Chicago, 1853. Member and dean faculty Hahnemann Medical College, 1861-1899. President of numerous medical organizations. Author of several medical books and editor of professional journals. Member of State Board of Health, 1877-1892.

Anson L. Clark, M. D.

ANSON L. CLARK, Elgin; born October 12, 1836, Clarksburg, Massachusetts. Was taken by parents to Palatine, Illinois in 1841. Graduated from Lombard College at Galesburg in 1858, and from Cincinnati Eclectic Medical Institute in 1861. First assistant surgeon 127th Illinois Infantry during Civil War. One of the founders of Bennett Medical College of which he was president from its organization in 1870 to 1910. Member 27th General Assembly, 1870-1871. Member State Board of Health, 1877-1893. Author of "Clark's Diseases of Women." Died April 11, 1910.

William M. Chambers, M. D.

WILLIAM M. CHAMBERS, Charleston; born April 11, 1814, Cynthiana, Kentucky. Graduated from Medical College of Transylvania University, Lexington, 1843. Went to Coles County, Illinois in 1855. Brigade surgeon, U. S. Army, 1861 to close of Civil War when he was brevetted Colonel for meritorious service. President of numerous medical organizations. Member State Board of Health, 1877-1881. Died in Charleston, November 12, 1892.

John Milton Gregory, LL. D.

JOHN MILTON GREGORY, Champaign; born July 6, 1822, Sand Lake, New York. Graduated Union College, 1846, A. B. Studied law, Schenectady, New York, 1846-47. Pastor Baptist Church, Hoosick Falls, New York, 1847-1850 and Akron, Ohio, 1850-1852. Principal Classical School, Detroit, 1852-1859; editor and publisher, Michigan Journal of Education, 1854-1859. Superintendent of Public Instruction, Michigan, 1859-1864. President Kalamazoo College, Kalamazoo, Michigan, 1865-1867. Regent (President) Illinois Industrial University, 1867-1880. U. S. Commissioner, Vienna Exposition, 1873. Illinois State Commissioner to Paris Exposition, 1878. Member and president (1881-1883) of State Board of Health, 1877-1883. Member U. S. Civil Service Commission, 1883-1885. Professor **Emiretus** of Political Economy, University of Illinois. Author of numerous pedagogical works. Died in Washington, D. C., October 20, 1898.

John Henry Rauch, M. D.

JOHN HENRY RAUCH, Chicago; born September 4, 1828, Lebanon, Pennsylvania. Graduated University of Pennsylvania, 1849. Member faculty Rush Medical College, Chicago, 1857-1860. Sanitary Superintendent of Chicago, 1867-1873. Chief medical officer under General Grant in his Tennessee and Virginia campaigns. At close of Civil War he was brevetted Lieutenant Colonel for meritorious services. Member president and secretary of State Board of Health, 1877-1891. Died in Lebanon, Pennsylvania, March 24, 1894.

Horace Wardner, M. D.

HORACE WARDNER, Cairo; born August 25, 1829, Wyoming County, New York. Studied at Cayuga Academy and Alfred University and graduated in medicine from Rush Medical College, Chicago in 1856. Began practicing medicine at Libertyville, Illinois in 1858. Returned to Chicago before the year was up and opened a private anatomical room where he taught medical students. Elected member faculty Chicago Medical College, 1859. Surgeon 12th Illinois Volunteer Infantry and staff surgeon in Grant's Tennessee Army during Civil War. Brevetted Lieutenant Colonel for meritorious services. Located in Cairo, Illinois in 1867. Appointed Superintendent Anna State Hospital, 1878. Member State Board of Health, 1877-1881.

Dr. George Cadwell.

Dr. Cadwell was a prominent citizen during the early period of Illinois history and participated in the first efforts to secure laws relating to the practice of medicine and to public health.

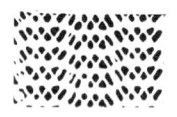

PUBLIC HEALTH ADMINISTRATION IN ILLINOIS.

The organization of the State Board of Health in 1877, marks the time when the conservation of the public health was first undertaken by the State of Illinois, and when a department of the State government was first charged with this function.

Prior to that time, the local township and municipal governments in the State had been given the power, either by special charters, or general legislation such as the Cities and Villages Act of 1872 to protect the public health, in their respective local communities. In some of the larger cities of the State, this authority had been exercised, and local boards of health or city physicians appointed to attend to this duty. Such action was usually taken during some epidemic of cholera or smallpox and after the danger from the epidemic had passed, the sanitary measures instituted lagged, the enthusiasm of the officials waned, appropriations for the work lapsed and were not renewed, with the result that it was discontinued, only to be renewed again with the next appearance of an epidemic.

This was the general history of the local health organizations in the State. Even Chicago was not an exception; there the board of health was abolished as late as 1860, "on account of the absence of any alarming conditions", but was reestablished in 1867 when cholera had visited the city and smallpox was reaching epidemic proportions.

The local medical societies took an active interest in instituting measures for the protection of their communities against pestilential diseases and in some localities attended to this work, without any form of health organization. Active members of these societies often served as members of the local boards of health. In this work as well as in their practice they came across the numerous unqualified persons who were practicing medicine, because as yet, there were no laws to prohibit this. It was this state of affairs that brought on the movement which resulted in the organization of the State Board of Health.

Genesis of the Public Health Law.

Public health work as a permanent function of the State government was first established in Illinois in 1877. On July 1 of that year two laws, one known as the State Board of Health Act and the other as the Medical Practice Act, became effective. The former was approved by the Governor on May 25 and the latter on May 29, 1877. Both laws had the same ultimate purpose in view and the State Board of Health, which was organized on July 12 of the same year, was charged with the responsibilities and duties in-

Shelby Moore Cullom, Governor of Illinois 1877-1883, who signed the first public health law enacted in the State and the first permanent law regulating the practice of medicine.

volved in the enforcement of both. This dual responsibility of regulating the practice of medicine and promoting sanitary and hygienic activities ordinarily referred to as public health service was a new thing for a state board of health in the United States, and it provoked considerable interest among sanitarians and the medical profession throughout the country.

The passage of these two public health laws was not an expression of a sudden burst of enthusiasm for more healthful conditions but rather the belated fruition of an idea that took root and provoked agitation among the people, especially the medical profession of Illinois in territorial days sixty years and more before. Proof of this is the fact that an ordinance or law regulating the practice of medicine was enacted by the territorial General Assembly in 1817 and duly signed by Ninian Edwards who was the territorial governor at the time. Furthermore the first State General Assembly passed a medical practice act in 1819 and another was passed by the General Assembly in 1825. Both were promptly repealed, however, by the next legislature succeeding the enactment. Bills introduced in later sessions of the General Assembly failed to become law until 1877.

Dual Conception of Public Health Work.

The idea of public health service as it was finally expressed in the first permanent statutes grew out of two very definite conceptions which have not always promoted harmony of action in this field of endeavor. One conception was and still is that good doctors are the dominant factor necessary to good public health and to secure the latter the state can best function by bringing about the former. This idea was expressed very well by Dr. Horace Wardner, as president of the State Board of Health in 1880, when he said.

"Through the work of the Board the profession has deliberately said to the people: 'Your greatest danger is from ignorance and the iniquity of pretending physicians, and we have sought, and are seeking, to protect the people at this point, by subjecting the qualifications of all persons desiring to practice medicine to reasonable and satisfactory tests;'"

and again by a committee of the State Board of Health appointed in 1880 to inquire into requirements for "good standing" of medical colleges which concluded that,

"We shall only fulfill our duty as a State Board of Health by promoting to the utmost that largest and most potential force in sanitary science and in public hygiene—a well trained and thoroughly educated medical profession."

The other conception was and is that sanitation, quarantine and hygiene are things the application of which will produce significant results in preserving and improving public health beyond the capacity of private medical practitioners, be the profession ever so efficient and well trained. Advocates of this conception believed that regulating the practice of medicine was incidental or subordinate to other public health functions of the State. A good expression of this conception is found in a paper read by Dr. E. W. Gray of Bloomington, before the Illinois State Medical Society in May, 1876, which reads:

"The people need to be enlightened; they need to be directed; in many cases they need to be restrained. A board of health organized, and provided with means to collect information, and diffuse among the people a better knowledge of the laws of health, and to discover to them the dangers to which they are exposed, would save thousands of poor victims from untimely death."[1]

The "good doctors" conception is much the older. It was the only one expressed in the territorial law of 1817. In the law of 1819 a section required the reporting of births, deaths and diseases but otherwise it was concerned only with providing "good doctors." The 1825 law was concerned with nothing but the regulation of the practice of medicine. Dr. George Cadwell, a prominent and useful citizen who came into Illinois because of his bitter animosity toward slavery, championed the law of 1819 while Dr. Conrad Will was the moving spirit behind the act of 1825. Dr. George Fisher was Speaker of the House of the territorial Assembly in 1817 and presumably had considerable to do with the law enacted then.

In 1856 and again in 1861 a committee was appointed by the Aesculapian Society of the Wabash Valley, which had originally been organized in 1846 as the Lawrenceville Aesculapian Society, to go before the State legislature asking for a law creating a State Board of Health to regulate the practice of medicine and to collect birth and death certificates. Both attempts failed to produce the desired results. Very likely the matter was agitated and brought before the General Assembly at other times during the fifty year period between 1827 and 1877.

The "good doctors" conception was revived by the Jersey County Medical Society in a communication addressed to the Illinois State Medical Society and read before that organization at its annual meeting in May, 1876. It advocated the organization of a State Board of Health for the purpose of regulating the practice of medicine and of collecting statistics of births and deaths. This communication was an important factor in crystalizing sentiment which resulted a year later in the Medical Practice Act of 1877.

It was not until after the Civil War that the sanitary and hygienic conception began to take root in this country. There is record of four meetings known as National Sanitary Conventions which were held in 1857, 1858, 1859 and 1860 in Philadelphia, Baltimore, New York and Baltimore but these were abandoned with the outbreak of hostilities and nothing further was done on a national scale until 1872 when the American Public Health Association was organized.

---
[1] P. 257, Trans. Illinois State Medical Society, 1876.

The very first public utterances on sanitation as an important factor in healthfulness took place in this country about 1850 when Lemuel Shattuck published his report on sanitary conditions in Massachusetts. It was 1857 before Pasteur, working in France, published his first report which opened up the field of bacteriology and it was ten years later before Lister, the celebrated English physician and pupil of Pasteur, began to attract public notice by his great success in the practice of antiseptic surgery. Prior to Pasteur and Lister, whose work related to bacteriology, was the German, Max von Pettenkoffer, founder of modern hygiene. He it was who recognized more fully than had ever before been recognized that health is impaired by factors not in ourselves but in our environment. This apostle of cleanliness was prominent enough in 1865 to be appointed head of the first institute for the study of hygiene which in that year was inaugurated at the University of Munich. It was doubtless the works of this man that stimulated the first agitation in America for sanitation as a public health activity. Bacteriology developed later and began to be appreciated on a significant scale in this country toward the closing years of the nineteenth century.

Born in Europe and finding ready disciples along the Atlantic seaboard in this country the new ideas of sanitary control over diseases began rapidly to filter into Illinois. Dr. John W. Rauch of Chicago manifested interest enough in the new movement to attend the organization meeting of the American Public Health Association which took place in New York on April 18, 1872. By 1876 Dr. E. W. Gray of Bloomington had become enthusiastic enough to prepare a paper on the subject addressed to the people of the State, which he read before the annual meeting of the Illinois State Medical Society in May. In this paper Dr. Gray advocated the establishment of a State Board of Health. As a result of this paper he was appointed chairman of a committee to memorialize the legislature on the subject of a state board of health. That the work of this committee was crowned with success shows that Dr. Gray and his colleagues carried their enthusiasm for sanitation to practical account.

While both the "good doctors" and "sanitation" conceptions of public health service prevailed among the medical profession the majority of opinion favored the former. The latter, however, appealed to the legislature strongly enough to bring forth a law creating the State Board of Health to which was incidentally delegated the power to regulate the practice of medicine. Indeed, provision was made in the Medical Practice Act for another type of administrative machinery and the Board of Health fell heir to that duty as a result of the success of the sanitary law.

This dual conception concerning public health service was important. It exercised a profound influence over the functions of the State Board of

Health; it also exercised a profound influence over the relations between the medical profession and the State health authorities.

As a result of the communication from the Jersey County Medical Society and the paper by Dr. Gray the Illinois State Medical Society passed the following resolution:

"*Resolved.*—That a Committee be appointed to memorialize the next legislature on the subject of the appointment of a State Board of Health; and that with proper modification, the act by which the Board of Health of Massachusetts was inaugurated be submitted to the same as a basis for the Illinois State Board.

"*Resolved.*—That as members to the State Medical Society, each one shall consider himself bound to urge the propriety of a State Board of Health upon the representative from his district."

This movement led directly to the enactment of the Medical Practice and State Board of Health laws in 1877 which vested in one body the authority and duties prescribed by both.

Proponents of the "good doctors" conception knew exactly what they wanted. Thus the Medical Practice Act was very definite, specifying what should and what should not be done under its provisions, giving the administrative agency reasonable discretion on technical points.

Provisions Relating to Sanitation.

Advocates of sanitation had little of a tangible nature, except the desire for vital statistics, which they could recommend in language that the average legislator could understand. Accordingly the first public health law grants to the State Board of Health the following powers:

"The State Board of Health shall have general supervision of the interests of the health and life of citizens of the State. They shall have charge of all matters pertaining to quarantine; and shall have authority to make such rules and regulations, and such sanitary investigations as they from time to time may deem necessary for the preservation or improvement of public health, and it shall be the duty of all police officers, sheriffs, constables, and all other officers and employes of the State, to enforce such rules and regulations, so far as the efficiency and success of the Board may depend upon their official cooperation."

This is the second of the fourteen sections of the original State Board of Health Act and it is the only section that deals with sanitation or hygiene. Six of the sections deal with vital statistics and the remainder with incidental matters relating to penalties, technique of the Board's procedures, appropriations, etc.

The sweeping authority—"general supervision of the interests of health and life of citizens" and "authority to make such rules and regulations and such sanitary investigations as they from time to time may deem necessary for the preservation and improvement of public health"—granted to the State Board of Health in the original law was a recognition by the legislature that public health work is highly technical in character and requires specially trained personnel. From this position the lawmakers have never retracted so that the laws are still broad, making the rules of the present State health organization tantamount to law. Time and again from the very outset the State health officials have found it convenient and necessary to initiate activities of an arbitrary character under the authority granted in this generalized section and the courts have generally upheld these measures.

It will be seen that the compromise of the General Assembly, which vested in one board the powers and duties representing two distinct schools of thought was not destined to unite and harmonize the two and that even a State Board of Health cannot serve two masters. Ultimately the State Board of Health lost its identity as an integral part of the State government and in its place were created two departments, the one to devote its full energy and resources to sanitary and hygienic activities and the other to regulate, among other things, the practice of medicine.

Development of State Health Service.

Three Periods.

State public health service in Illinois falls conveniently into three rather well defined periods. The first ended with the century in 1900. It may be described as a sort of probationary experience for the State Board of Health. During that time the State health organization was on trial, so to speak. It faced the problem of justifying its existence. Governors and lawmakers suffered it to continue through a sort of kindly tolerance. They were never warmed with sufficient enthusiasm for this new venture to unlock the treasury vaults for its benefit. The first appropriation was $5000 for the biennium. For the last fiscal year of the century, ended June 30, 1899, the appropriation to the State Board of Health for ordinary expenses was $9250. A contingency fund of $10,000 was available to draw on under specified conditions during a number of years in this period but those conditions rarely arose—at least not in the opinion of the Governor whose judgment in the matter was a lock on the purse strings.

The second period started out with the new century and terminated in 1917. For the State Board of Health these years may very properly be called the period of expansion and recognition. In 1901 the legislature appropriated a sum of $45,300 per annum for expenditure through the State Board of Health. For the fiscal year ended June 30, 1917, the available appropriation amounted to $166,589. Manifestly the people of the State and the legislature found in the State Board of Health something for which they were willing to pay considerably more than had been the case twenty-five years before. The 1901 appropriation amounted to 89 per 1000 persons per year while that drawn upon for the fiscal year ending June 30, 1917, amounted to nearly $25. The changes that took place in the amount of money made available for health service made a good measure for the amount of public interest in that work during those years.

The third and last period to date began with the adoption of the Civil Administrative Code by the Illinois state government and continues to this writing in 1927. It is called the period of maturity not in the sense that the State public health organization represents what might be considered a mature or adequate agency for combating disease and promoting health to the fullest practicable extent under present conditions but rather in the sense that it now is regarded as an essential factor in the State government and functions on a plane commensurate with that of any other department. The dominant characteristic of this period is the divorcement in practice of the "good doctors" from the "sanitation and hygiene" conception of public health service. Both continue to be important activities of the State administration but all matters relating to the registration of physicians and regulation of medical practice repose in the State Department of Registration and Education, while those concerned with sanitation, hygiene and vital statistics are in the hands of the State Department of Public Health.

Four Personalities.

The three periods of development of the public health machinery in the State are dominated by four personalities. About each of these revolve the policies, the character and the color of the State's participation in public health service during the period in which each was active. Each made significant contributions to the public health movement in Illinois.

The first of the four was Dr. John H. Rauch, moving spirit in the period of "probation." As his contribution he completely justified the existence of a State public health service. Few men have ever accomplished so much with such meagre resources. Blessed with a rare faculty for organizing, driven by an overwhelming enthusiasm for getting things done, guided by a wealth of medical and sanitary information which a passionate curiosity led him to seek, balanced by a capacity for sound judgment and endowed with tact and diplomacy Dr. Rauch literally made the public health service of his time. A disciple of sanitation and hygiene he also had a profound belief in the importance of good doctors so that under his influence the dual functions of the State Board of Health progressed harmoniously during the fourteen years of his service and carried over for several years afterward. The "probationary" period might very properly be called the "Rauch" period. Dr. Rauch's name will appear frequently on pages to follow that relate to the early health machinery of the State.

The second in chronological order of the four personalities was Dr. James A. Egan. He became the executive secretary of the State Board of Health in 1893 and belongs to and was largely responsible for the "period of recognition." Money getting was his unique contribution to the public health machinery of the State government. Before Egan's time, $12,000 per year, besides a contingency fund, was the largest appropriation that the legislature ever granted to the State Board of Health. The last General Assembly to meet during Egan's tenure appropriated $120,625, besides a contingency fund, for annual expenditure by the State Board of Health. As an opportunist, Dr. Egan took advantage of the phenomenal developments in sanitary and medical sciences that were taking place immediately before and during his time and turned them to good account for public health service in the State. Based upon highly scientific knowledge, successful public health services requires highly trained technical personnel and this requires money. Dr. Egan made a splendid contribution to public health service in Illinois, when he got the legislature in the habit of granting significant appropriations to the State Board of Health.

The third of the four personalities was Dr. C. St. Clair Drake. He became the executive officer of the State public health organization in 1914 and continued until 1921. His tenure was therefore partly in two of the major periods. By nature a propagandist, in the best meaning of that term, Dr. Drake popularized public health work in the State. He was a man who radiated enthusiasm. Endowed with a resourceful imagination, he managed to create ingenious mechanical models that carried fundamental public health messages into every part of the State. This exhibit material which was sufficient to fill one thousand square feet of display space was in demand at local fairs everywhere and it never failed to command attention and it left indelible impressions upon those who saw it. Furthermore, Dr. Drake initiated the Better Baby Conference movement in Illinois. He developed a motion picture library from which health films are circulated in the State. He inaugurated the "Health Promotion Week" idea that has come to be an annual event and one that has always attracted wide attention and a fine response. Under Dr. Drake the State Board of Health was reorganized into the State Department of Public Health and it was Dr. Drake who drew up the plans of organization which still characterize the Department. This movement, however, was initiated by Governor Lowden in his Civil Administrative Code scheme and was only incidentally a part of Dr. Drake's achievements. Dr. Drake was primarily a publicity expert. His donation was an educative method. He popularized public health activity.

Dr. Isaac D. Rawlings, appointed in 1921 as Director of the State Department of Public Health and the last of the four personalities brought system into the service. Vital statistics were far from satisfactory, and had been a bane to State health officers since the days of Rauch. Mortality returns were complete enough to be acceptable to the United States bureau of the census but no compilations or analyses of consequence were made by the State registrar before his coming. Birth reports were too incomplete to meet the federal requirements for recognition. Dr. Rawlings went methodically about the task of improving vital statistics, arranging for every division of the Department to cooperate to that end so that within eighteen months Illinois had been admitted to the United States birth registration area and fairly satisfactory annual compilations were forthcoming from the State registrar. Under Dr. Rawlings, regular staff meetings of division heads were started, the first board of public health advisors was appointed and met regularly, a central filing system of Department communications was installed, the official bulletin was established on a monthly basis in fact as well as in name, newspaper publicity was supplied regularly each week to the press of the State, a scheme of supplying local health officers with weekly morbidity reports was established, the method of recording morbidity reports was simplified and made much more serviceable, the routine investigation of every reported case of typhoid fever and smallpox was started—in short the work of the Department was systematized.

Each of these four sanitarians did other important public health services. Other executives of the State public health organization accomplished many things of importance and value. Justifying the existence of a board of health, wringing money from a sceptical legislature, popularizing health on a large scale and systematizing the public health service are the larger achievements that have marked the progress of officially organized preventive medical activities in Illinois and for these significant contributions Rauch, Egan, Drake and Rawlings were respectively responsible.

State Health Machinery.

Rarely may one find in history circumstances more favorable to the launching of a great public health movement than those which prevailed in Illinois in the "seventies". The severe losses of the Civil War in which disease caused far greater mortality than shot and shell was still fresh in the minds of men and especially in the memory of the medical profession. Disastrous waves of cholera had swept the country in 1852 and 1867. Highly fatal and widespread epidemics of diphtheria and scarlet fever came and went with the seasons while helpless communities sat grimly by until the infections burned themselves out by natural limitations. Typhoid fever was frightful, frequently striking whole families simultaneously. Yellow fever broke out periodically in the lower Mississippi Valley and was a perennial source of paralyzing fear to the citizens of Illinois. Immigration into the State from abroad was very heavy, establishing dangerous contact with European foci of smallpox, cholera and other infections that often in that day depopulated great areas of land, especially in foreign countries. Quackery was rampant in the State because the field was fruitful.

On the other hand an awakening to the possibilities of preventing and controlling communicable diseases through sanitation and hygiene was beginning to manifest itself here and there among research workers. Forward looking members of the medical profession and others in Illinois were already beginning to appreciate the significance of what Pettenkoffer, Pasteur and Lister were doing abroad. Vaccination as a preventive against smallpox was an established medical procedure.

Board of Health Organized.

If the time was opportune the members of the first State Board of Health, appointed by Governor Cullom were equal to the occasion and fully worthy of the confidence and trust reposed in them. They were Newton Bateman, LL. D., of Galesburg, intimate friend of Abraham Lincoln and an eminent educator and author, president of Knox College at the time of appointment; Reuben Ludlam, M. D., of Chicago, dean of the faculty of Hahnemann College and author of numerous medical treatises; Anson L. Clark, M. D., of Elgin, assistant surgeon in the Union Army, moving spirit in the organization of Bennett Medical College of which he was president for many years, president of a number of medical organizations and member of the Elgin Board of Education; William M. Chambers, M. D., of Charleston, brigade surgeon in the Union Army where he was brevetted Lieutenant Colonel and Colonel successively for meritorious services, president of a number of medical organizations and member of the American Public Health Association; John Milton Gregory, LL. D., of Champaign, ordained minister of the Baptist faith, eminent educator and author and many times commissioned by state and federal governments to fill important posts at home and abroad and president of Illinois Industrial University at time of appointment; John H. Rauch, M. D., of Chicago, highest ranking medical director on General Grant's staff in the Army of Tennessee, chief of the medical staff under U. S. Grant in his Virginia campaigns, sanitary superintendent for the board of health in Chicago; Horace Wardner, M. D., of Cairo, assistant medical director on General Grant's staff in the Army of Tennessee, member of faculty of Chicago Medical College. While not a member of the Board, Dr. Elias W. Gray of Bloomington, who had participated in the Civil War as an assistant surgeon, was elected the first executive secretary of the Board.

First Appropriations.

With an appropriation of $5,000.00 for the first biennium and authorized to spend moneys collected for license fees at the rate of $1.00 each from practitioners holding bona fide diplomas and $5.00 each from those who had to be examined, the State Board of Health, duly organized on July 12, 1877 with Dr. Rauch as president, set itself energetically to regulating the practice of medicine—the most obvious task at hand.

```
ORGANIZATION OF
STATE BOARD OF HEALTH
1877

    STATE BOARD OF HEALTH

        7 Members

    Members participating in
    the enforcement of Medical
    Practice Act with aid of extra
    help.

Clerical Service          1 Executive Secretary
  2 Clerks
```

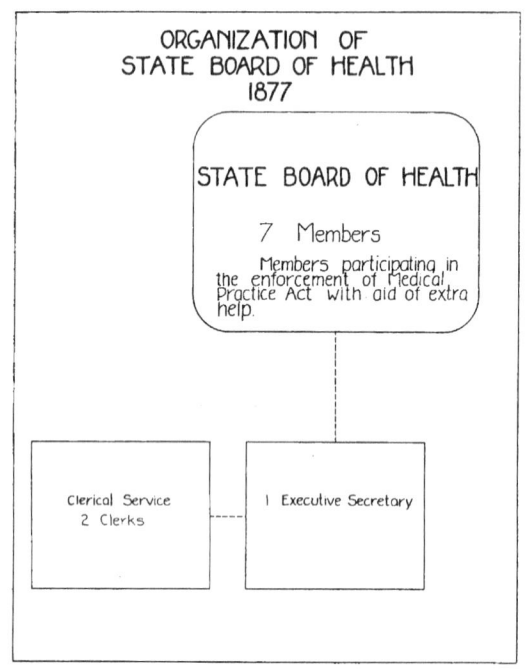

FIG. 8. Working strength of the first State health organization.

First Activities.

During the first six months of its existence the members of the Board of Health and its executive secretary, with very limited clerical assistance, made up the entire strength of the State's public health organization. The magnitude of the job of certifying doctors and the extreme meagerness of resources practically prohibited any significant attention to sanitary and hygienic matters. Presumably chafing under what he regarded as a neglect of its sanitary duties by the Board, Dr. Gray resigned as secretary on December 20, 1877. In accepting his resignation the Board emphasized its appreciation of Dr. Gray's interest in sanitation. Dr. Rauch acted as secretary from December, 1877 until May, 1878. Then Dr. Clark was secretary for about a year. Dr. Rauch then became secretary again in April 1879 and served continuously in that capacity until 1891.

At the beginning the resources of the State Board of Health were its own membership; such help as it could afford to employ with the sums appropriated by the legislature plus sums collected from applicants for license; all police officers, sheriffs and constables who were required by law to enforce the rules and regulations of the State Board of Health in so far as success depended thereon; voluntary assistance from interested citizens; the National Board of Health; such assistance as might be derived from interstate voluntary agencies; such active support as it was able to secure from commercial and industrial interests indirectly through legal authority to quarantine, etc.

The Rauch Regime

Dr. Rauch's amazing ability to utilize these resources to a remarkable degree constitutes the story of public health service in Illinois for the first fifteen years after its foundation. The legislature was never generous in providing funds. That body deemed it wise to clothe the Board of Health with extensive power and a small purse. For the first two years it allowed $5000 plus fees collected by the Board which amounted to less than $6000. For the next four years the appropriations amounted to $5500 per year exclusive of a standing contingency fund of $5000 that could be used only in the face of serious epidemic outbreaks. In 1885 the legislature granted the Board $9000 per year for the ordinary expenses and the usual $5000 contingency. For the next two years the appropriation soared to $24,000 for the biennium and a $40,000 contingency fund. This liberality was actuated by fear of a cholera epidemic. When the outbreak failed to materialize the annual grant fell again to $9000 but with the annual $20,000 contingency remaining. In 1889 the appropriations made for the ensuing biennium were $9000 per year for ordinary expenses and $5000 per year for emergency use.

The money appropriated during this period was scarcely enough to pay the necessary expenses involved in collecting and compiling vital statistics and in meeting the expenses of the Board which met as often as thirteen times in one year for the convenience of those who wished to be examined.

SECRETARIES
Illinois State Board of Health

Elias W. Gray, M. D.
JULY - DEC. 1877 ★

John H. Rauch, M. D.
DEC. 1877-MAY 1878 — APR. 1879-SEPT. 1891

Anson L. Clark, M. D.
JUNE 1878 - APR. 1879

Wm. R. MacKenzie, M. D.
AUG. 4, 1891 — SEPT. 24, 1891

No photograph of Dr. Gray was available.

Dr. Rauch was ambitious to raise the standard of medical practice to the highest possible level. He was no less anxious to put into operation every possible sanitary and hygienic measure calculated to prevent and control disease. Too energetic and resourceful to allow the lack of funds to thwart him in his purpose he set about wringing from the other resources at his command every ounce of activity and cooperation which was available.

General View of Problem.

It will be well to bear in mind that Dr. Rauch looked at sanitary problems from a national and even a world point of view. He would have gloried in the League of Nations because of its possibilities as an international health agency. He recognized, from a sanitary standpoint, no political lines of demarcation but only the great boundaries established by nature herself—the great oceans that separate whole races of people. He had a passion for inaugurating such things as immigrant inspection service at the ports of entry and for the requirement of a clean bill of health as an essential factor in a "passport" from abroad. "Concert of action" was a phrase dear to his heart and furnished the basis for most of his achievements. Perhaps his national point of view was too far reaching to be appreciated by the average State legislator and maybe that explains to some degree his inability to secure adequate appropriations for the execution of his plans. Even when he succeeded in alarming the law makers about the dangers from Asiatic cholera in 1887 the stupendous grant of $40,000 was so guarded with contingent clauses that it was not available for any practicable purpose.

Collecting vital statistics was the problem that led the State Board of Health first to connect up with the State's health machinery resources outside of its own immediate organization. In the law county clerks were required to collect certificates of births and deaths and to make returns to the State Board of Health. The Board put the county clerks to work on this job in the first year of its existence so that at the end of twelve months the functioning State health machinery consisted of the State Board of Health, which had met 13 times, and the county clerks. Small sums had been spent for the laboratory examination of drinking water supplies. In a few places local boards of health had been organized under the Cities and Villages Act of 1872.

Outbreak of Yellow Fever Starts Machinery for Control of Epidemics.

Dark clouds of epidemics and rumors of epidemics of yellow fever, Asiatic cholera and smallpox began to hover above the health horizon in the summer of 1878 and the yellow fever threat actually materialized into a disastrous outbreak that worked its way up the Mississippi Valley as far north as Illinois, invading Cairo. These conditions concentrated the thought of health officials everywhere upon sanitary matters. In Illinois the State Board of Health wanted to make the premises of every household clean and dry. It wanted to make every public and private water supply safe for drinking. It wanted every person in the State vaccinated against smallpox. It wanted everybody to believe in the cleanliness of environment as a preventive of disease and to practice it. It wanted immigrants inspected and vaccinated.

How to bring these things to pass was the question. The State Board of Health had no funds available to undertake such stupendous tasks with its own employes. A way out was found by the diligent and resourceful Rauch.

The yellow fever crisis of 1878, as it was regarded at the time, led the State Board of Health to test its power granted under that clause in the law which read:

"..... and shall have authority to make such rules and regulations, and such sanitary investigations as they may from time to time deem necessary for the preservation or improvement of public health......"

The Board made some rigid quarantine and sanitary regulations concerning the rail and steamboat traffic coming into the State from the lower Mississippi and it put the transportation interests to work at complying with these regulations. A few inspectors, temporary at first, were employed by the Board to see that the rules were carried out. Thus it was discovered that by making a rule, which had the weight of law, the State Board of Health could increase enormously the health machinery without any material increase in expenditure. This was the beginning of "rules and regulations" and we shall see how Dr. Rauch, with the support of the Board, turned this early experience to good account in carrying out his sanitary and vaccination plans.

Concert of Action.

When Dr. Rauch was elected secretary in the spring of 1879 the ambitions of the State Board of Health to "sanitate" and vaccinate the State began to resolve into plans and practical application. Cherishing his national point of view he took advantage of every opportunity and created opportunities to make contact with outside agencies. Thus in April, 1879, almost immediately after he became secretary of the State Board of Health, he went to Memphis and got himself elected secretary of the Sanitary Council of the Mississippi Valley, an interstate voluntary organization created at that time. Its function was to keep member health officers informed of all epidemic outbreaks, especially of yellow fever, and to draw up uniform sanitary rules and regulations which all members agreed to adopt and enforce in their several states. This strengthened the public health machinery in Illinois by adding the weight of group opinion to proposed plans and by providing timely information serviceable in promoting prompt action on local plans.

How an effective working contact was made with the National Board of Health, a federal agency created by Congress in 1878 with a $500,000 appropriation, in May and with transportation interests in July of 1879 is best described by Dr. Rauch, himself who gives this account in the second annual report of the State Board of Health:

"While the Illinois State Board, through its executive officer, was thus exerting its influence, beyond its own boundaries, to secure such a general sanitary reform throughout the entire valley as would prove the best safeguard against the introduction of epidemic disease from without, the National Board of Health, in anticipation of the act of Congress increasing its powers and resources, was seeking trustworthy information upon which to base such actions as the law might empower it to take in the discharge of its duties.*

"In response to a telegraphed invitation, received May 28, the Secretary repaired to Washington, for conference with the National Board, and on June 1 proceeded to New Orleans, under confidential instructions from the executive committee of that body. These instructions involved, among other matters, a report upon the general sanitary condition of New Orleans, and an inspection of the Mississippi quarantine station, seventy-five miles below the city. Returning to Washington, on June 8, two days were spent in consultation with the executive committee; and during this conference the situation in the Valley, from St. Louis to New Orleans, was thoroughly discussed, the various available sanitary agencies were duly canvassed, and divers plans were suggested for most efficiently extending the cooperation and aid of the National Government, through this organization, to 'State and municipal boards of health, in the execution and enforcement of the rules and regulations of such boards to prevent the introduction of contagious and infectious diseases into the United States from foreign countries, and into one State from another.'

"A code of rules and regulations was also prepared, and recommended for adoption, for ports designated as quarantine stations; for securing the best sanitary condition of steamboats and other vessels; also, the best sanitary condition of railroads, including station houses, road-beds, and cars of all descriptions; and the precautions to be enforced in a place free from inspection, having communication with a place dangerously infected with yellow fever; and when yellow fever is reported or suspected to exist in any town or place in the United States. As the general adoption of this code would tend to secure uniformity of practice throughout the Valley, and thus promote efficiency in preventive measures, the agency of the Sanitary Council, through its secretary, was invoked to attain this desirable result. The Sections relating to island quarantine were subsequently referred to a committee composed of Drs. H. A. Johnson, of Chicago, R. W. Mitchell, of Memphis, and S. M. Bemiss, of New Orleans, members National Board of Health. Representatives of other sanitary organizations, among them the Secretary of the Illinois State Board of Health, were invited to confer with this committee. The report is as follows:

"By invitation of the committee appointed to confer with the representatives of the railroad and steamboat interests of the Mississippi Valley, representatives of these interests met in the city of Memphis, July 2, 1879, and organized by electing Dr. R. W. Mitchell, Chairman, and Dr. John H. Rauch, of Chicago, Secretary. The following lines and companies were represented: Mr. James Montgomery, Louisville and Nashville Railroad; Mr. J. D. Randall, Memphis and St. Francis

---

* The act referred to was not approved until June 2, but the members of the Board, realizing the gravity of the situation, took such preliminary steps as were possible at this time.

River Packet Company; Mr. W. E. Smith, Memphis and Little Rock Railroad Company; Mr. M. S. Jay, Memphis and Little Rock Railroad Company; Mr. M. Burke, Mississippi and Tennessee Railroad Company; Dr. J. B. Lindsley, Chattanooga, Nashville and St. Louis Railroad Company; Mr. T. S. Davant, Memphis and Charleston Railroad Company; Capt. Ad. Storm, St. Louis Anchor Line Packet Company; Mr. R. A. Speed, Memphis and Arkansas River Packet Company; Captain Lee, Memphis and Friar's Point Packet Company; Capt. R. W. Lightbarne, Memphis and Cincinnati Packet Company. The 'rules and regulations for securing the best sanitary condition of steamboats and other vessels, also the best sanitary condition of railroads, including station-houses, road-beds and cars of all descriptions,'[*] were read separately, discussed, and unanimously approved. Assurance was given of the cordial cooperation of the railroad and steamboat interests in all measures adopted by the National Board of Health in their efforts to prevent the spread of contagious and infectious diseases. All that was asked was that all rules and regulations adopted by the National Board of Health be made uniform at all places and ports. The representatives also approved the recommendations made by the Mississippi Valley Sanitary Council as a special measure of protection to the Mississippi Valley, that *stations* of *inspection* be established at Vicksburg, Memphis and Cairo."

Thus by midsummer of 1879 a four cornered organization for fighting disease in Illinois had been perfected. It included the State Board of Health and such voluntary assistance as it was able to stimulate within the State, the Sanitary Council of the Mississippi Valley which furnished morbidity intelligence, the National Board of Health which formulated interstate sanitary requirements and the conference of Sanitarians and Transportation Interests which put into effect, through the resources of the common carriers, the sanitary measures agreed upon.

By utilizing every ounce of power that could be squeezed from these sources by means of persuasion and threats, Dr. Rauch was able to extend the influence of his sanitary ideas throughout the length and breadth of the Mississippi Valley. Within a few months from the time when the Sanitary Council was organized he was able to report:

"At the beginning of this section, 'Yellow Fever in 1879' there is given a comparative statement of freight movements over the Illinois Central railroad in 1878 and 1879, showing an increase of plus 37 per cent in the latter as compared with the former years. In this statement will be found an illustration of the effect upon commerce by the different systems in vogue in the management of yellow fever in the respective years. In 1878 there was a quarantine practically excluding everything that came from the south, while in 1879 it was one of sanitary inspection, including only dangerous articles. This result could not have been brought about without the cooperation of the National Board of Health, since neither the Illinois State Board nor the Cairo Local Board, without this cooperation, could have permitted the immense amount of material to be brought into the State from the south during the months of July, August, September and October. It required the constant presence of the Secretary at Cairo (especially in July), and repeated assurances to the local authorities that every precaution was being exercised by the National Board and the Louisiana State Board of Health at New Orleans, and other organizations along the entire route, to prevent the introduction and spread of the fever northward, to allay their fears, as this year a majority of the citizens of Cairo were favorable to a quarantine of exclusion. Such was the feeling of apprehension that fully one-third of the population of Cairo, from July 15 to September 1, was ready to leave the moment the first case appeared, no matter whether it was of foreign or local origin."

[*] These were based upon those adopted by the Sanitary Council at Atlanta, with such modifications as a more careful consideration suggested.

How he played one force against another is suggested in a telegram sent by Dr. Rauch on October 3, 1879, to the secretary of the National Board of Health. It read:

"I am almost constantly advised by telegraph, no matter where I am, of the condition of affairs throughout the whole Valley and I am, therefore, in position to judge intelligently of the situation."

The intelligence set forth in this communication was obtained through the operation of the Sanitary Council of the Mississippi Valley and the purpose of the message was to bring the National Board of Health to support Dr. Rauch's plan for combating yellow fever at the moment. Everywhere in the records of his work it is potent that Dr. Rauch kept well informed of epidemic outbreaks all over the world, so far as that was possible. Time and again he went before the national congress, the State legislature and other organizations with his plans and invariably he would recite stories of epidemics abroad, naming foreign cities with the familiarity of a native and quoting figures and relating circumstances like a local observer. Smallpox, cholera and yellow fever—these were the diseases he was fighting. When sanitary interest and activity in the State threatened to grow sluggish, Dr. Rauch would begin to search the skies for epidemic clouds. Invariably he found them, usually an Asiatic cholera thundercloud that flashed and rumbled with deadly threats.

Still catering to his national viewpoint Dr. Rauch resorted again to his "concert of action" idea in 1881 when smallpox outbreaks in the State began to take on serious aspects. This time he took it upon himself to call a conference which again is best described in his own words, taken from the fourth annual report of the State Board of Health, which reads as follows:

"Early in the following June, (1881), the Secretary—convinced by past experience of the futility of independent preventive measures, confined to States and municipalities, while the disease was increasing in the chief European ports, and thousands of unprotected immigrants were pouring into the interior, and after consultation with leading sanitarians—issued a call for a conference of health authorities, National, State, and local, with a view to co-operative action by all interested, and especially with reference to the arrest of further introduction of the contagion from abroad. This Conference, which was held in Chicago, June 29-30, was attended by representatives of the National Board of Health, and of eighteen other health organizations in fourteen different States. After full deliberation the Conference recommended that Congress incorporate into the laws regulating immigration, a provision requiring protection from smallpox by successful vaccination of all immigrants; that the National Board of Health consider the propriety of requiring the inspection of immigrants at the port of departure, the vaccination of the unprotected, and the detention of the unprotected exposed until it was certain that they were not carrying the germs of the disease on shipboard for the infection of the vessel and the transportation of the disease into the United States; that measures be taken for the quarantine detention of steamships bringing immigrants not provided with proper evidence of vaccinal protection; that local health authorities inspect all immigrants arriving in their respective jurisdictions, and enforce proper protective and preventive measures when necessary; and that, 'to meet present emergencies,' the National Board of Health secure the inspection of all immigrants, and the vaccination of the unprotected, before landing at any port of the United States."

PRESIDENTS
Illinois State Board of Health

John H. Rauch, M.D.
1877 -- 1879

Horace Wardner, M.D.
1879 - 1881

J. M. Gregory, LL. D.
1881 - 1884

Newton Bateman, LL.D.
1884 - 1887

As an outcome of the Chicago Smallpox Conference the National Board of Health inaugurated an Immigrant Inspection Service in June of 1882. It provided physicians, stationed at railway terminals throughout the country, who examined immigrants and vaccinated all of those susceptible to smallpox who were enroute to territory over which the inspector had charge. Dr. Rauch was appointed chief inspector for the western district. The inspection service continued only seven months but during that brief period 115,057 immigrants bound for Illinois were examined and 21,618 vaccinated against smallpox. While this service lasted the five inspectors located at Chicago and the two located at St. Louis and Indianapolis respectively, added great strength to the health machinery in Illinois and doubtless led to the coast quarantine service which subsequently relieved states from work and apprehension covering the health of immigrants to this country.

Comprehensive State Survey.

While working with interstate and national agencies for the sake of preventing the introduction of disease from the outside, the State Board of Health, through its secretary, was not idle in promoting sanitary activities within its own state boundary lines. In December of 1878 the Board adopted a form for use in making sanitary surveys. Plans for the use of these forms and what was expected to be gained therefrom are expressed in the first annual report of the Board as follows:

"This schedule of questions embraces everything appertaining to the sanitary interests of any city or town, and it can be carried out without a great deal of expense, as the local medical men or societies will no doubt cheerfully answer all the queries contained therein. The information asked for is necessary to a correct understanding of what is needful to be done to improve the sanitary condition of any city or town in this state. While this information is being obtained, it at the same time *stimulates the study of sanitary science all over the State.* It is therefore very important that this survey should be made."

The first survey forms were sent out to 8 communities in southern Illinois during the spring of 1879. After yellow fever broke out in the lower Mississippi Valley during that summer the forms were sent to 29 other municipalities. The percentage of response was rather disappointing but the idea of making sanitary surveys through local people continued to grow until it culminated during 1885 in over 300,000 inspections in 395 cities, towns and villages in 90 of the 102 counties. This stupendous task was made possible through services voluntarily rendered by hundreds of local physicians, school teachers and others who had been interested in the matter by fear of a cholera epidemic. Dr. Rauch himself had inspired this fear when he recited to the Board at its quarterly meeting in July 1884, the story of cholera in Europe during two preceding years, suggested that the disease seemed to be smouldering ready for a disastrous flare-up that might possibly leap the Atlantic and concluded that:

"......my own experience and observation lead to this conclusion that it is not judicious to place entire reliance on quarantine measures, no matter how administered, should the disease become epidemic in countries or points with which this country has close commercial relations. As Asiatic cholera, although it may invade places of good sanitary conditions, finds its most congenial habitat where filth in any form abounds, the best attainable sanitary condition; clean streets and premises; the prompt and proper disposal of organic refuse, night-soil and all forms of sewage; well ventilated habitations, with dry clean basements; a pure and sufficient water supply; and good individual hygiene, including personal cleanliness, proper diet and regular habits of life—these are the best safeguards against Asiatic cholera, as they are against most diseases."

This was the idea underlying the sanitary survey which brought to the State Board of Health detailed records of the environmental conditions of over 300,000 premises and much information concerning local epidemics and family health histories. The achievement of this stupendous task is significant here because it shows how the Board was able to bring into action hundreds of local people that put the State's health machinery into immediate touch with practically every household in Illinois.

Vaccination of School Children Required

Another illustration of the same means for expanding the health machinery of the State was based upon a resolution passed by the State Board of Health on November 22, 1881, which reads:

"RESOLVED, That by the authority vested in this Board, it is hereby ordered, that on and after January 1, 1882, no pupil shall be admitted to any public school in this State without presenting satisfactory evidence of proper and successful vaccination."

Acting upon this authority Dr. Rauch, as secretary of the Board, made ready such forms as were necessary for providing children with vaccination certificates and for collecting the desired reports for office records and study. Then he plunged into the task of communicating the order to all school officials and teachers in the State. So energetically was the job prosecuted that by January 24, 1882, he was able to say:

"I doubt if the people of any other state of equal age are as well protected against smallpox as those of Illinois at the present time."

In a complete report that was published later appears the assertion that:

"Nearly 500 individuals, embracing attending physicians, and municipal, town and county officers, have contributed, each in his proper capacity, to the information furnished as to the introduction of the contagion, its mode and extent of propagation, the measures resorted to for its suppression and their result, the cost, actual and constructive, and other noteworthy features. In like manner, the vaccinal history of 304,586 public-school children—based upon physicians' certificates of vaccination—has been furnished by over 8,000 teachers; 493 physicians have reported the results in 187,223 vaccinations at all ages; and the vaccinal status of 18,708 inmates of public institutions, private and parochial schools, colleges, academies, etc., has also been given—making an aggregate of 510,517 individual vaccinations and revaccinations."

This shows an amazing increase in the public health machinery which accomplished its purpose within sixty days after it was started resulting in an increase in vaccination of from 45 to 94 per cent of all school children. Power to so enlarge the health machinery was, of course, based upon an interpretation of the law giving the State Board of Health "General supervision of the interests of the health and life of citizens of the State."

Cooperation with Local Authorities

Another means employed by the State Board of Health to augment the available machinery for getting health work done in the State was the promotion of the organization of local boards of health, in the smaller municipal and rural communities. Nearly all the large cities had health organizations at the time, but it required stimulation to keep them going. Under pressure of local epidemic outbreaks and propaganda featuring possible dangers from cholera, smallpox and yellow fever, boards of health came into existence here and there from time to time.

Available records show that local organizations were formed in the larger communities in Illinois as follows:

Cairo	1818	Lasalle	1852
Belleville	1819	Waukegan	1852
Alton	1821	Aurora	1853
Urbana	1833	Elgin	1854
Chicago	1835	Freeport	1855
Ottawa	1837	Kankakee	1855
Bloomington	1839	Moline	1855
Danville	1839	Freeport	1857
Decatur	1839	Lincoln	1857
Quincy	1839 (As a town in 1825)	Centralia	1859
		Mattoon	1859
Pekin	1839	Champaign	1861
Peoria	1839	Rockford	1862
Springfield	1840	E. St. Louis	1865
Jacksonville	1840	Murphysboro	1867
Galesburg	1841	Kewanee	1872
Marion	1841	Streator	1874
Rock Island	1841	Maywood	1881
Blue Island	1843	Chicago Heights	1892
Joliet	1845	Harvey	1895
Canton	1849	Granite City	1896
Collinsville	1850 (town) 1872 (city)	Herrin	1898

By 1886 enough local interest in sanitary matters had been stirred up to bring 39 representatives of as many local municipalities to a sanitary conference called by Dr. Rauch to meet in Springfield on May 21st. Of those in attendance 15 were registered as health officers, 13 as members of local boards or committees of health, 7 as mayors and the other four as city engineer, town trustee, city attorney and city treasurer respectively. What transpired at the conference may be surmised from the report of a committee on resolutions which reads:

"1. That to insure the proper sanitary condition, it shall be the duty of the health officers to require a prompt special inspection of all buildings and premises within the corporate limits of town, village or city, to report same to proper authorities, and to cause all nuisances to be abated as far as practicable.

"2. All town, village, or city authorities should be informed touching the influence of such sanitary supervision of domiciles and places of labor, on sickness and death rates, and they are hereby requested to make a prompt and proper appropriation of means for the performance of this work.

"3. The registration of births and deaths having been too greatly neglected in the past, it is urged that ordinances and rules be made by the proper authorities on this subject, both for the procuring of necessary information, purposes of identification, and also to inform the sanitary authorities of the condition of the health of the neighborhood.

"4. The importance of vaccination and re-vaccination should be impressed upon all school authorities, and the laws of the State thereon should be promptly and vigorously enforced."

How primitive the ideas prevailing then about sanitation were, is shown in a question put before the conference by Dr. T. N. McIlvaine, health officer of Peoria, who wanted to know if pig-pens should be called a nuisance and in what towns they had been abolished.

This conference never resulted in a closely knit organization but it has continued to this day under various names; meeting sometimes regularly but more frequently with a lapse of some years between. Its purpose was manifestly to bring into effective cooperation the State and local health agencies by mutual discussion and understanding of common problems.

Rules and Regulations.

The very first use of the power vested in the State Board of Health "to make such rules and regulations . . . . as they may from time to time deem necessary . . . ." was peremptorily exercised by the president of the Board, Dr. John W. Rauch, at Cairo on July 29, 1878 when yellow fever threatened to invade the State. His action placed an absolute embargo on freight and passengers from the epidemic region into Illinois. In this action the Board later concurred.

From that time forward new rules were made and old ones modified as occasions arose until 1885 found the Board with a set of regulations which required all children in the public schools to be vaccinated against smallpox; quarantine, isolation, etc. of persons sick with smallpox, diphtheria, scarlet fever, typhoid fever, Asiatic cholera and yellow fever; the reporting of cases of contagious disease directly to the secretary of the State Board of Health; prohibition of transporting dead bodies of persons who had died from smallpox, cholera and yellow fever and any other dead bodies during the summer months except under specified conditions.

These rules and regulations, the development of which is recited in another chapter, have always formed the back bone of the State's health machinery. Schemes for making them work have always been the task that confronted executive officers whose duty it was to provide the machinery in sanitation and hygiene with the resources at their command.

Laws relating to health crept into the statute books from the very outset of organized government in Illinois. These were changed, repealed, modified and added to from time to time as the division of labor brought whole groups of persons to depend more and more upon other individuals and groups for supplies, the utilization of which had a direct influence over health and as sanitary and hygienic knowledge increased. By 1885 there were laws authorizing cities and villages to establish boards of health and making the supervisor, assessor and town clerk of every town a board of health to function outside of incorporated cities and villages. There were also numerous laws relating to food, milk, nuisances, etc. To promote desirable sanitary practice and uniformity of procedure throughout the State the State Board of Health drew up what was termed a Model Sanitary Ordinance and recommended its adoption. In this ordinance an attempt was made to codify all existing laws relating directly to health as well as the rules of the State Board of Health that had to do with quarantine, reporting of contagious disease, and sanitary conditions. It also embraced articles on vital statistics, burial permits, etc.

Attention to Water Supplies.

Water supplies attracted the attention of Dr. Rauch throughout the whole period of his association with State health service. Never was he too busy to think and talk about the importance of safeguarding drinking water from pollution. Frequently he found time to make extensive field studies himself. Often he arranged for others to do it. Scarcely a report came from his office that did not present data collected relative to some new investigation of water supplies. The very first annual statement of the Board contained an expenditure item of $19.20 for costs involved in the collection and analysis of samples of water taken from the Chicago River. During the years that followed samples of water were frequently taken from many other streams as well as from public and private supplies. Studies and observations, frequently carried out by Dr. Rauch himself, were often conducted for months at a time. Even after leaving the State Board of Health as its secretary, Dr. Rauch was employed by the Board to study the water supply question. He had much to do with providing a potable water in Chicago just prior to the Great World's Fair in that city

Educational Activities.

Education of the public through the publication and distribution of special pamphlets and through the newspapers was recognized from the outset as a valuable means for extending the public health machinery of the State. The early annual reports of the State Board of Health are replete with lengthy dissertations, reports and quotations on sanitation. Education was one of the chief purposes of the great sanitary survey which really began in 1878. In 1881 a circular entitled "Concerning the Prevention of Smallpox" was published and distributed widely throughout the State. By 1885 circulars on smallpox, diphtheria, scarlet fever and typhoid fever had been published and hundreds of thousands of copies distributed. Correspondence on these and other sanitary matters was voluminous.

The sanitary ideals toward which the first State health officials strove, and particularly Dr. Rauch whose ideas dominated the activity of the Board even before he became its executive secretary, were two-fold. On the one hand, the desire was to so educate the people that they could and would voluntarily, through personal action and local health officers, put into practice the sanitary and hygienic measures calculated to preserve and promote health and thereby make unnecessary a large corps of State health workers. On the other hand the desire was to bring into existence interstate, national and international machinery which would function so as to prevent the introduction of diseases from without and to keep the State health officials informed of world health conditions.

To the end of realizing these ideals the contacts heretofore referred to were made and the activities mentioned were undertaken prior to the close of 1885. This general scheme continued with but few and not very important exceptions, to govern the plans, policies, organization and performances of the State public health machinery in Illinois until the close of the nineteenth century.

Dr. Rauch continued as executive secretary of the State Board of Health until June 30, 1891, when he resigned and was succeeded by Dr. Frank W. Reilly of Chicago on September 24, 1891, Dr. W. R. MacKenzie of Chester, a member of the Board, filling in the interim.

Accomplishments.

Throughout the 14 years of his connection with the State Board of Health, most of which time was spent as its secretary, Dr. Rauch was easily the central figure of public health machinery and thought in the State. He exercised no insignificant influence over the sanitary and hygienic policies and practices in the nation and attracted notice of foreign countries. His ideas about yellow fever made an especial appeal in Europe and were made the subject of a lengthy and favorable editorial in the December 15, 1888, edition of the London Lancet. The extent and character of Dr. Rauch's activities as a sanitarian are succinctly expressed in a resolution, adopted by the State Board of Health when his resignation was accepted, which reads:

WHEREAS, Dr. John H. Rauch, after fourteen years continuous service, has severed his connection with the Illinois State Board of Health, having on the 30th day of June last, tendered his resignation as its Secretary, the following resolutions are hereby adopted, as in some degree expressing the sentiment of the individual members of the Board toward their friend and colleague:

Resolved, That Dr. Rauch's services in the cause of sanitary science and of the best interests of the medical profession have given the State of Illinois a gratifying pre-eminence not only in this country, but wherever the sanitarian and the physician are known and recognized as useful members of society.

Resolved, That Dr. Rauch's eminent attainments as a practical sanitarian, illustrated in his management and control of epidemics, his reformation of the theory and practice of quarantine, his establishment of a system of immigrant inspection on sea and land, his conservation of the purity of food supplies and products and his work in the domain of preventive medicine, place him in the front rank of those who devote their lives to the material welfare of their fellow men.

Resolved, That to Dr. Rauch's untiring energy, to his vigilance and to his intimate personal knowledge of the profession, both in his own State and in the country at large, are chiefly due the establishment of a body of efficient legislation, regulating the practice of medicine—legislation whose precepts and adjudicated cases have been copied, adopted and endorsed by older commonwealths.

Resolved, That his wise aggressiveness, his forethought, sagacity and persistence, in the face of manifold obstacles, have nowhere been more strikingly displayed nor more usefully employed than in his successful efforts to elevate the standard of medical education.

Resolved, That Dr. Rauch's personal sacrifices in the discharge of his duties as member, Secretary and President of the Illinois State Board of Health—sacrifices known to every member of the Board—are deserving of grateful recognition and substantial reward by the people of the State for whom he has so long and so faithfully labored.

Resolved, That the individual members of the Board, whose names are hereto appended, are unable adequately to express the regret caused by Dr. Rauch's resignation and the esteem in which he is held by them. They earnestly entertain the hope that he may long be spared to counsel and advise with them and their successors in matters touching the lives and health of the people of the state.

W. A. HASKELL, A. M., M. D., Harv.
NEWTON BATEMAN, LL. D.
ANSON L. CLARK, M. D.
R. LUDLAM, M. D.
WILLIAM P. MACKENZIE, M. D.
DANIEL H. WILLIAMS, M. D.
B. M. GRIFFITHS, M. D.

The things of noteworthy magnitude which had come to pass during Dr. Rauch's incumbency and which brought into action the available health machinery of the State were briefly as follows:

1. The State had been cleansed of unqualified practitioners of medicine. Physicians who were allowed to practice held bona fide credentials,

and medical education had been raised to a considerably higher level. This work was achieved largely by the State Board of Health itself whose members served without pay and met frequently in all parts of the State.

2. Practically every household in the State had been inspected from a sanitary point of view. This was accomplished through the voluntary services of local people.

3. Nearly every school child in the State had been vaccinated against smallpox. The law making it the duty of local officials to carry out the orders of the State Board of Health and that empowering the Board to make rules and regulations were invoked to bring success in this case.

4. Vital statistics such as reports of births and deaths were collected, compiled and published in great detail for the years of 1880 to 1886 inclusive. While estimated to be about 48 per cent incomplete for births and 31 per cent for deaths, the machinery for collecting them was set in motion and even in so incomplete a condition they furnish valuable data for comparison with present day conditions. This task was accomplished by putting county clerks to work at this task as the law required, and by utilizing the limited clerical resources available to the Board.

5. Rules and regulations concerning quarantine and sanitation had been adopted, their enforcement was promoted through a law creating local boards of health throughout the State.

6. Exhaustive studies of stream pollution in the State and of water supplies and sewer facilities, especially in Chicago had been made. This had been accomplished largely by the personal effort of Dr. Rauch himself and the analytical laboratory service which was paid for out of the general office expense fund.

7. The physical examination of immigrants for the special purpose of preventing smallpox, cholera and yellow fever was in general practice along the Atlantic seaboard and sporadically inland. This had come about, to some extent at least, because of contact with outside agencies.

8. The influence of the foremost sanitarians all over the country had made itself felt in Illinois. This had resulted from the prominent part taken by Dr. Rauch in organizing and participating in a dozen national sanitary movements.

Even after his resignation as secretary, Dr. Rauch continued to exercise a direct influence over the sanitary thought of the State and the policies of its health machinery. Indeed he was time and again called back to duty by the Board of Health in the capacity of Sanitary Counsel. Only death, which closed the career of this unique figure in the public health history of the country in March of 1894, could eliminate him as a master figure in the sanitary thought and activities of his State.

PRESIDENTS
Illinois State Board of Health

W. A. Haskell, M. D.
1887 - 1893

John A. Vincent, M. D.
1893 - 1894

Wm. E. Quine, M. D.
1894 - 1896

B. M. Griffith, M. D.
1896 - 1897

Dr. Reilly Secretary.

Dr. Reilly had been closely associated with the State Board of Health since 1878 when he was employed by it to work as a medical inspector in the yellow fever zone. For many years he was assistant secretary under Dr. Rauch. During his four years in office he carried forward the policies and activities that had been previously established. There was one notable exception in the continuity of policy. In 1892 an attempt was made to divorce the work relating to regulating the practice of medicine and that involved in sanitation and hygiene. The Board authorized Dr. Reilly to work with the legislature toward that end. The idea was to create a board of medical examiners and leave the State Board of Health to function only in the field of sanitation and hygiene.

Very rapid progress had been made in the science of bacteriology during the eighties and apparently Dr. Reilly was more inclined to put faith in the discoveries made in this field than was Dr. Rauch. It is easy to understand how a health officer with limited resources who believed in the possibilities for service disclosed by bacteriological discoveries would grow restive under conditions that required most of his time and effort to license doctors. An active imagination even in that early day of bacteriology could foresee opportunities for expending unbounded resources in prosecuting sanitary programs.

Dr. Reilly tended more toward the idea of building up a State health organization than did Dr. Rauch. Trying to get rid of the Medical Practice Act indicated this attitude. He also managed to employ out of the contingency funds a corps of immigrant inspectors which he stationed at Chicago. Dr. Rauch looked to the federal government for such service and probably regarded the latter as a principle. The immigrant inspectors constituted the only important change in the health machinery of the State under Dr. Reilly and this was discontinued when Dr. J. W. Scott of Chicago was elected secretary to succeed Dr. Reilly on July 5, 1893

Dr. J. W. Scott Secretary:

Under Dr. Scott the visitation of a general smallpox epidemic revived the compulsory vaccination rule that applied to school children which had been allowed to fall into disuse. This time its enforcement was accompanied by considerable litigation. Two suits are noteworthy. One was an action against a school board in Wayne County which was dropped upon advice of the State's attorney who felt that conviction was impossible. The other, a mandamus proceeding against a school board in Lawrence County went to the Supreme Court where the decision handed down in November 1895 was against the school board. This is important because it declared that the rule of the State Board of Health requiring evidence of vaccination before admitting children to the public schools could be enforced only when smallpox threatened or was imminent in a particular community. Henceforth the public health machinery which this rule had previously set in motion could be utilized only when smallpox appeared in a community.

Under Dr. Scott the conference of State and local health officers in Illinois was revived under the name of the State Board of Health Auxiliary Association. The fact that 108 representatives attended the meeting in 1894 showed that local health organization had grown considerably since the first meeting of this kind was held in 1888—when 39 representatives had responded to the invitation. At the meeting in 1894 a strong sentiment in favor of uniform procedures was manifested and to that end the Model Ordinance was reviewed and modified and its adoption recommended. So far the quarantine rules and regulations of the State Board were general, leaving specific matters to the discretion of local authorities.

In 1895 the means for enlarging the State's public health machinery were enhanced when the legislature appropriated $3,000 for the establishment of a vaccine farm and $5,000 for a water laboratory, both to be located at the State University. More detailed discussion of these projects appears in the chapter on laboratories.

Dr. Scott continued as the secretary of the State Board of Health until May 24, 1897 when he was succeeded by Dr. James A. Egan of Chicago who occupied that position until his death in March 1913.

There was no material change in the health machinery of the State between 1890 and 1900 except the beginning of the laboratory work. The strength of the State Board of Health was shifted from one problem to another. At one time a staff inspector was employed to examine immigrants as they came into the State. At another time a milk inspector would be put to work. Then attention would be concentrated on yellow fever with all hands busy in Cairo, making inspections of passengers and freight from the South. Again the examination of public water supplies and streams would interest those in charge and experts would be employed to carry out studies in that field. Smallpox flared up occasionally and stimulated field activity that involved expenses. Law suits developed from the enforcement of rules and this led to the employment of legal talent.

All of the personal service employed by the State Board of Health was temporary in nature, however, except that of the secretary, an assistant secretary and a small clerical staff. The total appropriation for the routine expenses of the State Board of Health during the last year of the nineteenth century was only $9,250. Of that sum $3,000 was for the salary of the

158   PUBLIC HEALTH ADMINISTRATION

secretary. The pay of a chief clerk reduced the total by $1,800 more. Two clerks were entitled by law to get $2,150 together. This left $2,350 for travel and other expenses of the Board members and secretary, printing, general office expense, other personal services not regularly employed, etc. There was a five thousand dollar contingency appropriation which the various secretaries tried to utilize from time to time. How successful they were depended upon the will of the particular governor in office at the time and upon the ability of the secretary to picture imminent danger from any of a group of diseases listed in the appropriation law.

Thus on July 12, 1900, the State's official public health organization was 23 years old. During that time this infant governmental function had survived apparently by reason of its stubborn refusal to die and a tenacious grip on life. From then on its growth was considerably accelerated.

Resume.

At the beginning of this short quarter of a century there was a State Board of Health with an executive secretary and a small clerical staff. At the end of it there was a Board, an executive secretary and a clerical staff a trifle larger. At the beginning the Board members met frequently—thirteen times the first year—but they received no remuneration except travel expenses. At the end of this period the Board members received a per diem pay, their travel expense and met less frequently, rarely more often than quarterly. Thus it is clear that the health work of the State devolved more and more upon the executive officer of the Board. An annual contingency fund made possible a medical and sanitary field service under epidemic conditions while sporadic work of this kind could be accomplished out of the routine funds.

During the 23 years the Board of Health had indulged the authority vested in it by law to make "rules and regulations" and a number of these efforts had been tested in the courts. Thus the limitations of the health machinery had been pretty well established, the courts leaning to the view that dangerous disease must be present in a community before drastic quarantine or sanitary rules may become operative.

Nearly everybody in the State had come into contact with the State health organization through the vaccination and sanitary survey projects so that the idea of doing public health work had taken root. Local boards of health had more than doubled in number during the period. At the same time the prevailing popular notion fixed the work of health officers to purely environmental cleanliness—collecting dead animals, causing abatement of nuisances, garbage removal, etc.

Sporadic efforts to collect vital statistics had been made. County clerks knew that it was their job to handle certificates of birth and death. Doctors knew that the law required these reports. The State Board of Health knew that it was legally required to receive and compile and preserve the statistics. This system never operated successfully enough to bring reasonably complete returns and no time was found by the State agency to compile and publish these records except for the years of 1880 to 1886 inclusive

Contact with outside agencies had been established and cultivated. This added the advantage of national and world intelligence of epidemic conditions as well as sanitary and hygienic developments to the State's machinery for doing health work.

This closed the probationary or Rauch period. Health work had become established in Illinois. Machinery for doing it was now regarded as an essential and permanent factor in the State's government. From now on it began to expand, take on new activities and developed into a strong agency relying more and more on its own resources to keep diseases under control and to preserve and promote good health.

The Egan Regime.

The predominating characteristic of public health service under Dr. James A. Egan, who became secretary of the State Board of Health in July 1897, was expansion. Regulating the practice of medicine and allied professions had reached a fairly satisfactory stage and still consumed 75 or 80 per cent of the time and energy of the State Board of Health. Dr. Egan wanted to get rid of it. He saw large possibilities for growth in the field of sanitation and hygiene. He began to examine the resources at his command and to plan for their enlargement.

Dr. Egan championed from the outset of his incumbency the idea of separating the regulation of the practice of medicine from the sanitary work and to this end he sought to create separate State machinery. He also wanted a larger State sanitary staff and better local health machinery. In a paper read before the State Medical Society at Galesburg on May 18, 1898, Dr. Egan declared that the people were indisposed to pass laws or spend money for sanitary improvement and the prevention of disease. This, he thought, was because of wide differences of opinion among sanitarians. In the same paper he advocated legislation, providing for the establishment of local boards of health and the separation of the State's functions relating to "medical practice" from those concerned with sanitation and hygiene. There was scarcely a meeting of the State Board of Health after Dr. Egan became secretary but the matter of getting relief from the duties involved under the Medical Practice Act was discussed.

Increased Appropriations.

The meeting of the General Assembly in 1899 gave Dr. Egan his first opportunity to begin his expansion program through legislation. What he wanted is outlined in a report from him to the Governor in January of that year which set forth seven specific requests. They were:

"*First:* The creation of a State Board of Medical Examiners to examine and license physicians and midwives.

Second: The creation of a local board of health in every city, village and town, and in every county not under township organization, certain duties to be imposed upon such Boards.

Third: The forbidding of the interment or cremation of a body dead from any cause, in any portion of the State, except upon a legal permit, the burial or cremation permit to be issued by the nearest health officer who shall be required to report monthly to the State Board of Health.

Fourth: Granting to the State Board of Health supervision over the sources of public water supplies and of sewage disposal throughout the State.

Fifth: Granting to the State Board of Health an appropriation commensurate in a degree with the sanitary duties the Board is expected to perform.

Sixth: Requiring that owners of cattle condemned for tuberculosis, should be adequately compensated by the State for the loss of the same when it can be shown that the owners were ignorant of the fact that the cattle were diseased when the purchase was made. Requiring also severe penalty against owners who fail to promptly report sick animals to the inspectors, or who oppose any attempt to the inspection of their herds.

Seventh: Amending 'An Act to Create and Establish a State Board of Health in the State of Illinois, approved May 25, 1877, in force July 1, 1877.' As under the recommendations outlined above, the majority of the sections of this Act will be amended, I would recommend that the entire act be amended. Section 2. (The Power and Authority of the Board), especially needs careful revision. In the opinion of the Attorney General, this section is weak and may often be found inoperative for a time at least."

Out of this ambitious program, Dr. Egan succeeded in getting an increase of $250 per year in appropriations and that went to the salary of two clerks. He had asked for an increase of $25,000. That was the beginning but Dr. Egan was destined to learn how to get the ear of the lawmakers and how to manipulate their purse string pulse.

But there were other resources. There was the contingency fund of $5,000 per year. It could be spent with the consent of the Governor "in case of an outbreak, or threatened outbreak of any epidemic or malignant diseases". To get it the task was only to convince the Governor that a malignant disease had appeared or threatened to appear in the State. This Dr. Egan could do. Prior to his time the contingency fund usually went back into the treasury untouched. From now on a year rarely passed when it was not drawn upon. It was used to pay physicians and quarantine officers appointed for special duty in connection with yellow fever alarms, smallpox outbreaks, typhoid fever and other diseases and for sanitary service in flooded areas along the Ohio, Illinois and Mississippi river bottoms.

Payment for Field Work Still Undecided.

But the State's machinery for getting sanitary work done was haphazard at best. Members of the Board of Health as well as the executive and clerical staff were heavily burdened with licensing doctors, midwives, pharmacists, etc. Then there were vital statistics to be collected and compiled. Epidemics more often invaded than threatened the State. Everybody agreed to the need of expert medical and sanitary services wherever infectious diseases became epidemic but nobody agreed upon who should pay for such services. A law required counties to pay for medical services in instances where the patients were unable to do so even though not classed as paupers. Another law appropriated money to the Board of Health for use in such emergencies. Who finally paid seemed to be a decision arrived at largely by skill in "buck passing". In December of 1898, for instance, a smallpox panic at Griggsville caused the secretary of the State Board of Health to employ Dr. Isaac D. Rawlings for duty in that area and Doctor Rawlings reported great difficulty in collecting his compensation and that of nurses employed in the emergency from the county commissioners. At another time a group of nurses employed a lawyer who appeared before the State Board of Health in October 1899 and presented a claim for pay for services rendered to smallpox patients in St. Clair County. In this case the Board paid the bill. Again the minutes of the Board at its January, 1900 meeting show that it paid claims aggregating $210 for work done in connection with smallpox quarantine in East St. Louis but refused to pay a supplemental claim of $159.50 for expenses incurred in the same procedure. This indicates that the public health machinery of the State was still so chaotic that nobody had a clear conception of whose duty it was to perform the sanitary work necessary to suppress disease and a still more confused notion about who should pay for it once the work had been done.

Miscellaneous Activities.

This confusion expressed itself in other ways. The State Board of Health had power to make rules and regulations. So did cities and villages. The one should not conflict with the other but in the face of alarming outbreaks when State help was not forthcoming the local people took matters in their own hand. Thus "pest houses" and "shot gun" quarantine came into vogue, especially where smallpox appeared and that disease seemed to pursue health officers in those days like an evil spirit.

An insatiable reader, Dr. Egan knew what was going on in the field of sanitation and he began to transform his information into plans as soon as he found himself in a position to be heard.

SECRETARIES
Illinois State Board of Health

Frank W. Reilly, M.D.
1891-1893

John W. Scott, M.D.
1893-1897

James A. Egan, M.D.
1897-1913

Amos Sawyer
1913-1914

C. St. Clair Drake, M.D.
1914-1917

Amos Sawyer acted as secretary for fourteen months prior to the appointment of Dr. Drake.

At the quarterly meeting of the State Board of Health in October, 1898, Dr. Egan presented a report concerning a recently established state tuberculosis sanitarium in Massachusetts. It was so favorably received that the Board instructed Dr. Egan to take up with the next legislature the matter of constructing such an institution in Illinois. The 1899 General Assembly declined to provide for the construction of a sanitarium but it did pass a joint resolution directing the State Board of Health to investigate the matter and report back to the Governor for that body. This indicated an awakening interest in sanitary matters. The leaven was at work.

In June, 1899 Dr. Egan arranged to spend $4,000 for making stream pollution investigations. His plan was to establish 20 observation stations along the Illinois River, hire an engineer to keep them functioning and pay for laboratory tests on the volume plan. This scheme was carried out, adding considerable volume to the State's health machinery. This piece of work, it may be observed, ultimately had an important bearing on the outcome of litigation between Illinois and Missouri upon the question of stream pollution and very probably was undertaken with that end in view.

Tuberculous cattle offered a field for expansion and Dr. Egan considered taking upon the State Board of Health the tuberculin testing of herds. He asked the opinion of the Attorney General in 1899, whether the Board had power to so do and received a favorable reply. Probably the reason he did not go into that work was lack of funds so he contented himself with agitating legislation on the subject.

The work of tuberculin testing herds started in May, 1899 by the State Board of Live Stock Commissioners and has since been continued under that agency which later lost its identity, becoming a part of the State Department of Agriculture created under the Civil Administrative Code in 1917.

The operation of the State's health machinery was simplified some and the power centering in the secretary of the Board considerably increased on January 17, 1899 when the State Board of Health passed a resolution which reads:

"*Resolved*, That the Secretary of the Board, Dr. James A. Egan, is hereby appointed executive officer of the Board and is empowered to act for and in the name of the Board when the same is not in session."

A similar resolution was passed the next year but was made unnecessary later by an amendment to the law in 1901 permanently providing the same thing.

This largely obviated the necessity of called meetings and at the same time gave the secretary a free hand to exercise his faculties. Health machinery in the State is drifting toward one man control.

Up to this time about 1900, nearly all requests and complaints reaching the State Board of Health had concerned the practice of medicine. Such expressions as:

"Three petitions, signed by fifty physicians, asking for an investigation of the unprofessional conduct, etc." and

Charges of unprofessional conduct have been received by the Board against nearly 100, etc."

appear in the early annual reports but few references are made to petitions begging for investigations of outbreaks and endemic prevalence of diseases and of insanitary conditions.

Beginning in the nineties the Board is called upon more and more frequently for help in sanitary matters. By 1899 every meeting of the State Board of Health brings questions about water supplies, milk, stream pollution, nuisances, infectious diseases. The deplorable sanitary conditions in penal and charitable institutions of the State are aired in the press. A committee of the Board investigates and reports. Floods at various places in the State at periodic intervals bring requests for sanitary investigations especially of water supplies. The public conscience is beginning to awaken. Possibilities of preventive medicine are playing upon the popular imagination. The time for expanding is opportune.

Lodging House Inspection.

A law making certain sanitary regulations concerning lodging houses in cities of 100,000 or more, which confined it to Chicago, was passed by the legislature in 1899 and placed under the State Board of Health for enforcement. The bill carried an emergency clause so that it became operative upon approval on April 21, 1899. No funds were appropriated for carrying out the provisions which enumerated minimum air space, maximum capacity, etc., for sleeping rooms. The enforcement of this would necessarily require the constant services of a considerable staff of inspectors. Work was started in a small way, however, when Homer C. Fancher and M. M. Jonas were appointed as chief inspector and assistant, respectively, on July 15, 1899, their pay to be drawn from the contingency fund. It was stipulated that their services should terminate on October 15th of the same year. Arrangements were made at that time to continue the work.

Fancher died during the autumn of 1899 and Edward J. Smejkal took his place as chief lodging house inspector. About this time Smejkal also became attorney for the State Board of Health. He was, therefore, brought into intimate contact with the operation of the Board. As chief lodging house inspector he experienced the unavoidable difficulty of getting pay promptly for his own services and those of his staff. This was because no funds had been specifically provided for that purpose and each claim

RATION 165

sometimes by the Governor
om three to six months were

rs were employed in lodging
ilties. Under these circum-
n securing for lodging house

F
EALTH

```
Lodging House
Inspection Service
1 Chief Inspector
3 Regular Inspectors
1-20 Temporary Inspectors
```

y-five years of existence.

from the General Assembly

General Assembly and soon
his established an important
and the appropriating body
ver subsequent events.

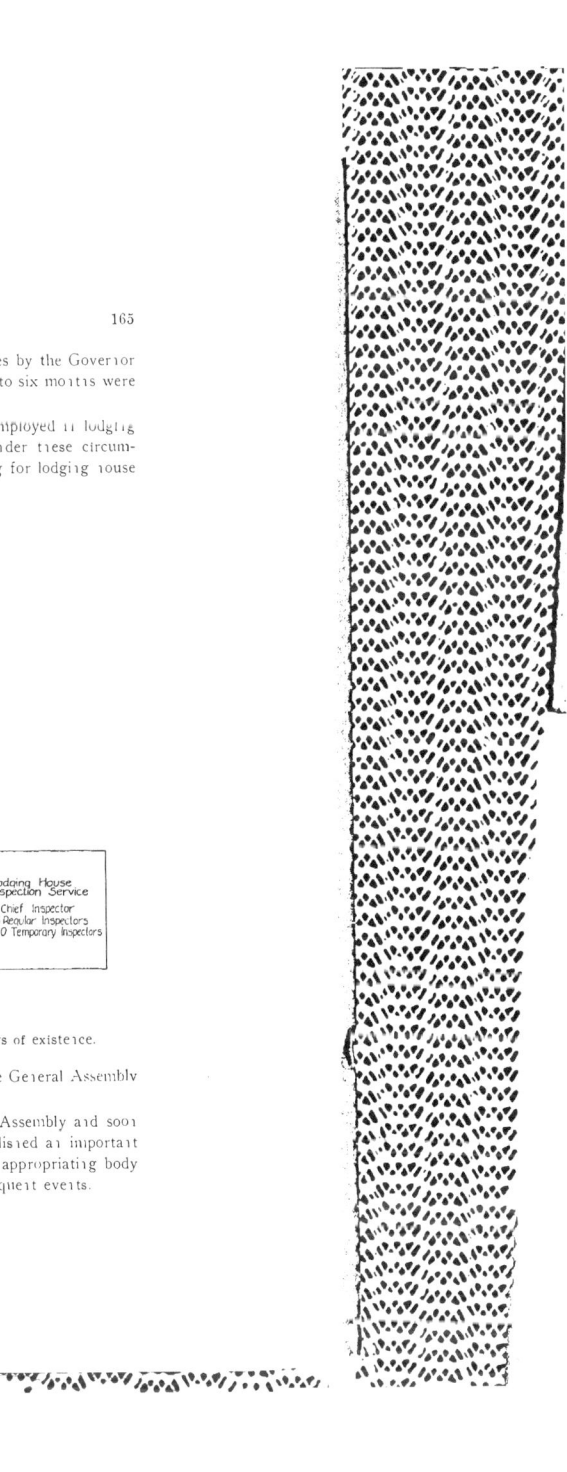

Communicable Disease Curative Measures.

In his annual report to the Governor for the year of 1900 Dr. Egan recommended virtually the same legislative program that was outlined two years before, adding the item of a state tuberculosis sanitarium.

This time the outcome was more favorable. The appropriation jumped from $9,250 to $22,500 per annum for routine expenditures while the contingency grant increased from $5,000 to $10,000 per year. These funds became available on July 1, 1901, shortly after the adjournment of the General Assembly.

Of the $22,500 a sum of $12,500 had been set aside in the law for lodging house inspection. This left but $10,000 for general work. On the other hand there was the $10,000 contingency. This justified a plan, at least, for building up the health machinery.

In July 1901, Dr. Egan reported to the Board at its regular quarterly meeting that:

> "Despite the fact that there is no available appropriation available for laboratory purposes, the necessity for a bacteriologic laboratory for the prompt diagnosis of tuberculosis, diphtheria and typhoid fever has become so urgent that the Secretary has diverted sufficient funds from the appropriations for investigation of contagious diseases, to equip a laboratory which is now in operation. Suitable quarters could not be obtained in the Capitol Building and offices were consequently taken in the Odd Fellows Building, in Springfield, the best equipped building in the city and convenient to the offices of the Springfield physicians. A limited but adequate equipment has been installed and the Board is now making diagnostic examinations of specimens for the physicians of the state without cost to them."

This is evidence that plans were materializing. About this time a plan for systematic service in connection with epidemic outbreaks was also evolved. A corps of physicians, located in various convenient places throughout the State, was selected. Arrangements were made to call upon anyone of them at any time when necessity required. Remuneration was on a per diem basis. Money could legally be drawn from the contingency fund to defray such expenses. The annual financial statements of the Board indicate that this was done. The system was somewhat like the reserve scheme in the national military organization.

No workable system for securing prompt and complete reports of communicable disease incidence had been evolved by the State Board of Health in 1902. During August of that year when Chicago found itself in the throes of a severe typhoid fever outbreak, the city health commissioner, Dr. Arthur R. Reynolds, requested from the secretary of the State Board of Health, Dr. Egan, information concerning the down state prevalence of the disease. Dr. Egan dispatched telegrams to health officers in 35 towns to get the desired information. The rules of the Board still required notification of diseases but the machinery was too feeble to enforce it.

Progress Made.

But with all of its inadequacy the health machinery was beginning to impress itself upon public men who were in a position to help it grow. The plan which worked best seemed to be that of starting something and then putting the matter up to the legislature for support. Thus the lodging house inspection work began. Now a diagnostic laboratory had begun. A chemist and a sanitary engineer had been employed sporadically and their investigations in stream pollution promised to be valuable in pending litigation between Illinois and Missouri. A corps of physicians known as sanitary inspectors were organized ready for duty when called upon. The machinery was there and it was too valuable to be without. How the political leaders felt about the situation in 1902 is expressed in a speech by Governor Yates, delivered at Anna on October 9th. Among other things he said:

"The sanitary work done by the Board must interest every citizen of the state. The Board now has, as for two years past, a corps of competent medical inspectors distributed throughout the state, prepared to investigate promptly all epidemics and all reports of any undue prevalence of disease. During the past four years the Board has had to contend with three epidemics of smallpox. Although, until the last year, handicapped by an inadequate appropriation—only $5,000 annually having been appropriated for this purpose, against $25,000 annually in the neighboring states of Indiana and Wisconsin—the Board has accomplished results of the greatest benefit and importance. Through its efforts, acting with the local authorities, the epidemic of smallpox has been kept well under control during the past year, notwithstanding the fact that the disease had reached an epidemic form in adjoining states. Smallpox is now widely prevalent throughout the Union, but there are comparatively few cases in the State of Illinois.

"Particular attention must be called to the sanitary investigations made by this board during the past three years, of the waters of the Illinois River and its tributaries, with special reference to the effect of the sewage of Chicago. Most exhaustive and elaborate tests and analyses of the waters have been made and the results, up to the summer of 1901, published in two comprehensive and complete reports. A report of the investigations made during the past year will be published within a month. Those disinterested and independent reports of a thorough chemic and bacteriologic analysis of water, the condition of which has excited so much controversy, have received unusual attention at home and abroad owing to the fact that they contain testimony of an unimpeachable character, given by a body which has but one object in view, namely, the truth. This testimony is of inestimable value, not only to the people of Chicago, but also to the people of the entire state. It demonstrates that the Illinois River, into which four-fifths of the sewage of Chicago is now turned, purifies itself through natural causes; that the influence of Chicago's sewage ceases long before the Mississippi is reached and that notwithstanding the enormous pollution 200 miles above, the Illinois River at its junction with the Mississippi is in better sanitary condition than the Mississippi at that point.

"This is the most important work ever accomplished by the State Board of Health. Not only has the Board demonstrated to scientists the self-purification of running streams and thus vindicated the wisdom of the people of Chicago in undertaking one of the greatest engineering projects of the century, but also, to use the language of a leading Chicago daily newspaper, 'has furnished the most conclusive testimony in favor of the contention of Illinois in the suit brought by the State of Missouri in the Supreme Court of the United States, that has ever been presented.' Through the expenditure of a few thousand dollars in scientific research, the State Board of Health has saved the tax-payers of Illinois very many thousands of dollars and has prevented years of litigation. The reports made by the State Board of Health on the effect of the drainage canal, the only published reports on the subject extant, will undoubtedly be accepted by the Supreme Court of the United States as trustworthy and conclusive testimony that there is little or no contamination in the water supply of St. Louis which can be attributed to the sewage which passes through the Chicago Drainage Canal."

This shows that the leaders were beginning to appreciate sanitary developments but science had traveled too fast for the public at large. Bacteriology had been born during the preceding fifty years but it had grown tremendously and especially toward the close of the nineteenth century. The causative organisms of tuberculosis, typhoid fever, diphtheria, malaria, dysentery, tetanus and other diseases had been isolated and described prior to 1900. Diphtheria antitoxin had been made available. Typhoid vaccine could be purchased. The means by which yellow fever, malaria, typhoid fever, diphtheria and a number of other infectious diseases spread had been clarified. Laboratory diagnosis of diphtheria, typhoid fever, tuberculosis and other diseases had been perfected. Great things in the control and prevention of diseases were possible. The practical application of knowledge at hand was the only necessary requirement. This depended upon public appreciation and support.

The public still clung to its traditional idea about disease, however, and indulged its consummate fear about some, such as smallpox, but calmly tolerated others as a necessary evil. Those who heard about the new scientific procedures were still sceptical. Otherwise funds for interpreting the scientific discoveries into practical terms and for applying preventive measures would have flown more quickly and more freely from the appropriating agencies.

The General Assembly in 1903 raised the appropriation for State health work $4,340 above that of 1901 but the items specified were still general except for lodging house inspection and clerical work. It is probable that the health officials had no very definite plan of organization and the members of the General Assembly had still less. In the year of 1905 new items find their way into the appropriations law. Assistant secretary, laboratory, registrar of vital statistics, bacteriologist were terms that appeared then for the first time. The total yearly sums granted, exclusive of contingency which remains at $10,000 have risen from $26,860 to $32,860. The plan of giving birth to an idea, nursing it along as an infant function and then turning it over to the General Assembly who had to accept the responsibility of feeding it or allowing it to perish is working well. An assistant director had been employed in 1904. During the same year the registrar of vital statistics had been placed in charge of the bacteriological laboratory. The expansion program is picking up momentum.

Antitoxin Distributed and Pasteur Treatments

Beside the enlargement of appropriation to the State Board of Health for sanitary purposes the 1905 General Assembly passed two other important laws which enlarged the health machinery considerably. One made it the duty of the State Board of Health to appoint one or more agents in every county who were required to keep on hand at all times a supply of diphtheria antitoxin certified to by the State Board of Health. This law further provided that the price charged for antitoxin should be reasonable and that the poor could have it at the expense of counties. The State Board of Health thus found itself in a position to exercise considerable influence in the choice of agents throughout the State and over manufacturers of biological products.

The other law appropriated $2,000 for the Pasteur treatment of poor people bitten by rabid animals. Supervision over the expenditure of this sum, which was to be handled through hospitals, was given to the State Board of Health. This was another public recognition of a feature of preventive medicine.

The antitoxin agents were duly appointed in 1906 but this arrangement did not satisfy the health authorities. Before a meeting in Springfield on October 18, 1906, of the State Board of Charities, at which Governor Deneen was present, Dr. George W. Webster, president of the State Board of Health, advocated the manufacture and free distribution of diphtheria antitoxin by the State. New York and Massachusetts had already begun that practice. Difficulty over the clause in the 1905 law which required counties to pay for antitoxin issued to poor people had already developed, the idea that the State was to pay, having prevailed generally. Thus in his annual report to the Governor for the year of 1906 Dr. Egan strongly recommended the free distribution of diphtheria antitoxin. This led in 1907 to an appropriation of $15,000 per annum for that purpose and thereby established a new and important piece of public health machinery. The law did not provide for the manufacture of antitoxin but for its purchase. This provision has continued from year to year and prevails to this day.

Monthly Bulletin Published.

Another important function that started in 1906 was the publication of a monthly bulletin by the State Board of Health. The advantage of such an educational medium had been appreciated for many years and attempts had previously been made to start it but they had proven temporary until now. From this time on some sort of monthly publication was printed and distributed with more or less regularity. It was distributed chiefly to physicians and health officers.

Duties of Board Extended.

Like Dr. Rauch, Dr. Egan realized the importance of safe water supplies and always found means to keep this subject prominent among activities undertaken. If he was unable to employ the technically trained personnel from the regular appropriation he managed to get hold of contingency money for that purpose. While the funds for ordinary expenses lasted he would draw upon them, calculating that the contingency purse string would be loosened for any necessary expenses involved in emergency epidemics. Later the State Water Survey of the University of Illinois offered an opportunity to get sanitary engineering work done and in 1906, an agreement was perfected, whereby the State Board could call upon the Water Survey Bureau of the University, to make investigations of water supply and sewerage systems as requested. Whatever the difficulties, the fact remains that Dr. Egan managed to keep this matter of safe water supplies and sewage disposal before the public. The litigation between Illinois and Missouri had ended favorably to Illinois in that year. The State Board of Health had engineered and paid for the stream pollution investigations which had been an important factor in the court decision and had received ample credit for that work. This added considerable prestige to the Board of Health as a sanitary agency. From this time on until it established a permanent sanitary engineering service of its own the Water Survey was largely depended upon to do that sort of work.

Again the appropriation for the State Board of Health went up at the hand of the General Assembly in 1907, the chief item of increase being $15,000 per year for the free distribution of diphtheria antitoxin. But this was not the most important extension of public health machinery in that year. A law amending the original State Board of Health Act was passed. It specified that the State Board of Health had supreme authority over quarantine matters in the State. It made it the duty of the State Board of Health to investigate the cause of dangerously contagious or infectious diseases. It gave the Board power to make such rules and regulations as the Board deemed advisable and required local health and other officials to enforce the rules. Furthermore, it gave the executive officer of the State Board of Health power to take charge of the situation wherever local health officials refused or neglected to take proper steps in combating an epidemic and to collect from the local community whatever expenses were involved in handling the situation. This same law gave the Board of Health specific authority to establish and maintain a chemical and bacteriological laboratory.

This law clarified matters considerably and established the State Board of Health very definitely as the supreme health organization in the State. From this time forth no rule, regulation or activity of local health officials relating to sanitation and quarantine could legally be in conflict with those of the State Board of Health. To become a powerful and adequate agency for combating diseases in the State the Board now needed only the necessary funds with which to build up an organization. The total annual appropriation in 1907 was $59,800. Of this $15,000 were for lodging house inspection in Chicago and another $15,000 for the distribution of diphtheria antitoxin. This left but $29,800 for other activities and $10,000 of that had the "contingency" string tied to it. When analyzed it is found, then, that less than $10,000 a year were easily available for field service of a really scientific nature and one-half of that was made up of the salaries of the secretary and assistant.

This same condition prevailed in 1913 when Dr. Egan died while still the executive secretary of the State Board of Health. The biennial appropriation to the Board in that year amounted to $243,319.25. But this enormous sum, compared with the $28,000 for the biennium when Dr. Egan came into office, did not change the complexion of the State's machinery for doing sanitary and hygienic work as much as might be expected. Potential resources were available but the organization of these resources was poor. A diagnostic laboratory, the lodging house inspection service in Chicago, the distribution of antitoxin and the vital statistics service were the only units in the State's public health machinery, except that involved in the regulation of the practice of medicine, which functioned systematically as a routine business in 1913. A corps of physicians located at convenient points in the State who accepted temporary duty when called upon were depended upon for field service in connection with epidemic outbreaks. There was no machinery operative for collecting reports of communicable diseases. The Water Survey at the University of Illinois was depended upon for field and laboratory work concerning water and sewer systems.

Cooperation With Other Agencies.

While manifesting primary interest in the expansion of the State's official public health service, Dr. Egan did not neglect outside agencies of interstate and national character nor did he overlook the importance of local health machinery in his own State. He preserved favorable contact with the American Public Health Association and with the organization which is now called the Conference of State and Provincial Health Authorities. He also maintained contact with other voluntary interstate organization which had come into being but for the most part died out after some specific problem had been solved. That was the experience of the Sanitary Council of the Mississippi Valley, long time defunct, and of the Conference of Western Boards of Health. These agencies gave way to better organized and better supported national movements.

In 1902 the Congress of the United States created the U. S. Public Health and Marine Hospital Service. This had a direct influence over the State health machinery in two ways. It provided an inspection service of immigrants at ports of entry into the country and it was made a part of its duties to call at least annually a conference of state and territorial health officers to meet with the Surgeon General. This latter provided a splendid means for the interchange of ideas, the dissemination of information concerning new discoveries and procedures, uniformity of practice throughout the country and harmonious cooperation. State health officers took advantage of this new piece of national health machinery when they initiated a meeting called by the Surgeon General in Washington on January 19, 1903, to consider problems brought before the country because of an outbreak of plague in Mexico and San Francisco. Dr. Egan participated in this conference and subsequent ones. He maintained close contact with this new federal agency, frequently calling upon the Surgeon General for advice and assistance, especially in regard to yellow fever outbreaks.

Local Boards in Rural Districts.

Largely through Dr. Egan's efforts there came into existence a law in 1901, which was amended in 1903, that created local boards of health in the rural districts throughout the State. In township organization the supervisor, assessor and town clerk of every town was made a local board of health to function outside incorporated villages and cities. The county commissioners in other counties constituted the board of health. This provided a definite local authority through which the State Board of Health could function. It remains to this day the machinery through which the State health officials work in rural areas.

Dr. Egan tried hard to get a law making it compulsory on cities and villages to appoint boards of health and also to get a state tuberculosis sanitarium but failed in both. A large number of sanitary and hygienic regulations in which Dr. Egan was interested and for which he worked was written into law. These related to stream pollution, free distribution of biologics, vital statistics, pure food, dairy products, common drinking cups, etc. There was a law passed in 1908 which enabled cities to establish public tuberculosis sanitaria

Resume.

Dr. Egan found the State Board of Health pretty well organized to enforce the Medical Practice Act and he left it so. This work increased enormously during his time but so did the resources. Fees collected for licenses could be used by the Board for expenses involved in regulating medical practice. These fees amounted to $10,000 or more per year. The work was performed largely by the Board members themselves with the necessary clerical and legal assistance. When Dr. Egan began, an attorney was chosen and paid for in accordance with the amount of work done. When he left there was provision in the appropriation law for hiring an attorney and a law clerk.

When Dr. Egan first took office there was no trained corps of sanitarians steadily employed to promote preventive measures against disease. At the end of his incumbency the same condition prevailed. There was this difference—Dr. Egan had a little larger appropriation for that sort of work and he had learned how to get hold of the contingency fund on the one hand. On the other hand he had designated a certain number of physicians throughout the State and upon whom he could call at will for temporary duty.

When Dr. Egan came into State health service there was practically no work being done on vital statistics. At the end of his time there was a state registrar of vital statistics and clerical assistants. The law had been changed several times, apparently from bad to worse, and was still unsatisfactory. But a considerable volume of records were secured and they were compiled and preserved in good shape for each year after 1902 until 1913.

At the beginning of Dr. Egan's term the practice was to employ sanitary engineers and chemists when studies of water supplies, sewer systems, etc., were desired. At the end of his time the University of Illinois had established a sort of bureau called the State Water Survey and arrangements were made for that agency to do the santiary engineering work of the Board.

No quarantine officers were steadily employed when Dr. Egan began and none were so employed when he quit.

During his time a lodging house inspection service, confined to Chicago, began to function and an embryonic diagnostic laboratory was established.

A system of agents through whom diphtheria antitoxin was distributed free throughout the State was established. A monthly bulletin devoted to sanitation, hygiene and the practice of medicine was published with considerable regularity.

This was the machinery which the State had built up by 1913 for the primary purpose of combating disease. It had expanded enormously since 1900. It was busy all of the time. Its money resources had increased over 700 per cent but it was poorly organized. It was without form but certainly not void. The most important contribution of the Egan regime to public health service in the State was the cultivation of the habit among legislators to grant money for that purpose.

THE DRAKE REGIME.

After a lapse of a little more than a year from the time when Dr. Egan died in March, 1913, during which period Mr. Amos Sawyer, chief clerk of the Board for many years, acted as secretary, Dr. C. St. Clair Drake of Chicago was appointed by Governor Dunne to take over the executive work of the State Board of Health. Dr. Drake was appointed in May of 1914 and took active charge on the first of June.

Several visits prior to that time had familiarized him with the situation. Few significant changes had taken place since Dr. Egan's death. The financing of the Board at that time was conducted on the following basis. Available money was drawn out of the State treasury, placed to the credit of the Board in a local bank and drawn upon while it lasted for whatever expenses were deemed necessary to incur. This practice had prevailed for 37 years. When the money appropriated for ordinary expenses was gone the Board either stopped functioning in sanitary and hygienic services or else managed to get hold of contingency funds which were likewise drawn out in lump sums and placed in the bank for expenditure as occasion demanded.

Reorganization and Budget.

When Dr. Drake arrived at the Capitol in June he brought with him a plan of organization, the first comprehensive scheme that had ever been introduced. Dr. Drake had been with the Chicago health department for many years. It was well organized. He had observed the systems employed elsewhere. He patterned his own plans of organization after that which prevailed in Chicago, making such modifications as the different circumstances demanded. Following this, there were bureaus under the State Board of Health each with specific duties and responsibilities and each allotted a specific sum of money. In short a budget system had been adopted.

Manifestly the new scheme could operate as planned to only a limited degree until recognized by the General Assembly in the shape of appropriations for full time personnel. This is exactly what happened within a year after Dr. Drake took charge. In a law enacted in the

PRESIDENTS
Illinois State Board of Health

Louis Adelsberger, M.D.
1897-1898

A. C. Corr, M.D.
1898-1899

Chas. B. Johnson, M.D.
1899-1902

George W. Webster, M.D.
1902-1914

John Albert Robison, M.D.
1914-1917

spring of 1915, making appropriations for the State Board of Health these per annum items are found:

Executive office	$18,680
Bureau of Medical Sanitary Inspection	16,300
Bureau of Vital Statistics	5,500
Laboratory (salaries)	2,640
Laboratory (supplies)	9,684
Laboratory (Branch Laboratories)	3,600
Vaccines, Sera and Antitoxins	38,000
Travel	21,750
Lodging House Inspection	11,075
Bureau of Sanitary Engineering	10,850
Miscellaneous including extra help per diem for Board members, rent, etc.	23,860
Contingency	4,650
Total	$166,589

All this was something distinctly new in Illinois health service. It represented a splendid step toward systematic prosecution of sanitary and hygienic work. The most significant feature was the provision for full time employment of personnel and the allocation of funds for specific purposes. Under each bureau the per annum salaries for a definite number of positions were itemized. In the bureau of medical and sanitary inspection, for instance, there were listed the salaries for four district health officers (this is the first appearance of that term), one epidemiologist, three dairy inspectors—two part time—and four clerks and stenographers. The bureau of vital statistics had a registrar and a clerical staff of four provided for while the laboratory drew a bacteriologist and messenger with extra funds for equipment. For the bureau of sanitary engineering there were listed a chief and two assistant sanitary engineers, one stenographer and miscellaneous supplies. For the executive office there were itemized the secretary, an attorney, a clerical staff of 10 and a messenger. This force was subject to duty involved in both branches of the Board's activities—those concerning licensure and those concerning sanitation.

Educational Propaganda.

Splendid as was the step toward organization and system, Dr. Drake's best efforts were in another direction. He was at heart an educational propagandist. The faculty for stimulating popular interest was his to an extraordinary degree. This faculty he put to work at once after coming into State health service.

At the Illinois State Fair held at Springfield in the autumn of 1914, a few brief months after his appointment, Dr. Drake put an exhibit in the space which had been occupied by the State Board of Health in previous years but it was a new kind of exhibit. It attracted the public eye with sufficient force to provoke front page newspaper comment. The exhibition was built up around six mechanical models of ingenious design and was graphic, impressive, fascinating.

Another feature of the exhibit equipment was its mobility. It could be transported, installed and dismantled easily. Year after year it increased both in size and popularity and was displayed many times in almost every county of the State with the exception of the extreme southern ones.

By January 1915 the monthly publication, which had been allowed to lapse after the death of Dr. Egan, was resumed under a new name, in a new style and for a new audience. What the purpose was and what

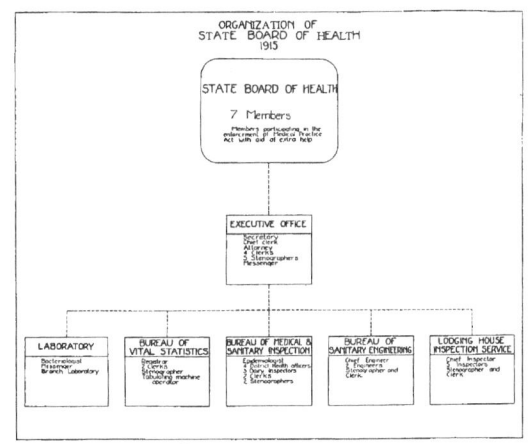

FIG. 10. This was the effective strength during the two years terminating on June 30, 1917 when the State Board of Health went out of existence.

subsequently was the character of the new publication that was named HEALTH NEWS are very well set forth on the title page of the first edition in these words:

> Health News is a continuation of the BULLETIN which, for several years, has appeared as the official organ of the Illinois State Board of Health. The change in title and the change in style foreshadow the new methods and new aims of the publication. The Bulletin sought to attain better health conditions throughout Illinois by the discussion of more or less technical subjects with the medical profession as its audience and, in addressing such an audience, the Bulletin very naturally contained many details of the activities of the Board and much material which would prove of interest only to physicians and persons of technical training.

Health News, with the same general purpose, seeks a new and larger audience. It hopes to bring the essential facts relative to "the promotion of health and the prevention of disease" to the men and women of Illinois; to reduce the technical science of preventive medicine to terms of practical application for the individual and the community.

Health News is merely a part of a definite campaign of popular, public health education contemplated by the State Board of Health. This program includes, aside from this monthly publication, the use of a public health exhibit which is now being employed and which is creating much interest throughout the State. There is also being operated a bi-weekly press service through which short, readable public health articles are published in the newspapers of Illinois. The various pamphlets and circulars of the Board, devoted to the prevention of the several communicable diseases, to the care of infants and kindred subjects, are being rewritten and made more acceptable to the public demand. The efforts of the individual communities to increase interest in public health affairs will be encouraged by public lectures by members of the State Board of Health and the office and field staff and, in many instances, these lectures will be illustrated by motion pictures and the stereopticon.

The policies set forth in this expression characterized the whole Drake regime. He followed it persistently and it popularized public health service in the State.

By autumn of 1915 Dr. Drake had struck upon another means of large potentialities for stimulating popular attention to sanitary and hygienic matters. This was the well baby conference. At the State Fair in that year was conducted the first baby conference in which the state government had ever participated. As a magnet for attracting public interest the baby conference was more than a match for the mobile exhibit. One careful look at a mechanical model satisfied more or less permanently the curiosity. Interest in a baby is immortal. The idea of helping him to keep well is appealing. Looking through spacious glassed openings at physicians and nurses busily engaged in examining babies is a sight of which the eyes never tire. The baby conference had come to stay and to grow. Soon it was a common feature of local fairs and other community events. Staff members of the State Board of Health were called upon to assist in this work. This practice added a considerable strength to the health machinery since it brought the idea of preventive medicine directly to thousands of mothers through personal contact.

Motion pictures and stereopticon slides were not overlooked as mediums through which to stimulate public interest in health matters. In 1916 a few motion picture films were purchased and a loan library started. This grew in popularity until now nearly 100 reels are maintained in the library and circulated widely.

The popularity of the exhibits promoted by Dr. Drake soon led to expansion. Before he left the state health service in 1921 the space allotted to the health exhibition at the State Fair embraced more than 1,000 square feet and in it was a motion picture theatre, specially constructed baby examination quarters and a score of booths. The mobile exhibits had traveled throughout the State and had been favorably received. Around them and the exhibits supplied by the city health department of Chicago and other health agencies had been built a mammoth exhibition known as the Pageant of Progress which drew hundreds of thousands of visitors to the Coliseum where it was staged.

A project called "Health Promotion Week" was another method initiated by Dr. Drake for cultivating public thought on preventive medicine. This idea materialized in a state-wide program in the spring of 1919. It was a new thing so the press of the State gave it generous space. It was perfectly planned. The General Assembly endorsed it with a joint resolution. The Governor certified that the movement pleased him. Endorsements were secured from a score of the most powerful civic and professional organizations in the State. A specific task for each day was described in the program which terminated with the item "Pageant". The idea was new in the health field so the press contributed space generously. Traveling representatives visited practically all communities in the State effecting local organizations.

The project was a tremendous success. Few if any other deliberate attempts to create public thought on health matters at a given time ever achieved its purpose so completely. It led to a permanent annual event by the same name but somewhat different in character. Health Promotion Week has come to be a sort of institution in Illinois. It is an occasion looked forward to by health workers all over the State as a time for starting new campaigns or for reporting to the public. It is a sort of revival project for local health workers.

Important Health Laws Enacted.

A number of important health laws were passed during the Drake regime. In 1915 a satisfactory vital statistics statute came into being, providing for the first time the legal machinery necessary to the collection of reasonably complete returns of birth and death records. At the same meeting of the legislature a bill known as the Glackin Law, which authorized counties to levy a tax and spend the revenue therefrom for constructing and maintaining tuberculosis sanitaria was passed and signed by the Governor. Still another law of 1915 provided for the establishment of health districts in one or more adjacent towns or road districts, making it possible to levy taxes and maintain modern local health organizations. Advantage of this law has been taken in Quincy and Berwyn while a privately endowed health department serving LaSalle, Oglesby and Peru exercises legal authority under it.

These three laws had a tremendous influence over the public health machinery of the State. This is especially true of the sanitarium law. It and the vital statistic statute are discussed in detail in another chapter. The district health law appeared to have come into existence more as a means of legalizing the LaSalle, Oglesby and Peru organization than anything else. It has never been regarded by State health officers as the best plan upon which to promote local health units. To make it apply in more than one town or road district the proposition must carry by popular vote in each. This makes it very difficult to work on a county basis and hence the county has been regarded by the Department as the most practical political unit in which to develop full time modern health departments for rural service. The larger cities are legally able to take care of themselves in health matters.

New Rules for Handling Contagious Diseases.

One of the very important things that Dr. Drake did early in 1915 was to revise the rules and regulations of the State Board of Health concerning communicable disease. Since the very early days of the Board's existence there had been rules requiring the notification of certain epidemic diseases but these had been general on the one hand and there had existed no local machinery through which they could be enforced on the other. Dr. Drake codified the rules and made a specific list of reportable diseases. He specified a time limit within which the diseases should be reported. He specified to whom they should be reported locally—health officer, health commissioner, chairman of the board of health, mayor, village president, supervisor, county commissioner, etc., covering every case. These officials, in turn, were required to forward the reports to the State Board of Health within specified time limits.

The rules also covered matters of quarantine, specifying time limits for isolation of patients and they specified sanitary and hygienic precautions that were required on quarantined premises.

General Plan and Personnel.

It will be seen, then, that Dr. Drake proposed to bring sanitation and hygiene into popular favor through educational channels and to apply modern disease control methods as rigidly as public sentiment would permit through an adequate organization. Prompt notification of communicable diseases was essential to the functioning of the State organization so far as epidemic outbreaks was concerned, so he provided for this contingency with his new rules. He was ambitious to concentrate all State health work under the Board of Health. This would include food, drugs, dairy inspection, tuberculin testing of cattle and stream pollution which were under various boards and commissions. He was even willing that the regulation of medical practice remain under the State Board of Health but this he would have separated into a department of its own, distinct from another department that would function only in the field of what might be called preventive medicine.

As soon as the 1915 appropriation law became effective Dr. Drake set to work organizing the health service in compliance therewith. This was slow for several reasons. In the first place the personnel had to be employed under civil service regulations and that took time. Secondly, it was difficult to locate suitably trained persons to fill the technical positions at the salaries provided. Furthermore there was lack of space in the capitol building to house the new machinery.

By early spring of 1916, however, the difficulties had been largely overcome and there was in existence the best organized force that the State had ever employed for doing straight public health work. There were five full time physicians in the bureau of sanitary and medical inspection each assigned to one of five districts into which the State had been divided for that purpose. In the same bureau there were milk inspectors and a clerical staff. There was a bureau of sanitary engineering made up of a chief and two assistant engineers and a stenographer. A bureau of vital statistics, headed by a registrar under whom was a corps of clerks, was functioning and had already put into operation the new law which required many new procedures. There was a central diagnostic laboratory, manned by a small staff, located in Springfield and two branch laboratories, the latter being operated on a contract basis with private laboratories already in existence. The agency system for the distribution of biologics now made easily available to every doctor in the State diphtheria antitoxin, typhoid vaccine, smallpox vaccine, silver nitrate for the prevention of blindness, mailing containers for laboratory specimens and circulars of information. In the central office there was a considerable clerical staff that divided its time between duties relating to health service and to licensure. There was the educational work of publishing a monthly bulletin and supplying copy to the press. All this was a splendid organization compared with what had gone before.

In the meantime national diplomatic difficulties with Mexico had led to a military complication which resulted in the mobilization of the National Guard. This incident involved the State Board of Health in camp sanitation activities and it is worthy of note that Governor Dunne twice delayed mobilization orders upon the recommendation of Dr.

Drake because sanitary facilities were incomplete. This was an expression of confidence in the State health authorities. Furthermore, the State Board of Health furnished smallpox and typhoid fever vaccine with which the troops were immunized against those diseases.

With the new year of 1917 came the Lowden administration with its reorganization plan that proposed to substitute a few departments, each headed by a director, for the manifold boards and commissions that constituted the State government and to put all governmental activities upon a budget system. Nothing could have pleased Dr. Drake better. He had an organization scheme already started. This opportunity allowed him to elaborate on it. He presented to the administration a plan that would have retained the State Board of Health to reign over two great departments—the one to do public health service and the other to regulate the practice of medicine. The administration chose to drop the Board, made two departments to carry on the work, and incorporated the Drake plan for health service into the Civil Administrative Code as the Department of Public Health and which still governs the organization as it functions today.

State Department of Public Health Organized.

While publicity was the work in which Dr. Drake excelled his success in that field was not the most important event, so far as the public health machinery was concerned, that transpired during his administration. The most significant single event was the adoption of the Lowden Civil Administrative Code by the State government in 1917. This converted the State Board of Health into two departments, the one to devote itself henceforth to sanitary and hygienic work alone and the other to handle all matters relating to licensures not only of physicians but of all other professions that required it. The State Department of Public Health was created by this division and it began to function in the field of sanitation and hygiene with an appropriation of nearly one half million dollars for the first biennium, a sum far in excess of anything that had ever been granted to the State Board of Health.

The adoption of the Civil Administrative Code divorced public health service and the regulation of medical practice. It established straight health work as one of the major departments of the State government and by doing so brought to an end the second period in the development of public health machinery in Illinois.

The new State Department of Public Health which came into legal existence July 1, 1917, fell heir to all the public health duties, powers and responsibilities that were formerly vested in the State Board of Health and had new ones added. Under the old law the responsibility for policies, rules, regulations, etc., was in a board of seven members. Under the new it was

Frank O. Lowden, Governor of Illinois, 1917-1921, whose Civil Administrative Code brought an end to the State Board of Health and put in its place the State Department of Public Health.

in one man, the director of the department. The Code provides for an advisory board but its functions, in a legal sense, are literally what the name implies—advisory. All decisions must ultimately be made by the director and upon him rests all the responsibility of the department.

The powers and duties of the State Department of Public Health under the Civil Administrative Code are, briefly as follows:

General Plan and Personnel.

"I. **Prescribed by the Civil Administrative Code.**
 1. To have general supervision of the health and lives of the people.
 2. To advise relative to public water supplies, water purification works, sewerage systems and sewage treatment works.
 3. To exercise supervision over water and sewerage nuisances and to make rules concerning same.
 4. To conduct sanitary investigations for the improvement of public health.
 5. To investigate nuisances and questions affecting public health.
 6. To maintain chemical, bacteriological and biological laboratories and to conduct examinations of milk, water, sewage, wastes, etc.
 7. To diagnose diseases when necessary for public protection.
 8. To purchase and distribute, free of charge, diphtheria antitoxin, typhoid vaccine, smallpox vaccine and other preventive and curative agents.
 9. To collect and preserve useful information relative to public health.
 10. To investigate the causes of disease.
 11. To keep informed of the work of local health officers and to assist local health authorities in the administration of health laws.
 12. To inform the general public in matters of health.
 13. To enlist the cooperation of physicians and health agencies to improve the public health.
 14. To make inspections of the charitable, penal and reformatory institutions and normal schools and to inspect all hospitals and other public institutions and to report their needs to public authorities.
 15. To print, publish and distribute documents, bulletins, etc., relative to public health.
 16. To exercise the rights, powers and duties vested in the former State Board of Health.

II. **Powers under the State Board of Health Act.**
 1. To declare, modify or relax quarantine.
 2. To prescribe rules and regulations for sanitation.
 3. To regulate the transportation of the dead.
 4. To investigate the cause of communicable diseases, especially during epidemics, and to take proper measures to suppress dangerously communicable diseases when local authorities fail to act promptly and efficiently.
 5. To prepare forms for the record of births, marriages and deaths.
 6. To inspect lodging houses, boarding houses, inns and hotels in cities of 100,000 population or more.
 7. To prescribe rules and regulations concerning the distribution and sale of antitoxin.

III. **Duties under the Vital Statistics Act.**
 1. To keep records of births, stillbirths and deaths.
 2. To establish registration districts and to appoint local registrars.
 3. To prescribe the form of register or record to be kept by cemeteries and to prescribe all forms of reports for births, stillbirths and deaths.
 4. To supply local registrars with blank forms and to issue instructions to secure uniform enforcement of the Act.
 5. To arrange and permanently preserve certificates of births, stillbirths and deaths.
 6. To publish annual reports of births and deaths.

7. To certify to county clerks the number of births, stillbirths and deaths registered in the county.

8. To furnish certified copies of records of any births, stillbirths or deaths.

IV. **Duties under the Ophthalmia Neonatorum Act.**

1. To provide all obstetricians with a prophylactic for opthalmia neonatorum.
2. To publish and distribute literature on the dangers from ophthalmia neonatorum.
3. To report violations of the Act to prosecuting attorneys.

V. **Duties under Miscellaneous Acts.**

1. The County and Township Board of Health Act authorizes the department to discharge the duties of local Boards of Health in case of failure or refusal to act in time of epidemic.
2. The Sanitary Health Districts Act requires the department to conduct examinations for health officers.
3. The Barbers' Act requires the department to approve sanitary rules for barber shops.
4. The Lodging House Act requires the department to formulate sanitary rules for inns, hotels and lodging houses.
5. The Occupational Diseases Act requires the department to furnish blanks for examinations for vocational and occupational diseases and to transmit such reports to the Division of Factory Inspection.
6. The Rabies Act requires the department to select institutions for the treatment of poor persons suffering from rabies.
7. An amendment to the Military and Naval Code authorizes the department to assume sanitary and health supervision over zones surrounding military camps, ranges or buildings used for military purposes."

For the purposes enumerated the General Assembly granted the State Department of Public Health $443,212 with which to function during its first biennium and the Governor appointed Dr. C. St. Clair Drake as the first director. Dr. George Thomas Palmer was made assistant director.

Seven divisions were named in the 1917 appropriation law with provided funds for each. The names of the divisions and the number and character of the personnel provided for were as follows:

I. **General Office.**
   1 Director,
   1 Assistant Director,
   1 Chief Clerk,
   5 Clerks and Stenographers,
   1 Messenger.

II. **Communicable Diseases.**
   1 Chief and Epidemiologist, M. D.
   1 Supervisor of Field Service,
   6 District Health Officers,
   2 Public Health Nurses,
   2 Quarantine Officers,
   5 Clerks and Stenographers.

III. **Tuberculosis.**
   1 Chief.

IV. **Sanitation.**
   1 Chief Sanitary Engineer,
   3 Assistant Engineers,
   1 Supervisor Surveys and Rural Hygiene,
   1 Farm Sanitation Advisor,
   3 Clerks and Stenographers.

V. **Diagnostic Laboratory.**
   1 Chief Bacteriologist and Pathologist,
   1 Bacteriologist,
   1 Laboratory Helper.

VI. **Vital Statistics.**
   1 Registrar.
   1 Assistant Registrar
   9 Clerks.

VII. **Lodging House Inspection**
   1 Superintendent,
   5 Inspectors,
   2 Clerks and Stenographers.

The Civil Administrative Code made possible a department for health work only. Dr. Drake organized that department in a way that gave it the capacity to participate in practically every phase of public health service and to extend its activities to all parts of the State. The rules and regulations pertaining to morbidity reports and quarantine which Dr. Drake had put into effect in 1915 linked together the State and local health machinery in a uniform, workable manner. The vital statistics law of 1915 provided a satisfactory means of collecting birth and death reports. Health had become popular through the educational activities of voluntary and official organizations. The stage was all set for the State to embark upon a splendid program of disease control and prevention. On July 1, 1917, the law which established the new order of things became effective.

War Activities.

A new contingency developed in 1917 when the nation had become embroiled in the World War a few months before the new health program was scheduled to start. This had a profound influence over every State governmental function. It brought new health problems for the new State health agency to solve. A number of new military camps sprang up overnight, almost, and old ones took on new life. This resulted in congested population at points where sanitary facilities were extremely inadequate giving rise to grave health dangers. Social hygiene became a problem. Industries, such as coal mining, started to operate at high speed and thus attracted an influx of labor in many communities and thereby introduced unusual health hazards. The call to arms began at once to deplete the staffs of organizations of all kinds and the newly created health department did not escape. Salaries and wages went soaring above the ordinary in all flexible concerns but for the health department the maximum rate of pay for every position was specified by law and the legislature would not meet again for two years.

Under these conditions the character and volume of public health service was considerably different from what might otherwise have been the case.

Instead of deliberately promoting contact with local peace time machinery it was of primary importance to line up with the military. Sanitary zones about the camps and cantonments were established and in these were concentrated most of the staff of the department. Careful sanitary surveys were undertaken in nearly all of the communities located near military posts and in a number of the mining towns. Thus the State Department of Public Health found itself under wartime pressure in a way considerably different from what had been anticipated. Instead of going deliberately into local communities, making contact with local officials, investigating water and sewer systems, promoting birth and death registration, stimulating close observance of quarantine and notification rules and regulations and encouraging the establishment of efficient local health organizations, the field staff was largely concentrated in the immediate vicinity of military camps and busily engaged in handling the emergency problems there.

Another event that modified both the course of public health service and the function of its machinery was the outbreak of epidemics of infantile paralysis in 1916 and 1917. The infectious nature of the disease made it a public health problem. Its crippling character made it the subject for specialists. To meet the situation, Dr. Drake arranged for a member of his medical staff, Dr. C. W. East, to go to Harvard Medical College for a special course in infantile paralysis.

Infantile paralysis in epidemic form was a new experience to many physicians and its wide prevalence made it of considerable public concern. This situation created a demand for instructive lectures. Dr. East was assigned to the task. He toured the State, disseminating the knowledge he had gained at Harvard, illustrating much of it with lantern slides.

The lectures led to a demand for clinics. Many physicians wished to bring patients in order to establish a diagnosis and for technical advice concerning special cases. Parents wanted to bring their children who were afflicted. Accordingly clinics were established at various points throughout the State and soon absorbed practically all of the strength of the division of child hygiene which had but a limited staff. Thus instead of devoting its strength largely to educational activities the Department found itself laboring with an acute problem that involved clinical service.

Venereal diseases constitute another subject that modified the course of public health service in the State. Under stress of the War the federal government launched against venereal diseases a tremendous program which reached every soldier in the army and spread over into the civilian population through the state governments. Since drying up the source of infections is a basic activity in this field the federal government appropriated large sums for the establishment of clinics. The plan of the federal government anticipated both educational and curative activity. It proposed to furnish money with which to start the work as a demonstration and then to withdraw as state and local agencies took over the matter.

Illinois joined in the plan and added a division of social hygiene to the organization of the State Department of Public Health on July 1, 1918. Funds which were provided by the federal government, became available November 1 of that year and the new division started to function at that time. Within a year five clinics had been established at as many different points in the State. These were of a permanent character, the equipment and the pay of the director, who was always a local physician, were furnished out of funds allotted to the State by the federal government.

Ultimately the number of clinics grew to more than a score and the State's government provided funds for continuing the work. An appropriation of $100,000 for that purpose was made by the General Assembly in 1919.

Here again the State Department of Public Health found itself involved in a task that required clinical service in order to fulfill the requirements of its program.

These clinical activities are important because they have been used to promote misunderstandings and conflicts between the medical profession and the State health officials.

If the great World War frustrated the carefully devised program for public health service in Illinois during the period of that emergency it produced compensating influences. The War gave to sanitarians the opportunity of an age of marvelous achievement. Soldiers were being mobilized in great numbers and were subject to rigid discipline. The civilian population was subject to unusual demands and was in a mental attitude that made easy the practical application of official dictates and suggestions in all fields of activity. Health was recognized by everybody as a predominating factor to success in the prosecution of the War.

Sanitarians were not slow to take advantage of the situation. Every soldier and every sailor was vaccinated against smallpox and against typhoid fever. Every trooper heard a lecture on social hygiene. Where safe water supply systems were not available the troops drank water from Lister bags that was well chlorinated. Wherever at all practicable water and fly tight latrines were constructed for troops. Food supplies were rigidly inspected. Sanitary officers inspected kitchens often. Medical officers inspected the

in the meantime the federal agencies at Washington were busy promoting health programs. The childrens' bureau had been created and had stimulated a lot of popular interest by carrying out a national baby week project. An inter-departmental social hygiene board had been created and given plenty of money with which to prosecute a vigorous anti-venereal disease campaign among civilians.

Post-War Activities.

Thus when the Illinois General Assembly met in 1919 it looked with greater favor upon public health programs than many such bodies had done in the past. This time Dr. Drake was able to get an increase in the biennium appropriation of $182,698 above that two years before. Of the increase $100,000 went to the support of the division of social hygiene, created a few months earlier through federal resources. The remainder went to the creation of four new small divisions. These included the divisions of biologic and research laboratories (which were from the outset combined with the diagnostic laboratory for practical purposes), child hygiene and public health nursing, surveys and rural hygiene and public health instruction. All of these divisions except that of the biologic and research laboratory had actually come into being on a small scale in 1917 through a legitimate manipulation of the funds appropriated for the Department, but the 1919 General Assembly was the first to recognize them officially.

This gave the State a well rounded public health organization. The total appropriation, which amounted to less than a nickel per capita per year, was not as unstinted as that which prevailed in some states. But it was much larger than anything that had gone before in Illinois and there was now authorized by law a staff, however small, to function in practically every department of the public health field.

While applying an organization plan and budget system to the official State health machinery Dr. Drake did not neglect either national or local agencies for adding strength to the public health movement. He maintained the favorable contacts that had been established with what were now great national organizations and made new ones whenever desirable opportunity arose.

Within the State Dr. Drake injected life into the legally established local health machinery—at least so far as reporting communicable diseases was concerned. There were laws that provided local health machinery in every community of the State. naming specific officials for the responsibility except in cities and villages where the appointment of boards of health was authorized. There was another law requiring all police and other officials to aid in carrying out the rules and regulations of the State health officials.

DIRECTORS
State Department of Public Health

C. St. Clair Drake, M. D.
1917 - 1921

Isaac D. Rawlings, M. D.
1921 -

C. St. Clair Drake, M. D.

C. ST. CLAIR DRAKE, Chicago; born January 23, 1870, St. Thomas, Ontario. Graduated Chicago Homeopathy Medical College, 1891. Statistician Chicago Health Department, 1895-1914. Member, secretary and executive officer, State Board of Health, 1914-1917. Secretary, Conference of State and Provincial Health Authorities, 1919-1922. Director, State Department of Public Health, 1917-1921. Member numerous medical and extra-governmental organizations.

Isaac D. Rawlings, M. D.

ISAAC D. RAWLINGS, Chicago; born April 29, 1869, Carrollton, Ill. B. S. and M. S., Illinois College at Jacksonville, 1890 and 1895 respectively. M. D., Northwestern University Medical School, 1893. Two years of graduate medical study in the universities of Vienna, Berlin, London and Dublin. Appointed instructor in bacteriology and director of the bacteriological laboratory in Northwestern University Medical School in 1895. From 1897 to 1918 held various positions on faculty at Northwestern University Medical School. Medical inspector, Chicago Health Department, 1899-1904; assistant chief medical inspector, 1904-1921. Director State Department of Public Health, 1921 to date. Member numerous organizations.

Under these laws Dr. Drake found ample authority for specifying certain persons in every community who were to receive reports of communicable diseases and to transmit them to the State health officer. He had field staff sufficient to stimulate the operation of this process. Dr. Drake also got himself appointed collaborating epidemiologist of the U. S. Public Health Service. This gave him the privilege of supplying local health officers with postage free cards for making reports. Then by 1919 the process of communicable disease reporting was functioning in a reasonably satisfactory degree. The vital statistics law of 1915 had created local registrars in practically all townships in the State and brought into operation new local machinery as well as greater facilities in the collection of birth and death reports.

Outside of official circles the old conference between State and local health officers was revived. This time it included extra governmental agencies and took on the title of "Illinois Public Health and Welfare Association." This was organized as a means of bringing together all the public health agencies in the State so as to coordinate, as much as possible, the work of all, and to keep some uniformity of practice. The organization never developed vitality enough to create a significant influence over matters in the State.

The great influenza epidemic in 1918 brought into local service a large number of public health nurses in the State who owed allegiance to the American Red Cross and the Illinois Tuberculosis Association. These nurses found such high favor in community life that they became permanent in many places and constituted a very large factor in the public health machinery of the State. In 1920 a plan for effecting a close cooperation between all of these public health nurses under the general supervision of the State Department of Public Health was perfected when Dr. Drake managed to secure a signed working agreement between the agencies concerned. This agreement was based on a national policy adopted by a conference between the National American Red Cross, the National Association for the Study and Prevention of Tuberculosis and the Conference of State and Provincial Health Authorities. It held great possibilities for extending the State's health machinery in a splendid way but never accomplished its full purpose because a State supervising nurse was never employed with regularity enough to develop and carry out a significant program.

There was also a plan to conduct schools of various sorts—one system for local health officers at regional points and another for public health nurses. The plan for the latter was to hold the school at Springfield during the summer when field work, particularly in the schools, was light. Neither project ever grew into anything of magnitude or permanence.

With all of the splendid progress in organization and magnitude of service since 1914 there was, at the end of the Drake tenure in February 1921, a distinct lack of coordination between the various divisions in the State Department of Public Health. It was not unusual, for instance, for a new staff member to be with the Department for months before he knew the other division chiefs with whom he was supposed to work. A district health superintendent might visit a town time and again where some recalcitrant local registrar obstructed prompt and complete returns of vital statistics without knowing of the difficulty. The field staff did not always know that the Department operated a free motion picture library or that Health News was available free to any citizens of the State who wanted it. The machinery for collecting and compiling vital statistics was all set up and functioning more or less satisfactorily but no comprehensive mortality statistics were forthcoming nor had the State been admitted to the U. S. birth registration area.

Furthermore, Dr. Drake never felt the need of official advisory council in determining policies and programs. The Civil Administrative Code provided for an Advisory Board of five members. None was ever appointed during Dr. Drake's time as State Director of Health. A staff meeting of division heads was never held. Business with each was transacted individually.

The divisions were located in half a dozen different places. One was in the arsenal, another occupied rented quarters down-town in Springfield, some were on one floor and some on another in the State House. Division chiefs made no reports of their activities except for copies of correspondence and the annual report. Discipline concerning work hours, time off, etc., for employes was a matter for the chief clerk to keep up with if he could.

Even *Health News* fell into the most irregular publication although the newly created Division of Public Health Instruction had the preparation of this bulletin as a principal function. In early December of 1919 a Chicago newspaper columnist humorously observed: "Now come to hand the October and November numbers of Doc Drake's 'Illinois Health News.' There is a chance for the printer to catch up this year, so here's hoping for the December number before Jan. 1." When Dr. Drake left the Department in February 1921, *Health News* was fully six months behind, according to records in the office.

Summary.

When Dr. Drake came to the Capital as the State's chief health officer he found a Board of Health dividing its time between regulating the practice of medicine and doing sanitary and hygienic work—about two-thirds to the former and one to the latter. When he left there was a State Department of Public Health, headed by one man who was responsible for its policies and activities, which devoted its entire resources to straight public health service.

At the beginning of Dr. Drake's tenure practically all the field personnel of the State Board of Health was on a per diem employment basis and there was nothing in the way of specialized headquarters service but a small diagnostic laboratory, a small staff for handling vital statistics and the general office force. At the end of his time all staff members and employes in the health service of the State were on a full time basis, functioning under a splendid plan of organization which divided the work of the Department into ten divisions.

When Dr. Drake became Secretary of the State Board of Health the rules and regulations of the Board concerning quarantine and morbidity reports were general and indefinite and the reports were incomplete and delinquent. When he gave up the office of Director of Public Health all the rules and regulations had been simplified and codified. Reporting of diseases was reasonably prompt and fairly satisfactory due in part to the codification of the rules, in part to the free mailing privileges granted by federal authorities who utilized the reports thus gathered and in part to the larger field staff that stimulated better reporting.

In 1914 the collection of vital statistics had fallen into a deplorable condition and there was no satisfactory law for helping matters greatly. Long before 1921 a splendid law was in effect and the necessary State and local machinery for collecting and compiling prompt and complete returns was in existence.

The number of public health nurses employed in the State outside Chicago in 1914 was inconsequential. More than 300 were at work in 1921 and a plan for coordinating their services under the general supervision of the State Department of Public Health had been agreed upon by all concerned.

In 1914 the State Board of Health operated a small diagnostic laboratory in Springfield and distributed a limited amount of biological products. At the close of 1920 there were half a dozen branch diagnostic laboratories beside the central one in Springfield which had broadened out to take on research work and the biological products distributed had increased considerably in number and volume.

In 1914 preventive medicine was little thought of or appreciated in the population at large. By 1921 it had become popular enough to lead newspapers, household periodicals and other publications to devote much space to it. In Illinois Dr. Drake had played a leading part in popularizing the subject.

Between 1914 and 1921 the State had discarded a cumbersome Board of Health with its chaotic ways of promoting public health and in its place had put a Health Department, ranking with any other department of the State government, with a splendid organization plan for systematic, co-ordinated, well balanced and up-to-date service. The main trouble was that the "system" and "coordination" were lacking.

THE RAWLINGS' REGIME.

A political change in the administration of the State government took place in January, 1921. It brought to the Department of Public Health its second Director, Dr. Isaac D. Rawlings, who took office on February 1. Like most of the executive officers of the State health service who had preceded him, Dr. Rawlings had been with the city health department in Chicago. Indeed he had spent over twenty years in the public health service of that city and had been closely associated with all of the great sanitarians since 1900 who had built up in Chicago one of the finest municipal health departments in the country and given to the city an enviable record for good health conditions.

In education and experience, Dr. Rawlings was better trained than any man who had preceded him with the possible exception of Dr. Rauch, who lived, of course, before the day when preventive medicine came into its own. Dr. Rawlings was a graduate of Northwestern University Medical School, one of the best in the country. Later he spent considerable time at the great medical educational centers in Germany, Austria and England. Then he taught for a number of years in Northwestern University Medical School and subsequently put in twenty years at public health work. He was, therefore, thoroughly familiar with the problems both medical and sociological, the technical procedures and the difficulties to be encountered in the field of public health service.

As native equipment, Dr. Rawlings had a love for routine system, a thirst for details, a passion for work and a tenacity of purpose that led him to carry out plans and policies in letter and spirit alike. If the law provided for a board of public health advisors which should meet quarterly he wanted a board appointed and he wanted it to meet on the first Tuesday of every third month and he wanted it to advise. If occasion required him to go before a legislative committee he was no man to say "Mr. Chairman, contagion is rampant in the State. We need twice the money we now get to make headway against it." No. He had to have with him a piece of paper bearing official statistics and with its help say "Mr. Chairman, smallpox left its scars on 8,536 persons in this State last year. That's too much. It's costing us close to a million dollars a year. In your own district, Mr. Chairman,

PUBLIC HEALTH ADMINISTRATION 195

there were 836 cases, a ratio much larger than that for the State." To satisfy this craving for system and this desire for details which were the tools of his mind that brought out his mental faculties to best advantage he was willing to begin before the sun rose and work far into the night, day in and day out. He was determined that his organization should put in honest hours and function so that results could be reduced to tangible records that would be available at any time for any necessary purpose.

The General Assembly was sitting when Dr. Rawlings assumed office. He asked for an enabling law that would permit counties to employ trained medical health officers to organize and direct county health departments. This the general assembly declined to do but did provide for 25 instead of 7 district health superintendents to work under the State Department of Public Health. Never before had so large an extension of the State health machinery been arranged for by any legislature.

Coordination of Forces.

As pointed out heretofore there was in existence when Dr. Rawlings arrived a splendid organization plan for the State Department of Public Health. The finances were budgeted and so were the functions. Appropriations were made for specific purposes and personnel, most of which was well qualified to perform the duties required, was divided into divisions to which special types of services were assigned. The main trouble was that the divisions were like so many independent units functioning under a general head. Coordination and systematization were necessary to make the Department produce maximum results.

As the first step toward unifying the health machinery, Dr. Rawlings started the practice of holding staff meetings of division chiefs each week. He laid before them his policies and mapped out his program. To every division was assigned the routine procedures which it was technically prepared to handle and such other duties as it might be able to perform in connection with general projects undertaken by the Department. This practice, which still continues keeps all members of the Department informed about activities within the Department and this greatly enhances the coordination of effort. It is particularly helpful to those employees who travel about the State and are frequently questioned about health matters.

By May 17, 1921, Dr. Rawlings had arranged for a meeting of all the field staff, consisting of 7 or 8 physicians with the division chiefs in Springfield. That was another step toward unification. Questions of policy were discussed. Each division chief outlined the services which he was prepared to undertake. Acquaintances were made for the first time between many of those present. This general conference of Department members became an annual affair and constitutes an important factor in the systematic operation of the State's health machinery.

Advisory Board.

Then there was the matter of an advisory board. The Civil Administrative Code provided for one, made up of five members, that should meet as frequently as deemed necessary but not less often than quarterly. The matter was laid before the Governor who appointed to the board on September 22, 1921, the full complement of members. It consisted of Dr. W. A. Evans and Dr. John Dill Robertson of Chicago. Dr. E. P. Sloan of Bloomington, Dr. C. W. Lillie of East St. Louis and Mrs. E. N. Monroe of Quincy. From the outset the board has met regularly and has participated energetically in the business of rendering advice about the health policies and problems of the State. Its contact with the professional and public life of the State enabled it to not only interpret public sentiment but to exercise considerable influence over the trend of sentiment concerning health matters. It has, therefore, proved to be an important factor in welding together the health machinery and of guiding the activities of the State Department of Public Health along a course that was both sound scientifically and wise sociologically.

Attempts to Improve Local Health Machinery.

Local health machinery was another important factor in the program of unification. The larger municipalities had fairly well organized health departments but the remainder of the State, divided into some 2,700 districts, had for health officers persons upon whom the law imposed this responsibility by virtue of some other office to which they had been elected—such as county supervisor, assessor, town clerk, village president, etc. Not only were these men untrained in public health work, generally speaking, but they frequently changed with local elections and the State Director of Health had no means of knowing about it.

Dr. Rawlings was ambitious to substitute the county for the township as the unit for local health organization and to create a demand for well trained medical health officers. The General Assembly turned down an enabling bill in 1921. Nevertheless Dr. Rawlings pushed forward his plans. By the end of 1921 he had created sentiment favorable to a county health service in Morgan County. With some financial help from the International Health Board and some from the State, Morgan County inaugurated the first full time county health service in Illinois in the spring of 1922. This Dr. Rawlings planned to use as a demonstration project both to other counties and to the General Assembly. It has pleased Morgan County well enough to be continued on a permanent basis.

MEMBERS
First Board of Public Health Advisors
Appointed September 22, 1921.

E. P. Sloan, M.D.

Mrs. E. N. Monroe
Vice-Chairman

Wm. A. Evans, M.D.
Chairman

Chas. W. Lillie, M.D.*
Secretary
*DECEASED

John Dill Robertson, M.D.

an annual affair and constitutes an important factor in the systematic operation of the State's health machinery.

Advisory Board.

Then there was the matter of an advisory board. The Civil Administrative Code provided for one, made up of five members, that should meet as frequently as deemed necessary but not less often than quarterly. The matter was laid before the Governor who appointed to the board on September 22, 1921, the full complement of members. It consisted of Dr. W. A. Evans and Dr. John Dill Robertson of Chicago, Dr. E. P. Sloan of Bloomington, Dr. C. W. Lillie of East St Louis and Mrs. E. N. Monroe of Quincy. From the outset the board has met regularly and has participated energetically in the business of rendering advice about the health policies and problems of the State. Its contact with the professional and public life of the State enabled it to not only interpret public sentiment but to exercise considerable influence over the trend of sentiment concerning health matters. It has, therefore, proved to be a important factor in welding together the health machinery and of guiding the activities of the State Department of Public Health along a course that was both sound scientifically and wise sociologically.

Attempts to Improve Local Health Machinery.

Local health machinery was another important factor in the program of unification. The larger municipalities had fairly well organized health departments but the remainder of the State, divided into some 2,700 districts, had for health officers persons upon whom the law imposed this responsibility by virtue of some other office to which they had been elected—such as county supervisor, assessor, town clerk, village president, etc. Not only were these men untrained in public health work, generally speaking, but they frequently charged with local elections and the State Director of Health had no means of knowing about it.

Dr. Rawlings was ambitious to substitute the county for the township as the unit for local health organization and to create a demand for well trained medical health officer. The General Assembly turned down an enabling bill in 1921. Nevertheless Dr. Rawlings pushed forward his plans. By the end of 1921 he had created sentiment favorable to a county health service in Morgan County. With some financial help from the International Health Board and some from the State, Morgan County inaugurated the first full time county health service in Illinois in the spring of 1922. This Dr Rawlings planned to use as a demonstration project both to other co and to the General Assembly It has pleased Morgan County w to be continued on a permanent basis.

MEMBERS
First Board of Public Health Advisors
Appointed September 22, 1921.

E. P. Sloan, M.D.

Mrs. E. N. Monroe
Vice-Chairman

Wm. A. Evans, M.D.
Chairman

John Dill Robertson, M.D.

An enabling bill authorizing counties to establish health departments failed again to pass the General Assembly in 1923 but a bill requiring county clerks to report annually to the State Department of Public Health the names and addresses of all local officials concerned with public health duties did become law. This linked up the Department more closely with local communities than any other one thing since the law creating local health officers was enacted.

In 1924 another attempt was made to stimulate the development of county health departments. This time arrangements were made with the United States Public Health Service and the International Health Board to help finance a certain number of units and Dr. Thomas Parran, Jr., surgeon on the staff of the United States Public Health Service, who had had a wide experience in the development of rural health service, was detailed to work in Illinois under the State Department of Public Health. Dr. Parran started to work in June and by July 1, Crawford County had employed a full time health officer and organized a department. Shortly afterwards Wabash County decided to do the same but difficulties arose over local authority to appropriate funds so that the plans didn't materialize. The department in Crawford was short lived. The attorney general of the State expressed the opinion that counties could spend money for the control of diseases in the face of epidemics but that they were unauthorized to do so for preventive activities when contagious infections were not present. This opinion settled the matter. An enabling law was necessary before progress could be made in building up county health departments. So far no such law has been enacted.

A full time rural health service was established in Cook County in 1924 and one in DuPage in 1925 as a result of efforts of the Department. Both have continued to date and appear to be permanent.

Dr. Rawlings now gave his attention to the improvement of municipal health service in the State. Under Dr. Parran a survey of the 15 cities ranging between 30,000 and 100,000 population was undertaken. It was certainly a different project from the Rauch survey just 40 years before. The Rauch survey considered alleys, back yards, cellars—environment. The Rawlings' survey measured the character of health service by the results obtained. It is interesting to note that both were patterned after the teaching of the American Public Health Association in their time.

As a means of creating interest in local health administration, the Rawlings' survey was the most successful single activity the State Department of Public Health ever undertook. Each city was rated on a percentage basis as a result of the findings and the newspapers devoured the reports. National magazines interested in the public health field commented extensively on it. More important still, the cities concerned took steps to make the improvements recommended. Evanston, for example, replaced a part time with a full time health officer. Other of the cities built isolation hospitals, put on public nursing services, started infant welfare projects and added such other improvements as seemed practicable under local circumstances.

In January, 1924 a system of clinics which the State Department of Public Health had been conducting for a number of years for the benefit of crippled children was discontinued. These clinics involved a consider-

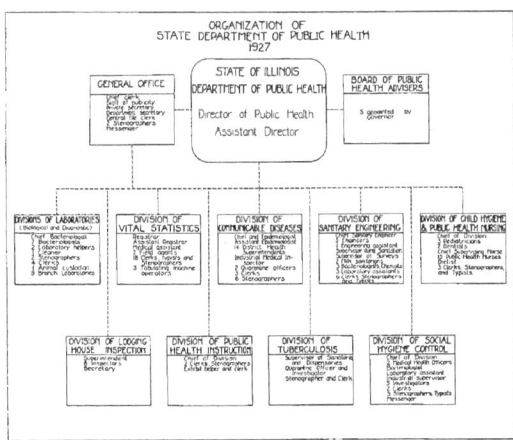

FIG. 11. Showing the available strength of the State Department of Public Health on July 1, 1927.

able amount of curative or corrective practice and this had caused some unfavorable feeling in the ranks of the medical profession. The work was continued under the auspices of voluntary agencies but its divorcement from the State service left the Health Department free to engage in purely preventive activities.

Maternity and Child Hygiene.

To stimulate activity in the field of maternity and child hygiene, Dr. Rawlings took advantage of the financial support offered by the federal government through the children's bureau under what is ordinarily called the Sheppard-Towner Act. A draft on the federal treasury in favor of the State of Illinois to the amount of over $19,000 was forwarded to Dr. Rawlings during the summer of 1922 but the State auditor had no legal authority to accept the funds and the legislature declined to ever grant that authority. Thus the State's child hygiene program had to be worked out with no outside financial support.

This was undertaken by the formation in 1925 of a State advisory committee on child hygiene. On it are represented the Illinois State Medical Society, the Illinois State Dental Society, the Illinois Federation of Women's Clubs, the Illinois Council of Parent-Teacher Associations and the State Department of Public Health. Through this committee, which has before it plans and programs concerning maternity and child health, a considerable amount of strength has been added to the State health machinery. It functions by informing the several organizations concerned about the programs and special campaigns undertaken by the State health officials and exercises no small influence in putting over definite projects. Through it, for instance, direct contact was made with club women and parent-teacher associations in every county of the State in connection with a diphtheria eradication campaign in 1926.

Another link in the chain that systematized health work in the State was welded when Dr. Rawlings succeeded in interesting the Illinois State Dental Society in a mouth hygiene program. The Illinois State and Chicago Dental Societies agreed to pay the salary of a dentist to work under the State Department of Public Health as a temporary demonstration of what could be done. The Illinois Tuberculosis Association contributed some funds to this project. The plan was carried out beginning in August, 1926. It culminated on July 1, 1927 when appropriations made by the 1927 General Assembly became available for continuing the program.

Other Activities.

In 1925 arrangements were made to open a branch diagnostic laboratory in Carbondale and in 1927 another was opened in Chicago. Prior to these dates branch laboratories had been established and maintained at various points but their work was confined to diphtheria. These two new branches were equipped to handle practically every kind of procedure common in public health laboratories. This step provided diagnostic laboratory facilities in easy reach of every part of the State so that physicians and the public could profit by prompt service whenever needed.

Vital Statistics.

When Dr. Rawlings was appointed State Director of Public Health in 1921 the most obvious shortcoming of the Department concerned statistics. Birth registration was 20 per cent deficient and accordingly was not recognized by the federal bureau of the census. To get Illinois into the United States birth registration area was the first extra-routine task that Dr. Rawlings undertook.

He went about the matter methodically.. The subject was thoroughly aired at staff meetings. A communication requesting cooperation and citing the birth registration law was directed to every practicing physician in the State. The 1,400 odd local registrars were advised of their duties and responsibilities. Birth records in the office of the State registrar were analyzed so that the amount of delinquency in every county and in all the larger municipalities was closely estimated. The Illinois Federation of Women's Clubs was prevailed upon to participate in the campaign by appointing local club women all over the State to make birth registration surveys. All the field personnel of the Department from whatever division were informed of registration delinquencies so that each could visit doctors and registrars in his district or along his itinerary. Local state's attorneys were called upon freely to handle the few legal cases that appeared unavoidable with recalcitrant offenders. Within eighteen months birth registration was so nearly complete and returns were so prompt that Illinois was admitted to the United States birth registration area and the 1922 statistics accepted by the federal bureau of the census for that purpose.

The chief significance of the birth registration campaign was its effect on the State health machinery. It had knit together the various divisions of the Department in a common purpose above that encountered in ordinary routine. It had brought into action a great potential strength for doing local health work and influencing public opinion—the women's clubs. It had awakened a lively interest among physicians. It had introduced the official legal talent of local communities to the laws governing public health service.

But birth registration was only one of the statistical problems that faced Dr. Rawlings. No detailed mortality rates had ever been computed in the State for official publication. Figures that were available had been compiled on a fiscal year basis so that they were incomparable with those of other states. This situation was remedied when Dr. Rawlings introduced into the Department a system of monthly and semi-annual reports from divisions and insisted on having the annual report when it was due. By the end of his first year in office Dr. Rawlings had succeeded in getting for publication a detailed infant mortality statement covering every county and every principal city in the State, the first report of the kind ever issued by the Department. By the middle of 1922 mortality tables showing the cause of each death in the State, puerperal deaths by counties and cities and detailed infant mortality rates for 1921 were available. This progress was continued from year to year, time limits being set for the delivering of similar reports, until 1927 finds tabulations and analyses of the State's mortality records in practically all standard forms.

Communicable disease reports likewise needed much improvement. They were incomplete on the one hand and not easily available for utilization on the other. Dr. Rawlings introduced a system of daily reports from the division chiefs to his own office. Then he put into effect a system of cross checking between mortality records and case reports. Furthermore he had brought together into one tabulation the cases and deaths from the principal reportable diseases for every county and city of 10,000 or more in the State. Then he began the practice of sending a field physician to investigate every reported case of smallpox, typhoid fever and chickenpox in adults. These procedures revealed the weak spots of notification and led not only to a distinct improvement in the completeness and promptness of reports from the field but also to the utilization of the data collected. To operate the system inaugurated records had to be kept in good shape and that is just what happened. By every available test it appears that communicable diseases are reported now (1927) in Illinois as satisfactorily as they are anywhere in the country.

Safe Milk Supplies.

The problem of safe milk furnishes another illustration of the system which Dr. Rawlings introduced into the operation of State health machinery. Sanitarians everywhere recognize the safety of milk supplies as scarcely second to safe water supplies in importance to general health conditions. With the exception of tuberculin testing, little had been done to promote the safety of milk outside of Chicago in Illinois prior to 1921. In that year the State Department of Public Health set to work on the problem. Dr. Rawlings appointed a committee representing several divisions to study the question. After consulting with experts in the Department of Agriculture and at the University of Illinois the committee drew up an ordinance suitable for adoption by municipalities. In August 1922 the ordinance was brought before and thoroughly discussed by a group of the most representative sanitarians and milk dealers of the State, gathered in Chicago at the Pageant of Progress to consider important public health problems, and received a vote of approval by that body. The ordinance was evidently about right.

MEMBERS
Present Board of Public Health Advisors

Wm A. Evans, M.D.

Mrs. E. N. Monroe
Vice-Chairman

Thos. D. Doan, M.D.
Chairman

E. P. Sloan, M.D.

Herman N. Bundesen, M.D.
Secretary

The next step was to get the ordinance adopted by local municipalities. This task was approached in the same way that proved successful in birth registration. Communications went out to mayors. Traveling representatives of the Department from whatever division who had opportunity to promote the idea were given assignments to meet with local officials, leaders, civic organizations etc. By 1927 a total of 60 cities with a combined population of 830,000 had adopted the ordinance.

But adopting an ordinance would not in itself provide safe milk. It had provoked thought, however, and soon the Department began to get requests for information about various municipal supplies. This led to a survey of all milk pasteurizing plants in the State by the division of sanitary engineering. The first survey was made in 1921 before much agitation for improvement had begun. Then in 1924 a sanitary engineer was assigned to do nothing but milk work. In 1925 a law that required the certification by the State Department of Public Health of all plants pasteurizing milk was passed. At the same time provision was made for employing a milk sanitarian and a milk bacteriologist and the purchase of a mobile laboratory to be used in that work. Thus by 1927 the Department of Health had considerably broadened its safe milk program and was in a position to prosecute the undertaking in earnest.

This milk project brought the State health machinery to operate systematically in a field that had been entered before only sporadically and in a haphazard kind of way. It brought milk dealers and producers into contact with health work more definitely than they had before experienced. Under Dr. Rawlings milk dealers became active agents of the State Department of Public Health because it would be an unwise business man indeed who could ignore a bad report on his milk pasteurizing plant and especially so when he was informed that responsibility for epidemic outbreaks that might be traced to his products would be put squarely up to him.

Appreciation of Departmental Regulations.

In 1925, following the development of a rather unusual incidence of typhoid fever attributed to contaminated oysters, an order was issued by Dr. Rawlings prohibiting the sale of oysters in the State for raw consumption. The effect of the order was nation-wide in magnitude and disastrous for the oyster industry. One conference between representatives of the oyster industry and public health officials followed fast upon the heels of another. With the Illinois Director of Public Health as the central figure the affair soon came to the attention of the United States Public Health Service and nearly every state health officer in the country. The result was a general sanitary improvement in the production and distribution of shell fish made necessary to meet requirements laid down by Dr. Rawlings and the Illinois Oyster Committee for any oysters allowed on the markets of Illinois. Indeed a cooperative state and national system of certifying oyster producing concerns was created and continues to operate under the general supervision of the United States Public Health Service.

This oyster business represented a new use of the authority granted to the State Department of Public Health to make rules and regulations concerning health matters. By such action the State health machinery extended its influence from coast to coast, causing a general sanitary advancement in a great industrial field.

Again in 1926 use was made of the same type of authority. This time the action related to stearate of zinc toilet powder. A few deaths of infants had been attributed to the accidental inhaling of this kind of powder. All cases, it appeared, could have been prevented had the powder containers been equipped with automatic safety caps. Accordingly it seemed wise to prohibit in Illinois the sale of stearate of zinc toilet powder except in safety containers. This was done and again the effect was nation-wide because the large manufacturers, engaged as they were in inter-state commerce, preferred to turn out a uniform product to all of their trade, including Illinois. Thus again was demonstrated the far reaching influence of the power of the State Department of Public Health to make rules and regulations.

Educational and Miscellaneous Activities.

Another activity that strengthened and extended the influence of the State's health machinery related to health education. In 1925 arrangements were made between the State Department of Public Health, the State Department of Registration and Education and the five State Normal schools to introduce courses of health instruction in the curricula of the institutions. The object of these courses, which have been introduced and expanded as rapidly as facilities permit, is to provide prospective teachers with the sort of sanitary and hygienic knowledge necessary for their personal health benefit and to equip them to not only impart knowledge to children but to exercise intelligent supervision over their health in the school room. This links up a great educational system with the State's health machinery and plants the seed of sanitary knowledge where they are apt to yield the greatest returns.

The foregoing references to projects undertaken by the State Department of Public Health under Dr. Rawlings by no means exhaust the field of activities which might be drawn upon but they are sufficient to illustrate very well the process of welding together the resources of the State for doing public health work which has characterized his entire administration. In every division the volume of work done has expanded very noticeably. On all sides a greater degree of coordination than had hitherto existed has prevailed.

Very few changes in the organization plan were made by Dr. Rawlings. During his first year he eliminated the division of surveys and rural sanitation, transferring the work and personnel to the division of sanitary engineering. Otherwise the divisional arrangement was unmolested. Each division grew in size and enlarged its volume of work but remained in the organization scheme as they were under the organization plan which prevailed when Dr. Rawlings became State Director of Public Health.

A line of 25 to 100 deep constantly flanked the entrance to the adult examination booths at the 1925 State Fair.

Appropriation.

The last appropriation made to the State Department of Public Health prior to the appointment of Dr. Rawlings, that made by the General Assembly in 1919, amounted to $720,810 for the biennium. In 1921 the biennial appropriation jumped to $1,179,712. After that it changed but little up to the present time August 1927. It fell back to $985,587 in 1923, due to anti-administration political maneuvers but 1925 found the grant back up to $1,138,887. In 1927 the General Assembly voted $1,187,684 for the general expenses of the State Department of Public Health during the ensuing two fiscal years. This is a substantial increase of money compared with the modest sum of $5,000 appropriated fifty years before to carry the infant

State Board of Health* along through its first two years of life. Compared with funds provided by many other states, including New York, Pennsylvania and Massachusetts, for public health purposes the amount appropriated by Illinois in 1927 is relatively small as she ranks twentieth along the States in her per capita expenditure for health although she is third in wealth and population.

The organization of the State Department of Public Health in 1927 is graphically shown by the illustration in Fig. 11. How this differs from the organization in 1917, the first year under the Civil Administrative Code, in

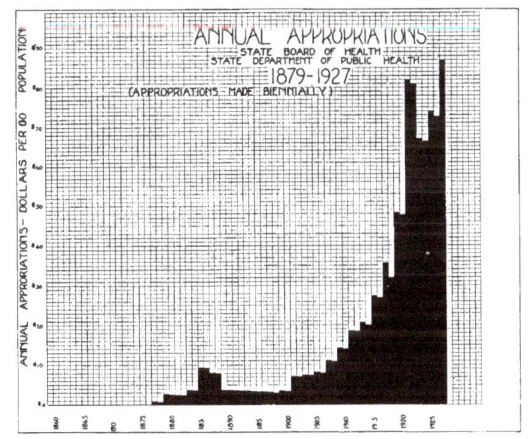

FIG. 12.

1915, the last year under the State Board of Health and in 1877, the first year under the State Board of Health may be observed by reference to Figs. 8, 9, and 10.

Summary

When Dr. Rawlings became State Director of Public Health in 1921 he found the Department functioning under a well devised organization plan with facilities for participating in practically every phase of public health

---

* The State Board of Health collected considerable sums from licenses which it was authorized to use.

service but it was loosely bound together. At the time this is written in 1927 with Dr. Rawlings still in office, the various divisions are coordinated into a unified Department which is capable of moving swiftly and efficiently toward the achievement of any general purpose and at the same time each division takes care of the routine problems within its own particular field with all other divisions fully informed of the work being done.

When Dr. Rawlings assumed office most of the divisions in the Department were very small and several of them were scarcely more than skeleton units. By 1927 all of them had been materially strengthened, giving the Department the capacity to perform promptly and effectively all of the activities in which it professes to engage.

The foregoing statements concerning the health machinery in the State suggest the way employed by Dr. Rawlings in binding it together into a systematic whole so that every unit of the State Department of Public Health and every other agency engaged on a significant scale in public health work meshed together in their programs and efforts like gear wheels that drive mechanical machines. Evidence that the job was well done is found in the accuracy, magnitude and promptness of returns of statistical data dealing with births, deaths and disease. Another evidence is found in reports of local participation in various campaigns inaugurated by the Department. A still more important evidence is the freedom which the State has enjoyed from epidemic diseases and the steady decline in infant mortality and the prevalence of such diseases as smallpox, typhoid fever and diphtheria.

Much detailed information concerning the organization, functions and activities of the various divisions may be found in the chapter on each division's history.

Infra-Departmental Organization of State Health Machinery

From the time when the State Board of Health was created until 1899 there was no distinct division of labor among the regularly employed personnel. In July of that year two men were appointed to devote their full time to the inspection of lodging houses. While these appointments were originally made on a temporary basis they proved to be permanent in character and became established as a distinct unit of the State health machinery when the General Assembly made a specific appropriation for lodging house inspection in 1901. This then was the first step toward a State health service organized into specialized units.

Along about 1902 or 1903 one member of the office staff of the State Board of Health was designated as State registrar of vital statistics but in 1904 the same man, W. H. Hoyt, was also designated as State bacteriologist and given charge of the small diagnostic laboratory which started then. Then in 1905 the General Assembly included "registrar of vital statistics" "bacteriologist" and "laboratory" as items for which specific appropriations were made. Yet it appears that no marked division of labor took place but that the technical and clerical employes were subject to routine duties of whatever character might be most pressing at the moment.

Subsequent to 1905 there appears to have been little or no attempt at organizing the resources of the State Board of Health into specialized units until 1915 when a definite plan of organization was adopted and five bureaus were created. These included "medical and sanitary inspection", "vital statistics", "laboratory", "sanitary engineering" and "lodging house inspection". Each of these was the forerunner of what became a division of the State Department of Public Health under the Civil Administrative Code adopted in 1917.

The first appropriation under the Civil Administrative Code, made in 1917, specifically, provided for seven divisions. These included "general office", "communicable diseases", "tuberculosis", "sanitation", "diagnostic laboratory", "vital statistics" and "lodging house inspections". As a matter of fact 10 divisions were created in 1917, including besides those listed above "child hygiene and public health nursing", "surveys and rural hygiene" and "public health instruction". To these was added the division of "social hygiene" in 1918. In 1927 the divisional designation was the same except that the division of "surveys and rural hygiene" had lost its identity in 1921 and the division of sanitation changed its name to "sanitary engineering". Details concerning each division are enumerated under its own title on the following pages:

GENERAL OFFICE.

The general office is made up of the Director, assistant director, chief clerk and corps of clerks. Up until 1917 the general office was about synonymous with the State Board of Health so far as sanitary and hygienic work was concerned. Sanitary engineering, diagnostic laboratory services and field medical activities were centralized under different heads and the first two occupied independent quarters. There was also a registrar of vital statistics but this work was done in the main office and came under the immediate supervision of the chief clerk of the State Board of Health.

Since 1895 the general office has been presided over by a chief clerk. Prior to the introduction of the division plan the chief clerk actually directed the office personnel employed in the State health service with the exceptions mentioned. After the introduction of the division system in 1917 the general office has been a headquarters unit through which divisional contact is maintained. Technical matters are left entirely to the division chiefs who are responsible to the director for matters of a scientific and technical nature.

All department records and correspondence are handled by the general office. Through it all accounts are settled including payrolls. In it is located the central filing system which was introduced by Dr. Rawlings in 1926. All personnel records are also kept there.

Although it was customary to have one person in charge of the clerical force prior to that time, specific provision for a chief clerk was first made by the legislature in 1895. Mr. F. A. Treacy was the first man appointed to hold that position, he being already in the employ of the State Board of Health, at the time the position was first recognized by the legislature in the appropriation law. He was succeeded in May, 1897, by Mr. Charles Ryan who in turn was succeeded on May 1, 1901, by Mr. Amos Sawyer. Mr. Sawyer has filled the office of chief clerk continuously from the time of his appointment to date.

Mr. Chas. Ryan.

Division of Communicable Diseases.

The work of this division, as the name implies, is concerned directly with the control of contagious and infectious diseases. It has charge of morbidity reports, quarantine, rules and regulations relating to reporting and quarantine, epidemiological investigations, promotion of local health machinery and the distribution of biologics such as antitoxin, vaccine, silver nitrate, etc.

While activities of the character of those performed by the division have been participated in by the State health agency since its creation in 1877 the work was not centralized nor carried on in a systematic way until 1915 when the bureau of medical and sanitary inspection was established. Prior to that time the field work was done by the secretary himself or physicians or lay quarantine officers employed on a per diem basis. Sometimes the physicians so employed were members of the State Board of Health. More often they were not. Beginning about 1900 a scheme was devised whereby a number of physicians, located at convenient points in the State, agreed to accept appointment for temporary duty whenever called upon and receive therefore remuneration at a stipulated per diem rate. This method of handling communic

Dr. J. J. McShane.

able diseases continued until July, 1915, when it was converted into the bureau of medical and sanitary inspection with a definite amount of money appropriated sufficient for employing a medical staff of five and specific duties assigned to it.

By early spring of 1916 the necessary civil service examinations had been held and the five appointments made. They included Dr. E. S. Godfrey, who was designated as State epidemiologist, Dr. C. E. Crawford, Dr. C. S. Nelson, Dr. Clarence W. East and Dr. I. N. Foster. These physicians were assigned to field duty, each covering one of five districts into which the State was divided for that purpose and all were placed under the general supervision of Dr. Godfrey. Besides these district health officers, as they were called, there were attached to the bureau three dairy inspectors, one on a full and two on a part time basis and a small clerical staff.

In 1917, with the adoption of the Civil Administrative Code by the State government and the consequent reorganization of the health service, the bureau of medical and sanitary inspection became the division of communicable diseases which title it has retained. Funds sufficient to employ one chief, one superintendent of field service, six district health officers, two nurses, two quarantine officers and a clerical staff of five were appointed to the division. All of these positions were filled although the two nurses and one physician were utilized in another type of service and for med what developed into the division of child hygiene and public health nursing. Dr. J. J. McShane became the first chief of the division, on August 1, 1917, as a result of a civil service examination. Dr. McShane has continued in that capacity to date.

During the ten years ended with June 30, 1927, the field personnel of the division varied considerably, due to small salaries provided in the early part of that period and fluctuations in the appropriations made from time to time. In 1919 a total of $16,000 per year was granted for the employment of district health officers, with maximum salaries specified at $2500. The next General Assembly, that of 1921, raised the appropriation for medical field personnel to $100,000 per year, set $4,800 as the maximum salary and changed the title of the positions to district health superintendents. The difficulty of securing trained men delayed the filling of these places, however, so that the field strength never exceeded about 20 men. Then in 1923 the sum appropriated for district health superintendents was set back to $30,000 per year and raised again to $50,000 in 1925. In 1927 it remained at $50,000 with the maximum salary placed at $4,000, where had been set in 1923.

The amount of strength actually employed varied about as the appropriations but never up to the maximum provided for. On July 1, 1927 there were 13 district health superintendents, including a chief at work. In addition there were the division chief, an assistant epidemiologist, two quarantine officers, one industrial hygienist and a clerical staff of ten.

All of the personnel of the division is employed on a full time basis. The State is divided into districts equal in number to the number of district health superintendents employed. Each of the latter maintains headquarters in the district to which he is assigned so as to facilitate field service.

It has been the practice since 1921 to hold meetings of the field staff periodically in order to increase the efficiency of the force by permitting general discussion of their problems and bringing to them the proper interpretation of policies, plans, programs and procedures included in the Department's services. These conferences are held at least annually and sometimes oftener.

Rules and Regulations Promulgated.

When the State Department of Public Health was created in 1917 the division of communicable diseases was charged by the Director of Public Health with making rules and regulations governing quarantine and reporting of diseases, with the collection and compilation of morbidity reports and with epidemiological investigations. It was also made responsible for the distribution of such biological products as the Department furnished to the citizens of the State. Its duties also included the promotion of local health service.

The history of the rules and regulations dates back to 1877 when health work first began as a function of the State government. For 38 years, however, there was nothing very specific about them except in special cases. When yellow fever threatened; rules were promulgated in regard to quarantine at Cairo. When smallpox broke out there were rules that required isolation of patients. At one time, prior to 1895, rules required the vaccination of all school children but this was later annulled by a court decision. Furthermore, and of great importance, there was no machinery for enforcing rules once they were made. Cities and villages had authority to make rules and regulations concerning disease control and the same power was granted to counties later. Up until 1903 the local regulations frequently conflicted with those of the State and then confusion arose.

About the only rule that really operated satisfactorily before 1915 was that relating to the burial of dead. This rule required permits from local registrars before burial and its purpose was to promote complete filing of death notices.

In 1915 all the quarantine rules and regulations were codified, and the proper local officials specified as the person to whom reports should be made

This step clarified the air of confusion making it plain what the rules were and to whom reports should be made. Length of quarantine, sanitary precautions on quarantined premises, diseases for which quarantine should be established and like matters were definitely specified.

Under the early system there was difficulty in getting reports of contagious diseases. Altogether some 2,500 local officials were included in the list of those who should receive reports. Many of them did not know it. Others who received reports had little inclination to pay the postage necessary to send them in to the State Board of Health. At times the State Board of Health sent out communications asking for the required information. Sometimes it was returned and sometimes not and its reliability was questionable at best.

In 1917 two things happened that helped matters. The State Director of Public Health was appointed collaborating epidemiologist for the U. S. Public Health Service with privilege of supplying local health officers with postage free report cards. The other thing was the establishment of the division of communicable diseases with its field staff on a full time basis. Reports began at once to improve.

There was still the difficulty of knowing who the local health officers were. This was corrected by an amendment to the State Board of Health Act in 1923, new sections being added as follows:

"Section 21. The county clerk of every county under township organization shall, annually before the first of May furnish the Department of Public Health the names and postoffice addresses of the supervisor, assessor and town clerk of every township in the county, the date when their terms of office expire and the township of which each is an official. The county clerk of every county not under township organization shall, annually before the first of December furnish the Department of Public Health the names and post office addresses of the county commissioners and the date when their terms of office expire.

Section 22. The clerk of every city, incorporated town and village shall, annually before the first day of May furnish the Department of Public Health the name of the mayor or president of the board of trustees, the clerk, the health officer and the members of the board of health and this list shall indicate which person is charged with the enforcement of quarantine regulations.

Section 23. The county, city, incorporated town or village clerk shall promptly inform the Department of Public Health of vacancies in the offices named in sections 21 and 22 of this Act and appointments or elections to fill such vacancies."

From 1923 on reports have steadily improved in both promptness and completeness.

With improvement in the character of municipal health departments it appeared wise to permit a wider use of local discretion in connection with quarantine than the strict letter of the rules would permit in all cases. Thus in 1923 a system of what is known as modified quarantine regulations was inaugurated. By means of this arrangement local health officers who are able to satisfy the State Director of Health that they have the facilities for adequately handling the local situation may receive permission to practice modified quarantine. This system permits the isolation of a patient in a room to himself with attendant and the free use of the remainder of the house by other members of the quarantined premises.

Another instance of the changing character of the rules was the inclusion of carriers of disease within their scope. Thus persons found to be chronic carriers of typhoid fever are required to stay out of occupations that bring them into direct contact with food supplies of other people.

Contagious Disease Reports.

Subsequent to 1915 when the rules were first codified and made specific they have been revised many times in order to conform with the ever increasing knowledge about handling disease and with the changes in habits and customs of the people. The scope of the rules has increased also, new diseases being added to the notifiable list from time to time and new uses being made of the rules as preventive measures. Thus in 1925 a rule prohibiting the sale of oysters for raw consumption in Illinois was placed in effect and another in 1926 prohibiting the sale of stearate of zinc toilet powder in any but safety top containers.

Reports received at the office are immediately compiled on forms arranged for that purpose so that daily totals are made showing the incidence reported by counties, principal cities and the State. These daily reports in turn are compiled into weekly, monthly and annual summaries. The filing system enables reference to be made to counties, cities and townships. This office system was started in 1921 so that reliable data are available back to that time but figures for previous years are more incomplete.

A system of spot maps and weekly prevalence charts was adopted in 1924 and a system of notifying local health officers of the prevalence of disease in the State was started in 1926. The latter is a weekly service which keeps local health officers informed of all reported cases of the principal diseases and the foci of infections as well.

Laws Applying to Work of Division.

The important laws affecting the activities of the division are not many. First in importance was the State Board of Health Act of 1877, which reads in part, as amended in 1907, as follows:

"The State Board of Health shall have the general supervision of the interests of the health and lives of the people of the State. They shall have supreme authority in matters of quarantine and may declare and enforce quarantine when none exists, and may modify or relax quarantine when it has been established. The board shall have authority to make such rules and regulations and such sanitary investigations as they may from time to time deem necessary for the preservation and improvement of the public health, and they are empowered to regulate the transportation of the remains of deceased persons. It shall be the duty of all local boards of health, health authorities and officers, police officers, sheriffs, constables and all other officers and employees of the State or any county, village, city or township thereof, to enforce the rules and regulations that may be adopted by the State Board of Health.

It shall be the duty of the State Board of Health to investigate into the causes of dangerously contagious or infectious diseases, especially when existing in epidemic form, and to take means to restrict and suppress the same, and whenever any dangerously contagious or infectious disease shall become, or threaten to become epidemic, in any village or city and the local board of health or local authorities shall neglect to refuse to enforce efficient measures for its restriction or suppression or to act with sufficient promptness or efficiency, or whenever the local board of health or local authorities shall neglect or refuse to promptly enforce efficient measures for the restriction or suppression of dangerously contagious or infectious diseases, the State Board of Health or their secretary, as their executive officer, when the board is not in session, may enforce such measures as the said board or their executive officer may deem necessary to protect the public health, and all necessary expenses so incurred shall be paid by the city or village for which services are rendered."

Prior to this, in point of chronology, was the Cities and Villages Act of 1872 that gave these municipalities authority to establish boards of health. Then came the law of 1901 that created boards of health in rural districts by making county commissioners, supervisors, assessors and town clerks constitute boards of health.

A law was enacted in 1911 which required employers of labor to protect employes from undue exposure to poisonous chemicals used in manufacturing processes.

The State health officials were required to receive reports of occupational diseases under this law and to transfer the notice to the State factory inspector for disposition. This same law requires monthly physical examinations of all employees engaged in certain occupations where they are exposed to lead and other poisonous chemicals.

In 1917 there was enacted a law authorizing the establishment of local health departments by popular vote in one or more adjacent towns or road districts. Under this law taxes may be levied, collected and spent for health purposes only.

In 1905 a law was enacted providing free Pasteur treatment for poor people bitten by rabid animals and in the same year the State Board of Health Act was amended so as to require the appointment of antitoxin agents in every county. Then in 1907 a clause was added to the appropriation law providing for the free distribution of antitoxin. In 1911 typhoid vaccine was added to the free list and silver nitrate in 1915. Later the law on this subject became general so that the Department is in a position to purchase and distribute whatever biologics may be deemed necessary for the preservation and improvement of the public health.

In 1915 what is known as the Ophthalmia Neonatorum Law was enacted. This law defines ophthalmia neonatorum and makes it the duty of physicians and midwives to report all cases immediately upon discovery.

Distribution of Biologics.

The distribution of free state biologics began in 1907, when the legislature appropriated $15,000 to the State Board of Health for that purpose. Diphtheria antitoxin was the only product included at that time.

Distribution was accomplished through a system of agents, usually a local druggist. This agency system began in 1905 when a law was passed requiring their appointment and providing that they shall handle antitoxin approved by the State Board of Health. Then after the 1907 act they became the agents for distributing diphtheria antitoxin supplied free by the State. By 1927 these agents, who number 477, were handling antitoxin, toxin-antitoxin, silver nitrate and typhoid vaccine.

The biologics provided by the State in 1922 included the following:

Diphtheria Antitoxin, in both immunizing and curative doses.
Diphtheria Toxin-Antitoxin, for active immunization against diphtheria.
Schick test material to determine susceptibility to diphtheria.
Silver Nitrate Solution to be used in new born babies' eyes, as a preventive of Ophthalmia Neonatorum.
Typhoid Vaccine for immunization against Typhoid Fever.
Smallpox Vaccine as a preventive of Smallpox.
Antirabic Vaccine for prevention of rabies in humans.

The antirabic treatments are available free to poor people only but the other products are free to every citizen who needs any of them for therapeutic use.

Table 23 shows the amounts of biologics distributed during recent years.

Table 23.

Biologics Distributed July 1, 1918–Dec. 31, 1926.

Antitoxin.

	1,000 unit pkgs.	3,000 unit pkgs.	5,000 unit pkgs.	10,000 unit pkgs.	20,000 unit pkgs.	Hosp. sz. 10,000 unit pkgs.	Hosp. sz. 20,000 unit pkgs.	Total
July 1, 1918–June 30, 1919	13,501	4,915	10,526	7,474		1,540	450	8,816
July 1, 1919–June 30, 1920	14,166	4,859	9,717	8,996		853	730	39,306
July 1, 1920–June 30, 1921	22,539	2,445	16,564	15,586		1,187	1,078	6000
July 1, 1921–June 30, 1922	28,844		20,504	21,863		1,858	1,717	75,814
July 1, 1922–June 30, 1923	28,701		30,437	24,590		2,443	3,289	79,500
July 1, 1923–June 30, 1924	18,842		10,774	13,589		447	295	41,907
July 1, 1924–June 30, 1925	12,337		5,732	10,109		427	412	29,947
July 1, 1925–June 30, 1926	12,479		6,342	10,669		885	870	0,865
July 1, 1926–Dec. 31, 1926	6,740		3,540	5,340	452	365	93	16,630
Total Distribution	157,149	12,219	104,256	118,615	452	9,949	8,934	411,594

Typhoid-Vaccine.

	Style A Syringe pkg.	Style B Ampule pkg.	Hosp. sz. Style C in vials	Total
July 1, 1921–June 30, 1922	2,000?	4,200?	4,192	4,649
July 1, 1922–June 30, 1923	168	8,139	437	8,744
July 1, 1923–June 30, 1924	265	10,340	74	11,679
July 1, 1924–June 30, 1925	2,515	7,779	418	10,742
July 1, 1925–June 30, 1926	2,485	9,793	114	12,392
July 1, 1926–Dec. 31, 1926	2,280	8,721	50	1,051
Total Distribution	13,713	48,972	1,542	6457

Silver-Nitrate.

	Six ampule pkgs.	Twelve ampule pkgs.	Total pkgs.
July 1, 1921–June 30, 1922	3,800	200	4,000
July 1, 1922–June 30, 1923	19,000	635	19,635
July 1, 1923–June 30, 1924	14,300	700	15,000
July 1, 1924–June 30, 1925	13,362	649	14,011
July 1, 1925–June 30, 1926	13,067	1,441	14,508
July 1, 1926–Dec. 30, 1926	6,751	963	7,714
Total Distribution	70,280	4,578	74,858

HEALTH ADMINISTRATION

Table 23—Continued.

TOXIN-ANTITOXIN.

	Style A single tr.	Style B three tr.	Style C ten tr.	Total.
	4,106		2,433	6,539
	588		1,147	1,735
	793		2,513	3,306
	1,069		2,679	3,748
	212	5,929	2,053	8,194
	6,768	5,929	10,825	23,522

HICK TEST MATERIAL.

	No. pkgs.	Total tests.
	181—50-tests ea.	9,050
	128—50-tests ea.	6,400
	285—50-tests ea.	14,250
	295—50-tests ea.	14,750
	889 pkgs.—50-tests ea.	44,450

SMALLPOX VACCINE.

	No. pkgs.	Total points.
	1,443—10-points ea.	14,430 points
	1,464—10-points ea.	14,640 points
	202—10-points ea.	2,020 points
	3,109	31,090 points

ANTIRABIC TREATMENT.

No. pkgs.	Total.
56 paid for by state, 0 paid for personally	56
90 paid for by state, 31 paid for personally	121
77 paid for by state, 19 paid for personally	96
223 paid for by state, 50 paid for personally	273

DIVISION OF TUBERCULOSIS.

The division of tuberculosis has never been more than a skeleton unit of the State Department of Public Health. Like most of the others it came into being with the organization scheme that was adopted July 1, 1917. From the beginning it has been inseparable from the general office, having as its titular head, the assistant director and occupying space in the main office.

In 1917 a salary of $2,800 per year for a chief of the division was appropriated. That was dropped in 1919 and an item of $1,320 per year for a supervising nurse took its place but no nurse was ever appointed, the entire sum lapsing back into the treasury. In 1921 there were two items in the appropriation—one of $3,000 per year for a supervisor of sanatoria and one of $1,200 for a stenographer. From that time on there was no change made in the appropriations for the division until 1927 when an item of $1,800 per year was added for a quarantine officer and investigator.

Dr. George Thomas Palmer.

The principal activities of the division have been rather of a liaison character between the State Department of Public Health and other agencies. There is a strong voluntary tuberculosis association functioning in the State, forty-eight counties having taken advantage of the law authorizing a tax levy for the construction and maintenance of sanatoria. In the following counties the Glackin Law has been adopted by a referendum vote. In fifteen of these counties sanatoria have been built. In the others, with few exceptions, there is a fund for the care and treatment of the tuberculous:

Dr. Thomas H. Leonard.

Adams	Crawford	Knox	Menard	Shelby
Alexander	DeKalb	LaSalle*	Montgomery	Stephenson
Boone	DeWitt	Lee	Morgan°	Tazewell*
Bureau	Douglas	Livingston*	Ogle	Vermilion
Champaign*	Fulton	Logan	Piatt	Whiteside
Christian	Grundy	McDonough*	Pike	Will*
Clark	Henry	McLean*	Randolph	Winnebago*
Clay	Jackson	Macon*	Rock Island*	Woodford*
Coles	Jefferson	Madison*	Sangamon	
Cook*	Kane*	Marion	Scott	

* Counties having sanatoria.

This being the case it has been unnecessary for the State Department of Public Health to maintain a strong organization for service in that particular field.

Dr. George Thomas Palmer, assistant director of the State Department of Public Health from 1917 to 1921 acted as chief of the division during that period. In August 1921, Dr. Palmer was succeeded in his dual capacity by Dr. Thomas H. Leonard who has continued to date in the position.

Division of Sanitary Engineering.

Previous to the establishment of the division of sanitary engineering, the State Board of Health carried on occasionally in a limited way some of the phases of public health work which are now handled by the sanitary engineering divisions of modern health departments. These activities relating to sanitary engineering were carried on almost entirely by engaging temporary outside assistance or by cooperative arrangement with State or outside agencies.

In 1879 the State Board of Health gave some attention to the pollution of the Illinois River by the city of Chicago. In 1880 the Board had stream-pollution investigations made at Chicago, Peoria, Springfield, Quincy, Rock Island, and Rockford. The records indicate that in 1883 some further sanitary inspections of streams were made. The legislature in 1885 appropriated a contingent fund to engage services of analysts, observers, and other assistants for examination of water supplies and polluted streams in the State. In 1888 an analytical study was made of the quality of the larger rivers in Illinois that were more or less polluted, the samples being collected over a period of six months. In 1900 engineers, not regular employees of the Board, were engaged to investigate the contamination of Mississippi River at Chester by sewage from the Southern Illinois Penitentiary.

Paul Hansen.

The need for sanitary water, sewage, and stream-pollution surveys apparently becoming more and more realized and the procedure of engaging part-time occasional outside assistance proving not sufficient, the Board adopted a resolution in 1894 favoring an appropriation by the legislature of money to the University of Illinois for making analyses of samples of water and polluted streams at the laboratories of the University. As a result such analytical studies were undertaken at the University in 1895 under the supervision of Prof. Arthur William Palmer. The appropriation to the University at that time for additions and improvements to the chemical laboratory was $5,000. The chemical studies of the waters of Illinois at the University possibly not fully meeting the needs of the State Board of Health, the Board in 1899 adopted a resolution preliminary to the engagement of the services of Prof. John H. Long, of Northwestern University Medical School and Jacob A. Harmon, a civil engineer of Peoria, to investigate the quality of the waters of Illinois River. Previous to this time the Board had some stream-pollution studies made by Professor Long and the results of these investigations of the Illinois River are included in a report of the Board issued in 1901 entitled "*Sanitary Investigations of the Illinois River and Tributaries*".

The decision of the United States Supreme Court in favor of the State of Illinois and the Sanitary District of Chicago in the action brought by the state of Missouri because of the discharge of sewage from Chicago into a tributary of Mississippi River was handed down on February 19, 1906. The report and studies made by Professor Long and his associates at the request of and by arrangement with the State Board of Health were major items of evidence in this litigation and the favorable outcome of the State of Illinois, was based to quite an extent upon these investigations.

Harry F. Ferguson.

In a further effort to increase the extent and value of chemical studies of waters and streams of Illinois, the Board in 1906 entered into a cooperative agreement with the State Water Survey located at the University, and which had developed into a separate unit although administered by the University trustees since the chemical studies of the waters of Illinois were started in 1895.

Sanitary Engineering Bureau Established.

By 1915 the need of full-time systematic engineering activities became so apparent that the legislature in that year appropriated funds for the establishment of a sanitary engineering bureau under the State Board of Health. An integral part of modern public health activities is sanitation, especially that relating to water supply, sewerage, and stream pollution, and experience apparently had shown that full efficiency and effectiveness could not be obtained, especially to meet increasing demands caused by the increase in population in the State, by the engagement of outside occasional services and cooperative agreements with other agencies located miles away from the Board headquarters.

The first appropriations for the sanitary engineering bureau provided for a chief engineer, an assistant engineer for field studies, an assistant engineer for a water and sewage laboratory, and a stenographer. Paul Hansen was appointed by the Board of Health upon the recommendation

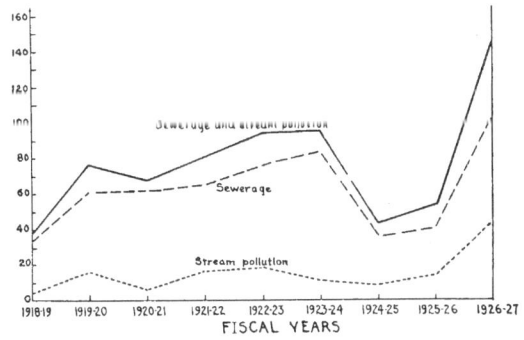

Fig. 13. Number investigations made by sanitary engineer relative to existing and proposed sewerage installations and stream pollution.

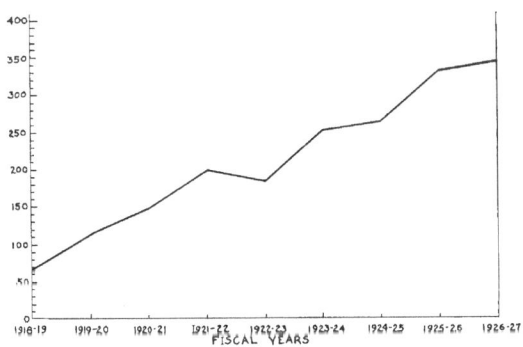

Fig. 14. Number of investigations made by sanitary engineers of existing and proposed public water supplies by fiscal years.

224   PUBLIC HEALTH ADMINISTRATION

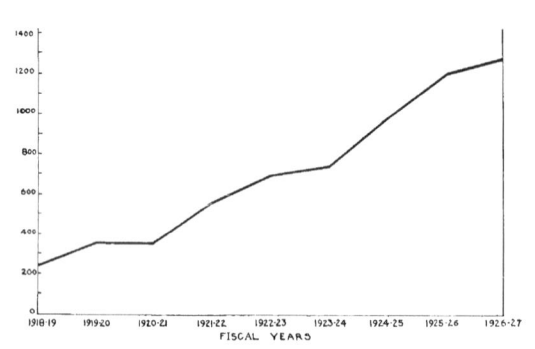

Fig. 15. Number of inspections made by sanitary engineers for all purposes by fiscal years since July 1, 1918.

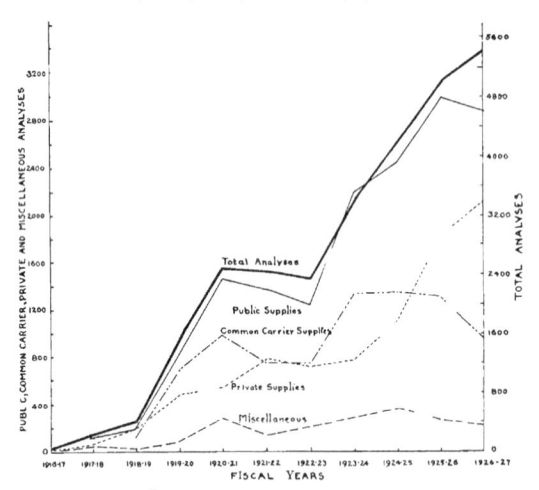

Fig. 16. Number of water analyses.

of Dr. C. St. Clair Drake to serve as chief engineer to organize the new bureau and later Mr. Hansen agreed to continue in that position and the appointment was confirmed by the civil service commission after holding an examination. He resigned in 1920 and was succeeded on May 15 of that year by Harry F. Ferguson, then principal assistant engineer, who has continued as chief sanitary engineer to date.

That the establishment of a sanitary engineering bureau by the 1915 legislature was a sound step and the sanitary engineering activities met a need throughout the State is perhaps best evidenced by the fact that the following legislatures have from time to time increased the appropriations for that division so that on July 1, 1927 the positions in the division had increased from three engineers and one stenographer to seven engineers, three bacteriologists and chemists, one supervisor of rural sanitation, two milk sanitarians, six clerks and stenographers, and four other assistants.

Previous to the adoption of the Civil Administrative Code in 1917, the activities of the bureau of engineering were regulated by the law creating the State Board of Health as amended and especially that portion of the law which provided that the State Board of Health shall have "general supervision of the interests of the health and lives of the citizens of the State" and "authority to make such rules and regulations and such sanitary investigations as they may from time to time deem necessary for the preservation and improvement of the public health".

In accordance with this law the Board in 1916 adopted the following rules and regulations relative to water and sewerage installations:

"(1.) No municipality, district, corporation, company, institution, person or persons, shall install or enter into contract for installing, waterworks or sewers to serve more than 25 persons until complete plans and specifications fully describing such waterworks or sewers have been submitted to and received the written approval of the State Board of Health and thereafter such plans and specifications must be substantially adhered to unless deviations are submitted to and receive the written approval of the State Board of Health.

"(2.) No municipality, district, corporation, company, institution, person or persons, shall make or enter into contract for making, any additions to, or changes or alterations, in any existing waterworks serving more than 25 persons, when such additions, changes, or alterations involve the source of supply or means for collecting, storing or treating the water, until complete plans and specifications fully describing proposed additions, changes or alterations have been submitted to and received the written approval of the State Board of Health and thereafter such plans and specifications must be substantially adhered to unless deviations are submitted to and receive the written approval of the State Board of Health.

"(3.) No municipality, district, corporation, company, institution, persons or person, shall make or enter into contract for making, alterations or changes in or additions to any existing sewers or existing sewage treatment works, serving more than 25 persons, until complete plans and specifications fully describing such alterations, changes or additions have been submitted to and received the written approval of the State Board of Health and thereafter such plans and specifications must be substantially adhered to unless deviations are submitted to and receive the written approval of the State Board of Health.

"(4) Any municipality, district, corporation, company, institution, person or persons, owning or operating a water purification works or sewage treatment works shall submit to the State Board of Health monthly records showing clearly the character of effluents produced.

"(5.) No municipality, district, corporation, company, institution, person or persons, shall offer lots for sale in any subdivision, unless within the boundaries of an area incorporated as a municipality or sanitary district, until complete plans and specifications for sewerage, drainage and water supply, have been submitted to and received the written approval of the State Board of Health and thereafter such plans and specifications shall be substantially adhered to unless deviations are submitted to and receive the written approval of the State Board of Health.

"(6.) No natural ice shall be furnished or vended to the public for domestic purposes until the source of the ice supply has received the written approval of the State Board of Health, which approval is revocable upon evidence being presented or discovered of undue contamination entering the source."

The Civil Administrative Code placed upon the Department of Public Health all of the duties and powers of former boards of health insofar as the sanitary engineering activities were concerned, and in addition provided more definite duties relative to water-supply and sewerage installations by providing that the Department of Public Health shall have authority as follows:

"To act in an advisory capacity relative to public water supplies, water-purification works, sewerage systems, and sewage-treatment works, and to exercise supervision over nuisances growing out of the operation of such water and sewage works, and to make, promulgate, and enforce rules and regulations relating to such nuisances:

"To maintain chemical and biological laboratories, to make examinations of milk, water, sewage, wastes, and other substances as may be deemed necessary for the protection of the people of the State".

The water supply and sewerage rules adopted in 1916 have never formally been repealed, but they are practically void in view of the provisions of the Civil Administrative Act of 1917. In accordance with that Act rules and regulations relating to sewage nuisances have been adopted.

In 1922 the Department of Public Health adopted a Railway Sanitary Code in conformance with a Standard Railway Sanitary Code prepared and recommended by the Conference of State and Territorial Health Officers in cooperation with the United States Public Health Service.

The legislature in 1925 enacted a law relating to milk-pasteurization plants and instructing the Department of Public Health to adopt and enforce minimum requirements for pasteurization plants in accordance with the law. These minimum requirements have been prepared and the work required by the law and the enforcement of the requirements have been carried on by the sanitary engineering division.

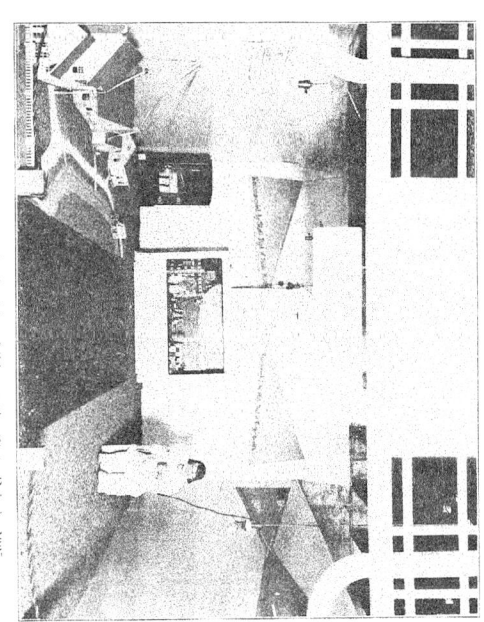

One of the many attractive health exhibits at the State Fair in 1925.

Principal Activities.

The following are the principal activities of the division of sanitary engineering:

1. Investigation and approval of proposed new or improved public water-supply projects and examination of and advice relative to existing public water supplies, including water-purification plants.

2. Investigation and approval of proposed new or improved public sewerage projects, including sewage-treatment plants, and examination of and advice relative to existing sewer systems including sewage-treatment plants.

3. Investigation of stream pollution.

4. Investigation of methods for the purification of water, sewage, and other liquid wastes.

5. Water and sewage laboratory service.

6. Examination and certification of water supplies for use on common carriers in cooperation with the United States Public Health Service.

7. Investigation and advice relative to rural sanitation including water supplies, sewage disposal, camps, summer resorts, fairgrounds, country schools, etc.

8. Examinations of and advice in regard to swimming pools and bathing beaches.

9. Investigate and report on the prevalence and control of mosquitoes, especially in those areas where malaria is a public health problem.

10. Investigate milk-pasteurization plants and issue certificates to those plants complying with the State law.

11. Advice relative to municipal plumbing ordinances.

12. Advice relative to local nuisances and insanitary conditions.

13. Investigation of diseases that may be water-borne, such as typhoid fever and enteritis, in cooperation with the division of communicable diseases.

14. Investigation of sanitary condition of school buildings.

15. Investigation of sites for tuberculosis sanatoria with special reference to water supply, sewage disposal, and drainage, as a basis for approval of such sites as required under the State law.

16. Studies of city waste collection and disposal and street cleaning.

17. Filtration and distribution of State House drinking-water supply.

18. Educational work by means of publications, addresses, exhibits, and correspondence.

The number of total investigations made by the staff of the division since statistical records were kept are graphically shown in Figures 13 and 14, and the number of investigations made relative to different subjects included in the divisional activities, are illustrated in Figures 15 to 18.

No attempt will be made to indicate any outstanding activities of the division during the twelve years that it has been functioning as a part of fifty years of public health work by the State of Illinois because some activities which may appear to be more important possibly are less important than some other apparently minor activities of the division if all the results obtained could be definitely measured. For example, the activities of the division during floods and tornadoes which have occurred in different parts of the State are more or less spectacular but the net result from the standpoint

PUBLIC HEALTH ADMINISTRATION 229

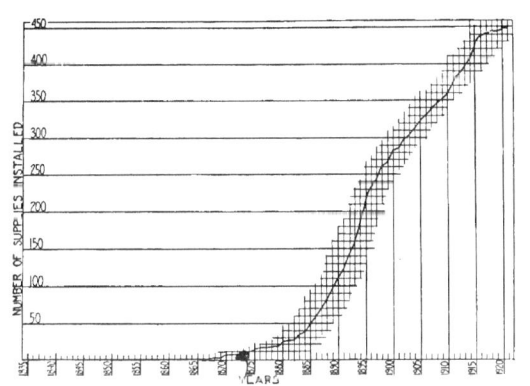

Fig. 17. Public water supplies installed by years in municipalities in Illinois.

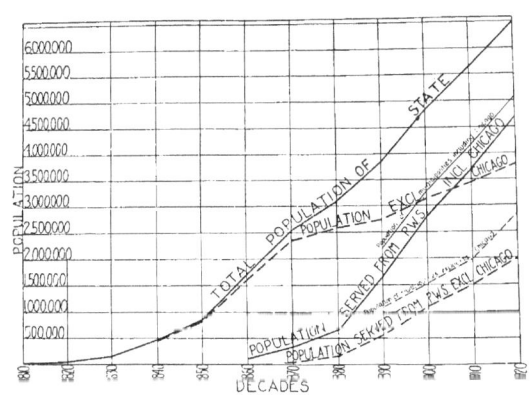

Fig. 18. Population served from public water supplies in Illinois.

of lowered morbidity from preventable diseases and better and more healthful conditions may be actually less than that resulting from routine work and what might be termed by some as "minor activities" such as bringing about the abandonment of cross-connections between polluted and safe water supplies here and there as they are found, the routine checks on the quality of public water supplies and sanitary disposal of sewage, advice and assistance relative to rural sanitation, routine inspections of milk plants, and other features making up the daily activities of a modern sanitary engineering division.

The installation of public water supplies in municipalities and the populations served from such supplies during the early period compared with the later decades are an index of the advance in sanitation and the civil and sanitary engineering activities throughout the State during the period since and even previous to the establishment of the Board of Health.

In a chronological record or history of public health activities accompanying this treatise on fifty years of public health in Illinois some of the activities of the division of sanitary engineering are included, but as stated above the net result in the decrease in the morbidity and mortality rates from certain diseases and the general improvement in public health may not be as great from some of these items as from the routine activities which have not been listed but which would be too numerous to include in a chronological record of that kind.

Division of Vital Statistics.

The registration of births and deaths was from the very beginning an important factor in the agitation for State public health service. It has, therefore, been a matter of concern to the State health officials since the creation of the State Board of Health in 1877.

Probably no other problem has been so complex and puzzling and few things in the whole history of public health service have been the object of so much legislation.

How to get complete and prompt returns of births and deaths has been the perpetual question that pursued the executive officer of the State health service year in and year out. Some made valiant attempts to collect and compile the statistics while others appear to have regarded the task as too great to justify the expenditure of efforts necessary to its achievement and let it go at that.

W. H. Hoyt.

Early Efforts to Collect Records of Births and Deaths.

Thus at the very beginning in 1877 an honest effort was made to collect vital statistics. In December of that year forms were prepared by the State Board of Health and sent out to county clerks. The law required all certificates of births and deaths to be filed with the county clerks whose duty it was to make summaries of their records and forward them to the State Board of Health on forms supplied for that purpose.

The whole business was new so that it required some little time to get the procedure started with any degree of satisfaction. The indomitable and indefatigable Rauch, who was secretary of the Board for most of this early period, kept steadfastly at the job, however, until he was able to get sufficient returns in 1881 to publish the data collected for that year. The tables list death statistics for 93 of the 102 counties for 1881 and for 78 in both 1882 and 1883. There were 86 counties listed in the tables for 1884 while the returns for 1885 and 1886 presumably represented registration from all of the counties. Birth reports were published for some of these years.

Orin Dilly.

But registration was far from complete during any of this time. In 1885 the secretary of the State Board of Health estimated the deficiency in birth registration was about 48 per cent and that for deaths about 31.

After 1886 no birth or mortality statistics were prepared for publication until 1902. In the meantime there seems to have developed the attitude that it was practically impossible to get reliable data under the law and little time was lost in trying. Dr. Rauch recognizing the weakness in the law, reported to the Board in 1886 that he had been too busy with other matters to engineer an amendment or a new law through the legislature.

At the quarterly meeting of the State Board of Health in January, 1899 the secretary, Dr. Egan, reported:

"Under the law now in force, all physicians and accouchers are required, under penalty of ten dollars to be recovered in any court of competent jurisdiction in the State, at suit *of the County Clerk*, to report to said clerks all births and deaths which may come under their supervision. The County Clerks are required also to report to the Board all births and deaths reported to them. This system of collecting statistics is so imperfect as to make the returns of no practical value. The law has been inoperative for over ten years. When an attempt was made to enforce it, it was found that very few physicians complied with the statutes, and that this Board has no power to compel them to do so."

There were two principal factors that operated against satisfactory registration of vital statistics during all of these years. One was an inadequate law and the other was lack of clerical machinery

Work Lags.

Thus the opening of the nineteenth century found both the system and the registration of vital statistics in a rather chaotic condition. About that time matters began to take on a brighter aspect. Dr. Egan, secretary of the State Board of Health, managed to get a new law enacted in 1901. It required burial permits from county or town clerks, according to the type of government organization in the counties. It also provided a fee of 25 cents each to go to the person making the report to the local registrar. The burial permit feature was the backbone of the system and its enforcement would have the desired results.

About this time Dr. Egan also employed W. H. Hoyt to have charge of the vital statistic work of the Board. In 1905 an item for "registrar of vital statistics" appeared in the appropriation law and from that time forward provision was regularly made for a registrar.

Dr. Egan went further. He sent Mr. Hoyt to study the vital statistics system employed by the State Board of Health in Michigan, which was considered very good. As a result of this study a satisfactory method of handling the statistics was introduced in Illinois.

The 1901 law operated with a fair degree of satisfaction to the State Board of Health but it provoked formidable opposition in the counties not under township organization where burial permits could be issued only by county clerks. That often entailed considerable hardship and delay in connection with funerals so that a general political movement to repeal the law entirely was set in motion. This movement was strong enough to force a revision so a new law was enacted, one drafted by the secretary of the State Board of Health.

Sheldon L. Howard.

This law provided for birth reports to be made direct to county clerks, except in cities of 50,000 or more where they should go to the health commissioner, and for deaths to be reported direct to the State Board of Health except in municipalities enforcing a burial permit ordinance. A fee of 25 cents each was paid to the one making the report.

Under this law statistics were complete enough to justify compilations and reports for the years 1902 to 1913 inclusive.

The last law affecting vital statistics, the one now operating and known as the model vital statistics law, was enacted in 1915 after having failed in two preceding attempts. It provides for a system of local registrars located at convenient places in all parts of the State. Fees of 25 cents each are paid to the local registrars while physicians and others are required to make reports as a part of their professional duty to society.

Up until July, 1902 vital statistics received by the State Board of Health were summaries compiled by county clerks on forms sent out by the Board. Such analysis, recording and filing as was possible from these records was a relatively simple matter and required a relatively small amount of clerical work.

On August 28, 1902, a communication was directed to the county clerks making a change. It requested the county clerks to send the original certificates to the State Board of Health specifying that this would be construed as fulfilling the requirements of the law. This change was effective July 1, 1902.

Manifestly the new method made necessary a much larger amount of clerical work on the part of the State Board of Health and required some one to supervise the classification, compiling and recording of the certificates. Thus a registrar of vital statistics was employed. He began to function in the spring of 1903. The man chosen for this work was W. H. Hoyt who was given charge of the bacteriologic laboratory started in 1904 and was referred to in the dual capacity of registrar and bacteriologist in the minutes of the Board for July 1904.

Mr. Hoyt continued as registrar of vital statistics until May 15, 1910 when he was succeeded by Dr. C. C. Ellis who was followed in turn on March 1, 1911, by Dr. T. H. D. Griffitts. He occupied the position until 1915 when Orrin Dilly took over the work. Mr. Dilly was succeeded in 1917 by Sheldon L. Howard who has continued to date as registrar of vital statistics.

Thus it is seen that the work of the division of vital statistics is as old as the State public health service itself. About 1903 it became sufficiently systematized and voluminous enough to require a special corps of workers under the supervision of a registrar. Then in 1915 it became an important unit of the original organization plan of the state health service and received a special appropriation of $5500 per year as the bureau of vital statistics. That amount provided for a registrar and four clerks.

Improvement After New Law Was Passed

The bureau of vital statistics became the division of vital statistics in 1917 with the creation of the State Department of Public Health and fared well in the appropriations. A registrar, and assistant registrar and five clerks were provided with $12,800 per year as total salaries. This continued to grow until 1927 found the division with a staff of 26, including the registrar, assistant registrar, medical assistant, two field agents and clerical staff.

Statistics that were not complete and never so regarded but which were complete enough to show the general trend of health conditions were collected, compiled and published for the years of 1902 to 1913 inclusive. After that a period of confusion and uncertainty set in, due to the death of the secretary of the State Board of Health in March, 1913, and the change in the vital statistics law in 1915. Accordingly no compilations were made for the intervening years between 1913 and 1916. Summary statistics for births and deaths were made up for 1916 and 1917 but no analyses were made.

Illinois Admitted Into Registration Area.

By 1918 the registration system was working satisfactorily enough to justify the federal bureau of the census to accept Illinois into the U. S. registration area for deaths, a minimum of 90 per cent completeness being required for that purpose.

It was slower for births but after a long drawn out campaign the State was admitted to the U. S. birth registration area in 1922.

Detailed statistics are available from the mortality reports of the bureau of the census for 1918 and subsequent years. The division has published detailed statistics of its own since 1921. Infant mortality rates have been published by the division annually since 1921 and the tables include figures for 1920. The federal reports include these figures for 1922 and subsequent years.

Division of Child Hygiene and Public Health Nursing.

This division was officially created by the legislature in 1919 but like several of the others it had come into existence prior to that time. An effort had been made to secure an appropriation for work of that type in 1915, but it failed in the General Assembly. In 1917 an item providing for a chief of a division of child hygiene and public health nursing passed the legislature but was vetoed by the Governor.

Necessity, however, was the governing factor in bringing together a staff that really began child hygiene and nursing work as early as 1916. In the late summer of that year an epidemic of infantile paralysis appeared in the State and caused the State Board of Health to begin work that was calculated to relieve the children affected. A recurrence of the epidemic in 1917 led to the definite

Dr. C. W. East.

creation of a division of child hygiene and public health nursing with Dr. C. W. East as chief and two nurses on the staff, all of whom were borrowed from the division of communicable diseases.

This arrangement continued until July 1, 1919, when an appropriation of $22,480 for salaries and wages for two years became available for the division. In 1921 an equal sum was appropriated to meet the salaries and wages of the division during the ensuing two years, in 1923 there was granted $45,600 and in 1925, the sum of $47,640. The appropriation in 1927 for salaries and wages in the division for the ensuing biennium was $123,820 and provided for a staff of four physicians, sixteen nurses, one dentist, one dietist and three clerks.

The infantile paralysis work which precipitated the creation of the division involved the establishment of clinics at more than a score of points in the State. The staff traveled from one place to another, holding clinics weekly or less often as circumstances permitted, and giving such aid as could be provided for cripples of all kinds and particularly the victims of poliomyelitis. This work soon began to necessitate considerable curative or corrective service.

Demands for crippled children's work increased instead of diminishing after the epidemic subsided and formed a major part of the work of the division until February 1, 1924, when it was taken over by the Illinois Crippled Children's Society, a voluntary organization.

The purposes of the division of child hygiene as set forth in the organization scheme of the Department are to combat the high mortality among children by promoting child health service in the various communities throughout the State, establishing infant welfare stations and visiting nurse service; to promote medical inspection of school children; to disseminate information and advice on the care of children and investigate local conditions affecting child life. Also, to have general supervision of the nursing service maintained by communities and by extra-governmental agencies; to investigate orphanages, homes and hospitals for children; to assist in the management of baby health conferences, baby week programs, etc., and to supervise the practice of midwives with special reference to the prevention of blindness from infection of the eyes of the newborn.

Dr. C. W. East who had served the State Board of Health in the capacity of district health officer and as acting chief of the division of tuberculosis initiated the child hygiene work and served as the chief of the division until February, 1924. Dr. R. C. Cook was acting chief from February to July 15 when Dr. Edith B. Lowry was appointed temporarily to the position. In October, 1925, Dr. Grace S. Wightman of Chicago became chief of the division as a result of the civil service examination held for the purpose of fill-

Nursing Service.

In 1919 a state supervisor of public health nurses was first employed. Two more cities were added to the list of cities having a public health nursing service. A movement for the standardization of public health nursing service was initiated in 1920. This initial step took the form of an agreement between State agencies and private and local governmental agencies employing public health nurses.

By this time the division had influenced and assisted nine cities in establishing well organized public health nursing services. In addition to this a large number of visits were made by the different members of the division to nursing associations for demonstrations and instructions. It was not easy to measure specifically the value of this service but face to face contact and personal service was found to be the very strongest agency available in building up the public health throughout the State.

In 1922 the public health nurses in the State were organized into district associations through the activity of the State supervising nurse. Twelve new communities were influenced to establish public nursing services.

The next year a survey of public health service in the State was carried out and a successful campaign for enlarging this service was conducted. Every city in Illinois with 8,000 or more population with the exception of two had some form of active nursing service in the public schools in 1923.

In 1924 the State was divided into four public health nursing districts and a State nurse assigned to each. The policy of the Department was that the State nurses should visit the counties in turn in a consulting and advisory capacity. Realizing that the various communities had somewhat different problems, the division attempted to help select and establish the particular service best suited to the local needs.

All public health nurses were encouraged to communicate freely with the Department relative to local problems, so that every possible assistance might be rendered. That year twenty-two counties had no public health nursing service of any character. A survey in 1927 showed that the number of counties with public health nursing service totalled 73, while 60 counties had rural public health nursing service. The total number of public health nurses in the State was 418.

Better Baby Conferences.

The first better baby conference held by the State Board of Health was in 1915, when 250 children were examined. With the inauguration of the division this work naturally fell under its supervision.

In 1921 the holding of better baby conferences, which had previously been confined largely to the State fair was extended to include any point in the State where demands existed. Physicians and nurses assisted in thirteen such conferences in as many counties during that year.

The next few years showed a rapid development of this activity. In 1922 a physician from the division organized and directed 65 better baby conferences in the State with a total of 7,647 children examined. In 1923 seventy-nine conferences were held at which 7,851 children were examined.

In a number of ways the 1926 conference at the State Fair differed from those held in former years. In order to do both careful and painstak-

The State Fair Better Baby Conference in action—1925.

ing work the number of children entering it was definitely limited. The Illinois State Medical Society cooperated in selecting a pediatrician who acted as consultant to mothers whose babies presented defects and faulty habits about which they should be especially advised. A total of 613 children were examined against 1,485 in 1925. The limitation of numbers did not appear to produce the advantages anticipated, however, so that in 1927 the conference was again thrown open to as many as desired to come.

The opportunity for research and investigation was unexcelled in connection with these conferences. In order to determine the relative health conditions prevailing among rural and urban children an analysis was made in 1923 of the baby conference records which gave sufficient detail to be classified. As a result of this undertaking it was found that a group of 3,193 rural pre-school-age children had a total of 6,800 significant physical defects, while a group of 2,130 city children of similar age had a total of only 3,488 defects. This indicates that children in rural areas have greater need for an extension of the public health service than do their city cousins.

Maternity and Infant Hygiene Service.

Although the State of Illinois did not accept the provision of the Shepherd-Towner Act, maternity and infant hygiene services were not neglected. In 1921 a special maternity and infant hygiene program involving the promotion of public health nursing service and infant welfare stations was inaugurated. In 1923 four new infant welfare stations were opened, one at Wilmington, one at Steger, and two at Freeport, one of the latter was for white children and the other for colored. A series of nine prenatal letters were prepared covering the important phases of prenatal care, and sent to any prospective mothers in the State who made application or were listed for the series.

The first "Young Mother's Club" was formed at St. Charles and the plan is to form similar clubs in every county in the State. The object of these clubs is to bring to young mothers the very best scientific information available on the subject of child care and to stimulate frequent examination of babies by the family physician.

Eight additional young mother's clubs were organized the same year; two at Diquoin, two at Mounds and others at Hamilton, Dallas City and Bowen.

Medical Examination of School Children.

The medical examination of school children was a logical sequence of the work done at the better baby conferences. In 1921 a uniform "school record card" for this work was adopted. The next year members of the staff assisted with the medical examination of the 50,000 rural school children, while the number in 1923 reached 60,000.

In 1925, the uniform record card was somewhat modified to assist in obtaining the correction of defects. This class room health card was designed to meet the request of teachers for a record to be left in the school room and also to impress upon the children the importance of obtaining and maintaining a definite standard. An especially designed button having on it "Illinois Health 1925" was presented to the children coming up to the standard requirements.

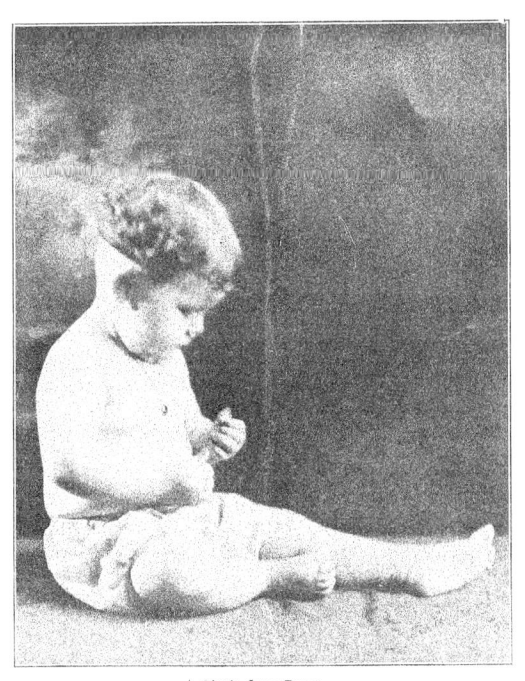

Gloria June Esper,
The first of the two children who were each given a one hundred per cent perfection rating at the Illinois State Fair. Examined in 1923.

Because of a gap between the better baby conferences and the examination of school children, in 1925 the pre-school examination of children was inaugurated.

A pre-school examination card was adopted after careful consideration by a committee from the Illinois State Medical Society, Illinois State Dental Society, Illinois Federation of Women's Clubs and representatives from the division. During the year 1926 more than 40,000 cards were requested by public health nurses, club women and parent-teacher association groups.

A five year pre-school health campaign was undertaken jointly by the Illinois Federation of Women's Clubs, Illinois State Medical Society, Illinois State Dental Society and the Illinois State Department of Public Health. Up to date members of the division have assisted with the examination of over 7,000 pre-school age children and about 10,000 school children.

Educational Activities.

The educational activities of the division of child hygiene and public health nursing have been numerous and diverse. Very early in its history, the division prepared literature on a variety of subjects much of which is still being distributed after many reprintings and revision.

Demonstration work naturally centered around the public health exhibits and in connection with special health programs in local communities. At the State fair in 1918 a total of 250 consultations were given to mothers by the chief of the division and the medical assistant and in 1923 this number reached 900. Similar consultation work was conducted at practically every fair and exposition where better baby conferences were held.

A very important and rather new activity was the inauguration in 1927 of a breast-feeding demonstration in McLean County. This was done under the auspices and with the full cooperation of the McLean County Medical Society and is intended to function for two years. A nurse from the division especially trained for the work was assigned to work in the county.

Lectures assumed a large place in the educational work. Either with or without moving picture reels and lantern slides, members of the division were in great demand not only in connection with fairs and expositions but at meetings of women's clubs, parent-teacher organizations and the like. The subjects included in these lectures covered a wide range, such as child hygiene and nursing problems and allied subjects such as the model milk ordinance and the toxin-antitoxin campaign.

Courses of instruction to nurses and teachers seemed to be especially popular. An eight weeks course for graduate nurses in community nursing service was conducted in 1918.

James Robert Craycroft,
The second of the two children who were considered perfect in physical development at the Illinois State Fair. Examined 1924.

In 1925 an infant mortality survey was made in the counties reporting an infant death rate for 1923 of 100 or more. There were nine such counties. Personal visits or addresses at county medical society meetings afforded the opportunity to present the matter to physicians, women's clubs, parent-teacher associations, etc.

A goitre survey was made during 1927 in the Western Illinois University at Normal, Illinois; also at Decatur among both high school and grade school pupils. In this survey over 3,000 pupils were examined.

A child hygiene committee consisting of Dr. Harold N. Smith, Chairman, representing the Illinois State Dental Society, Dr. B. V. McClanahan, Galesburg, representing the Illinois State Medical Society, Dr. Lena K. Sadler, Illinois Federation of Women's Clubs and Mrs. Blanche Bulig, the council of Illinois Parent-Teacher Associations met with the chief of the division once every month to discuss ways and means, policies, cooperative plans and other important measures related to child health needs in Illinois. Among the specific accomplishments of this committee was its work in promoting the toxin-antitoxin campaign.

The chairman of the educational committee of the Illinois State Medical Society sent letters of information to the officers of the county medical societies. The Dental Society through letters and its official journals urged the cooperation of dentists in distributing literature. The president of the parent-teacher association sent out over 700 letters to officers of her organization asking their help in distributing 80,000 circulars on toxin-antitoxin to the membership.

The child welfare chairman of the federated clubs wrote letters to the child welfare chairmen of the 750 component clubs, outlining the plans of the State Department for the toxin-antitoxin campaign and placing 80,000 educational leaflets for distribution to parents of young children.

Other Activities.

In 1923 practical demonstrations in oral hygiene were carried out in four of the largest cities in the State, namely Mattoon, Decatur, Elgin and Springfield by a federal field service unit working at the request of the State Department of Public Health. The unit consisted of Major Butler (who died during his stay in Mattoon) and Miss Verna Thornhill. From 200 to 300 children were examined in each city.

In connection with these demonstrations the staff of the dental unit carried out a very definite educational program in the schools and gave talks on mouth hygiene before organizations wherever opportunity was presented.

An important expansion of the activities of the division in 1926 was the creation of a section on dental hygiene. This new undertaking was financed for one year by the Illinois State and the Chicago Dental Societies. The major emphasis of the program was educational, aiming at prevention of dental disease through fundamental requirements for securing the development of hard, durable teeth. The State Dental Society through letters and its official journal urged the cooperation of dentists in distributing literature. The 1927 General Assembly provided for taking over this work by the State.

Among the many miscellaneous activities of the division was the rendering of emergency nursing service in the area devastated by the tornado in Murphysboro and West Frankfort in 1925. Nurses were stationed in this territory for months and assisted in the prevention of epidemics, school inspections and made home visits.

Division of Surveys and Rural Hygiene.

The division of surveys and rural hygiene came into being in 1917 when the sanitary zones established around military posts created a demand for sanitary surveys of an intensive character. Its functions included the making of house to house sanitary studies of communities that expressed a desire for that sort of research as a preliminary step toward improving local health conditions. Such studies were carried on in Rockford, Freeport, Waukegan, East St. Louis, Alton, Moline, and Quincy in the order named, the first being done in 1917 and the last in 1921. The surveys were exhaustive in character requiring from four to six months in one community.

Paul L. Skoog.

Personnel attached to the division was never large. Sometimes the division chief had an assistant and sometimes not. He always had a stenographer. Field work was accomplished on a cooperative plan, the local community providing a corps of five to ten investigators.

Paul L. Skoog had charge of the division from the time it was created until March, 1920. From that time until the division lost its identity, being fused with the division of sanitary engineering in the spring of 1921, B. K. Richardson acted as its chief.

Laboratory Work.

The year 1877 has a double significance for Illinois. When the State Board of Health was established one of the first undertakings was the laboratory examination of water supplies,—an activity that later grew into the modern laboratory. The same year at Urbana Prof. Thomas J. Burrill introduced into his course of botany at the University of Illinois the study of bacteria. Prof. Burrill was the first teacher in the United States to officially recognize bacteriology by including it in a college course and thus initiate what was to develop into an entirely new science having a profound influence on public health practice.

Prof. Thomas J. Burrill.

The foundation of public health laboratory work was laid by Pasteur in France in the period of 1865 to 1870, when he demonstrated the germ theory of disease. In England Lister began his studies on aseptic surgery in 1867 transforming surgical methods "from a purgatory to a paradise". In 1875 Koch first grew the anthrax bacillus in pure culture while other investigators were working with other diseases. In 1881 Koch discovered the poured plate method of isolating bacteria, following which in rapid succession came the demonstration of the bacilli of tuberculosis (1882), Asiatic cholera (1883), diphtheria, tetanus and better recognition of the typhoid bacillus (1884) followed by many others.

Development in the United States was not rapid at first. In 1876, the year before the founding of the Illinois State Board of Health, Bowditch published a *Centennial Survey of the State of Public Hygiene in America* in which no mention of bacteria was made and but one reference to the germ theory of disease which was in connection with yellow fever. Although Burrill began teaching his students about bacteria in 1877, it was apparently not until 1884 that the term "bacteriology" was coined. In 1884 and 1885, several colleges and universities began teaching the new science as a separate course.

The first municipal public health laboratoty was opened in 1888 in Providence, R. I. but for several years this devoted itself entirely to the study of water supplies. Credit for the first modern municipal diagnostic laboratory, therefore, goes to New York City in 1893, followed closely by the laboratory of the Chicago health department in 1894. The first state public health laboratory was that of Rhode Island established the same year.

Laboratory Work by Illinois State Board of Health.

The history of laboratory work of the Illinois State Board of Health begins with the establishment of the Board. In 1877, the financial statement of expenditures included an item of $19.85 for collecting water samples which were submitted for analysis to Prof. H. A. Weber, chemist of the Industrial University of Champaign. In 1880 the records of the Board mention the investigation of water supplies at Chicago, Springfield, Peoria, Quincy, Rock Island and Rockford. In 1883 the legislature appropriated a contingent fund to secure the services of analysts, observers and other assistants for examination of water supplies. The same year a systematic observation of the varying character of the water supply of Chicago was made under the direction of the Board. Chemical examinations were made weekly by Dr. John H. Long, Professor of Chemistry, Northwestern University Medical School. For the next fifteen years Prof. Long continued to analyze water at intervals for the State Board of Health, culminating in the study in 1899 and 1900 in connection with the Chicago Drainage Canal. Dr. F. Robert Zeit, Professor of Bacteriology and Dr. Gustav Früterrer, Professor of Pathology, at the Northwestern University Medical School also took part in this investigation.

Dr. Walter G. Bain.

Since no laboratory was available in the early days for the routine analysis of water samples, citizens were given a method whereby they could test their own sample. Report of committee on school hygiene minutes of State Board of Health, 1894.

"For examining water by a simple method take a sample of the water in a bottle cleansed by boiling water and provided with close fitting glass stopper, and a lump of loaf sugar and place it in summer temperature in the rays of the sun. If the water becomes turbid after a weeks exposure organic matter has decomposed and bacterial multiplied, the water cannot be regarded as wholesome and must be boiled or filtered."

On December 6, 1894 the committee on legislation of the State Board of Health Auxiliary Sanitary Association prepared a report on "needed legislation", and, among other recommendations, passed the following resolutions:

"Whereas, It is a fact of familiar knowledge, that certain diseases of great fatality are caused by elements of pollution in drinking water;
"Whereas, Such diseases are plainly preventable by proper attention to the purities of the sources of supply"

"Whereas, Such attention can be given with maximum efficiency and minimum expense by the University of Illinois, under the direction and authority of the State Board of Health; therefore, be it

"Resolved, that the Illinois State Board of Health and its Auxiliary Sanitary Association, earnestly recommend the legislature of the State to make suitable appropriation for the establishment and maintenance of work of this kind in the institution."

Also the following resolution

"Resolved, That any question as to purity of food and medicines, be also referred for analysis to the authorities of the University of Illinois under the direction of the State Board of Health."

While there is no record of any action taken on the latter resolution, the legislature in 1895 provided $5,000 to equip and maintain a water laboratory at the State University. Professor A. W. Palmer of the Department of chemistry was put in charge. The State Water Survey, as it was known, continued as the agent of the State Board of Health until 1915, working in close co-operation with the State and local boards of health. In the latter year the bureau of sanitation and engineering of the State Board of Health was formed, which took over the analysis of water for the Board although the Water Survey still continued sanitary examination for many local boards of health.

Food analysis appears in the records of State Board of Health in 1885, when on July 31, Prof. John H. Long reported the results of a chemical analysis of meat in a ptomaine poisoning outbreak causing the death of one person and the illness of thirty-seven others. He also made microscopical examination of sections of the meat, reporting the presence of bacteria.

Food laws had been on the statute books since 1817. In 1885 the legislature passed an additional act to protect the public from imposition in relation to canned or preserved foods. Since no laboratory facilities were available, the resolution quoted above in regard to analysis at the State University was recommended, but apparently not accepted by the legislature.

In the early nineteen hundreds the State food commission was organized with a laboratory in Chicago. In 1907 this Commission was reorganized with broad powers concerning food control and ample laboratory facilities. Co-operation between the food commission and State Board of Health was intended by Section 32 of the pure food law, which reads:

"The State Board of Health may submit to the superintendent or any of his assistants samples of food and drink for examination or analysis, and shall receive special reports showing the results of such examination or analysis".

The first mention of the examination of diphtheria cultures appears in the records of the Board for 1894. On the program of the State Board of Health Auxiliary Sanitary Association for Nov. 14, of that year, appeared the name of Dr. Adolph Gehrmann, bacteriologist of the newly formed laboratory of the Chicago health department. In his paper on the "Bacteriological Diagnosis of Diphtheria" he presented the feasibility of establishing in every city and town which has a board of health, facilities for the prompt and positive diagnosis of every case of diphtheria, at trifling expense. Demonstrations of his method were carried on in the laboratory of St. Johns' Hospital at Springfield.

In 1895, according to the Board minutes for January, 1896, measures had been adopted in the city laboratory in Chicago for the prompt and accurate diagnosis of all cases of diphtheria as soon as reported, and stations established where a supply of diphtheria antitoxin could be promptly obtained, free of charge to those unable to pay. This work was started in September of the preceding year.

The above incidences naturally stimulated a demand for laboratory assistance in the diagnosis of diphtheria in other communities, for the following item is found in the minutes mentioned above:

"Requests were received from Dixon and Grayville, Ill., for bacterial examination of membranes from typical cases, from diseases prevailing in those cities, with a view to settle the dispute as to their character. As is known, the Board has no facilities for making such diagnosis, but through the kindness of Dr. L. C. Taylor, Bacteriologist of St. John's Hospital, Springfield, your secretary was enabled to furnish the desired information."

Laboratories Established.

In 1904 the State diagnostic laboratory was organized, and in 1915, the first branch laboratory was established.

In 1917, when the division of sanitation and engineering, as it was then called organized as part of the State Department of Public Health, a water and sewage laboratory was created which has worked in close connection with the diagnostic laboratory, but as a separate unit.

The biological and research laboratories were established in 1919.

In 1921, the division of social hygiene obtained money for additional laboratory service, whereby the services of three technicians for venereal disease work in Chicago were made available to the Chicago health department.

Dr. Thomas G. Hull.

The laboratory work of the State Department of Public Health is divided as follows:

Division of diagnostic laboratories.
This includes two branch and eight diphtheria diagnostic laboratories.
Division of biological and research laboratories.
For the purposes of convenience the above are referred to as the division of laboratories and administered under the direction of the chief bacteriologist of the biological and research laboratories.
Division of engineering.
Water and sewage laboratory.
Division of social hygiene.
Three laboratory workers loaned to the Chicago health department.

Laws Under Which the Laboratories Operate.

The original Act of the legislature creating the State Board of Health in 1877, did not specify the maintainence of a laboratory. In 1907 the following was enacted by the legislature:

"The State Board of Health may establish and maintain a chemical and bacteriologic laboratory for the examination of public water supplies, and for the diagnosis of diphtheria, typhoid fever, tuberculosis, malarial fever and such other diseases as they may deem necessary for the protection of the public health."

When the Department of Public Health was formed in 1917, the Civil Administrative Code (Sec. 55, p. 29) included the following:

"To maintain chemical, bacteriological and biological laboratories, to make examinations of milk, water, sewage, wastes, and other substances, and to make such diagnosis of diseases as may be deemed necessary for the protection of the people of the State;
"To purchase and distribute free of charge to citizens of the State diphtheria antitoxin, typhoid vaccine, smallpox vaccine and other sera, vaccines and prophylactics such as are of recognized efficiency in the prevention and treatment of communicable diseases;
"To make investigations and inquiries with respect to the causes of disease, especially epidemics, and to investigate the causes of mortality and the effect of localities, and to make such other sanitary investigations as it may deem necessary for the preservation and improvement of the public health."

Biological and Research Laboratories.

One of the great developments in the application of bacteriology to public health occurred in the period of 1890 to 1895 with the production of diphtheria antitoxin. Attention was focused on the phenomenon of immunity obtained through the use of vaccines and serums in preventing and curing disease. Smallpox vaccine had been known since 1796, and its efficacy well established by the time the State Board of Health was formed. Its use was continually recommended by the Board and in 1889 there was an item of $500 to be expended for free vaccination against smallpox.

Reliable smallpox vaccine was not available at that time however. The science of bacteriology was barely in its infancy and the aseptic technic of Lister had not been adopted by veterinarians. Supervision of biological products was not attempted by the federal government till 1902. Hence much of the vaccine of that period was lacking in both potency and purity.

An interesting report depicting the conditions of the times was made by Dr. George Tullo to the State Board of Health concerning an inspection in June, 1894, of the Oak Park Vaccine Farm.

"The stable in which the heifers are kept during the incubation period is a common country stable for about twenty animals, presenting a low ceiling, unplastered and uncoated walls, with a few small windows and a wooden floor with two outlets for stable refuse. Special provisions for ventilation, flushing or disinfecting the stable are not to be seen there, but on the other hand, no accumulation of filth is noticeable. In other words, the broom seems to rule there exclusively.

"The operating room contains an apparatus of two planks and a strap for wedging in the animal while standing. In one corner was an ice box for storing lymph in the warm season; some pieces of soap were lying on a window and some rags hanging on a rope.

"In the storing room on one side a wooden box filled with clean points in frames; on the other side, an open place for drying lymph on the points and two paper boxes with vaccine points, one 6 bladed rusty knife for sacrification, one kitchen knife, a crystal vase, two hair brushes and a fruit jar. No disinfectants could be shown . . . . .

"Test of lymph just collected from two heifers showed by microscopical examination, broken down tissue, cell detritus, abundant micrococci, some solitary bacilli and a multitude of non-pathogenic micro-organisms frequently observed in the dejecta of the human body."

Included with this report were suggested rules for the application and sale of vaccine virus in Illinois, but no record appears of the Board adopting them.

The State Board of Health Auxiliary Sanitary Association in 1894 voted to "Ask the legislature to make provisions for the establishment of a vaccine farm in connection with the University of Champaign, under the controlling supervision of the State Board of Health."

By an act of the legislature, approved June 15, 1895, and in force July 1, 1895, it was made the duty of the trustees of the University to establish and manage "a laboratory in connection with the State University for the propagation of pure vaccine virus." It was provided in the Act that "the State Board of Health shall exercise supervision of the methods of propagation and certify to the purity of the products." An appropriation of $3000 was made to establish and maintain the laboratory. Dr. Thomas J. Burrill, Professor of Botany and Horticulture and Dr. Donal McIntosh, Professor of Veterinary Science, both took an active interest in the management of the plant.

On Oct. 30, 1896, Dr. Edgar P. Cook reported the results of an inspection of the plant to the State Board of Health. It read in part as follows:

"We indorse the following excerpt taken from a recent circular letter sent out from the laboratory; 'The laboratory, an isolated building to be used for no other purpose, has been provided and properly equipped to attain the purposes of the law. The most careful attention has been given to everything which can facilitate freedom from contamination. The ceilings, walls and floors of the operating and animal rooms are so finished that they can be frequently washed with hose and scrubbing brush and otherwise thoroughly disinfected. A crematory is provided for burning all litter and other organic matter. None but animals bred by the University, or of well known parentage, and selected with great care, will be used. Everything is being done to secure bacterial cleanliness and insure the preservation of the virus in a state of reliable purity.

"Careful examination verified the correctness of the above statement. The building had been constructed for and used by the Veterinary Department. Some necessary changes were made in its arrangements adapting it very well to the purpose of a vaccine laboratory. It is very pleasantly located in a grove nearly equi-distant from the University Hall and the buildings of the University Experimental Farm. In its exterior it has the appearance of a neat cottage being extended in one of its dimensions by that part of the structure that is the temporary home of the juvenile bovines in whose living laboratory is produced an animal immunizing agent—vaccine virus. The grounds, like all others about the University, are neatly kept. The interior of the building is pleasing. It is a model of neatness; with office, operating room and room adjoining, equipped with modern facilities for sterilizing, etc. The rooms for the heifers—we can not call them stalls—are convenient, well lighted and ventilated. The degree of cleanliness of all approaching very nearly that of one of our modern hospitals. The heifers selected are the best obtainable, and their care and treatment the best possible.

"Their preparation for inoculation, the operation, subsequent care and process of securing and preserving the lymph are as aseptically done as possible. We only need to add that Sec. 3 of the Act establishing the Laboratory reads: 'That the product of the Vaccine Laboratory shall be furnished all physicians and health officers within the State at the cost of propagation.'"

Apparently the vaccine laboratory was given up soon after this, for there is no further record of it in the minutes of the Board. The purchase of smallpox vaccine is noted from time to time, until in 1923 it was included in the specifications for biological products to be purchased under contract and distributed free of charge.

Diphtheria antitoxin, dating from 1890, came into general use after 1894. In 1895 the Chicago Health Department provided stations throughout the city where it could be obtained without delay, and where it was given free of charge to those unable to pay.

In 1905 the legislature amended the Act of 1877 creating a Board of Health, providing that "it shall be the duty of the Board of Health of the State of Illinois to appoint one agent in the county seat of each county in the State who shall have for distribution a supply of diphtheria antitoxin, certified to by said Board, etc." and further providing for the sale at a reasonable price or for the free distribution to poor persons on certificate of the overseers of the poor. In 1909 antitoxin was given free to all. Massachusetts was the only state up to this time which distributed diphtheria antitoxin in this manner.

In 1913, typhoid vaccine and silver nitrate were added to the free list to be distributed by agents. Smallpox vaccine in 1915, Schick test material in 1916, diphtheria toxin-antitoxin in 1921 and antirabic vaccine to poor persons in 1923, came in turn.

Provision for the free treatment of poor persons bitten by rabid animals was provided for as early as 1905, when the legislature passed "an act to provide for the treatment and care of poor persons afflicted with the disease called rabies." It was necessary for such persons to go to a hospital with which the State had a contract for the administration of anti-rabic material, the long trip often being inconvenient to the patient as well as expensive to the county in railroad fare and maintainence of patient and attendant. In 1923 the distribution of the vaccine to the local physician who could administer it to the patient at home was inaugurated and proved a great saving in expense to all concerned.

In 1919 the biological and research laboratories were established to manufacture the various biological products which heretofore had been purchased under contract and to investigate problems pertaining to public health work. Because of the lack of proper personnel and quarters, this idea has never been fully realized.

In 1920 quarters were obtained in the plant of the former hog cholera serum laboratory five miles from the State House and preparations made for the manufacture of typhoid vaccine and some other products. It was later decided however, to continue the purchase of these materials. The quarters there were used for a few years for Wassermann work, preparation of mailing containers, housing of animals and the like, but later given up because of inaccessibility.

RESEARCH WORK: The necessity for research has always been recognized. In the *Annual Report of the State Board of Health* in 1906 the following statement is made.

"It is the belief of the Board that, had the laboratory not accomplished, in its two years existence, anything more than it has done in placing aerial disinfection upon a sound and scientific basis, the time and money devoted to it would have been well spent."

Research activities have been somewhat limited due to inadequate personnel and quarters. It has been necessary to use the personnel of the biological and research laboratories largely for routine diagnostic work, devoting what little time was available to problems that could be picked up and dropped according to pressure of routine. In fact, a study made in 1921 by the Carnegie Foundation on research facilities of the State of Illinois recommended that all research activities of the State be confined to the State University, while other branches of the State government devote themselves strictly to routine activities. This of course, was impossible to put into practice.

252 PUBLIC HEALTH ADMINISTRATION

The first result of research was published in 1920, since which time eighteen other contributions have appeared, as shown by the following list:

INVESTIGATIONS CONDUCTED IN THE BIOLOGICAL AND RESEARCH LABORATORIES.

1920. The Sachs-Georgi Test for Syphilis.
Thomas G. Hull and Eva E. Faught.
Journal of Immunology, Nov. 1920, 5, 521-527.
This was an attempt to make more workable one of the early precipitation tests for syphilis.

1922. Anthrax in Shaving Brushes.
Thomas G. Hull.
Fifth Annual Report.
Illinois Department of Public Health, p. 190-191.
Ten cases of human anthrax led to a study of shaving brushes. While the more expensive brushes showed no contamination, many cheap brushes were found to be badly contaminated.

1922. A Study of the Typhoid Epidemic at Kewanee, Ill.
Thomas G. Hull and Kirby Henkes.
Illinois Health News, 1922, 8, 196-199.
Twenty-five cases of typhoid fever on one milk route led to the detection of a carrier on the farm.

1923. Preserved Cultures in the Widal Test.
Thomas G. Hull and Hugh Cassiday.
Abstracts of Bacteriology, 1923, 7, 3.
A report presented to the Society of American Bacteriologists to the effect that dead cultures were not as reliable as living typhoid cultures in the performance of the Widal test.

1923. The Widal Test in Tuberculosis.
Thomas G. Hull and Kirby Henkes.
Abstracts of Bacteriology, 1923, 7, 28.
A report presented to the Society of American Bacteriologists that persons afflicted with tuberculosis sometimes gave peculiar and characteristic reactions with the Widal test.

1923. Intracutaneous Reactions in Pertussis.
Thomas G. Hull and Ralph W. Nauss.
Journal of American Medical Association, June 23, 1923, 80, 1840-1841.
The intracutaneous injection of a dead culture of pertussis bacilli was found unreliable for the early diagnosis of whooping cough.

1923. Agglutination of the Flexner Dysentery Bacillus by the Blood Serum of Tuberculous Persons.
Thomas G. Hull and Kirby Henkes.
American Review of Tuberculosis, Nov. 1923, 8, 272-277.
Persons in the incipient stage of tuberculosis, apparently carry in their blood stream a substance capable of agglutinating the Flexner dysentery bacillus while persons in the advanced stage of the disease do not.

1924. Another Milk-Borne Typhoid Epidemic.
Thomas G. Hull.
Illinois Health News, July 1924, 10, 197-206.
A typhoid outbreak at Litchfield, Ill., where two carriers were found on the dairy farm.

1924. The Control of the Public Health Laboratory.
J. J. McShane and Thomas G. Hull.
American Journal of Public Health, Nov. 1924, 14, 950-953.
The report of a committee appointed by the advisory board to study methods employed in other states of co-operating with or controlling private laboratories doing public health work.

1924. The Effect of Heat on the Staining Properties of the Tubercle Bacillus.
Thomas G. Hull, Kirby Henkes and Luella Fry.
Journal of Laboratory and Clinical Medicine, Nov. 1924, 10, 150-153.
Steam pressure at 15 pounds for 8 hours or dry heat at 150° for one hour and forty minutes did not cause the tubercle bacillus to lose its acid-fast staining properties.

1925. Agglutination Reactions of the Paratyphoid-Dysentery Group in Tuberculosis.
Thomas G. Hull, Kirby Henkes and Hugh Cassiday
American Review of Tuberculosis, March 1925, 11, 78-84.
Agglutination reactions with blood serum from persons in various stages of tuberculosis were obtained with certain members of the paratyphoid dysentery group.

1925. The Schick Test and Scarlet Fever.
Thomas G. Hull.
Journal of Laboratory and Clinical Medicine, Dec. 1925, 11, 260-261
An attack of scarlet fever appears to destroy the diphtheria antitoxin in the blood stream, causing the Schick test to become positive.

1926. Laboratory Differentiation of Smallpox and Chickenpox.
Thomas G. Hull and Ralph W. Nauss.
American Journal of Public Health, Feb. 1926, 16, 101-106.
Smallpox may be differentiated from chickenpox by the intracutaneous injection of immune rabbits with serum from the pustule of the patient.

1926. The Widal Test as Carried out in Public Health Laboratories.
Thomas G. Hull.
American Journal of Public Health, Sept. 1926, 16, 901-905.
The Widal test needs standardizing according to a study of methods used in 53 public health laboratories.

1926. The Control of Private Laboratories.
Thomas G. Hull.
The Nation's Health, Dec. 1926, 8, 809-10.
A discussion of certifying private laboratories doing public health work.

1927. Undulant Fever as a Public Health Problem.
Thomas G. Hull and Luther A. Black.
Journal of the American Medical Association, Feb. 12, 1927, 88, 463-464.
Among 70 serums tested with bacillus abortus antigen, 5 reacted positively in high dilutions, indicating infection with bacillus abortus.

1927. Twenty-six Thousand Kahn tests Compared with the Wassermann.
Thomas G. Hull.
Journal of the American Medical Association, June 11, 1927, 88, 1865-1866.
The two tests gave relative agreement in about 98 percent of instances. Treated cases of syphilis gave the most discrepancies.

1927. Seasonal Prevalence and Control of Rabies.
Thomas G. Hull.
The Nation's Health, June 1927, 9, 21-24.
Rabies is on the increase throughout many portions of the United States. March is the month of greatest prevalence in many communities.

Diagnostic Laboratory.

In August of 1904, Dr. James A. Egan, secretary of the State Board of Health was successful in acquiring funds originally intended for sanitary investigations and using them for opening a laboratory. This was located in the Odd Fellows' Building in Springfield and Mr. W. H. Hoyt a medical student was put in charge. Specimens for the diagnosis of diphtheria, typhoid, tuberculosis and malaria were examined.

In 1905, an appropriation of $1,200 was secured from the General Assembly for the services of a bacteriologist and $1,800 per annum for "expenses of laboratory for investigation of diseases."

The one room in the Odd Fellows' building soon became inadequate to house the rapidly developing work and on Nov. 15, 1906 quarters were secured in an apartment house located within one block of the State House and directly opposite the site of the Supreme Court building. Here a six room apartment was shared with the bureau of vital statistics.

The next change in location was made to the State House where the laboratory remained for a number of years in a small room on the second floor. In 1917 it was moved to the sixth floor where it shared quarters with the division of sanitary engineering which were supposed "to be adequate for many years". So rapid was the increase of laboratory examinations however, that the space soon became cramped and an attempt was made to relieve congestion by moving some of the work to the former plant of the hog cholera serum laboratory five miles north of the State House. This division of work did not prove practical and gradually the workers were re-called and the quarters at the serum laboratory were given up in 1925. Additional space on the sixth floor of the State House was acquired in 1926, which made possible the necessary expansion of activities.

In the 23 years that the laboratory has existed, ten different individuals have been in charge as follows:

```
W. H. Hoyt .................................1904- 5
H. C. Blankenmeyer, M. D...................1905- 7
Walter G. Bain, M. D.......................1907- 9
Flint Bondurant, M. D......................1909
W. S. Crowley, M. D........................1909-10
N. E. Wagson, M. D.........................1910
W. H. Holmes, M. D.........................1910-11
Geo. F. Sorgatz, M. D......................1911-18
Martin Dupray, M. S........................1918-19
Thomas G. Hull, Ph. D......................1920-to date
```

In 1904 when the laboratory was first started only 171 examinations were made during the fall months, covering diphtheria cultures, sputum examinations for tubercle bacilli, blood examination for malaria parasites and Widal tests for typhoid fever. The volume of work increased very markedly during the next dozen years, especially in sputum examinations but with almost no increase in scope. Unfortunately no records are available for the years 1908 and 1909.

In 1917, came the war with its venereal disease program and free Wassermann tests and gonorrhea examinations, and general emphasis on all things of a laboratory nature. With the return of physicians from military service the demands on the laboratory for all kinds of work in-

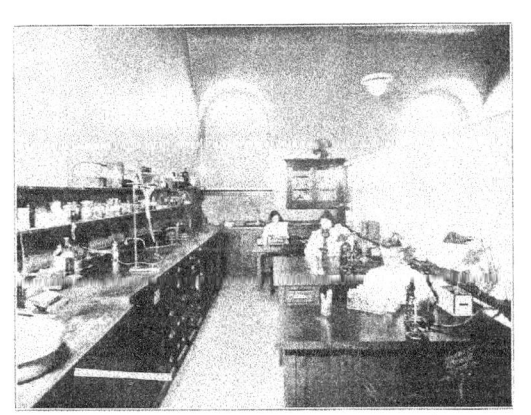

A section of the main laboratory at Springfield where general diagnostic service is done free for the citizens of Illinois (1924)

creased markedly. In 1920 routine examinations for all contagious diseases for which laboratory tests were available were being made, including the complement fixation tests for gonorrhea and tuberculosis.

In 1926, after considerable experimentation, the Kahn precipitation test for syphilis was adopted as a routine in addition to the Wassermann test. In June 1927, the Wassermann test was dropped as a routine procedure; except where there was a special request for it. It was soon found that there were no such requests.

The interest of veterinarians in public health laboratory work had been confined mainly to rabies for some years. In 1924 the contagiousness of bacillus abortus of cattle for man was shown in several human cases in Illinois. A demand upon the laboratory for routine testing of cattle for contagious abortion was immediately made by veterinarians. Since the Department had neither the facilities nor personnel for this additional burden, only a small number of blood specimens from cattle were examined. In all matters relating to animal diseases, the closest co-operation was maintained with the division of animal pathology at the University of Illinois.

Table 24.

DIAGNOSTIC LABORATORY—TOTAL EXAMINATIONS, 1904-27.

	Main laboratory Springfield.	Branch laboratories.	Social hygiene.	Total.
1904	171			171
1905	1,425			1,425
1906	2,370			2,370
1907	3,275			3,275
1908	? ?			? ?
1909	? ?			? ?
1909-10	4,024			4,024
1910-11	4,037			4,037
1911-12	4,249			4,249
1912-13	4,442			4,442
1913-14	4,222			4,222
1914-15	4,611			4,611
1915-16	7,579	1,409		8,988
1916-17	6,013	2,429		8,482
1917-18	10,499	2,399		12,898
1918-19	12,003	3,058	4,628	15,061
1919-20	31,494	3,412	84,749	39,543
1920-21	52,008	7,691	20,205	79,904
1921-22	83,630	8,442	27,128	119,200
1922-23	82,840	4,576	27,893	115,309
1923-24	84,104	5,520	79,736	169,360
1924-25	78,311	4,611	93,726	176,648
1925-26	99,259	9,037	52,725	161,021
1926-27	134,200	5,845	84,749	224,794

The following is a list of examinations made by the diagnostic laboratory showing the year when they were begun:

Diphtheria cultures	1904	Dysentery cultures	1918
Sputum for tubercle bacilli	1904	Meningococcus cultures	1918
Widal tests	1904	Pneumococcus typing	1918
Malaria examinations	1904	Tuberculosis fixation tests	1920
Rabies examinations	1909	Gonococcus fixation tests	1920
Wassermann tests—blood and spinal fluid	1917	Colloidal Gold tests	1920
Pus for gonococci	1917	Diphtheria virulency tests	1920
Treponema pallidum	1917	Kahn precipitation tests	1926
Typhoid cultures feces, urine and blood	1918	Vincents' angina	1927

Occasional examinations have been made since the period 1917 to 1920 of specimens which have not been numerous enough to list as "routine", but classed under miscellaneous, including examinations for anthrax, chancroid, glanders, streptococcus, sore throat, Vincents' angina, also the Weil-Felix test for typhus fever, blood cultures, oyster examinations, food poisoning investigation, etc.

Previous to 1920 a certain number of routine urine analyses was done as were also blood counts, together with an occasional tissue examination. Since that time these activities have been confined to instances where a communicable disease was involved, leaving the routine specimens to clinical laboratories.

Previous to 1922 very few milk examinations were made. In that year in conjunction with the milk campaign, bacterial plate counts and sediment tests were made in several cities and since then milk specimens have been examined at irregular intervals in considerable numbers, culminating in the use of a mobile milk laboratory in 1927 for field work.

BRANCH LABORATORIES: In 1915, it seemed advisable to establish branch laboratories to improve the service, especially in diphtheria work. Accordingly, contracts were drawn up with the Burdick-Abel Laboratory in Chicago and with Dr. W. H. Gilmore in Mt. Vernon, to examine diphtheria cultures for diagnosis at the rate of 50 cents each. Cultures for quarantine release or for survey work as in schools, were sent to Springfield. Similar contracts were later made with other laboratories to include not only diphtheria diagnosis but also Widal tests, malaria and gonorrhea specimens. Because of lack of funds the scope of the branch laboratories was confined to diphtheria diagnosis. Later in 1922, instead of paying for each culture examined most of the laboratories were paid a stated sum each month on the basis of the amount of work previously done.

In 1925 a definite change in branch laboratory policy occurred when the Palestine Laboratory, connected with the Crawford County Health

Unit and the southern branch laboratory at Carbondale were opened. All procedures connected with public health work were provided for. The Palestine laboratory, under Dr. J. A. Ilkemire, was later discontinued when the Crawford County Health Unit was given up. The Carbondale laboratory established in an emergency was made permanent to fill the demand for service as the result of work done by the field laboratory sent to southern Illinois for tornado relief. When the rest of the Department activities were discontinued the laboratory remained as the southern branch.

In 1927 arrangements were completed for a branch laboratory in Chicago at the State Research Hospital with Dr. Lloyd Arnold in charge. While the laboratory is independent of the medical school and hospital certain material from the laboratory will be used for teaching purposes.

Following are the branch laboratories which the Department has maintained since 1915:

DIPHTHERIA DIAGNOSTIC LABORATORIES.

Chicago	Theodore C. Abel, M. D., 7 W. Madison St.	1915–1927
Mt. Vernon	W. H. Gilmore	1915–1922
Urbana	F. W. Tanner, Ph. D., University of Illinois	1916–to date
Galesburg	S. G. Winter, M. S., Galesburg National Bk. Bldg.	1916–to date
Rockford	W. H. Cunningham, M. D.	1917–1918
Moline	Maude Vollmer, M. D., Lutheran Hospital	1918–to date
Ottawa	R. T. Pettit, M. D., Illinois Valley Laboratory	1920–to date
East St. Louis	Earl Brennan, M. D., City Health Department	1922–to date
Decatur	Decatur & Macon Co. Hosp., B. S. Stackford, M. D.	1924–1925
	C. R. Smith, M. D.	1925–to date
Kankakee	St. Mary's Hospital	1927–to date

BRANCH LABORATORIES—ALL EXAMINATIONS.

Palestine	Crawford County Health Unit, J. A. Ikemire, M. D.	1925–1926
Carbondale	Holden Hospital, Eva Faught	1925–to date
Chicago	Research Hospital, Lloyd Arnold, M. D.	1927–

FIELD LABORATORY WORK: The field laboratory was instituted to satisfy the demand for laboratory service during epidemics in communities where no local laboratory existed and where it was found inconvenient or impossible to send specimens a distance to the main laboratory.

In 1915, a chest was built combining the minimum necessities for making diphtheria, typhoid, and meningitis cultures. Several trips each year were made with this equipment with very distinct advantage. Not only were typhoid, diphtheria and meningitis epidemics solved, but also other work such as glanders and venereal disease diagnosis, milk bacteriology and general laboratory work taken care of. Among the towns visited were Litchfield, Anna, Carbondale, Peoria, Rock Island, Rockford, Kewanee, Marshall, Taylorville, Belleville, East St. Louis, Granite City, Streator, Belvidere and Galena.

Equipment and personnel for setting up a field diagnostic laboratory are ready at all times to respond to emergency calls. The picture shows the field unit about to be off from the Capitol Building to Rock Island in 1923.

An interesting trip was made in 1923 to Rock Island. A few days before Christmas a telephone call requested urgent help in controlling a diphtheria outbreak. While the branch laboratory was available at Moline, supplies for several thousand cultures were not at hand nor could they be shipped by train because of the tremendous congestion of Christmas packages in both post office and express office. In but a few hours culture media for the entire work was ready and loaded into the laboratory car. By driving all night two bacteriologists with necessary supplies and equipment were on the scene the next morning.

The tornado of 1925 in southern Illinois caused an acute situation making the presence of laboratory service indispensable. Equipment sufficient to take care of any emergency that might arise was dispatched by automobile and installed in the Elks' Club at Carbondale.

Through the co-operation of the National Guard, the laboratory equipment of the 108th Medical Regiment was pooled with that of the State Department of Public Health and placed at the disposal of the Department. While the main laboratory was maintained at the Elks' Club in Carbondale, sufficient technicians were available from the National Guard to establish sub-laboratories in the various emergency hospitals in Murphysboro, West Frankfort and at Holden Hospital in Carbondale. With the closing of the emergency hospitals and the withdrawal of the National Guard, the laboratory was moved from the Elks' Club to the temporary offices of the State Department of Public Health at 222½ South Illinois Street. So well did this laboratory function during the next few months, not only in the storm area but all over the southern part of the State, that its abandonment was out of question. Definite arrangements were made with the Holden Hospital where commodious quarters were provided and the southern branch laboratory was thus established.

The field laboratory equipment was augmented from time to time to take care of special emergencies so that it eventually consisted of more than half a dozen chests, packed ready with sterilizers, incubator, acetylene gas tanks for burners and other necessary materials. One or all the chests were taken according to the nature of the emergency and amount of equipment that might be found locally.

The milk campaign initiated in 1922 resulted in various milk surveys in different communities. These were discontinued because of lack of laboratory personnel and funds to satisfy the demand. The campaign resulted in the passage of the milk pasteurization law, the enforcement of which required a complete laboratory. Such a laboratory has been installed in an automobile bus, with a milk bacteriologist in charge and is now ready to start out on a tour of pasteurization plants. While this mobile laboratory was built primarily for milk work, it was so constructed and equipped that it can take care of any emergency that may arise.

Status of Laboratory Work in Illinois.

The activities of the State Department of Public Health are so closely interwoven with innumerable other agencies that it is difficult to disentangle the relationships. The laboratories of the State Health Department are by no means the only ones doing laboratory work of a public health nature. Various municipalities maintain laboratories while hospital and private clinical laboratories do a large amount of work.

The Chicago health department established the first public health diagnostic laboratory in the State and the second in the country in 1894. Since that time eleven other cities have provided for laboratory work, some with technicians on a full time basis, some part time and some by contract with clinical laboratories. Evanston equipped its laboratory in 1908, Elgin in 1912, Rockford in 1915 and Oak Park in 1917

Following is a list of cities making provision for laboratory work·

Chicago health department, fifty workers, full time, about 375,000 examinations in 1926.
Rockford health department, one worker, full time, about 8,500 examinations in 1926.
Oak Park health department, one worker full time, about 1,700 examinations in 1926.
Aurora health department, one worker, full time, about 2,500 examinations in 1926.
LaSalle, Peru and Oglesby Hygienic Institute, one worker, full time.
Elgin health department, one worker, full time.
Evanston health department, one worker, part time, about 2,000 examinations in 1926.
East St. Louis health department, one worker, part time.
Peoria health department, one worker, part time.
Joliet health department, contract with local laboratories.
Quincy health department, contract with local laboratory.
Decatur health department, contract with local laboratory.

The modern clinical laboratory dates almost from the same time that the public health laboratory does. In 1894 there were very few clinical laboratories, in the modern sense of the word, in existence either in hospitals or under private auspices. The Columbus Laboratories in Chicago, one of the oldest, was founded in 1893. A few hospitals had laboratories, but their activities were apparently not numerous. In 1895 St. John's Hospital in Springfield employed Dr. I. C. Taylor as bacteriologist

At the present time there are clinical laboratories as follows·

Hospital laboratories—Chicago 52
Hospital laboratories—Downstate 70
Clinical laboratories—(private) Chicago 53
Clinical laboratories—(private) Down-State   13

Most of the clinical laboratories are prepared to carry out many of the procedures of a public health nature, such as milk, water and communicable disease control. Because of the competition of the free municipal and State laboratories, however, there are a good many instances where specimens requiring more elaborate procedure, as the culture of stool specimens for typhoid and even the Wassermann test, are not attempted by the clinical laboratory but sent to the nearest public health laboratory or to the State laboratory.

The competition of municipal and state laboratories has been the basis of much criticism by many clinical laboratory workers. The controversy has centered largely around the Wassermann test. In 1925 the Illinois Medical Laboratory Association attempted to turn more work to the private laboratory by passing a resolution requesting the Director of the State Department of Public Health to require the name and address of the patient with every Wassermann specimen done in the state laboratory. The Director referred the matter to the State Medical Society where adverse action was taken upon it.

There are four groups into which laboratories in Illinois fall.

1. Clinical laboratories maintained by a competent clinical pathologist with a medical degree.
2. Hospital laboratories, either in charge of a competent clinical pathologist or, as is the case with small hospitals, a laboratory technician supervised by a physician.
3. Public health laboratories either in charge of a competent pathologist, bacteriologist or chemist, or a laboratory technician supervised by a medical health officer.
4. Clinical laboratories outside of hospitals in charge of technicians which have no medical supervision.

Laboratories falling in the first group are at present eligible for approval by the American Medical Association. The program of the Illinois State Department of Public Health includes groups one, two and three. The two organizations, however, try to co-ordinate their activities so that a laboratory is not approved by one which does not meet the requirements of the other.

The following laboratories have been issued certificates of approval by both the American Medical Association and the State Department of Public Health.

Chicago Laboratory—Chicago.
Lincoln-Gardner Laboratory—Chicago.
Medical Research Laboratory—Chicago.
The Murphy Laboratories—Chicago.
National Pathological Laboratories—Chicago.
Dr. Homer K. Nicoll's Laboratory—Chicago.
Quincy Clinical Laboratory—Quincy.
Rockford Hospital Laboratory—Rockford.
Rockford Laboratories for Medical Research—Rockford.

A bacteriologist at work in the diagnostic laboratory established in the Lurnado zone in 1925.

In addition to the above list the following laboratories have been certified for certain procedures by the State Department of Public Health:

Rockford Health Department Laboratory—Rockford.
Decatur and Macon County Hospital Laboratory—Decatur.
Lake View Hospital Laboratory—Danville.
Our Saviors Hospital Laboratory—Jacksonville.
Lutheran Hospital Laboratory—Moline.
Elgin Municipal Laboratory—Elgin.
Aurora Municipal Laboratory—Aurora.
Brokaw Hospital Laboratory—Bloomington.
Prescription Shop Laboratory—Joliet.
Holden Hospital Laboratory—Carbondale.
Illinois Valley Laboratory—Ottawa.
St. Anthony's Hospital Laboratory—Rockford.
St. Mary's Hospital Laboratory—Kankakee.
Methodist Hospital Laboratory—Peoria.
St. Francis Hospital Laboratory—Peoria.
St. John's Hospital Laboratory—Springfield.

In 1924, the State Department of Public Health took an active part in the formation of the Illinois Public Health Laboratory Association. The name was later changed to the Illinois Medical Laboratory Association as being more descriptive, but the objects of the organization remained the same. Dr. Thomas G. Hull, chief of the diagnostic laboratory, served as president for two years and then as secretary.

One of the objects was to reach the technician isolated in a laboratory in a small city, who if a member of a national technical society, rarely obtained the opportunity to attend. Frequent meetings in different parts of the State were intended to interest and stimulate these technicians to better work.

The certification of laboratories by the State Department of Public Health came about in 1925 when the Illinois Medical Laboratory Association passed a resolution requesting the Director of the State Department of Public Health to issue certificates of approval to laboratories found competent to do public health laboratory work after proper inspections had been made. The Director agreed to this arrangement, limiting inspections only to laboratories from which requests had been received. Many conferences were held with the committee on education and hospitals of the American Medical Association, which was also carrying out a national program of certifying clinical laboratories. The program of the Department of Public Health went farther than that of the American Medical Association, however, in that frequent inspections were made, "unknown" specimens for examination submitted and reports returned, certain biological reagents furnished and the advice of a bacteriologist offered in times of necessity. The local laboratory, on its part, agreed to use only approved methods, to make annual statistical reports to the Department and to assist in certain ways in times of epidemic.

Division of Hotel and Lodging House Inspection.

The inspection of lodging houses, taverns, hotels and inns began in 1899 as a result of a special law enacted in that year for the purpose of preventing serious overcrowding and gross insanitation in the poorer hostelries operated in Chicago. At that time the city was growing very rapidly and deplorable conditions existed in some quarters where persons of small means were given shelter at low rates. The work of inspecting these places was confined to Chicago by making the law apply only to cities of 100,000 or more population.

The duties and responsibilities of the lodging house inspectors are all specifically enumerated in the law and the division maintains headquarters in Chicago. The number of employees and the money provided are specified in the law. The work is associated with the State Department of Public Health principally because the law puts it under the general supervision of the Department.

At the outset, July, 1899, two inspectors were employed. Homer C. Fancher was designated as chief and paid out of the general funds granted to the State Board of Health. Mr. Fancher was succeeded by Edward J. Snejcal in December of 1899. He managed to get a staff of 10 inspectors at work during 1900 but most of them were on a temporary basis.

In 1901 an appropriation of $12,500 per year was set aside for the inspection of lodging houses and from that time on the service was known in appropriation laws as "supervision and inspection of lodging houses" etc. until 1917 when along with all other units in the State Health machinery it was designated as a "division". Mr. Snejcal was succeeded as chief inspector by William G. Laub in the fall of 1901 who was succeeded in 1904 by John W. Utesch. George Delvigne began as chief inspector on October 1, 1913 and continued until 1917 when the position of chief inspector was abolished and in its place, as the head of the division of lodging house inspection, was established the position of superintendent of lodging house inspection. To that place was appointed W. W. McCulloch. In October 1923 he was succeeded by Arch Lewis who has continued to date.

The work of this division has changed very little during the long period of its existence except in volume. Funds provided for carrying the service have increased from $12,500 per year in 1901, to $35,615 in 1924.

DIVISION OF PUBLIC HEALTH INSTRUCTION.

Education in health matters was regarded as a fundamental activity of the State health service from the time of its creation and every executive officer of that service gave to it as much time and thought as possible. The publication and distribution of circulars was a favorite way of handling the matter from the outset and continues to be important.

Education was always stressed by Dr. Rauch as one of the most important results of his survey of the State during the middle eighties. He also distributed millions of leaflets on smallpox and large numbers on other diseases.

The annual reports of the Board which were issued with more regularity than almost anything else that it ever undertook were prepared with a view to their educational value.

Earl B. Searcy.

From time to time attempts were made to publish a periodical bulletin prior to 1900. The few numbers that came from press were called *State Medicine*. This idea was revived in 1903 when two numbers, the March and April, of a monthly publication called the *"Bulletin"* were issued. Again it dropped out of the activities only to be revived in 1906 on a permanent and more or less regular basis. From that time until December 1912 a number of the *"Bulletin"* was published for every month and bound by years.

Then the publication succumbed to another lapse and was revived again in 1915 under the title of *"Health News"*. From that time until 1920 it was issued for each month but quite irregularly at times. Beginning with 1921 and continuing to date *Health News* has come from press and been mailed during the month of its date with but one or two exceptions.

Dr. Henry B. Hemenway.

Prior to 1915 the publication was prepared for a medical audience and distributed among physicians almost exclusively. Since that time it has been popular in character. On the mailing list the laymen outnumber physicians and include teachers, farm advisers, members of women's clubs, nurses, social workers, local officials, etc.

PUBLIC HEALTH ADMINISTRATION

All of the publicity work was handled directly by the secretary or his assistant until 1917 when an item providing $1,200 for a medical editor appeared in the appropriation law. On the basis of that fund a division of public health instruction was created and consisted of one individual in the person of Earl B. Searcy who was a newspaper man and began work on September 24, 1917. His job was to edit *Health News* and prepare material for the newspapers.

Mr. Searcy went to war on April 12, 1918 and Dr. Henry B. Hemenway acted as editor of Health News until Mr. Searcy returned on April 21, 1919. After the brief period of three months he took a six months leave beginning July 1, 1919 and never close to return. He was succeeded on July 28, 1919 by Samuel W. Kessinger who received a temporary appointment. As a result of civil service examinations, B. K. Richardson was appointed to succeed Mr. Kessinger on December 1, 1920. Mr. Richardson has continued in the capacity of chief of the division to date.

Samuel W. Kessinger.

The division staff has never been large. At first it consisted of one person who was trained to do publicity work. Then in 1919 a stenographer and exhibit helper were added. Another stenographer was added in 1923. In 1927 the staff consisted of these four members.

Beginning in 1917 the work done by the division relieved the Director more and more of the detailed activities incidental to the preparation of publicity material and at the same time the scope of the publicity service was gradually increased.

Thus by 1927 the division had the responsibility of securing and preparing for the printer material suitable for publication in *Health News*. It is published monthly and usually runs 32 pages to the number.

It was preparing as a weekly routine function a story and a sheet of pointed paragraphs for the newspapers of the State. This service has continued uninterruptedly since January 1, 1921.

B. K. Richardson.

It exercised supervision over a motion picture library in which are maintained some eighty odd films on health subjects. These are loaned free throughout the State, and are found very useful in health educational work

PUBLIC HEALTH ADMINISTRATION

The division was arranging programs and handling publicity for special events like Health Promotion Week, diphtheria eradication and other campaigns; also the better baby conferences at the State fair. In addition it managed the mobile exhibit equipment maintained by the Department.

Furthermore the division exercised supervision over the publication of educational pamphlets. These have been issued in large quantities, covering more than a score of subjects. It also accepted responsibility for editing the various reports of the Department.

DIVISION OF SOCIAL HYGIENE.

There is but little doubt that the division of social hygiene came into existence as a result of the startling figures given out by the government showing the alarming prevalence of venereal diseases among recruits mobilized for military duty in the World War. Records reaching the Adjutant General's office at Washington showed that three per cent of the first million men mobilized had a venereal disease when they reported at their respective camps. Those from some of the states showed an even higher percentage. It was a part of a general effort to control, suppress and eradicate venereal disease that the division was created July 1, 1918. It actually began to function on November 1, of that year when the first federal funds became available.

With a subsidy from the government of $66,307.50 for the year ending June 30, 1919, the second year allotment however was conditioned upon an appropriation by the State legislature to be matched dollar for dollar with an equal amount of federal funds. The 51st General Assembly appropriated for the use of the division of social hygiene the sum of $100,000 for two years ending June 30, 1921. This was matched by an allotment of $50,000 for the second year's work from the federal government, so that there was available for the year ending June 30, 1920 the sum of $100,000.00. The work of the division has proceeded along lines established during the first year conforming in general to the venereal disease program suggested by the Interdepartmental Social Hygiene Board, which was created by act of congress.

Dr. G. C. Taylor.

Dr. C. C. Copeland.

Treatment of Disease Carriers.

Due to the accepted fact that there exists a lack of proper information concerning the serious character of the complication and sequellae wrought by venereal disease carriers, an endeavor was made to place before the public facts pertaining to these diseases, and along these lines, clinics were opened in the following cities:

    Chicago—2   Decatur
    East St. Louis   Springfield
    Rockford

In the year 1920 there were in addition to the above named clinics, the following:

Alton	Chicago Heights	Rock Island
Cairo	Litchfield	Waukegan
Carlinville	Moline	West Hammond
Chicago—5	Peoria	

The following year clinics were in operation at Princeton and Quincy. Later clinics were opened at DuQuoin and Robinson.

From the year 1921 it has been the policy of the division to operate clinics in such a manner as not to pauperize the public or infringe upon the legitimate practice of any physician. This is obviated by having the endorsement of local medical societies before taking action upon application of city or county officials requesting that clinics be opened. Clinics are established wherever the Department is assured that for every dollar of State funds subsidized, there will be double the amount appropriated from city or county funds.

Repressive Measures.

It is a known fact that in order to prevent the spread of venereal disease it is necessary to render non-infectious the carriers of the disease. In order to carry out such a program, it is essential to have the cooperation of city and county officials. In order to acquaint officials of the respective communities as to prevalence of these diseases, vice investigations are made, and the results of such surveys are confidentially given them. In a number of instances, the city officials have seen fit to pass local ordinances which deal with male offenders as well as prostitutes. From a public health viewpoint, every reduction of the amount of irregular sexual intercourse means just so much less exposure to venereal disease. One of the main methods of reducing these exposures is the preventing of professional prostitutes and loose women of all kinds from any opportunity to do business, as these women are the most prolific carriers of venereal disease.

Education.

Syphilis, gonorrhea, chancroid, the chief venereal diseases are caused by germs which can be identified through means of the microscope. For these diseases there is a definite curative treatment which, if begun promptly is usually successful. The most serious results come from improper or delayed treatment. The connection of these dangerous communicable diseases with sexual immorality has prevented proper discussion of the means of preventing and curing them and has delayed the building up of effective prevention and treatment in the interest of public health.

The social and economic loss caused by these diseases mark them as one of mankind's greatest scourges. When it is taken into consideration that frequently more cases of venereal disease are reported than that of measles, it may give the public a general idea as to the prevalence of venereal disease. There have been reported in Illinois from physicians and clinics, 194,808 cases of venereal disease during the period July 1, 1918 to July 1, 1926, while the number of cases treated at the clinics showed a stupendous total of 349,047.

The number of lectures given during this period was 1,814. The educational measures used to combat these diseases are carried on by the use of placards, pamphlets, motion pictures, exhibits and lectures.

To show the interest manifested by social workers and others interested in the venereal disease problem, there was held in Chicago during March 13-18, 1922, a Venereal Disease Institute. This was conducted under the auspices of the United States Public Health Service and the Illinois Department of Public Health. The attendance was over one thousand.

The audience was composed of representatives from every walk in life and included doctors, nurses, educators, social workers, judges, business men, mothers of families, clearly showing that the efforts to arouse interest in the subject of venereal disease had been successful.

Generally this subject has been of interest only to doctors, but on this occasion the lecturers recognizing that a general knowledge of the medical side of venereal disease is necessary to those who would fight it, so presented the subject that it could be grasped by all in attendance.

One of the best features of the program was the series of noonday luncheons, at which prominent representatives of the various agencies interested in combating venereal disease, presented their views as to how the work could best be carried on. The church press and various social welfare organizations were represented, and suggestions were made and conclusions reached which will be of inestimable value if put into practice in the different communities.

PUBLIC HEALTH ADMINISTRATION

A striking feature of the Institute was the changed attitude of the audience. A short time ago it was impossible to frankly discuss social diseases and allied subjects before so varied an audience, but those present at the conference showed by their whole attitude that the time has come when it is no longer necessary to veil the matter under a cloak of false modesty; that it can be approached with unaffectedness and ease.

The Social Hygiene Bulletin which had been published monthly since September 1, 1920, was discontinued after the June issue in 1923 due to decrease of appropriations for the biennium.

Two very important bills relating to venereal disease were passed by the 53rd General Assembly. The one approved June 21, 1923 amends section 57 of the Criminal Code to provide that any one who keeps, leases, or patronizes any disorderly house shall be fined not more than $200.00 or imprisoned not more than one year.

The other, approved June 27, 1923, amends section 1 of the Divorce Act by adding as a ground for divorce the fact that one spouse has infected the other with a communicable venereal disease.

Summary.

The following chronology is given for the purpose of presenting the activities rendered by the division in a more precise manner:

1918. Division of social hygiene was created on a fifty-fifty federal subsidy basis.
1919. The establishment of venereal disease clinics at various parts of the State was begun. Six were established during this year.
1920. Additional venereal disease clinics established in State, sufficient in number to bring the total to nineteen.
1922. A one week intensive course relating to social hygiene was conducted in Chicago. More than 1,000 persons registered as being in attendance on the lectures.
1923. Standards of infectivity in reference to venereal diseases, which were created by a special committee of experts at the request of the State Director of Public Health were adopted and put into effect.

A stringent law pertaining to vice was enacted.

The *"Social Hygiene Monthly"* publication which began in 1920 was discontinued during this year.

A bill providing for the acceptance of federal aid to almost the amount of $14,000.00 in social hygiene service failed to pass the legislature. A decrease of $28,000 from the last preceding appropriation limited the activities of the division for the biennium.

1923. Law passed, amending Section 57 of the Criminal Code, and which is directed at the very center of the venereal disease evil. Law provides heavy fines and imprisonment for patrons, owners, leasors, proprietors or other persons directly influencing the operation of houses or quarters for prostitution. If enforced, this will reduce very greatly the possibility of venereal disease infections. This, in turn, would make more and more unnecessary a large number of clinics for treating such diseases.

Standards of infectivity, relative to the treatment of venerally infected persons, worked out by a committee consisting of Doctors W. A. Evans, Herman N. Bundesen, Louis Schmidt, C. C. Pierce and others.

Standards of infectivity pertaining to venereal diseases officially adopted as a part of the rules and regulations of the Department. Standards printed in pamphlet form and available to physicians, health officers, social workers, lawyers and judges of the courts.

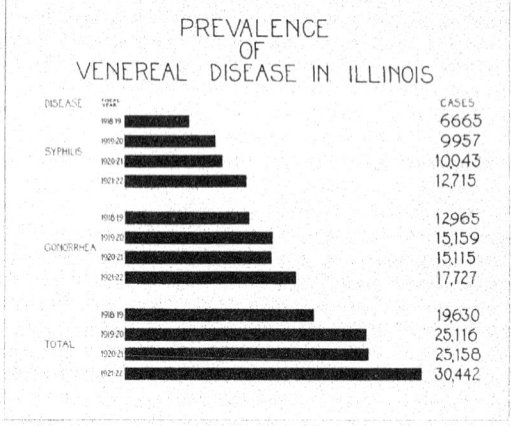

PREVALENCE OF VENEREAL DISEASE IN ILLINOIS

DISEASE	YEAR	CASES
SYPHILIS	1918-19	6665
	1919-20	9957
	1920-21	10,043
	1921-22	12,715
GONORRHEA	1918-19	12,965
	1919-20	15,159
	1920-21	15,115
	1921-22	17,727
TOTAL	1918-19	19,630
	1919-20	25,116
	1920-21	25,158
	1921-22	30,442

Fig. 27.

MEDICAL PRACTICE ACT.

Instinctively the people look to their state government for protection against frauds of all kinds and especially for protection against quacks and cults. Unless the state measures up to its responsibilities, many incompetents and some rascals, as well as the trained ethical physicians use the title "Doctor." The public, unable to dicriminate, and believing all are using the title legally, are liable to fall into incompetent hands, when in case of illness they come to select their medical advisor.

The ethical, trained physicians of Illinois, recognizing the public need for this protection, and being ever the guardians of the health and welfare of the people, early began to agitate the need for medical practice laws.

The Practice Act of 1817.

The Third General Assembly of the Territory of Illinois, elected in 1816, met at Kaskaskia on December 2 and adjourned on January 14, 1817. A second session of the same assembly began December 1, 1817, and ended on January 18, 1818. It was but a few years before that an Act of Congress dividing Indiana Territory into two separate governments, revived the name of Illinois which had officially disappeared after the organization of the Northwest Territory in 1789, and only five years previous had the Territory been given actual governmental powers.

The House of Representatives that sat at Kaskaskia in the Third General Assembly was made up of but seven members, and was presided over by Dr. George Fisher, a physician who had migrated from Virginia in 1800. This was the same Dr. Fisher who had been Speaker of the First General Assembly of the Territory of Illinois, which met in Kaskaskia in 1812.

This little handful of law makers was brought together, however, by the stern necessities of the infant Territory, and their sessions, informal as they were, placed an indelible imprint upon the future government of Territory and State. Perhaps no member of the Assembly appreciated so keenly as did the Speaker of the House, Dr. Fisher, the necessity for the restriction of itinerant and ignorant medical practitioners throughout the Territory, and if he did not cause the introduction of the territorial Medical Practice Act, it is certain that he lent his influence to it.

Among the important laws passed by this Third General Assembly was one regulating the practice of medicine. This pre-state Medical Practice Act bearing the signature of Dr. George Fisher, Speaker of the House, and Pierre Menard, President of the Legislative Council (which corresponded to our present Senate) and the approval under date of December 01, 1817, of Ninian Edwards, Governor of the Territory of Illinois, read as follows:

(273)

"LAWS OF ILLINOIS TERRITORY—1817-1818.

"AN ACT *to incorporate Medical Societies for the purpose of regulating the practice of Physics and Surgery in this Territory.*

"WHEREAS, Well regulated medical societies have been found to contribute to the diffusion of true science, and particularly the knowledge of the healing art, therefore be it

"Enacted, By the Legislative Council and House of Representatives of the Illinois territory, and it is hereby enacted by the authority of the same, that this territory be and is hereby divided into two medical districts, and shall be called the eastern and western districts; the eastern district shall be composed of that part of the territory lying east of the meridian line running due north from the mouth of the Ohio; and the western district of that part lying west of said line.

"Section 2. Be it further enacted, That it shall and may be lawful for the following persons: J. D. Woolverton, J. E. Thrognorton, Thomas Shannon, Henry Oldham, James Wilson, John Reid, Amos Chipp, Samuel R. Campbell, Harden M. Wetherford in the eastern district, and Joseph Bowers, Dr. Todd of Edwardsville, Dr. Hancock of St. Clair, Caldwell Carnes, George Fisher, William L. Reynolds, Dr. Heath of St. Clair, George Cadwell and Dr. Paine of Kaskaskia, to meet together on the first Monday of May, in the year of our Lord eighteen hundred and eighteen, at the towns of Carmi and Kaskaskia, in their respective districts, and being so convened as aforesaid, or any of them, being not less than five in number, shall proceed to the choice of a president, vice-president, secretary and treasurer, who shall hold their offices for one year, and until others shall be chosen in their places; and whenever the said societies shall be organized as aforesaid, they are hereby declared to be bodies politic and corporate, in fact and in name, by the names of the 'Medical Society of the district,' where such society shall be respectively formed; and by that name shall in law be capable of suing and being sued, pleading and being impleaded, and answering and being answered unto, defending and being defended, in all courts and places, and in all matters and causes whatsoever, and shall and may have a common seal, and may alter and renew the same at pleasure; and the said medical societies shall and may agree upon the times and places of their next meeting, which shall thereafter be the anniversary day of holding their respective meetings.

"Section 3. Be it further enacted, That the medical societies established as aforesaid are hereby respectively empowered to examine all students who shall or may present themselves for that purpose, and give diplomas, under the hand of the president and seal of such society, before whom such student shall be examined; which diploma shall be sufficient to empower the person so obtaining the same, to practice physic or surgery, or both, as shall be set forth in the said diploma, in any part of the territory. And the person receiving such diploma, shall upon the receipt of the same pay to the president of said society, the sum of ten dollars, for the use of said society.

"Section 4. Be it further enacted, That it may be lawful for the medical societies established as aforesaid, at their annual meetings, to appoint not less than three nor more than five censors to continue in office each year, and until others are chosen; and it shall be the duty of each one of them, carefully and impartially to examine all students who shall present themselves for that purpose before each of them, and report their opinions respectively in writing to the president of said society, and upon such report of any one of said censors, if favorable, the president is hereby authorized to license such student to practice physic or surgery, or both, until the next annual meeting of the medical society; and for such license, such student shall pay one dollar to the president for the use of the society.

"Section 5. Be it further enacted, That from and after the organization of the said medical societies in the respective districts, no person shall commence the practice of physic or surgery in either of the aforesaid districts, until he shall have passed an examination and received a diploma, or license as aforesaid; and if any person shall so practice without having obtained a diploma or license for

Where the remains of Dr. George Fisher rest in undisturbed peace on a bluff near Modoc in Randolph County near St. Leo's Church, enacted in Illinois in 1817. *(Illustration used by courtesy of Dr Lucius H. Zeuch.)*

tiat purpose, he siall forever tiereafter be disqualified from collecting any debt or debts incurred by such practice, in any court, or before any magistrate in the territory.

"Section 6. Be it further enacted, That it shall and may be lawful for the medical societies which shall be established by virtue of this act, to purchase and hold any estate, real and personal, for the use of the societies respectively; *Provided*, such estate as well real as personal, which the said societies are hereby respectively authorized to hold, shall not exceed the sum of twenty thousand dollars.

"Section 7. Be it further enacted, That it shall be lawful for the respective societies to be established by this act, to make such by-laws, rules and regulations, relative to the affairs, concerns and property of said societies, relative to the admission and expulsion of members, relative to such donations and contributions, as they or a majority of the members at their annual meetings shall think fit and proper; *Provided*, the by-laws, rules and regulations be not contrary to, nor inconsistent with the ordinance, and laws in force in this territory; nor the Constitution and laws of the United States.

"Section 8. Be it further enacted, That the treasurer of each society established as aforesaid, shall receive and be accountable for all monies that shall come into his hands, by virtue of any of the by-laws of such society; and also for all monies that shall come into the hands of the president, for the admission of members or licensing students; which monies the said president is hereby required to pay over to the said treasurer, who shall account therefor to the society at their annual meetings; and no monies shall be drawn from the treasurer unless such sums and for such purposes as shall be agreed upon by a majority of the society at their annual meetings, and by a warrant for that purpose, signed by the president.

"Section 9. Be it further enacted, That it shall be the duty of the Secretary of each of the medical societies to be established by virtue of this act, to provide a book, in which shall be made an entry of all the resolutions and proceedings, which may be had from time to time; and also the name of each and every member of said society, and the time of his admission, and also the annual report relative to the state of the treasury, and all such other things as a majority of the society shall think proper, to which book any member of the society may at any time have recourse, and the same together with all books, papers, and records, which may be in the hands of the secretary, and be the property of the society, shall be delivered to his successor in office.

"Section 10. Be it further enacted, That it shall be lawful for each of the medical societies to be established by virtue of this act, to cause to be raised and collected from each member of such society, a sum not exceeding ten dollars, in any one year, for the purpose of procuring a medical library and apparatus, and for the encouragement of useful discoveries in chemistry, botany, and such other improvements as the majority of the society shall think proper.

"Section 11. Be it further enacted, That nothing in this act contained, shall be construed to prevent any person coming from any state, territory or country from practicing physic or surgery in this territory; such person being duly authorized to practice by the laws of such state, territory or country, and having a diploma from any such medical society.

"Section 12. Be it further enacted, That it shall be in the power of the legislature of this territory, and of the legislature of the state, to be formed out of this territory, to alter, modify and repeal this act, whenever they shall deem it necessary or expedient.

"Section 13. Be it further enacted, That this act shall be and hereby is declared to be a public act, and to take effect from and after its passage.

"GEORGE FISHER,
Speaker of the House of Representatives.
"PIERRE MENARD,
President of the Legislative Council.

"Approved—December 31, 1817."

The law required each group to meet on the first Monday in May, 1818. The eastern group met at Carmi, the western group at Kaskaskia. It required five to make a quorum, and the officers consisted of president, vice-president, secretary and treasurer.

It is generally supposed that Dr. George Fisher was the father and prime mover in the various steps necessary to place this Medical Practice Act on the statute books.

Practice Act of 1819.

When this legislation came to a natural death with the termination of the territorial government, it is reasonable to believe that this group of 18 men, who constituted the membership of the two boards for enforcement of the provisions of the early pre-state Medical Practice Act, knowing from experience the great need for the control of medical practice, were largely instrumental in having the first State legislature in 1819 pass an "Act for Establishment of Medical Societies," among the provisions of which were the licensing of physicians and the reporting of births and deaths. Indeed, the 1819 Medical Practice Act in many particulars is quite similar to the territorial law of 1817.

So it would seem that he who, in later years, spoke of Illinois as "the pioneer in practical medical education," but who was unaware of the precocity of the State in the control of medical practice, placed his words of praise upon a commonwealth which, probably earlier in its history than any other state, enacted medical practice laws for the protection of its people.

The Act of 1817, which died with the termination of territorial government, but which was resurrected in 1819, to die again after an unsuccessful attempt to enforce its provisions in a land of unmeasured prairies and wood lands, and of sparsest settlement, is of more than passing interest to the historian. It was the initial law, the blazed tree in the trail of medical advancement, and it served a practical purpose in directing the policies along this line for later general assemblies. It indicated that during the earliest infancy of the State, the control of medical practice was regarded as essential to the best government, and that impression has remained to bear fruit in a later day and generation when the enforcement of law is a far simpler matter than at the time when Illinois developed "from an Indiana county into a territory of the second grade."

Repeal of the 1819 Act,

In 1821, the Act of 1819, which provided for the organization of medical societies, with certain powers to regulate the practice of medicine, with the object of providing improved medical standards and attention to public health, was repealed. This was a tremendous back-set to the regulation of medical practice in Illinois. An attempt to pass a law similar to the one that had been repealed was made in 1823, but did not succeed. A second law, known as "an Act prescribing the mode of licensing physicians" was passed in 1825, but was promptly repealed at the next session of the legislature.

How badly a law regulating medical practice was really needed is suggested by this statement by William Blane in his "A Tour in Southern Illinois," published in 1827:

"Persons who have not visited the western states cannot have any idea of the general ignorance of the practitioners of medicine. A young man, after an apprenticeship of a year or two in the shop of some ignorant apothecary, or after a very superficial course of study at some school or college is entitled to cure (or kill) all the unhappy backwoodsmen who may apply to him for advice. To become a doctor it is only necessary to have a cabin containing 50 to 100 dollars worth of drugs."

The following partial statement from Zeuch's "History of Medical Practice" indicates that wholesale barter in certificates to practice medicine developed in the State in the absence of laws regulating the practice of medicine:

"When this Thomsonian system was at its height a great number of certificates were sold, ...

"Joseph Chapman was the holder of the certificate, which shows one of the methods employed in the olden times in creating a practitioner of medicine. When the tide of the Thomsonian school was at its flood, a large number of these certificates were sold, giving the holder thereof the right to practice medicine. Without any medical study except such as was furnished with this certificate, any man who would pay the price was permitted to prescribe for the sick and administer such remedies as were endorsed by this particular cult, which was founded on the use of remedies of vegetable origin only, discarding all remedies which belonged to the mineral kingdom.

"No. 1398   Seventh Edition

"This may certify that we have received of Joseph Chapman, Twenty Dollars, in full for the right of preparing and using, for himself and family, the Medicine and System of Practice secured to Samuel Thomson, by Letters Patent from the President of the United States; and that he is thereby constituted a member of the Friendly Botanic Society, and is entitled to an enjoyment of all the privileges attached to membership therein.

"Dated at Alton this 19th day of . .   . . 1839.

"R. P. Maxey, Agt. for Pike, Platt & Co., Agents for Samuel Thomson."

Early Efforts to Get a Medical Practice Act.

That there remained the hope of securing a medical society as the nucleus for promoting a successful campaign for a Medical Practice Act, is indicated by the House Records of the General Assembly for February 5, 1839, which say "Mr. Webb of White County presented the petition of P. H. Brady, for the incorporation of a medical society, which on a motion was referred to Committee on Education."

Again in 1842 efforts were made to get a Medical Practice Act passed. The reports of the General Assembly show that:

"Mr. Anderson from the select committee, to which was referred the petition of sundry physicians of Shawneetown praying for the passage of a law regulating the practice of medicine, etc., made a report at length on the subject, and reported a bill for 'An Act to incorporate the Illinois State Medical Society' which was read the first time, and a second time by its title.

"Mr. Logan moved to amend the bill by striking out all after the enacting clause; and inserting the following: 'That no physician, surgeon or lawyer shall hereafter be entitled to sue for, or recover by action of law, his or their fees for services rendered as such physician, surgeon or lawyer.'

"The report, bill and proposed amendment were laid on the table by yeas and nays; 55 yeas; 50 nays."

The Illinois Medical and Surgical Journal in October, 1844, in an editorial commenting on the approaching meeting of the State Legislature respecting medical practice, said in part as follows:

"As the period for the session of the Legislature approaches we perceive a disposition of many members of the profession to agitate the subject of medical legislation. * * * There is at present no special legislative enactments relating to the practice of medicine in the State of Illinois. Every one is entitled to assume to himself the title of 'M. D.' to prescribe any or all substances in the three kingdoms of nature to any who call on him for advice. * * * *"

Added impetus to the agitation for a Medical Practice Act resulted from the organization in 1850 of the Illinois State Medical Society at Springfield in the library of the Capitol Building. The Chicago Medical Society was organized the same year.

In 1856 a committee was appointed by the Aesculapian Society of the Wabash Valley from among its membership to go before the Illinois legislature and urge upon that body the propriety of enacting a law creating a State Board of Health regulating the practice of medicine and providing for the registration of births and deaths. The committee did the duty assigned to it, but its work was without immediate tangible effect. Early in 1861 a second committee was selected for the same purpose and consisted of Doctors D. W. Stermont, William N. Chambers and John Ten Brook. But the labors of this committee, like that of its predecessor, bore no immediate perceptible reports.

However, at a meeting of the Illinois State Medical Society held at Champaign in 1876, a committee was appointed for a purpose similar to those of the Aesculapian in 1856 and 1861. The sentiment for a medical practice act expressed in 1856 did not crystallize into concerted action by the medical profession until a quarter of a century had passed. Apparently the organized medical profession of that day finally became convinced that to enforce adequately a medical practice act, if secured, a State Board of Health would be required. At least the following indicates that these two subjects were jointly in the minds of some of the members of the State

Medical Society. The Transactions of the 27th Anniversary Meeting of Illinois Medical Society in 1877, page 255, says:

"The Jersey County Medical Society of Illinois sends greetings to the Illinois State Medical Society, pledging our vigilant exertions in helping to secure the enforcement of such laws as you may be able to secure the enactment of, by either the State or National Legislature, looking to the establishment of

"A State Board of Health.

"Causing the registration of births and deaths and certificates as to the cause of the latter.

"Preventing those persons unqualified to practice medicine from doing so

"Creating a State Board of Medical Examiners."

On the twenty-first day of May, 1877, the legislature—after a lapse of over fifty years from the date of the repeal of the short, imperfect Acts of 1819 and 1825, placed upon the statute books an act to regulate the practice of medicine in the State of Illinois, approved May 29, 1877, and in force July 1, 1877.

That the Medical Practice Act came none too soon and that the patient of 1877 who came into the hands of the many sub-standard practitioners of medicine fared none too well, are deductions that may well be permitted by the ideas expressed in the following quotation from the December 17, 1877, edition of the Chicago Inter-Ocean daily:

"It is hardly necessary to say that the city of Chicago has become noted, not only for the immense number of villainous quacks, but for the ignorant and imperfect manner in which the register of births and deaths has been kept. The infant who was reported as having died of 'canker rash, diphtheria, dysentery and consumption,' and another whose cause of death was returned as 'five doctors,' doubtless had good reason to die; and 'delicate from birth,' 'infancy,' 'stoppage,' 'fits,' 'Colerafantum,' 'collocinphanton,' 'cholry fanton,' 'bled,' 'direars' (diarrhea), 'billirm (delirium) fever,' 'artry lung busted,' 'feusson,' (effusion), 'canker on brane,' and 'infermation lungs,' probably convey some ideas to the persons who write the terms; but such returns cannot be of much use from a statistical point of view. The importance of correct and intelligent registration cannot be underestimated, as modern sanitary science owes its existence to the registration of deaths and the localization thereby of insanitary conditions. It is right that the enforcement of the two bills, passed by the Legislature of the State, that will make such radical change both in medical profession and the method of registering births and deaths, should demand considerable attention."

Governor Cullom promptly appointed a Board of Health in conformity with the new law of 1877 and the appointees met in Springfield on July 12 of that year when they organized with Dr. John H. Rauch as president.

The State Board of Health, immediately after its appointment, weighed the urgency of the duties and obligations placed upon it by the newly enacted laws and decided that its first duty was to enforce the Medical Practice Act. The knowledge that over half of the 7,400 persons practicing medicine in 1877 were non-graduates (about 3,800) and that 490 were practicing medicine under fraudulent credentials, or even under assumed names, made this decision relatively easy.

Not only did the Board of Health decide first to center its chief attention on the enforcement of the Medical Practice Act, but a careful perusal of the minutes of the Board of Health from 1877 down to 1917, indicates clearly that this feature of their legally prescribed duties consumed fully three-fourths of the time, energy and resources of the Board.

On November 15, 1877, the following resolutions were adopted by the State Board of Health.

"That on and after July 1, 1878 the Board will not consider any medical college in good standing which holds two graduating courses in one year.

"Also, that on and after July 1, 1878 the Board will not recognize the diplomas of any medical school which does not require of its candidates for graduation the actual attendance upon at least two full courses of lectures at an interval of six months or more."

This was the first official step taken by the Board for higher medical education.

During the first year (1877) certificates totalling 5,374 were issued by the State Board to practitioners and midwives. By 1880, enforcement of the Medical Practice Act had materially reduced the number of quacks and itinerant vendors. Likewise the number of graduates in Illinois who were from reputable medical schools had increased from 3,600 to 4,825.

In the Annual Report of 1881, the Board printed for the first time a complete official register by counties of physicians registered to practice medicine, also a directory of medical societies in Illinois in 1881, and a roster of midwives registered, listed by counties. An alphabetic index of physicians is also printed in this report.

By 1882 the certificates issued to practitioners and midwives totalled 7,766, an increase of 2,392 since the end of 1877.

STANDARDS FOR MEDICAL EDUCATION.

In 1881 minimum standards for preliminary education of entrants into medical schools and requirements for medical colleges in good standing were established. An examination of all candidates with diplomas from medical schools not meeting these requirements, was required.

At the close of the year 1885, there were in round numbers 6,000 practitioners of medicine in the State. The Official Register, published and revised to February 10, 1886, contained the names, addresses, etc., of 5,915, to which are added some 150 others, exempt from the clause requiring certificates. Of this number 454 were added during the year; 114 applicants for certificates failed to comply with the law and were refused; and the certificates of eight practitioners were revoked for unprofessional and dishonorable conduct.

Revised Medical Practice Act Adopted.

The Act to Regulate the Practice of Medicine, adopted in 1877 was amended on June 16, 1887, and in force July 1, 1887. The amendments struck out the provisions of the original act relating to the appointment of boards of examiners by State medical societies, provided for three classes of certificates instead of two. The third class applied to persons who were licensed to practice on account of 10 years previous experience. It also provided that such certificates should be applied for within six months after the act went into effect, and that all persons holding certificates on account of 10 years of previous practice, should be subject to all requirements and discipline of the act.

The fee for the issuance of certificates without examination was raised from one dollar to five dollars, and a provision was made for the issuance of certificates to midwives, for a fee of two dollars.

Minimum requirements for schools of midwifery were adopted May 24, 1889.

A comparative table published in 1890 gives the status of the enforcement of the Medical Practice Act and the registration of physicians as follows: For purposes of comparison, the following totals from each of the five registers are here presented:

	Jan. 14, 1880.	Dec. 29, 1881.	Dec. 1, 1884.	Feb. 9, 1886.	Jan. 1, 1890.
Total number engaged in practice	6,029	6,037	6,148	6,115	6,215
Graduates and licentiates of medical institutions	4,282	4,488	4,882	5,098	5,524
Licentiates upon examination of State Board of Health	191	183	159	145	116
Exempts, non-graduates, certificated	948	896	757	672	575
Exempts, not certificated	*608	*470	*350	*200	,0

* Since the completion of this Register, a careful examination has disclosed the fact that there were about fifty more non-graduates in the state than were supposed, consequently this number has been added in the above table to the number of 'exempts, not certificated' for each of the years 1880, 1881, 1884, and 1886.

, No exempts under the law at this time—and no certificates based on years of practice, will be issued hereafter."

From the above tabular statement it will be seen that the number of those engaged in medical practice in the first 10 years of the Board's activities is nearly the same, notwithstanding that there was marked increase of population; also while the aggregate number of practitioners has not materially varied, there were some noticeable changes in the numbers of the different classes. Thus, there was a gain of 1,167 graduates and licentiates— these forming 91 per cent of the total number in 1890, as against about 76 per cent in 1880; the number of licentiates upon examination of the State Board was largely diminished—mainly by their transfer to the number of graduates, very many of them having subsequent to their examination attended lectures and obtained diplomas; also to the fact that few are added to this class owing to the increased severity of the examinations given by the Board.

The following summary, from the first Register, and corresponding figures from the 1890 report, exhibit these changes for the whole period since the Medical Practice Act went into operation:

	July 1, 1877.	Jan. 1, 1890.
Total number engaged in practice	7,400	6,215
Graduates and licentiates	3,600	5,640
Non-graduates	3,800	575
Percentage of graduates and licentiates in 1877		48
Percentage of graduates and licentiates January 1, 1890		91
Percentage of non-graduates in 1877		52
Percentage of non-graduates January 1, 1890		9
During the period of its existence or up to January 1, 1890, the Board has issued certificates to physicians		10,453
To graduates and licentiates of medical institutions		8,949
To exempts on years of practice		1,228
To licentiates upon examination, State Board of Health		246

"Diplomas or licenses have been presented by those now in practice in the state from 151 medical colleges and licensing bodies in the United States, from 18 in Germany, 18 in Great Britain and Ireland, 13 in Canada, 8 in Switzerland, 6 in Russia, 4 in Austria, 2 in Sweden, 2 in France, 1 in Denmark, 1 in Norway, 1 in Maderia, 1 in Spain, 1 in Bolivia, 1 in Italy, 1 in Belgium, 1 in Uruguay—making a total of 230 graduating or licensing bodies represented."

In 1892 the State Board of Health recommended for the consideration of the legislature, the desirability of relieving the Board from the enforcement of the Medical Practice Act by the creation of a Board of Medical Examiners, whose duty it should be to determine the fitness for the practice of medicine in the State, by examination of candidates, without reference to when, where or how they attained their fitness.

A resolution was also adopted providing that all applicants for a State certificate to practice midwifery in Illinois must pass a satisfactory examination given by the Board.

The proposition of establishing a separate licensing board was again taken up in 1896, when a committee was appointed representing the Illinois State Medical Society; the Homeopathic State Society; the Illinois State Eclectic Medical Society, and the State Board of Health, for the purpose of considering a plan to be presented to the legislature to amend the Medical Practice Act so as to require an examination by an impartial board, of all applicants to practice medicine in the State of Illinois. At the same time, the committee on administration of the Medical Practice Act submitted the rules and regulations governing the recognition of schools of midwifery.

A resolution was adopted that no medical college shall be recognized as in good standing for the purpose of the Illinois Medical Practice Act, that does not require of all matriculates, after January 1, 1897, as a condition of graduation, a four years' course of lectures in four separate years:

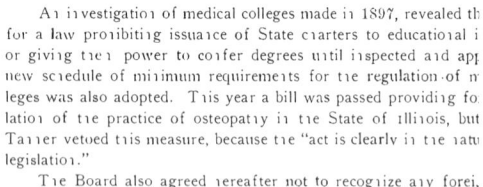

An investigation of medical colleges made in 1897, revealed th[at the need] for a law prohibiting issuance of State charters to educational i[nstitutions] or giving the[m] power to confer degrees until inspected and app[roved. A] new schedule of minimum requirements for the regulation of m[edical col]leges was also adopted. This year a bill was passed providing fo[r the regu]lation of the practice of osteopathy in the State of Illinois, but [Governor] Tanner vetoed this measure, because the "act is clearly in the natu[re of class] legislation."

The Board also agreed hereafter not to recognize any forei[gn diploma] as a basis upon which to issue a certificate to practice medicine a[nd surgery] in the State, and that all applicants holding such diplomas shall b[e required] to pass an examination.

Interstate reciprocity was adopted in 1899. The Medical P[ractice Act] was amended again this year and broadened so as to provide for th[e examina]tion and licensing of persons who desire to practice any other system of treating human ailments.

At the annual meeting of the Illinois State Medical Socie[ty held at] Quincy, May 20-22, 1902, a proposed Bill for an Act to Establi[sh a State] Board of Medical Examiners was presented and received appro[val of the] Society as a whole.

The Medical Practice Act was further amended in 1907 by [adding] a provision empowering the State Board of Health to determine [the stand]ard of literary and scientific colleges, high schools, etc., to be ac[cepted as] preliminary education of medical students, and to require the en[forcement] of a standard of preliminary education by medical colleges; also [providing] for reciprocity and granting of the compensation to members of th[e examin]ing board for their services.

In 1915 a law was passed amending the Medical Practice Act [giving] the Board jurisdiction over certificates issued to all physicians [in] the State under the various medical laws.

OTHER PRACTITIONERS.

Neither the Medical Practice Act of 1877 nor that of 188[7 make] mention of or give provision for licensing "other practitioners."

In the 1903 report of the Board of Health on page XLIII w[e find the] following:

"REQUIREMENTS FOR 'THOSE WHO DESIRE TO PRACTICE AN[Y OTHER] SYSTEM OR SCIENCE OF TREATING HUMAN AILMENT[S]'

Instructions to Applicants.

"State Certificates authorizing persons who do not use medicine[s internally] or externally and who do not perform surgical operations, to treat [human ail]ments, are issued by the State Board of Health, on complying with [certain re]quirements, based upon the Act to Regulate the Practice of Medic[ine in the] State of Illinois, in force July 1, 1899."

Midwives.

While the 1877 Medical Practice Act referred only to persons practicing medicine in any of its departments and made no reference to midwives, the State Board of Health at a Cairo meeting on November 15, 1877, made the following statement:

"The Board in entering upon the enforcement of the medical practice act, considered it imperative to attend to the demands made upon it by general practitioners, and paid little attention to midwives. Four hundred and twenty four certificates have however been issued to midwives, a comparatively large number, taking into consideration that owing to the amount of time and labor needed for issuing of certificates to medical practitioners, the systematic work of licensing midwives did not begin till a very recent date. In many counties of the state the proportion of midwives to general practitioners of medicine is very large—and much remains to be done to secure their complete licensing and registration."

And again at the first annual meeting January 10, 1878, we note this comment

"By vote of the Board it was resolved that midwives be placed upon the same basis under the law, so far as the requirement for certificates to practice are concerned, as practitioners of medicine."

The 1887 Medical Practice Act makes no specific requirements for licensing midwives but under Fees for Examination says:

"The fees for the examination of non-graduates shall be as follows: Twenty ($20) dollars for examination in Medicine and Surgery. Ten ($10) dollars for an examination in midwifery only."

The 1899 Act in the second section provides: "No person shall hereafter begin the practice of medicine or any of the branches thereof, or midwifery in this State without first applying for and obtaining a license from the State Board of Health to do so."

The official register of midwives having a State certificate issued by the Board since 1877 totalled 1,470 in 1896

Embalmers.

The official rules of the State Board of Health for the transportation of the dead based on an "Act providing for the Regulation of Embalming and the disposal of dead bodies" approved May 13, 1905, were promulgated and given wide publicity in 1907, and all concerned were informed:

"It is the duty of every Embalmer in the State of Illinois to thoroughly familiarize himself with every provision of these rules, the rigid enforcement of which is essential to the proper operation of the law under which they were created."

REGULATION OF MEDICAL PRACTICE TRANSFERRED TO DEPARTMENT OF REGISTRATION AND EDUCATION

Through the enactment in 1917 of the Administrative Code, the responsibility for "the rights, powers and duties vested by law in the State

Board of Health relating to the practice of medicine, or an[y]
thereof, or midwifery, * * * * the regulation of the embal[ming]
of dead bodies, and for a system of examination, registra[tion]
of embalmers," was transferred to the Department of Regi[stra]tion. Thus for the first time since 1877, the State Dep[artment of]
Health which was created by this Act, was free to give t[he sub]ject of public health the fair share of the attention it merit[s.]

AUXILIARY HEALTH AGENCIES.

In the promotion of health in Illinois the State and local departments of health have had the aid of many health agencies. Some of these are arms of government and some are not. Some are known as health agencies and act directly as such. Others are known by other names and their contribution is more indirect. Some are national and some are local.

The legislature in providing health laws and the courts in interpreting them have made their contribution. The collateral administrative officers in other departments have made theirs. The contribution of governors and of the heads of the departments of education, agriculture, public welfare and labor, have been outstanding. Among the national organizations that have helped to promote health in the State are the United States Public Health Service, Children's Bureau, U. S. Department of Labor, U. S. Department of Agriculture, the International Health Board, American Public Health Association, American Child Health Association, National Tuberculosis Association and National Educational Association. Among the more active agencies operating principally within the State are those, some of the activities of which are detailed on the following pages.

Quasi Public Health Agencies.

ILLINOIS MEDICAL SOCIETY.

The Illinois Medical Society has been in continuous existence since 1850. While their main objective is the education of physicians in the methods of curative medicine, keeping them abreast of the times and otherwise promoting the professional interest of their members, they have not been unmindful of the duties of the medical profession in the field of prevention. For many years one of the sections of this Society has been that of preventive medicine. The Journal of the Society carries the papers read in this section to the offices and homes of all the membership. There are those who hold that in the division of labor in the field of preventive medicine the medical societies can justify themselves in a policy of limiting their work to education of physicians in preventive measures and keeping them abreast of all advances in this field. This activity the Illinois Medical Society does through the Section on Preventive Medicine, but they do other work as well.

Their large share of credit for the law creating a State public health service is referred to elsewhere. Their committee at Springfield has lent its support to legislation for the public health at every session of the

General Assembly for many years. The expense of this is borne in part out of Society funds and in part out of subscriptions and donations by individual members of the profession.

In 1903 the Chicago Medical Society organized a course of lectures on health subjects for lay hearers. These lectures were held in the public library weekly for about two years.

In 1922 the Illinois Medical Society provided for a similar activity under the auspices of an Education Committee. This Committee began work in 1923. Their report for January 1 to May 12, 1927 made in May 1927 indicates the nature of their state wide activities.

Seven counties in the State have made definite use of the service offered through the Educational Committee during these four and one-half months. The other counties have made use of the service indirectly.

Eighty-eight requests for speakers have been filled to date. The members of the speakers' bureau have appeared before such groups as Kiwanis, Lions, Rotary, Optimist clubs, women's clubs, churches, parent-teacher associations, teachers' institutes, home bureaus, Y. M. C. A., Y. W. C. A. groups, and boy and girl scouts.

A speakers' bureau of colored physicians and another of foreign speaking physicians have been organized in order to widen the circle reached through health talks.

Thirty-nine newspapers are using the health articles released from the office of the Educational Committee as a regular feature. These articles appear in all cases under the signature of the local medical societies. Eight hundred health articles have been released to the newspapers in the State.

Fifty-nine radio programs have been arranged for over stations, WGN, WHT, WLS, WMAQ and WQJ. Reports have come from Wisconsin, Iowa, Michigan and Indiana as well as from many parts of Illinois commending these programs most highly.

Forty-two moving picture films have been scheduled for use by lay groups. These have been obtained from the State Department of Public Health, the American Dental Association, the University of Wisconsin, and the Society for Visual Education.

Five communities have had splendid poster exhibits in connection with special health day programs through the courtesy of the Educational Committee.

Cooperation has been given to certain projects of the State Department of Public Health, such as furnishing speakers, films and posture exhibits for various groups during Health Week.

The Committee has worked with the Illinois Federation of Women's Clubs in urging club women to cooperate with county medical societies in all health activities. Letters have been sent out emphasizing the importance of educating the public on the subject of cancer.

Approach has been made to all county societies where baby conferences have been held in cooperation with the child hygiene division of the State Department of Public Health. Through this introduction county societies were enabled to work out their own plans with the State Department of Public Health.

The committee serves as a clearing house in making contacts with lay organizations.

During National Baby Week programs were arranged and speakers supplied for several department stores in Chicago. Special radio talks were also given by physicians and dentists.

One hundred dentists were given complete physical examinations at the annual meeting of the Chicago Dental Society in 1927. Twenty-five physicians were examined at the meeting of the Illinois State Medical Society at Moline in May of the same year.

The promotion of periodic physical examinations has been one of the more recent public activities of the Illinois Medical Society.

Illinois Federation of Women's Clubs.

This organization has been of material support in furthering health measures. About 1912 when the war on consumption down-state was in need of friends, the Federation through its local clubs and district organizations made a survey of tuberculosis throughout the State. The facts revealed by this survey and the local interest stimulated by it was largely responsible for the County Tuberculosis Sanitarium bill and for support of the county sanatoria throughout the State. At this time they are especially interested in promoting the physical and mental examination of children of preschool age.

Illinois Society for the Prevention of Blindness.

In 1915 in Chicago ten babies became blind as a result of neglected ophthalmia neonatorum. This led to the formation of the Illinois Society for the Prevention of Blindness. Before 1915 only 30 cases a year of ophthalmia neonatorum were reported. During 1926 nearly 600 such cases were reported. This does not mean that there is more of the infection, it means only that the cases are now recognized and properly treated. There has been a marked reduction in the number made blind yearly and also in the number of grave infections.

The Society's first task was to promote the passage of a law requiring that gonococcal infections of the eye be prevented by the compulsory use of nitrate of silver and that cases of the disease be reported. They have helped in the enforcement of the law. The preventive is now supplied free by the State Department of Public Health.

The Society has promoted trachoma surveys and clinics, also examination of children for usual defects. They have conducted work in Chicago and in the State outside Chicago.

The other interest of this Society is in the poor vision found among school children. The Society works down-state as well as in Chicago, in making surveys of existing conditions, securing relief for those who are handicapped by eye defects and in helping them to useful occupations, and also in educating and interesting people in the prevention of poor vision.

CHICAGO TUBERCULOSIS INSTITUTE.

The present Chicago Tuberculosis Institute had its beginning in the Visiting Nurses Association in 1902. Miss Fulmer, the superintendent of nurses wrote her board calling their attention to the great amount of time and money spent by their organization in nursing and otherwise helping persons sick with consumption. She suggested that some money, brains and energy spent in prevention would eventually save something in money, brains and energy spent in care and occasional cure.

As a result of this communication the Visiting Nurses Association called a meeting of physicians and other interested persons, members of their board to convene in the rooms of the Association on January 21, 1903. This meeting organized a committee on tuberculosis. The Association voted $2,000 as a part of funds necessary to start the work. The plan of activities adopted was that proposed by Dr. A. C. Klebs. In March, 1903, this Committee began to function in rooms adjacent to those of the Visiting Nurses Association. By October, 1903, the Committee reported 67 cases of consumption under their direction. In November, 1903 it was reported that a course of lectures on tuberculosis had been arranged for.

In March 1905, this Committee sent a letter to the Visiting Nurses Association proposing that the Tuberculosis Committee form a separate organization. The Visiting Nurses Association replied that they considered that the time had come to consummate that.

At the third annual meeting of the Tuberculosis Committee of the Visiting Nurses Association held January 27, 1906, the Chicago Tuberculosis Society was formed to take over the activities of the Committee. This was in effect nothing more than creating a new form and selecting a new name for the old Committee and its work. The change was made with the approval of the Visiting Nurses Association because it was thought the work could be better done by a separate organization. Most of the old committee members continued active in the new organization and two of them, Mrs. E. C. Dudley and Dr. W. A. Evans have been in continuous service since and are still active.

March 1, 1906, the name was changed to the Chicago Tuberculosis Institute. It was chartered March 17, 1906.

At first the Society did nothing except educational work, study and propaganda.

On September 1, 1906, they established a temporary sanitorium or camp on the grounds of the Durand Institutions. It was known as Camp Norwood and it served the public in a small way from that date until March 31, 1907.

The Institute inaugurated a free dispensary service on May 15, 1907. This was gradually extended as to the number of dispensaries operated and the variety of service given until September 1, 1910 on which date the service in its entirety was handed over to the Municipal Tuberculosis Sanitarium.

On May 27, 1907, after an interruption of about two months the Institute went back into the business of operating a philanthropic sanitarium through their acceptance from Mrs. Keith Spalding of Edward Sanitarium at Naperville, Illinois.

In the beginning the activities of the Committee, Society and Institute were supported by funds from the Visiting Nurses Association and donations from the public at large.

In 1908 the system of raising money by the sale of Christmas seals was inaugurated. This has been the principal, in fact almost the sole means, of raising money since that date. Seals have been sold each December with the exception of 1918 in which year by special arrangement the funds were supplied out of the nation-wide community chest collected for the purpose of supporting all philanthropic home activities in war time.

On April 16, 1910, a meeting to organize a State Tuberculosis Society was held in the offices of the Chicago Tuberculosis Institute. This meeting was attended by Doctors Sala of Rock Island, Hardesty of Jacksonville and Wallace of Peoria and a number of persons from Chicago; it was voted to organize a new Society out of the old State Society for the Prevention of Tuberculosis. The Chicago Tuberculosis Society agreed to stand all the preliminary expense of this reorganization. On June 10, 1910, the new State Society was organized (out of the old Society) (taking over its charter). It was then voted that the offices of the new society should be in the rooms of the Chicago Tuberculosis Institute and that the superintendent of the institute also serve the State Society as its superintendent without expense to the State Society for either rent or salary of the superintendent. At a later date the State Society occupied separate rooms but adjacent to those of the institute. Later on they employed a full-time superintendent, still later the offices were removed to Springfield.

December 30, 1918, the officers of the Illinois Society for the Prevention of Tuberculosis completely separated the Chicago Tuberculosis Institute from affiliation with them creating Cook County as a separate jurisdiction for the sale of Christmas seals and the doing of tuberculosis work. On January 11, 1919, this action of the State Society was approved by the executive committee of the National Tuberculosis Society.

Among the acts and activities of the Chicago Tuberculosis Institute found recorded in the minutes in addition to those narrated above are the following:

Propaganda before the legislature for a State sanitarium and for a tuberculosis bureau in the State Department of Health. Propaganda in support of the Glackin law for a municipal sanitarium in 1909. Activity in the campaign on the referendum under this law which vote established the Municipal Tuberculosis Sanitarium. Council in the organization of the sanitarium activities under that act.

On July 17, 1907, the Chicago Tuberculosis Institute turned over to the city health department their street index file of tuberculosis and the filing cabinet in which this was kept, the city health department promising to keep this file alive.

They helped in the passage of the Glackin county sanitarium bills, the pasteurization ordinance and various laws for the repression of bovine tuberculosis, they organized study classes for tuberculosis in industry and for the scientific and clinical study of the disease, they conducted exhibitions and issued leaflets and pamphlets. Their present major activities are as follows:

A general nursing service in more than one-half the county. This service is active in the control of all forms of contagion. This service is rendered in cooperation with the county and local health departments. A health service rendered by physicians attending a number of health centers. A follow-up service for persons who have arrested tuberculosis. A health survey service. A course of lectures on public health for nurses in training. An employment agency for nurses trained in tuberculosis work. An educational and propaganda service. A sanitarium service and other miscellaneous services.

THE ILLINOIS TUBERCULOSIS AND HEALTH ASSOCIATION.

The voluntary organization which has done more to promote general public health improvement than any other non-official agency in the State is the Illinois Tuberculosis and Health Association. Originally established for the purpose of concentrating its efforts against tuberculosis this organization became in time a powerful factor in the general field of public health service through the stimulation of local public health nursing services. It changed its name three times but its functions, while emphasizing tuberculosis work in particular, have included general activities for the greater part of its life.

Through the sale of Christmas seals this organization has had more resources than any other voluntary agency for doing health work in the State at large. These have been used to good advantage, resulting in the establishment of local voluntary health organizations, local nursing services, tuberculosis sanitariums and the promotion of health education. Always the policies and activities have conformed with standard practices set up by the organized medical profession and the public health authorities

The organization had its beginning in 1903 when Dr. J. W. Pettit of Ottawa, Illinois, read a paper on consumption before the Illinois State Medical Society. Following this he was appointed by the Society to the chairmanship of a committee on tuberculosis with instructions to carry out whatever plans seemed practical and advisable.

The National Tuberculosis Association had just been organized in New York and encouraged with the interest of the State Medical Society, Dr. Pettit sent out a letter on December 6, 1904, calling a meeting for the purpose of organizing an Illinois tuberculosis association. This meeting convened at the Great Northern Hotel, Chicago, December 14, 1904. Seventeen attended. The outcome was a plan, which later materialized into reality, to organize an association to function on a state-wide scale.

The organization was called the Illinois Association for the Prevention of Tuberculosis. Dr. A. C. Klebs was elected president and Dr. N. A. Graves, secretary.

The first work of the organization was concentrated on legislation looking toward the establishment of a State tuberculosis sanitarium. The further objects were to stimulate the formation of and provide assistance for local societies in all the towns of the State and to cooperate with the national association for the study and prevention of tuberculosis.

Funds were secured through the sale of Christmas seals. The first sale was conducted in 1905 and the total amount raised was $1,200. President James of the University of Illinois was elected president of the Association in 1905.

On April 16, 1910, a reorganization meeting was held, using the old charter which was dated February 7, 1905. Dr. W. A. Evans, Chicago was elected president and Mr. Frank E. Wing of Chicago, secretary.

Four local organizations applied for affiliation. The purpose of the organization was again stressed emphasizing educational work and nursing service instead of material relief for consumptives.

In 1914 the Modern Health Crusade movement was launched as the outcome of a survey made in White County.

In 1914 the organization cooperated with the State Department of Public Health in a health exhibit at the Illinois State Fair, a practice that has continued to date.

In December 1918, Cook County was created as a separate organization for the sale of Christmas seals, and early in 1919 the office of the Illinois Association for the Prevention of Tuberculosis, as it was called at that time, was moved to Springfield and the name was changed to the Illinois Tuberculosis Association.

Some of the tangible results of activities for which the Association was entirely or largely responsible, according to records available in August 1927, include the following:

Public health nursing services in 72 counties,
Tuberculosis sanatoria in 16 counties,
Affiliated organizations in 104 different localities,
Modern health crusade functioning in 87 counties,
Two summer camps operating for undernourished children,
Christmas seal sale organizations in every county.

In 1919 the executive secretary of the Illinois Tuberculosis Association was employed by the State Department of Public Health to direct a state-wide project known as Health Promotion Week. Both organizations put a very large share of their joint resources behind the undertaking which resulted in a very general public response. This project developed into an annual affair, conducted by the State Department of Public Health, which has doubtless exercised considerable influence on the volume of public health educational achievements in the State.

Other activities of the Association include the publication of a monthly health educational bulletin called the "Arrow", the promotion of legislation calculated to result in substantial improvement of public health, the carrying out of tuberculosis surveys (such surveys have been made at least once in every county), the launching of "open window" and anti-spitting campaigns annually and cooperation with legitimate public health movements generally.

For example of the latter, the Association contributed $250 toward the salary of a dentist who was employed by the dental profession of the State and placed on the staff of the State Department of Public Health in 1926 as a demonstration of what could be done by promoting dental hygiene. This demonstration resulted in legislative provision for carrying on the work by the State Department of Public Health.

Parent-Teacher Associations.

This is an organization composed of teachers in the grade schools and the parents of the pupils therein. It is a liaison organization between the schools and the home. Its plan is to have a local society for the parents and teachers of each school to consider everything that makes for the physical and mental welfare of school children. A recent amendment to the plan provides for the preparation of children for the school by having them examined physically and mentally, having their physical defects corrected and having them vaccinated against such diseases as diphtheria and smallpox all before they reach six years of age in order that they may enter the first grade in the best possible state of health and bodily vigor

National Safety Council.

The National Safety Council calls Illinois its home state. The preliminary meeting to organize this Council was held in Milwaukee in 1912. The first meeting under a completed organization was held in Chicago in 1914 under the presidency of R. W. Campbell of the Illinois Steel Company.

Today the Council has 4,312 members and spends more than half a million dollars annually.

The preliminary meeting in 1912 was addressed on the subject of "The Illinois System of Factory Inspection" by Edgar T. Davies. It was principally by virtue of the Health, Safety and Comfort Act that this Illinois department was able to function.

The National Council stimulated the formation of a Chicago Industrial Safety Council to function in Chicago and elsewhere in Illinois.

The principal work of the Safety Council is to lessen the number of industrial accidents, through propaganda and education of the employers and employees and promotion of the general use of safety devices and safety methods. They have devoted some time to an objective not quite so directly in their field, namely, the prevention of public accidents such as accidents on the streets and public highways and in the home.

They likewise promote better first aid service. Since 1914 there has been a very marked decrease in industrial accidents both fatal and non-fatal in the State. The Safety Council feels that this field of need is being covered in a way that is satisfying. Not so the field of street or public accidents. The fatal accident rate composed principally of public or street accidents is now one of the leading causes of death.

Chicago Heart Association.

The Chicago Heart Association was organized in October, 1922, the purposes being stated as follows—education of the public, second—coordination of all organizations having to do with heart diseases and the establishment of new organizations and promotion of research in the problems of heart disease especially as it relates to public health. Since 1922 twelve cardiac clinics have been developed and 15,000 to 25,000 pamphlets have been distributed yearly; 2500 numbers of a quarterly bulletin are sent out four times a year.

The Association has assisted in procuring facilities for the care of cardiac convalescents and vacation camps for cardiacs. In 1926 they made a study of cardiacs in industry.

While the greater part of the present program relates to the care of those already having heart troubles it is preventive in that it plans to prevent incapacity due to heart disease by reason of broken establishment. The Association plans to try prevention of heart disease as soon as the basic facts are established.

State Heart Society.

There is a State Heart Society, of which Dr. C. H. Diehl is president, but it has not functioned yet.

The Chicago League for the Hard of Hearing.

The Chicago League for the Hard of Hearing was founded in January 1916. It now has a membership of seven hundred and sixteen. The activities of the League are, teaching lip reading, testing apparatus for the aid of hearing, making surveys of the degree of hearing of school children, the conditions of ears, nose and throat in school children and securing care for school children who have infections of the ears, nose and throat.

State and Local Dental Societies.

The State and local dental societies have contributed something to the improvement of health and physical vigor by aiding health departments and schools to secure dental clinics in the schools and elsewhere and by educational and propaganda campaigns.

Laboratories and Universities.

The laboratories and universities have contributed to the betterment of health by research work and by teaching and by education of the public.

The health departments eagerly seize on every fact established by research either in laboratory or in hospital or in universities whether in Illinois or elsewhere. Some part of the improvement is due to indirect aid from all institutions of these types.

The universities and colleges further contribute by maintaining a health service for students which service is largely in fact principally preventive in character.

INDUSTRIAL PHYSICIANS.

The industrial physicians have an opportunity to apply preventive medicine to large bodies of men and women under the very best of circumstances. Their recommendations of changes in methods and in environment made to the management are generally needed. Their advice to employers made both directly and indirectly through foremen carry weight and influence. The industrial physicians have helped the health campaign.

PRACTICING PHYSICIANS.

No other group renders so much service as an auxiliary agency as do the practicing physicians. They are constantly rendering service in prevention through their direct contacts with their clients. They periodically render such service indirectly through their local medical societies.

ILLINOIS SOCIETY FOR MENTAL HYGIENE.

The Illinois Society for Mental Hygiene was founded in 1909. Its first staff consisted of one nurse who had a desk in the woman's club in Chicago. In 1911 some additional personnel was availed of by means of funds set aside for the purpose by the County Judge of Cook County. This work in the Cook County courts was taken over by the court in 1915. In 1923 the need of definite practical training in mental hygiene for social workers was demonstrated to the social service agencies in Chicago. A (health) demonstration of the relation of mental hygiene to personality difficulties was made in a Chicago high school. Local mental hygiene committees were organized in two Illinois communities.

A survey was made of the mental hygiene conditions in the schools of LaSalle, Illinois.

The Society helped to bring about the organization of the State Institute for Child Research. Much of the energy of the Society is expended in popular education and propaganda for mental health.

AMERICAN RED CROSS.

The American Red Cross first entered the field of rural nursing in 1912. Their activities in home nursing were increased when the State troops were called to the border in 1916. A program of development on a large scale was adopted in 1919. While most of the work of the rural nurses takes the form of bedside nursing of the sick much of it is preventive in character.

In April 1927, public health nurses were employed in 77 counties as county, school or community nurses. In fifty-nine of these counties the American Red Cross participated in inaugurating the service. There were seventeen Red Cross chapters employing public health nurses. Eight of these nurses are financed entirely by the Red Cross and nine jointly by the Red Cross and other agencies. The Red Cross conducts nearly five hundred classes yearly in home hygiene and care of the sick—issuing certificates to about 11,000 persons yearly.

The following are some of the principles of the nursing service: "The protection of the public health is fundamentally a governmental problem but at the same time, it is one that requires the intelligent and active cooperation of the individual citizen. The function of the Red Cross is the promotion of individual and community health through personal service, group instruction and general health propaganda." The duties of these nurses are given as—"eradication of communicable diseases, health education, nursing care of the sick, of mothers, of new born babies, of the tuberculous and school nursing."

AMERICAN SOCIETY FOR THE CONTROL OF CANCER.

The American Society for the Control of Cancer was organized at the Clinical Congress of Surgeons held in New York City in 1912, (about). Soon after that an Illinois branch was formed. Dr. Gilbert Fitz-Patrick, present chairman of the Illinois branch, sets September, 1926 as the time of rejuvenation of that branch. At that time he appeared before the council of the State Medical Society and secured their endorsement. Since then sixty-three county branches have been organized and 500 meetings attended by 150,000 people have been held. "The campaign has for its prime objective teaching the people ways of checking their disease liabilities against the health assets through the physical examination yearly." Cancer has proven the best wedge and the worst topic with which to open for discussion the topic of better health.

ILLINOIS SOCIAL HYGIENE LEAGUE.

On July 15, 1916, three Chicago men, Budd C. Corbus, M. D., Mr. Samuel Carson and Mr. Roger Sherman received articles of incorporation for an organization whose objective was defined as "devoted to the scientific observation and study of diseases and cures therefor," but whose constitution limited its work "to the study, prevention and treatment of venereal diseases."

At the first annual meeting Robert H. Gault, professor of criminal law and criminology at Northwestern University was elected president. An active campaign of prevention and education, particularly in the camps at Fort Sheridan, Camp Grant, Grant Park, Great Lakes and Municipal Pier, was carried on.

Prophylactic stations were opened at the League's first permanent home, an old house of prostitution at 118 West Grand Avenue, Chicago, and at the Northwestern depot. Cooperative relations were established with the Illinois State Council of Defense, the British Recruiting Mission and the United States Examining Boards.

Exhibits were installed, lecturers trained and sent out, hundreds of thousands of pamphlets printed, and lantern-slides made.

A comprehensive survey of the hospitals and dispensaries of Chicago with reference to the facilities for the diagnosis and treatment of the venereal diseases was made in behalf of the League by Dr. Mary C. Lincoln and published, April 24, 1917.

The name was changed to the Illinois Social Hygiene League early in 1919. Since then the yearly expenditures for charitable treatment and education have grown to nearly $50,000 and the number of treatments given yearly from 3,302 to 28,222 in 1926.

When Professor Gault left Chicago, Mr. Charles S. Dering became president and under his wise leadership and that of Dr. Louis E. Schmidt, who succeeded him, the constructive contribution of the League to the welfare of society increased materially.

In April, 1927, the League moved into its own building a comparatively new four-story brick business structure ideally located and constructed for teaching, treating and training purposes. This purchase was made possible by contributions from the president, Mr. E. S. Meyer, a member of the board of directors, Mr. Albert Kuppenheimer of Chicago and other generous Chicago citizens.

Here the League conducts separate clinics for venereally diseased men, women, and children, an exhibit room and lecture hall, with one floor devoted to education and preventive work. Four full-time physicians provide the service in return for post-graduate instruction plus an honorarium while ten or twelve medical men and women of experience and ability provide the instruction and medical supervision. Over 100 patients a day are treated here for syphilis and gonorrhea while over 100,000 instructive pamphlets are distributed yearly by the educational department, 100 lectures given and many exhibits set up. The League has a film library of 35 reels of educational films which is in constant use. Research work in cooperation with the U. S. Public Health Service has been organized and an efficient laboratory provided where it is carried on with the assistance of the League staff and students from Northwestern University Medical College.

Plans are afoot for a further increase of activity looking toward a comprehensive program for the ultimate eradication of the venereal disease if such a thing is possible.

The work done in Illinois outside of Chicago is limited to propaganda and educational activities.

Children's Hospital Society and Milk Commission.

In December 1902, following the visit of Dr. A. Lorenz of Vienna, a movement was set on foot by the Woman's Club reform department to provide Chicago with facilities for sick children.

This meeting resulted in the organization of the Children's Hospital Society of Chicago. Dr. Frank Billings was elected president. Mrs. Harold McCormick, secretary, Mr. E. G. Keith, treasurer and Mrs. Flora G. Moulton, chairman of the Membership Committee.

In May, 1903, this Society organized the Milk Commission of Chicago. This Milk Commission remained active thereafter although the parent society (the Children's Hospital Society) appeared to have lapsed.

Mr. and Mrs. Nathan Straus of New York donated to this Society a pasteurizing plant which through the courtesy of the Chicago Board of Education was located in the basement of the Thomas Hoyne School, Cass and Illinois streets, Chicago.

Dr. I. A. Abt was chairman of this Commission and Mrs. Plummer and Mrs. Moulton were in control of the plant. They began distributing milk on July 7, 1903, and continued until November 28, 1903. In this time they distributed 222,000 bottles of pasteurized modified milk. It was sold below cost through thirty-one milk stations.

The laboratory work on this milk was done without cost by the Columbus Medical Laboratory through Dr. Adolph Gehrman. At a public meeting to promote this activity held at the Chicago Woman's Club, May 26, 1903, speeches were made by Mrs. Chas. Henrotin, Dr. F. Billings, Miss Jane Addams, Mrs. Geo. Plummer, Mr. Steve Sumner of the milk drivers union, Mr. H. B. Farmer of the milk shippers union, J. E. Allen, Chicago and North Western Railroad, Professor E. O. Jordan, Dr. A. R. Reynolds, Dr. I. A. Abt, James Cheeseman, Dr. W. S. Christopher, Mr. H. B. Gurler and Dr. Rosa Engelman.

In 1903 the Commission continued distributing milk. They inaugurated inspection of farms, visitation of babies in the homes, mothers' meetings and a series of educational articles in the Chicago Tribune. The secretary pronounced the work of the Commission as "An educative benevolent one of instruction, example and protection where no mere law can reach." In their minutes we read that Northwestern University medical school established a diet kitchen in December, 1902.

Also that as the years passed by St. Louis and other cities established commissions modeled after that of Chicago.

In May 1904, one of the educational articles was on the subject of State supervision of milk by E. N. Eaton.

From this article we learn that the Illinois legislature passed a law in 1874 which prohibited the adulteration of milk under a penalty of $500. In 1879 they passed a law prohibiting the selling of impure milk and also the selling of milk from diseased cows. The penalty was $100.

In 1897 they provided for State standards for milk. In 1899 another law created the office of State food commission and gave them some control over milk.

An interesting report on the work of 1903 is a report of the home and dairy visits of a field worker. Much of her time was spent in instructing mothers how to keep their babies well.

This type of activity was continued for several years. On July 24, 1908, the Commission was chartered. In its year book for December 31, 1911 the Milk Commission says, "For eight years (since 1903) the Milk Commission for Chicago has successfully carried on its work."

Chicago Infant Welfare Society.

On March 10, 1911, the Infant Welfare Society was formed by a reorganization of the Milk Commission. The milk stations were closed and the new organization continued the policy of instructing mothers in the home and in stations, but stressing this type of activity especially.

Judge Julian Mack resigned as president January 31, 1911, and Mr. Lucius Teter succeeded him. Two important conferences with representatives of the Chicago Medical Society are referred to in the minutes. On December 28, 1908, a joint meeting was held to discuss the confusion which seemed to be arising relative to the use of the terms medical commission, milk and certified milk, commission milk. This seems to have been adjusted by naming the Milk Commission recommend some persons to membership of the Milk Certifying Commission of the Chicago Medical Society.

This source of friction was entirely removed little more than two years later when the Milk Commission changed its name and stopped supplying milk.

Another consultation with representatives of the Chicago Medical Society was held February 2, 1909. This was with reference to the system of consultation days and hours for mothers and babies. The plan appears to have met the approval of the representatives of the medical society.

On March 15, 1910, a joint meeting of the Milk Commission and the Children's Society was held to work out a plan for infant welfare stations that would be more comprehensive than that in use.

On March 29, 1910, Dr. W. A. Evans, health commissioner of Chicago asked the Milk Commission to participate in a city wide "Save the Babies Campaign" during the summer of 1910. This campaign was to operate through infant welfare centers as agencies. The Society accepted and participated.

In December 1910, the superintendent, Miss Ahrens, made a report based on a four months study of the local situation. She recommended a reorganization of the work of the society under a medical director. This was done.

The final transformation of the Commission into the Infant Welfare Society in 1911 has been referred to above.

The Society has functioned since on that basis.

Its objects are stated as:—"To reduce the infant death rate and improve the health of the coming generation by keeping the baby well, before its birth by caring for the mother and after its birth by teaching her how to feed and care for her child."

The types of care given in 1926 are prenatal care, infant care, care of pre-school children.

The number of infant welfare stations operated in 1926 was given as twenty-three. Of these nine stations gave all three kinds of work. Seven gave service only to preschool children. Six served infants only and one gives prenatal and infant care only

In 1926 prenatal care was given to 1,298 mothers, infant service was given to 12,901 babies, and preschool service to 2,429 children.

A part of the service rendered since October 1925 is in mental hygiene.

Elizabeth McCormick Memorial Foundation.

The Elizabeth McCormick Memorial Foundation specializes in promoting health work among children. Having observed the operation of open window schools in the Graham school in 1908 and 1909 they spent several years in active propaganda for fresh air and open window schools.

They next became active in propaganda and promotion of the Emerson plan for improving the nutrition of school children. More recently they have been promoting more general procedures principally aimed at improving the nutrition of school children.

...S OF PROFESSIONAL HEALTH WORKERS.

...Dr. J. H. Rauch there has always been one or more ... the State. Most of the times these societies have ...ns. At times they have functioned satisfactorily ...re are three of them. The health officers have an ...s annually to discuss methods of doing health work— ... to promote the efficiency of health officers and to ...ention done by them.

...rculosis and Public Health Association has some ... addition to their tuberculosis work. They hold ...issue a periodical.

... Society has some funds in the treasury and main-

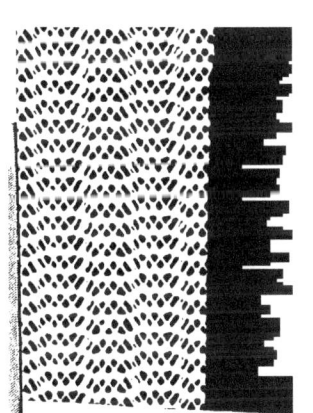

HEALTH CONDITIONS IN ILLINOIS AFTER 1877.

Few changes in the history of Illinois have been so pronounced as the differences between health conditions that prevailed fifty years before and fifty years after 1877. Prior to that date the territory included within the boundary lines of the State went through a period when it rightly provoked the reputation of being one of the most unhealthful portions of the United States. Practically no improvement in mortality and sickness rates took place before 1877 although malaria, the predominating factor in the early evil reputation, had begun to decline noticeably. Indeed the prevalence of such infections as typhoid fever, tuberculosis, diphtheria and most of the other communicable diseases grew worse. The fertility of the soil and other economic resources such as coal made so strong an appeal to settlers that immigration poured in regardless of health hazards. It was true, furthermore, that the diseases which beset humanity in Illinois after the plague of malaria became more tolerable were common everywhere so that there was no point in avoiding the State because of them.

At the end of the first fifty years subsequent to 1877, Illinois enjoyed the reputation of being one of the most healthful commonwealths in the United States. Mortality statistics uphold this reputation. While many factors are present that prevent mortality statistics from portraying an absolutely accurate picture of health conditions they do, nevertheless, reveal what may be accepted as approximately correct information. The factors present in the Illinois statistics are, moreover, to be reckoned with in the data from every other State so that comparisons are justified.

The mortality records published by the United States Bureau of Census give Illinois a lower death rate for 1926 than the United States and a rate lower than any other of the seven states with an estimated population of 4,000,000 or more. Furthermore, the average annual death rate in Illinois for the six years ended with 1926 was lower than the average for any other of the same group of states for the same period. The figures are:

MORTALITY PER 1,000 POPULATION.
(U. S. Bureau of the Census.)

States*.	1921.	1922.	1923.	1924.	1925.	1926.	Average.
California	13.2	14.1	14.3	14.5	13.6	13.6	13.9
Illinois	11.1	11.3	12.0	11.2	11.5	11.8	11.5
Massachusetts	12.2	12.8	13.0	12.0	12.5	12.6	12.5
Michigan	11.6	11.3	12.4	11.6	11.5	12.7	11.8
New York	12.3	13.0	13.0	12.7	12.8	13.4	12.3
Ohio	11.3	11.3	12.3	11.2	11.4	12.3	11.6
Pennsylvania	12.4	12.3	13.3	12.3	12.4	12.7	12.5
United States	11.6	11.8	12.3	11.8	11.7[a]	12.1[a]	11.9

* With 4,000,000 or more estimated population in 1925.
[a] Provisional figures.

Texas comes within the population classification indicated in the table but that state was not included in the United States death registration area during the period for which statistics are given.

The data cited show that health conditions in Illinois were equal to if not better than those which prevailed in the country at large after 1920. Similar statistics for earlier periods are not available but there are other evidences of a profound change for the better after 1877. For one thing the average length of life increased very noticeably. Only four and seven tenths per cent of all deaths recorded in 1880 were among persons over 75 years old. In 1925 the percentage was fifteen and three tenths. In actual numbers the deaths among the older than 75 age group went up from 2131 in 1880 to 12,545 in 1925, an increase of nearly six fold during a period when the total population only doubled. Furthermore, deaths among children less than five years old fell from about forty-five per cent of all mortality in 1880 to about fifteen per cent in 1925. Again, the experience of industrial insurance companies, who pay more regard to dollars and cents than to theories, shows an increase of about 11 years in the average span of life of policy holders between 1910 and 1926.

Another evidence of increasing longevity is the greater number of people who die from old age diseases. Heart disease, cancer, nephritis and cerebral hemorrhage, particularly the first two, caused a far greater percentage of deaths in 1926 than they did twenty, fifty or one hundred years before. In 1880 mortality from heart disease was less than three per cent of the total deaths and that from cancer was scarcely more than one per cent. In 1925 heart diseases were credited with more than seventeen and cancer with more than eight per cent of the total mortality, or twenty-five percent together. This is clear proof that people live longer because these diseases are insignificant causes of death for people under forty.

Then there is the seasonal phenomenon of mortality. All statistics applying to death rates in Illinois prior to 1900 show unmistakably that the hot months were the most hazardous for life. August and September were nearly always the months of heaviest mortality. About 1900 a gradual transformation became noticeable. Long before 1927 August and September had become the period of lowest mortality and the time when people were freest from sickness. This change resulted from a diminution in the prevalence of such diseases as cholera, typhoid fever, diarrhea and other intestinal disturbances

There are no general mortality data available which furnish a reliable basis for comparing health conditions in Illinois during the various periods referred to. All of the statistics relating to the State as a whole are fragmentary for the years prior to 1918. That was the date when Illinois was admitted to the United States death registration area a manifestation that mortality reports were sufficiently complete to warrant federal recognition. Before that date they had ranged from sixty to eighty per cent incomplete. That much discrepancy made unreliable any conclusion that might be drawn from general mortality rates based upon the published records of death.

With all of their incompleteness, however, the statistics for specific diseases provide valuable basis for conclusions regarding the public health. These data, together with information collected from other sources, furnish material for tracing the trend of man's conquest of disease in Illinois and the success that has attended his efforts. This is set forth in the chapters that follow.

The two factors which contributed more than any other to the fall of communicable diseases in Illinois after 1877 were the requirements of case reports and the development of bacteriological laboratory service. Quarantine and the isolation of patients helped, but nowhere in the whole category of infectious ailments was progress toward eradication so pronounced as it was with those diseases for which laboratory facilities provided aids in diagnosis and specific products for cure or prevention. Malaria is a possible exception and in this case the great change in environment that drove out the disease might be thought of as the unconscious operation of a great sociological laboratory. Smallpox is perhaps another exception but here by a happy circumstance of clever observation man was able to employ a procedure stripped of specific bacteriological information which in relation to another disease would have waited for the results of laboratory research.

Tuberculosis, typhoid fever and diphtheria are the three diseases against which the most phenomenal progress toward eradication was made. The marked receding prevalence of each set in after the introduction of laboratory service concerning each. Toward the end of the period covered by this volume, the laboratory developed facilities helpful in controlling scarlet fever and pneumonia. Time had not permitted any considerable results from these processes although scarlet fever had already responded indirectly to laboratory procedures in that milk supplies were subjected to sanitation thereby.

Venereal diseases can be diagnosed in laboratories and that fact contributed enormously to such success as attended the efforts of control but the peculiar sociological connection of these diseases prevented their decline in degrees characteristic of some others.

No infectious disease endemic in Illinois, again with the exception of malaria, declined to any significant degree until health authorities required the notification of cases and developed machinery for enforcing the requirement. Knowledge of location of cases permitted the application of all the control measures available to health officers.

In the summer of 1927 a general revision of the rules and regulations relating to communicable diseases was made by the State Department of Public Health. A more general dependence on laboratory procedures, a more rigid requirement of case reports and a substitution of indeterminate for specific long-time quarantine periods featured the revision. Results of laboratory examination of specimens and clinical evidence were the factors specified to determine length of isolation rather than dependence on an arbitrary time period.

Smallpox and Vaccination.

Smallpox is a disease for which preventive measures, such as vaccination and revaccination, isolation of cases and the observation and quarantine of susceptible persons who have come in contact with a case, are absolutely effective. The usefulness of these measures was generally recognized by sanitarians when the State Board of Health was organized in 1877, but public opinion had not been awakened to the necessity of carrying out these simple procedures. As a result, vaccination was neglected, and local authorities, upon whom falls the responsibility for the enforcement of public health regulations in this State, were often negligent in carrying out the other preventive measures referred to above, such as isolation and quarantine, even in the presence of a local outbreak. This was the state of affairs when the Board was organized in 1877, but it did not long remain that way, for in 1881 to 1882 there occurred an epidemic of smallpox of such proportions that the entire State was roused to action, so that it became relatively easy for the State Board to enforce general vaccination.

But in time, especially when a feeling of tranquility began to prevail on account of the relative absence of smallpox, these measures were neglected and later even attacked in the courts with the usual result, that conditions soon became ripe again for another outbreak.

The history of smallpox in the State is graphically shown by the chart in Figure 18-A, which shows the course of the disease from 1860 to date, as indicated by the decennial or annual mortality rates as far as these are available.

Smallpox Not Prevalent.

Smallpox not being especially prevalent during the first two years of the Board's existence, did not demand any special attention. Conditions soon changed, however. Immigration into the State from Europe was heavy. The population was unvaccinated. The appearance of an epidemic was only a matter of time. This time arrived about 1880. By 1881 the situation was completely beyond control. Smallpox was rampant.

General conditions as well as those in the State were grave enough to lead Dr. John H. Rauch, Secretary of the State Board of Health, to take it upon himself to call a general conference to be held in Chicago on June 29-30, 1881, to consider the smallpox situation. In answer to his call 18 health organizations from 11 different states responded. The federal government was represented by members of the National Board of Health, an organization that was in existence at that time. The meeting was held

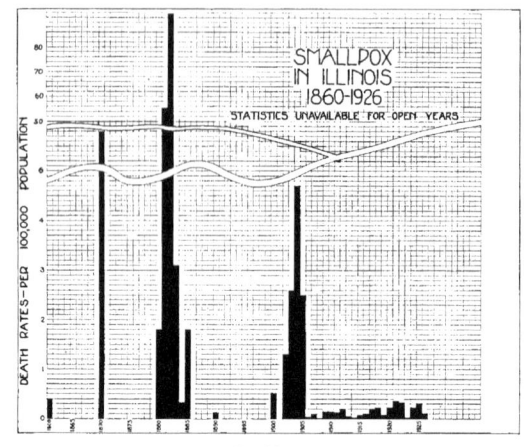

FIG. 18-A.

at the appointed time, and after full deliberation, the Conference recommended that Congress incorporate into the laws regulating immigration, a provision requiring protection from smallpox by successful vaccination of all immigrants, also that the National Board of Health consider the propriety of requiring the inspection of immigrants at ports of departure, the vaccina-

HEALTH CONDITIONS AFTER 1877   309

of vaccinal protection; that local health authorities also inspect all immigrants arriving in their respective jurisdiction and enforce proper protective and preventive measures when necessary, and that the National Board of Health take steps to secure the inspection of all immigrants and the vaccination of the unprotected before landing them at any port in the United States. A considerable part of this program was carried out later. An immigrant inspection service, for instance, was established in the United States for the six months of July to December 1882. Physicians were posted at railway terminals throughout the country. Dr. Rauch was superintendent for the Western District and caused the inspection of 115,057 and the vaccination of 21,618 immigrants bound for Illinois. This work was done largely at Chicago and St. Louis, the railway terminals leading into the State.

Table 25.

CASES OF SMALLPOX REPORTED IN ILLINOIS.

Year	Jan.	Feb.	Mar.	Apr.	May	June	July	Aug.	Sept.	Oct.	Nov.	Dec.	Total
1917	556	910	526	657	811	411	312	114	146	168	93	292	4,996
1918	742	744	645	557	571	189	103	73	26	42	36	114	3,842
1919	322	284	465	567	554	442	183	135	232	260	648	779	4,871
1920	776	842	748	1,063	1,232	909	383	212	198	326	553	1,294	8,536
1921	1,960	1,659	1,760	1,204	1,027	412	102	29	23	39	120	261	8,536
1922	373	360	228	197	238	113	113	40	8	75	176	133	2,118
1923	369	121	64	50	69	128	39	24	9	28	15	21	937
1924	37	46	95	111	164	242	168	48	42	187	58	166	1,362
1925	210	299	220	215	150	194	46	30	20	30	79	137	1,630
1926	177	164	108	165	135	105	93	21	26	5	25	51	1,077
1927	172	118	213	113	150	63	67						

Outbreak of 1881 and 1882.

The average prevalence of smallpox during the years 1877 to 1880 was relatively low, but early in 1881 it began to increase, and by the end of the year a total of 3,000 cases was reported, of which number 1,180 occurred in Chicago.

At a special meeting of the State Board of Health, in November 1881, the notification of smallpox or other epidemic disease was made compulsory. Local health officers were required to collect the reports from practicing physicians and transmit them promptly to the Board. It cannot be said, however, that either cases or deaths were reported with any large degree of completeness because no machinery for collecting reports existed. There were very few local health officers.

The situation was serious and required vigorous action. Recognizing school children as a large section of the population which could easily be reached with the least effort and in the quickest time, the Board ordered that no child be admitted to public schools in the State after January 1 without giving evidence of successful vaccination or a history of smallpox.

The plan worked. Within sixty days after the order went into effect the percentage of vaccinated school children rose from about 45 to 94 per cent. A considerable number of adults, particularly employees of large industries like the railway companies and inmates of State institutions were also vaccinated. The epidemic subsided. The people became absorbed in other problems and promptly forgot all about the compulsory vaccination order and ignored it although the Board had put it into effect as a permanent procedure.

Events ran true to form so that in the course of time neglect of vaccination resulted in widespread outbreaks of smallpox again as soon as the in-

Table 26.

DEATHS FROM SMALLPOX IN ILLINOIS BY MONTHS.

Year.	Jan.	Feb.	Mar.	Apr.	May.	June.	July.	Aug.	Sept.	Oct.	Nov.	Dec.	Total.
1917												2	10
1918	4	1	4	1			1						14
1919	1	1	2	1									5
1920	1	2		3	1	1		1		2	1	3	16
1921	4	2	5	3	4	1					2	5	26
1922	2	5	6	4	1	4	1						23
1923				1								1	2
1924	1		2	3	6	2	1	1					16
1925	1	2	2	7	2	6	2						23
1926	1			1	3	2					1		8

fluence of the wholesale vaccinations of 1882 began to wane. In the early nineties the situation had again grown serious and again the Board attempted to handle the matter by demanding compulsory vaccination of school children. This time the outcome was not so happy for sanitarians. Enough pupils were vaccinated to check the epidemic but two law suits were started by parents who objected to the coercive character of the vaccination procedure. One against a school board in Wayne County was dropped by the defendants. The members of the school board had been fined by a justice of the peace and appealed at two different times. Both suits were dropped, however, upon advice of the local state's attorney who opined that a reversal of decision was improbable.

A mandamus suit was started in Lawrence County against a school board, to compel it to admit the children excluded from the schools be cause they were not vaccinated. The case was first decided against the school board. The decision was affirmed by the circuit court of Lawrence County, and appealed to the appellate court. It was then taken to the Supreme Court, which rendered a decision against the school board in November, 1895. This decision declared unconstitutional the requirements of vaccination as a contingent to attendance on public school so that the rule of the Board was voided. The subsequent practice, which has been upheld by the courts, has been to require either vaccination or quarantine of all school children during the period of immediate danger after smallpox has actually appeared in a community.

Table 27.

DEATHS AND DEATH RATES FROM SMALLPOX IN ILLINOIS.

Year.	No. deaths.	Rate per 100,000 population.	Year.	No. deaths.	Rate per 100,000 population.
1850			1909	8	0.14
1860	8	0.4	1910	8	0.14
1870	170	6.7	1911	8	0.13
1880	45	1.4	1912	12	0.20
1881	1,723	54.6	1913	3	0.05
1882	2,641	81.8	1914	20	0.03
1883	103	3.1	1915	5	0.08
1884	11	.32	1916	6	0.09
1885	63	1.8	1917	10	0.02
1890			1918	14	0.23
1900	25	.1	1919	5	0.08
1902	67	1 3	1920	16	0.23
1903	135	2 6	1921	26	0.37
1904	242	4 7	1922	23	0.34
1905	131	2 5	1923	2	0.03
1906	2	0.03	1924	16	0.23
1907	5	0 09	1925	23	0.31
1908	1	0.02	1926	8	0.11

By an act of the legislature, in force July 1, 1895, it was made the duty of the trustees of the University of Illinois to establish and maintain a State vaccine propagation station. The law also provided that the State Board of Health should exercise supervision of the methods of propagation and certify to the purity of all products manufactured at this plant. An appropriation of $3,000 was made to establish and maintain the vaccine farm in connection with the State University. This project was short lived, however.

All the troops sent from Illinois for duty during the Spanish-American War in 1898 were vaccinated against smallpox through the activity of the State Board of Health.

Smallpox in 1903 and After.

In 1903, a total of 1,664 cases of smallpox were reported and it was estimated by the Board that this number represented probably not over two-thirds of the cases occurring in the State.

Another law suit grew out of a smallpox epidemic at Hyde Park, Chicago in 1907. This involved a city ordinance which required vaccination as a contingent upon school attendance. Here again the Supreme Court decided in favor of the plaintiff, holding that neither local health officers nor cities had the authority to make or enforce such ordinances.

Thus it was made very clear that compulsory vaccination would not be tolerated in Illinois under prevailing laws. It was up to health officials to find some other way to control smallpox.

This situation resulted in the practice of requiring either vaccination or quarantine of exposed persons in a community where smallpox was actually present. The courts have generally upheld this procedure. It is still in vogue and operates fairly satisfactorily when the State health officials are alert. Practically everyone in a community may be regarded as exposed to smallpox when the disease is present so that the method practically amounts to compulsory vaccination on the installment plan, the installments coming due when epidemics threaten.

Since 1905 smallpox has fluctuated with the years, varying with the degree of success that attended various schemes for stimulating vaccination. In general the disease has been mild although malignant cases were introduced into Illinois in 1922 and again in 1924. Mortality has steadfastly remained below one death per 100,000 people, however, during the period.

The last significant step toward preventing smallpox in Illinois was taken in 1921 when the State Department of Public Health under Dr. Isaac D. Rawlings began the practice of making a personal investigation of every reported case of smallpox and every reported case of chickenpox in adults. Field physicians are assigned to these duties as they arise from time to time so that the control methods described above can be applied promptly and effectively.

State and local health officers have indulged in sporadic campaigns agitating voluntary vaccination and these efforts result in considerable success.

By combining the last three methods mentioned the health officials have been able to manage smallpox about as satisfactorily as could be expected under existing conditions. No alarming outbreaks developed up to this writing subsequent to 1921.

History of the Chicago Smallpox Epidemic of 1893 1894 and 1895 With Side Lights and Recollections.

[By Arthur R. Reynolds, M. D.*]

A serious epidemic of smallpox occurred in Chicago during the years 1893, 1894 and 1895. Not the most serious in the city's history, for three great epidemics had previously occurred, one in 1864, another in 1872 and a third in 1882. All were much more serious than that of 1893-1895. Each had more cases compared with the population, all were more fatal and none of them were so speedily suppressed. During the prevalence of smallpox in 1880, 1881 and 1882, a total of 6,835 cases were reported. In the 1893-1895 epidemic the cases numbered 3,754 in a population more than three times greater than in the early eighties.

Dr. Arthur R. Reynolds.

There was no smallpox in Chicago during 1890 and 1891. In the following year eight cases were reported, two in May, one in June, three in September and four in December. Concerning these the chief medical inspector, Dr. Garrott, in his annual report, wrote, "We were able in every instance to trace the source of contagion to other countries."

Onset of Epidemic and Vaccination.

In January, 1893, there were three cases followed by three in February and five in April. The onset of the epidemic of 1893-1895 has ordinarily been given as June 12, 1893, because from that time on there was a continuous monthly occurrence of cases. Undoubtedly the disease had been smouldering for two years previously in the form of unrecognized cases for on July 6, cases were found in three widely separated localities and none could be traced to their origin. In August there were nine cases, in September three, October nine, November thirty-five and in December sixty-six.

It was the year of the World's Fair. Throughout 1892 the Fair was in course of building. Thousands of workmen and others came to the city and of course they brought whatever contagion they had with them. Exhibitors and others from every country were coming for a year before the Fair opened in 1893. Indeed the formal opening of the Fair was in October, 1892. It is fair to assume that smallpox was one of the things the Fair brought to Chicago.

---

* Dr. Arthur R. Reynolds was appointed Commissioner of Health for Chicago by the elder Mayor Carter H. Harrison, April 17, 1893, and served until June 13, 1895. He was again appointed by Carter H. Harrison, Jr., April 19, 1897, and reappointed every two years until June 27, 1905.

There had been great neglect of vaccination for 10 years previously. In the last six months of 1893 nearly one hundred thousand vaccinations were done by the department and that was more than had been done in several years before, all told. Meanwhile every means that the department could devise was employed to arouse the public to the necessity of vaccination. Letters were written to the superintendents of public schools, to the parochial schools, to private schools, to the head of business concerns, factories, the railroads, etc., urging that they see to it that those whom they employed or were under their control were vaccinated. From all came hearty responses and promises of cooperation. In newspaper interviews the necessity for vaccination was constantly stressed. The foreign language press was appealed to and innumerable local publications were also addressed and from all valuable help and cooperation was obtained.

By January 1, 1894, the public was thoroughly aroused. Every physician in the city was vaccinating. This valuable start was made without any increased expense to the department except for the vaccine that was distributed free to all who would use it.

The country was in a period of great financial stringency. Repeated requests for appropriations of money brought no results. Finally the mayor told me to cut loose and do whatever was necessary. It was realized that the entire city must be vaccinated immediately. Several hundred physicians and senior medical students were employed to vaccinate. The city was divided into districts and those again into sub-districts and men put to work until the entire city was covered by vaccinators who went from house to house and from group to group. Five hundred were employed at one time and more than half a million vaccinations were done in three or four months.

Among this corps of vaccinators were some of the city's ablest medical men, others who later became prominent practitioners. Dr. John Dill Robertson was a vaccinator for the department in 1894. In 1915 he became commissioner of health for Chicago and held the office seven years with a good record. He is still proud of having been a vaccinator for the department in his early career.

Later the city council appropriated $100,000 but a rough estimate of expenditures revealed that the entire sum had been spent or contracted for when the appropriation was made.

Progress, Hospitalization and Other Incidents.

An emergency hospital was erected and soon beds were available for every patient and thereafter every case was hospitalized. By May, 1894, the backbone of the epidemic was broken. From then on there was a dim inishing number of cases each month. The last case occurred in December, 1895.

It must not be presumed there was no faultfinding or criticism of the department and its head. There was plenty of it and it was persistent but we knew that we were on the right road and that the public as a whole were with us and stood firmly behind us. There was in fact great apprehension in the city as there always is in time of peril, but it had to be faced.

The department was fortunate in gathering together a force of men who knew no hours but worked unceasingly, who did as much as the commissioner and other officers. They all worked as partners in the enterprise. Among these must be mentioned the late Dr. Frank W. Reilly who was appointed assistant commissioner in January, 1894, to whom I give all praise for wise guidance throughout the rest of my service which ended in June, 1905. Credit is also due to the late Dr. Erasmus Garrott and the late Dr. Henan Spalding.

The late John P. Hopkins, then Mayor, stood like a rock behind us. In no way did he interfere with the selection of the force of employees. He attended every meeting when requested and there were many of them. They were called to discuss features of the work when it seemed to clash with some interest or another.

Hon. Martin B. Madden was then an alderman and chairman of the finance committee of the city council, he had great courage and furnished a wise balance in many a clash. He then largely controlled the city's finances, held a firm hand over them but was generous as could be expected. For many years he has been in the Congress of the United States where he now keeps a wise and restraining hand upon National expenditure.

The details of the epidemic are told in the reports of the department and need not here be recounted. There are, however, many side lights of that time remaining in my memory that may be told.

In 1893 the appropriation of money for the department of health was only about one-tenth of the amount in recent years when compared on a per capita basis of population. There were 84 people all told employed in the department; 44 of these were connected with store, tenement house and factory inspection, 10 were meat inspectors, 10 fumigators, 8 medical inspectors and 4 were funeral directors. From the distribution of these assignments to various duties may be seen the status of public health work and disease prevention in the public mind of that time. Sewer gas was the great bugbear to be combated, although ventilation and cleanliness of homes were always stressed. Ten fumigators fumigated infected rooms or houses by burning sulphur after sealing up all cracks about windows or doors. After 24 hours the windows and doors were opened and instructions given for a thorough scrubbing of the floors and a general house-cleaning.

Contagious diseases were reported by physicians in a rather desultory way and warning cards were placed on the front door of houses where the disease was present. An investigation of the fate of these warning cards revealed that they were sometimes taken from the front door and tacked up on the basement door where they could not be seen. Another trick was to take the card from the front door and place it on the back door. Another was to take it from the outside of the door and put it on the inside of the same door and very frequently they were destroyed altogether. The department of health was generally considered the fifth wheel of the municipal chariot. The present day efficiency and standing of public health work had not even dawned when the city council made the appropriation for 1893. Before the year was out and the public awakening was on, it was frequently pointed out to the commissioner of health that he had the power to command the entire resources of the city if necessary to control smallpox.

The inadequate smallpox hospital was soon overcrowded. Walled and floored, tents heated and fully equipped were set up in the rather spacious hospital grounds, but soon these were filled. A new temporary hospital was quickly built and equipped with an ample supply of tents for summer use, and from that time on there were beds for all. The new hospital was not ready until the time when the new cases came in decreasing numbers.

When the smallpox hospital became crowded there was public clamour demanding that another building be fitted up for temporary use as a hospital. A school building was suggested and a public meeting held in the rooms of the Board of Education. A discussion pro and con was had. Those in the neighborhood of the school objected, and some one said the building was too good for such purpose. The late Mr. Thomas Brennan, presiding, answered: "No building was too good for the care of the sick." But it was soon found that the idea was not practicable for several reasons, the chief of which was that the refitting would be too expensive.

Mrs. Dudley, wife of Dr. E. C. Dudley of Chicago, was then at the head of the Visiting Nurse Association. She came and offered to furnish the nurses for the new hospital and pay their salaries. The offer was promptly accepted. The nurses were retained until the hospital closed in 1895 and after that the city paid the salaries of the nurses.

Smallpox was prevalent in a section of Chicago where there were factories for ready made clothing. At a meeting of the clothiers it was suggested that clothing shipped should have a label saying the goods were free from smallpox contagion. Dr. Reilly at once protested that such a label cast suspicion on the goods and would be ruinous to the trade. It was announced that no infected goods of any kind would be shipped from Chicago or sent to any place within the city

At another meeting of the clothing industry a representative of the State demanded that the department of health burn all clothing that had been in the hands of home workers where there might be contagion. The department of health agreed to burn everything that the State recommended for such fate, provided the State guaranteed to indemnify the owners for any unnecessary loss that subsequently might be proven. That ended that.

There was much speculation on the danger of infection in the factories of the ready-made clothing industry and several meetings of those interested were held. At one of these meetings at which Mayor Hopkins was present Mr. Hart of Hart, Shaffner & Marx offered to raise $5,000 and present it to the city to battle the contagion. After the meeting the Mayor was asked what he thought of Mr. Hart's offer. He answered, "The city cannot afford to accept the offer although it is most generous."

In the winter of 1894 communities and states surrounding Chicago were concerned about the spread of smallpox from Chicago. Frequent visits were made to Chicago by health officials and finally a meeting was called in Chicago of state and city health officers. Quarantining against an infected city, town or state was then in vogue though not so popular as formerly and an officer who would "slap on a quarantine" was displaying great erudition and efficiency.

As we met in conference it was plain that our visitors were imbued with the thought that there was something wrong with Chicago in its trials. The discussions were inane. There were no suggestions of assistance or help of any kind. One illustration will suffice. The secretary of the conference who was also the executive officer of the State Board of Health of Illinois, when asked what the State was doing said—"When any community in the State fails to stop an epidemic, then the State steps in." What it would step into or any word of what should be done was not mentioned.

There was one notable exception. Our great crusade to vaccinate the entire city was then in full swing. It was explained to the visitors. Finally Dr. Ernest Wende, Commissioner of Health of Buffalo, New York, arose and said: "Gentlemen, there is just one thing that will stop smallpox and that is vaccination, from what I have heard today. The scope and system of vaccination in Chicago covering the entire population is without parallel in the history of previous epidemics. I am satisfied the disease is now practically under control. I am going home and will make an effort to do the same thing in Buffalo."

Disinfection.

Mattresses, comforters and other things of small value that could not well be otherwise disinfected were burned and the owners paid for them if they had any value. Cotton goods were boiled and the rooms subjected to sulphur fumigation.

During the course of the epidemic the department was offered the use of a long tubular steel chamber in a convenient location that had been used for drying lumber. It was fitted with steam pipes, so that the interior could be raised to a high temperature and was therefore suitable for use as a disinfecting chamber. It had a conveyor that carried its load from the entrance to the exit at the other end; the front was fitted so that live steam could be turned in. This plant was accepted and used for the disinfecting of bedding, clothing and similar articles. The goods were hauled to it, put in the steam chamber and were taken out from the other end by clean hands, put into a clean conveyance and sent back to the owners.

Hospitalization.

Hospitals in 1893 were not as popular as they are now and smallpox hospitals generally designated as "pest houses" were to be avoided at all hazards. No human being would then or now voluntarily go to a pest house. No department rules or statutory law could overcome the horror of a pest house. Fear of the pest house led to the secretion of cases. Sick children were wrapped up and carried through the alley to a neighboring house when the family saw the health department conveyance arrive for their removal. Open violence was early threatened and occasionally attempted. An ambulance was also a thing to be avoided. Removal, however, was logical and necessary.

Familiarity with these facts naturally led to the consideration of other methods than force to hospitalize the sick. Nicely upholstered carriages drawn by a pair of horses were purchased and put to use in the work. That helped some.

In the better neighborhoods the argument that non-removal left the family in more danger from their neighbors than from the authorities was very effective. The common sense of the difficult situation was that there was some influence, some person or persons in every community that could overcome the fear or the prejudice of every terrified or recalcitrant individual or family in any proposition that was right, just and humane. These influences were sought and found and put to good purpose in the removal of the sick to the hospital when finally ample hospital facilities were provided. Different communities and different nationalities required different management. In one foreign speaking community Sisters of Charity were of the greatest help. They acted as interpreters and pointed out the advantage of removal so the sick could have special care and the premises cleaned up. They helped secure vaccination and in every way were efficient helpers. A group of lay brothers who were teachers in a parochial school gave the

save special and efficient service. Every case of smallpox was removed to the hospital when there was room for them. Mothers of small children were taken along to the hospital when they would go. Telephones were installed so the sick could talk to the folks at home.

Vaccination.

This epidemic occurred nearly one hundred years after the immortal Jenner had discovered vaccination but there was a woeful lack of accurate knowledge as to what constituted a true vaccination. It was not generally known that a true vaccination left a typical scar unlike that from any other cause. The patient's word was generally accepted as to whether he was vaccinated or not. Those upon whom vaccination had ever been attempted considered themselves vaccinated. Anyone with a scar on the arm at the site of vaccination considered themselves vaccinated and the bigger the scar the more certain they were.

There was little knowtledge even in the profession of what constituted a true Jennerian scar. Jenner it is true had painstakingly described it, but medical colleges had not taught it and Jenner's works were not studied.

Before the epidemic was over the large number of cases reported in vaccinated persons and the frequent use of the word varioloid, meaning smallpox modified by vaccination caused inquiry to be made, together with a careful study of the scar, following vaccination. It was ultimately found that persons with a typical Jennerian scar did not contract smallpox at all, not even varioloid. From that day to this there was little, if any smallpox reported in the truly vaccinated. It was found too that the large scars were made by some extraneous infection and that in such cases there was often no true vaccinal result. It was prior to the day of glycerinated vaccine lymph. The vaccine used was dried on bone points and naturally there were some sore arms, not, as we then pointed out, due to the vaccine but as a result of infection either on the point or introduced afterward by the fingers of the patient.

Large groups were afraid to be vaccinated, others objected on religious grounds and anyway nobody wanted to be meddled with. Then there were those who called themselves antivaccinationists, who made a sort of cult of it and worked themselves up into a fine frenzy of indignation over it. How they got that way is hard to understand. They were the most unreasoning and cantankerous of the lot. However they generally faded away when danger of smallpox was imminent.

One very charming lady visited the commissioner of health to voice the objection of the religious organization in which she was a leader. She said her people had other means of preventing disease and that they did not quail before smallpox. She also said she and her church were law abiding but wanted to talk it over. Among others of her arguments she said that Christ did not say anything about vaccination. She was told, with sacrilegious risk, that vaccination was not known till Dr. Jenner discovered it less than one hundred years ago but that nearly all the followers of Christ were in favor of it now. Later it was learned that her organization gave instructions to submit to vaccination when the authorities demanded it but prayed that it might do them no harm.

The department was frequently urged by this group or that to forcibly vaccinate the objectors. The fact was we never had the authority to vaccinate by force nor does that power exist now. We did have the authority of law to quarantine any who refused to be vaccinated. That power was used in one notable instance where a hotel full of a religious group were shut in for weeks.

A total of 3754 persons had smallpox during the two and a half years of its reign. Of these 1213 died. The survivors had their usefulness impaired in many instances. Many were seriously poc-marked and their faces less lovely to look upon. The expense to the city was great. The impairment to traffic and commerce was, however, rendered almost nil. There was the toil and trial of those in the department who cared for the sick and suppressed the disease. Had it any influence on the present or any lesson for the future? We think it had and that not only Chicago but the world learned a useful lesson.

The Lesson.

The epidemic was due to the neglect of vaccination. It demonstrated anew that none who were truly vaccinated contracted the disease and that a successful vaccination left a scar typical of vaccination and unlike any other scar; also that in cases of skin eruption, where a diagnosis was difficult, the presence of a typical Jennerian scar, made the decision that it was not smallpox practically certain. It showed that everybody could be vaccinated when it was properly presented and hence vaccination by force was poor policy and unnecessary.

Experience showed that vaccination with pure vaccine did not cause a bad sore and left only a small scar and that large scars were due to extraneous infection and as a rule did not protect.

Cholera

1884 and 1885 in its efforts to prevent the invasion of Asiatic cholera. This disease had frequently invaded Illinois prior to 1877, the year in which the State Board was established.

The Cholera Danger in 1884.

As early as July, 1883, the danger of an invasion of Asiatic cholera into the United States and Illinois was noted by the State Board, and preliminary action was taken with reference to measures necessary to resist its introduction and to prevent its spread.

The safeguards determined upon as the most promising for success were two-fold. The first was an intra-state measure and was to take the form of a state-wide sanitary survey to determine the sanitary needs, and a sanitary "clean-up" if data obtained through the survey indicated that this was needed. The second was inter-state and related to aiding and insistence upon enforcement of quarantine requirements and inspection methods along the Gulf and Atlantic coast, together with efforts to secure improved sanitation and cleanliness of the various neighboring states.

The cleanliness campaign was based on the prevailing theory in regard to origin and spread of cholera, and was possibly also conducted with a view that it would have a good effect in the saving of lives from other filth diseases far in excess of the mortality from the cholera itself, unless it should spread beyond all expectation.

The Board inaugurated this campaign with the following statement to the public: "An epidemic spread of Asiatic cholera now seems imminent. Mention is made of cases in England and France. Whether the disease will cross the Atlantic from the East will depend upon the efficacy of measures employed to confine contagion to the present localities."

To guard against the invasion, the secretary of the State Board made the following statement and recommendation:

"My experience and observation lead to the conclusion that it is not judicious to place entire reliance on quarantine measures, no matter how administered, should the disease become epidemic in countries or points with which this country has close commercial relations. As Asiatic cholera, although it may invade places in good sanitary condition, finds its most congenial habitat where filth in any form abounds, the best attainable sanitary condition; clean streets and premises, the prompt and proper disposal of organic refuse, night-soil, and all forms of sewage; well ventilated habitations, with dry, clean basements; a pure and sufficient water supply; and good, individual hygiene, including personal cleanliness, proper diet, and regular habits of life these are the best safeguards against Asiatic cholera.

"I have to respectively recommend that a thorough and systematic sanitary survey of the State be inaugurated by the first of January, 1885."

The results of the efforts made in 1884 to secure a general inspection and improvement of sanitary conditions were as follows:

Reports from 230 cities, towns, and villages were received in reply to the circular sent out, and an immense amount of work was accomplished in remedying the defects disclosed by the inspections. The secretary personally inspected a number of the State institutions, and found them in as good sanitary condition as could be expected in view of faulty construction, or location, from a hygienic standpoint. Suggestions for improvement were given and carried out as far as practicable.

SANITARY SURVEY: At the next meeting of the Board, the secretary by resolution was authorized "To prepare the necessary blanks and instructions, and to distribute the same to the proper authorities of counties, townships, and municipalities, for a thorough and systematic sanitary survey of the State, to be begun by January 1, 1885, or as soon thereafter as practicable."

The secretary explained that it was proposed to begin work in the southern portion of the State, and to work northward as rapidly as the weather would permit, so that by May 1 the sanitary condition of every dwelling in all of its parts, of all premises, outhouses, wells, cisterns, and other belongings should be made known, the remedy of defects be pushed, and the authority of the State Board be exerted wherever necessary to supplement the efforts of the local authorities of the State to resist the threatened invasion of Asiatic cholera.

A much greater share than usual of the labor of the Board in 1885 was devoted to purely sanitary work and efforts to prevent the invasion and spread of cholera. The records show that a total of 300,000 houses and premises were inspected in 395 cities, towns, and villages. These inspections were made from March to December, 1885, and embraced 96 of the 102 counties.

The thoroughness of these inspections made at that early period would do credit to any state-wide sanitary survey, and the relatively low cost of this survey is remarkable for even that period.

These inspections embraced every material condition affecting health, individual and public; site of house; its age, material, ventilation, condition, especially of basement or cellar, of cesspools, sinks, drains, outhouses and water supply; of the yard and stables, barns, etc.; the vaccinal status of occupants; the occurrence of certain diseases, etc. They disclosed in 382 places from which reports were received at the end of the year, a total of 484,831 defective conditions and nuisances prejudicial to health, of which number 441,593, or over 90 per cent, were reported abated or remedied.

The sanitary surveys of cities and towns were begun early in June, and the house-to-house inspection was resumed in the extreme southern portion of the State as soon as the weather permitted, and was by midsummer, successfully prosecuted throughout its entire area.

These surveys were at first largely tentative and experimental; but they were the means of discovering, in many cases, a multitude of defects and evils, the dangerous importance of which had been overlooked or whose existence had not been suspected. They gave a distinct impetus to the house-to-house inspections. They aroused communities to the importance of their sanitary conditions. The series of circulars prepared by the secretary, and the Schedule of Questions—revised from that originally prepared by a committee of 28 prominent sanitarians under the direction of the American Public Health Association were, in not a few instances, the first sanitary instruction to receive a practical application.

The surveys included all data necessary to a complete description of the city or town as to its location, population and climate; topography, water supply; drainage and sewerage; streets, alleys and public grounds; habitations; gas and lighting; disposal of garbage and excreta; markets and food supply; slaughter houses and abattoirs; manufactories and trades; hospitals and public charities; police and prisons; fire establishments; cemeteries and burials; public health laws and regulations; municipal officials; registration and statistics of deaths and diseases; municipal sanitary expenses; and public schools; the whole embracing nearly 600 separate questions grouped under 19 general heads.

The total cost of these inspections was estimated at about $50,000 for everything except the work actually done or caused to be done by the householder, tenant, or owner. In Chicago it was a little less than 17 cents for each inspection, including pay of inspectors, wages of laborers, hire of teams, cost of disinfectants, printing, stationery, etc.

Dr. Oscar De Wolf, health commissioner of Chicago, reported that the death rate from the filth diseases in Chicago was reduced 15 per cent, and stated that there can be no question that much of this decrease in the preventable mortality was due to the house-to-house inspection and kindred efforts which were made possible through the special appropriation in the anticipation of cholera.

It is believed to be entirely within the bounds to say that at the close of 1885 the State was in a cleaner and, consequently, healthier condition than any equal population had ever been before at the same period of occupancy of the soil.

During 1886 the Board was still in fear of invasion of Asiatic cholera. The work of the sanitary survey was continued. The house-to-house inspections were completed where not finished the year before, and extended to new territory, so that they embraced an aggregate of nearly half a million inspections and reinspections of houses and premises, in about 400 cities, towns, and villages.

While the Board had been thus successful in organizing and promoting sanitary work by municipalities and individuals, it continued the effort to supplement such local action by prosecuting the investigation into the water supplies of the State, the disposal of sewage, and pollution of streams. These were matters affecting large areas of territory in common, and yet, in the nature of the case, they were such as could not be controlled by the independent action of the communities.

At the close of the year, an aggregate of 499,832 inspections and reinspections had been made, embracing every important item pertaining to the sanitary status of 335,547 premises in 398 cities, towns and villages, with an aggregate population of 1,677,734 inhabitants. In all but three of these places work was begun prior to 1886, but at the close of the previous year, the aggregate number of inspections—exclusive of Chicago—was only 224,260, so that the increase during 1886 was considerably over 100 per cent. A large number (164,285) of these, however, were reinspections, the actual number of additional premises inspected, amounted to 113,162.

QUARANTINE MEASURES PLANNED: While this extensive sanitary survey and clean-up was going on within practically every county of the State, the Board was also energetic in trying to keep cholera from entering the United States and especially Illinois.

Provision was made for guarding against any introduction of the disease, by defining a system of border quarantine inspection. For this purpose the Thirty-fourth General Assembly made a contingent appropriation of $40,000 to be used, upon the recommendation of the Board, in case of the outbreak or threatened outbreak of any epidemic or malignant disease, such as Asiatic cholera, smallpox, yellow fever, or to defray the expense of preventing the introduction of such diseases, or their spread from place to place within the State, and suppressing outbreaks which might occur, and in investigating their causes.

In the event of such outbreak or threatened outbreak, it was planned to establish quarantine inspection stations at 24 designated points of entrance of important railroad lines along the eastern and southern boundaries of the State, and at points upon the Ohio and Mississippi Rivers—or at so many of these as might be necessary—for inspecting, quarantining, disinfecting and caring for cases of epidemic disease.

At the meeting of the Sanitary Council of the Mississippi Valley, similar action was urged upon the health officials of neighboring states. Satisfactory action was taken by the Council upon this recommendation, and thus another step was taken in perfecting the protection of the State against an epidemic of imported contagious or infectious disease.

Cholera Invades United States in 1887.

These cholera cases arrived late in the year (end of September) and a total of 34 cases had been recorded in New York and vicinity by October 11, 1887.

It is uncertain how much credit should be given the Board and its activities in preventing Asiatic cholera in the State, but it is nevertheless a fact that the local epidemic in the New York quarantine zone did not reach Illinois. The Board took no chances, but made a determined effort to protect the health and lives of the people by maintaining a state-line quarantine by inspections of passengers on railways coming from infected cities.

Cholera Invades United States in 1892.

In 1892 a conference of Western State Boards of Health was called, which met and drafted seven agreed rules for inter- and intra-state procedure to be followed in the then existing emergency in regard to cholera.

Dr. F. W. Reilly was elected to act as secretary of the conference. He was authorized to act for the Board in the case of a threatened pandemic of Asiatic cholera, in the interim pending the next meeting and to call an emergency meeting of the members at his discretion.

After the adjournment the secretary engaged in a telegraphic correspondence with the New York City Board of Health and with Dr. John H Rauch, who was at the time in that city. As a result of the information thus obtained, and after consultation with Dr. Griffith, the secretary furnished the following statement for publication:

Chicago, September 14, 1892.

"While the intelligence of five deaths from Asiatic cholera among residents —not immigrants—of New York City, one of these eight days ago, was a most unpleasant surprise to Western health officials, still there is nothing in the situation to cause panic or even excitement. The delay in admitting the existence of the disease was natural, but it does not appear that any precaution has been neglected on this account. From the first suspicion the cases have been treated as if it was known that they were genuine Asiatic cholera. Premises have been disinfected, inmates kept under strict surveillance and the most rigid care has been exercised.

"In its own interest New York cannot afford to have any spread from these cases, nor from others which may be now reasonably anticipated before the advent of cold weather.

"As to any immediate danger to the country from these sporadic cases, there are these facts to be considered:

"1· The cases have occurred among a class of persons not likely to start an exodus from the localities and so to spread the infection.

"2· As already recited, reliance may be placed on the natural interest of New York to make every effort to prevent any spread.

"3· Every day brings us nearer the season when cholera, at least in this country, is checked by a low temperature.

"4· The history of the disease on this continent shows that, while it has repeatedly effected a foothold on the mainland in the fall of the year, it has never been until repeated introductions that it has spread as an epidemic. In the epidemic of 1854 it took eighteen months after the first cases on the mainland to effect a lodgement and become epidemic.

"5· The sanitary defenses of the country were never so well organized to battle with and suppress an epidemic of any preventable disease.

"The practical deduction from these considerations is that, as already said, there is no occasion for panic or even excitement.

"What remains, as the lesson of the situation, is that every community and commonwealth should realize in practical effort, that its immunity from cholera, as from other preventable disease, rests with itself. It must work out its own salvation and not rely upon any vicarious protection of quarantine. Every source of filth, of pollution of water, soil or air, must receive prompt and effective attention, and not only must municipalities exert themselves, but every householder for himself must put his own house and premises in order.

"No cleanly city, town or village—with a proper disposal of excreta and with a pure water supply—need apprehend a visitation of cholera. In all human probabilities there remains from now until next spring in which to perfect the work of sanitation already well under way throughout the length and breadth of Illinois. With the present warning, the municipality which fails to utilize these intervening months will be culpably criminally derelict in an obvious and imperative duty.

"The Illinois State Board repeats: There is no occasion for panic—there is every occasion for a general cleaning up."

In view of this situation, it was decided to keep a strict check on all immigrants entering the State. In pursuance to this plan, all immigrant-carrying transportation companies were notified in September, 1892, not to bring into the State of Illinois any immigrant, nor the personal effects and belongings of any immigrant, without first receiving satisfactory assurance that such immigrant and his or her personal effects and belongings are free from the danger of introducing the contagion of an epidemic, contagious or infectious disease.

The companies were further instructed to accept only, as satisfactory assurance, the certificate of an inspector of the United States Marine Hospital Service, setting forth that the individual immigrant has been under observation long enough to determine that he or she has not the germs of cholera in the system, and that he or she is vaccinally protected against smallpox; that all the personal effects and belongings of said immigrant have been subjected to proper disinfection; and, furthermore, that, in the professional judgment of the inspector, the individual immigrant referred to and his or her belongings are free from any danger of conveying contagion or infection to others.

At the December, 1892, meeting, the Board passed a resolution requesting the legislature to provide a contingent fund to be used in case of the invasion or threatened invasion of cholera.

At the January, 1893, meeting of the Board, much concern was expressed by the secretary, Dr. F. W. Reilly, concerning Chicago's financial inability to continue to inspect all trains carrying immigrants, in order to protect Chicago and Illinois against invasion of cholera and smallpox. On March 23, 1893, he wrote a letter to Governor Altgeld, informing him of this condition, and in reply received instructions to continue the immigration inspection as a preventive measure against cholera, etc., the expense to be defrayed out of the contingent fund appropriated for kindred purposes.

The health commissioner of Chicago was duly advised of the Governor's approval, and was authorized to select and appoint eight inspectors, who should receive pay at the per diem rate of two dollars and a half ($2.50) for each day of actual service, the expense to be defrayed out of the contingent fund of the State Board of Health. This service was continued until the end of the following June.

Thus ends the history of cholera in Illinois. In fact it was not a history of cholera at all, since the State Board was established in 1877, but a chronicle of measures instituted to prevent the invasion of the State by this disease. No cases of the disease occurred in the State during this period. Twice cholera invaded the United States, once in 1887, and again in 1892.

The elaborate precautions which were started by the State Board of Health in 1883, under Dr. Rauch's direction, apparently helped to prevent the spread of cholera into the State in 1887, when immigrant inspection and the machinery for the control of epidemics, was not perfect or so well organized on a national basis as in later years. This was a time when every state and community had to be on guard for such national invasions of pestilence.

The 1892 invasion of cholera and its prompt restriction and check at the vicinity of the port of entry, is evidence of the effectiveness of modern methods of disease control, based on accurate knowledge of the causes and mode of transmission of infectious diseases and augurs well of what would occur should the State again be threatened with the invasion of any such pestilential disease, now or in the future.

Yellow Fever

The panicky situation concerning yellow fever in the South in 1878 was the first big public health problem to divert temporarily the attention of the State Board of Health from its activities in the enforcement of the Medical Practice Act.

A description of the yellow fever epidemic of 1878 at Cairo, the point of greatest incidence in Illinois, can best be visualized by quoting from John M. Lansden, a resident of Cairo at the time and an eyewitness of the outbreak. In his history of Cairo, Illinois, he writes in part as follows concerning the epidemic:

"The ten days beginning with July 9, 1878, were probably the hottest ten successive days in the history of the City. During that time the writer was kept at home by an attack of illness and was treated by Dr. W. R. Smith, whom most of us remember as one of our most prominent citizens and physicians. On entering the room one of those days and while wiping the perspiration from his face, he said, 'John, we are likely to have yellow fever in the south within a month or two.' The doctor's prophecy came true. The first case occurred in the south about the first of August. It moved on northward and soon appeared at Natchez, Vicksburg, Memphis, and Hickman, and reached Cairo September 12. It is said by many persons that Mr. Oberly, the father of the Hon. John H. Oberly, died of the fever a few days before the 12th. On the 12th there were two deaths; one of them, Mr. Thomas Nally, editor of the Bulletin, and the other, Mr. Isaac Mulkey, a son of Judge John H. Mulkey, and also of the Bulletin office. Those deaths caused a panic in the city, and the afternoon and evening of that day witnessed the departure of hundreds of people from the city.

"For some three or four weeks prior to that time there had existed in the city an unseemly controversy as to whether the fever would probably reach Cairo or not. Were one to turn to the files of the Bulletin and the Cairo Evening Sun for the last half of August and the first twelve days of September of that year, he would see what a state of feeling existed in the city; the one party insisting that there was little or no danger and the other that there was very great danger and that every possible effort should be put forth to keep the dreaded disease out of the city. The Bulletin led off as was its custom and criticised with unnecessary severity every one who close to differ with it. It was strongly supported by a few of our prominent citizens who felt that it was their duty to maintain our supposed immunity.

"I can best describe that peculiar state of things preceding September 12th by saying that it was not quite as bad as the yellow fever itself. I had been attending court at Jonesboro and was told by the conductor, on offering to go aboard the train at Jonesboro to come home, that he could not take me on account of the quarantine at Cairo. I prevailed upon him and came, and on reaching the northern part of the city I saw the levees patrolled by armed guards. One or two of them went through the train to ascertain who might and who might not be permitted to go on into the city.

"When I reached the city, I was surprised beyond measure to see the state of things prevailing. On every hand were seen all kinds of vehicles carrying trunks and every other description of baggage to the railroad stations. They were driven, some of them, almost at furious rates of speed. In a word—there was a panic, which I need not attempt further to describe.

"I left on the same Illinois Central train about eight o'clock that evening, on which were Mr. Oberly and hundreds of other citizens of the town. I remained away until the 2d of October, when I returned home, having seen in the Cairo Evening Sun, of September 24th, the following notice:

"The Cairo public schools will open on Monday, September 30th under the superintendency of Prof. G. G. Alvord.'

"The schools opened at the time announced, but were discontinued October 4th. On Sunday and Monday, October 6th and 7th, there were six deaths, among them Miss Marie Powers, one of the public school teachers. These deaths occasioned another exodus, not quite so panicky nor quite so large; and it was not until the latter part of October that the people began returning home, and it was not until far into November that all had gotten back.

"The Bulletin had suspended publication with its issue of September 12th, and did not resume publication until the first day of November. Mr. D. L. Davis, the editor of the Cairo Evening Sun, and his family had also gone from the city, and had left Mr. Walker F. McKee in charge of the paper. Walter, for most of us were accustomed to address him by that name, remained at his post and gave the city a very faithful account of what was daily taking place. As bad as the news often was which it contained, the residents were eager for its appearance in the evening, and most of them forwarded copies to their friends who had gone from town and who were anxious to know the state of things at home. Mr. Davis removed from Cairo to Chicago a few years afterwards, and kindly handed to me all the numbers of the 'Sun' which covered the yellow fever period.

"The facts are just as above given. There were about one hundred cases and about fifty deaths.

"I have devoted these few pages to the epidemic of the fever because it was an era in the city's history. One-third of the people left the city. Many remained who could and should have gone. Their reasons for remaining were various; and sometimes they could give none at all. It was a simple disinclination to leave home. There was a continuing hope that the danger would soon pass, but it persisted instead. To some it was a question of means; for to go and remain away even for a short time required money for the trip and board. Many had no friends or relatives to whom they could go. Few persons from the surrounding country desired to see any from Cairo. Many whole families would not go because they could not decide who should remain, and they feared leaving their homes unprotected.

"Business was suspended; only just enough done as seemed actually necessary for the people at home. The days were unusually bright, in sharp contrast with the doubly dark and silent nights. Part of the time persons could not be abroad at night without passes of some kind from the authorities. In a word, everything spoke plainly of the reign of pestilential disease.

"The city government of course went on. It had to. Mayor Winter was equal to the occasion, and to be equal to such an occasion seems capability for almost anything, but he seemed made for it as for some special occasion. Jack, like so many public men of the country, liked to do things in a kind of showy way, not exactly spectacularly, but that word expresses something of the idea. Jack had been so harrowed by the Bulletin and others about the fever, that he seemed somehow to be glad that they had not he had proven false prophets; and when the fever came he met it with an undaunted face. He could not rescue its victims; but he and the few trusty men he had, buried them in the shortest possible time and yet with all the care and ceremony of which the deadly situation would admit. But it must not go on further or attempt to describe the pestilence that walked in darkness or the destruction that wasted at noonday.

"Jack Winter was no better than many of the rest of us; but if at the end of all things there is a balancing of accounts for every man, Jack's account will have opposite September and October, 1878, a very large credit. Of the rather few persons on whom he relied for attention to families in need and for other aid to the city authorities, I may mention Mr. William H. Schutter. I do so because of my personal knowledge of much of his work. Of the many persons who remained out of a sense of duty to those who could not go or did not choose to go, I may mention the Rev. Benjamin Y. George, of the Prebyterian Church and Father Zabel of St. Joseph's Catholic Church, of whose constant care and devotion to the stricken families of the town it would be impossible to say too much. Doctor Roswell Waldo, of the Marine Hospital, gave up his life in the work he did, which extended alike to all persons needing his service. He died at St. Mary's Infirmary October 18th, after a long illness which kept the community alternating between hope and fear for his life. The Sisters of St. Mary's Infirmary did everything in their power, as they always do. It may not be so, but it sometimes seems that they take pleasure in such times as those were. They look upon every opportunity for doing good as a blessing to themselves. Did not this happiness come to them, how could they devote their lives to such work?

"The Sun of Monday, November 25, 1878, gives an account of the presentation to Dr. J. J. Gordon of a gold medal in recognition of his very faithful services during the prevalence of the fever. The presentation took place at the Arlington House, afterward The Illinois, and now The Marion. It gives the names of the thirty-five donors, and speaks of Mayor Winter, the Rev. Mr. George and other persons present."

A general report on the yellow fever epidemic of 1878 at Cairo was made by Dr. Wm. R. Smith, Sr., of Cairo, Illinois, to Dr. John R. Rauch, President of the State Board. Dr. Smith was a practicing physician in Cairo at the time of the epidemic, and speaks from experience inasmuch as he remained in the infected territory throughout the entire outbreak and took a heroic part in administering to the sick, and later as an inspector at Station 3 in the Cairo district.

330   HEALTH CONDITIONS AFTER 1877

In summing up his observations in regard to the epidemic, Dr. Smith reported in part, as follows:

"Cairo is situated at the confluence of the Mississippi and Ohio Rivers at an elevation of 325 feet above the sea, in latitude 37, longitude 89.12. Its site is from eight to 15 feet below high-water mark, and to protect it from overflow, is surrounded by a levee. During high-water in either river, all the low ground within the levee is covered with 'seep water' from one to six feet deep. To prevent th collection of rain water and to remove the 'seep water,' large sewers underlie

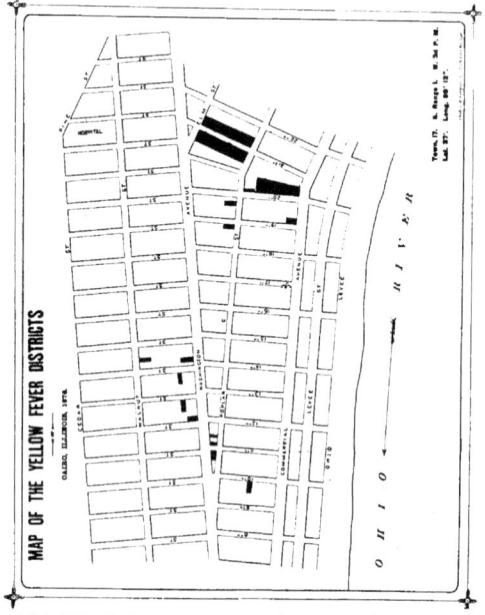

MAP OF THE YELLOW FEVER DISTRICTS
CAIRO, ILLINOIS, 1878

Commerical and Washington Avenues, with outlets into the Ohio River. Opposite Cairo, on either side, are extensive swamps, and all the land for eight to ten miles is subject to overflow.

QUARANTINE: "On July 29, 1878, the city Board of Health established a quarantine by visitation. All steamers from the South were visited by a physician, and if all were well, were permitted to land. Also all trains were visited. During the quarantine, the steamer 'Porter,' from New Orleans, landed here and discharged her crew, slipped another, and went to St. Louis. One of the crew died at the hospital on Walnut Street, (see map), August the 12th.

"In about a week the 'Porter' returned from St. Louis with several cases of yellow fever on board. Part of her crew again left her here and she went up the Ohio River, spreading death wherever she touched. After the fever became epidemic at Memphis and Granada, no steamers were permitted to land and all trains were stopped at Cairo. There were two violations of quarantine by steamers the 'Jas. D. Parker' and 'Batesville.' One of the passengers on the 'Parker,' a Mr. C......, landed here and died of the fever at C. on Poplar Street, August 24th (see map).

METEROLOGICAL: "The year 1878 will be in after years reverted to by 'the oldest inhabitants' as 'the hot year.' Its winter was very mild and we had a summer temperature during its spring. The summer was excessively hot. And, furthermore, the high temperature was distributed over a wider belt than usual.

"The following table shows the mean and highest thermometer, humidity, prevailing winds and rainfall at Cairo during the months of June, July, August, September, and October, 1878:

	Thermometer.		Humidity.	Wind.	Rainfall.
	Mean.	Highest.			
June.........................	74	89	69	S.	4.6 inches
July..........................	83	96	72	N.	2.81 inches
August.......................	81	94	70	S. W.	3.45 inches
September...................	76	88	70	S.	2.99 inches
October......................	59	81	69	S.	2.59 inches

"The above table shows that we had for four months a temperature and just about enough moisture, to maintain (if not generate) yellow fever.

"Although the quarantine was as perfect and as stringent as it was possible to make it, with so much shore line to guard, violations of it by individuals were quite frequent.

THE BEGINNING: "The first local case of yellow fever was J. M. ...., taken on September 7; next T. N. ...., September 8; next J. C. ...., September 12; next J. S. ...., September 13. T. N. .... was editor of the Bulletin, and the other three were printers who worked in the same building (see B. B. on map). There were no more cases until the 21st, when M. H. M..... was taken at 1. The fever then gradually spread from the Bulletin center B. B. to 2, 3, 4, 5, 6, 7, 8, 9. On the 25th of September a case occurred at M. on 21st Street, and from that center the fever spread so fast that it is impossible to give names or location of cases, but the black on map will show the extent of territory it took in.

"From whence came the fever? T. N. ......, visited C......, who died on Poplar Street, and 15 days afterward M...... was taken with the fever. and in 16 days afterward N...... was taken, and in 20 and 21 days C...... and S... were attacked. They were all employed on the Bulletin and worked in the same room.

"So we may safely say that the yellow fever was brought from Memphis by the steamer 'Jas. D. Porter.' "

The quarantine established by the State Board of Health practically excluded everything that came from the south unless it passed inspection. The transportation of freight and passengers across the Ohio River, between Fillmore, Kentucky, and Cairo was also subjected to the same regulations.

Thousands of fugitives from Memphis and below were allowed to come into Illinois and Missouri, and although 28 of these died of the disease in Illinois, there was not a single case contracted from refugees nor their effects outside of Cairo.

The reports to the State Board of Health show that 62 officially reported deaths from yellow fever occurred during the outbreak at Cairo. Five cases and three deaths from fever occurred at Centralia, 100 miles north of Cairo, among those who were engaged in transhipping hides from Shreveport, Louisiana. One fatal case was reported from Rockford, Illinois. The history of this case was that the husband contracted yellow fever and died in Decatur, Alabama. The wife nursed him, and the day after he died she returned to her home in Rockford and died in one week of yellow fever, contracted in Decatur, Alabama.

After the Cairo Outbreak.

Following this tragic experience in 1878, the Board of Health was always on guard in subsequent years, to prevent the recurrence of this dread disease. In 1879, Dr. John H. Rauch was appointed delegate from the Illinois State Board of Health to attend the meeting at Memphis on April 30, of the various state boards of health in the south, to consider the best methods for the control of the yellow fever scourge.

Rules and regulations recommended by the National Board of Health were adopted to secure the best sanitary condition of steamboats and other vessels, railroads, their station houses, cars, freight, and passengers.

A system of sanitary inspection was maintained in the southern part of the State. One sanitary policeman was stationed at Mound City, and two at Cairo. One medical inspector was appointed to assist in carrying out the rules and regulations of the State Board of Health. Dr. Frank W. Reilly was appointed sanitary inspector July 28 and stationed at East Cairo. Dr. W. R. Smith of Cairo was appointed inspector and assigned to Station No. 3, Cairo, July 1.

Dr. John H. Rauch was elected secretary-treasurer of an interstate organization, known as The Sanitary Council of the Mississippi Valley. The function of this organization was to keep health officers in all states within the yellow fever zone informed concerning outbreaks of epidemic diseases, particularly of yellow fever, and to make rules and regulations which were expected to be adopted by all the member health officers.

The Board adopted rules and regulations concerning yellow fever, requiring critical inspection of health certificates of passengers on trains and boats. The regulations concerning the inspection of boats were strictly enforced. In regard to these the captain of the "Belle St. Louis" remarked: "If it wasn't for these inspections, boats wouldn't be paying expenses—they'd be shut off of so many ports, now open to them on account of their health bills."

The report of a single case of yellow fever in the south caused a shrinkage of the provision market in Chicago alone, which amounted to a million dollars within 24 hours.

A summary of the quarantine measures taken against yellow fever in 1879, is contained in the following letter to the Mayor of Cairo, giving instructions as to necessary precautions:

"Sir:

"In transmitting the accompanying summary statement of inspection and other service at the Quarantine Inspection Station, Mississippi River, below Cairo, during the season this day closed, the Illinois State Board of Health begs to express its appreciation of the aid, both material and moral, which the National Board of Health has rendered it in protecting the State, possibly not from an invasion of yellow fever, but must assuredly from such interruption of travel and traffic as have hitherto uniformly followed a threatened invasion of that disease. Precisely what such interruption amounts to it would be difficult to state in dollars and cents; but an inkling of it is given in the figures in the summary statement, from which it will be seen that, whereas the average vessel tonnage arriving from below at the time the inspection system was begun, amounted to only 967.66 tons per diem, it had risen to 2,166.67 tons per diem during the last 31 days, and this in spite of an unusually low stage of water. Last year the commerce of the port at Cairo during the month of October amounted to only 48,967 tons northwise and eastwise as well as southwise, while this year it amounts to 87,127 tons for the same period. (The tonnage of barges, lighters and flats is not included in these figures, while it is in the figures in the summary statement.)

"During the period while the Inspection Station was in commission this year, 1,162 vessels of all kinds (exclusive of barges, lighters and flats) entered at the port of Cairo; as against only 707 vessels during the same period last year; and notwithstanding this quarantine of exclusion in 1878, yellow fever obtained access to the port with a total mortality of 62 recorded deaths. This year not a single case of the disease has developed among the 3,098 persons allowed to come into Cairo, nor among the 20,776 persons passed through the Inspection Station from below, notwithstanding fever prevailed at 43 distinct points in the Valley during the period.

"Intercourse with all ports below Tiptonville, Tennessee, 120 miles south of Cairo, was practically suspended at the port when inspections were begun; but as confidence in the system was established by observation of its workings and results, one by one the interdicts were removed, until by Sept. 1 the sole requirement for entry of passengers or freight into the State of Illinois from southern ports, was a clean bill of health (or certificate of inspection) from the station. A comparison of the figures shows the steady restoration of river business from below. In August, 56 vessels, with an aggregate capacity of 44,966.87 tons, presented themselves for inspection; in September, 80 vessels, with an aggregate capacity of 57,824.50 tons; and in October, 100 vessels, with an aggregate capacity of 69,667.85 tons."

The sum of $500,000 was appropriated in 1879 and placed at the disposal of the National Board of Health for the control of yellow fever, of which sum $160,000 was wisely and successfully employed in combating the epidemic that year.

Measures to prevent the introduction of yellow fever from the South were continued in the summer of 1881. The Board ordered that after July 1, Dr. W. R. Smith, inspector at Station No. 3, below Cairo, put into commission said station and that after said station had been put into commission the secretary of the State Board of Health be directed to notify the authorities of all ports in this State not to allow boats to land from points below Cairo, unless upon presentation of a clean certificate of inspection as to cargo, officers and crew.

The Yellow Fever Scare of 1888.

In the fall of 1888 it was reported that yellow fever had developed in the south. The secretary of the Board of Health found it necessary to make active efforts to check the public alarm that developed immediately. The yellow fever epidemic had occurred in Florida, but it was late in the Fall. Nevertheless, millions of dollars were lost from foolish quarantines, interference of travel and a general feeling of apprehension, all unnecessary even in the light of the then known facts about yellow fever.

It is worthy of note that a status of public panic developed in southern Illinois, especially in the vicinity of Cairo, as a result of reports of yellow fever in Decatur, Alabama, and that the secretary of the Board spent several days in that vicinity restoring public confidence and preventing a costly quarantine from being unnecessarily set up. The secretary's stand was based upon meteorological grounds that were sound and were proved so by subsequent developments, namely that yellow fever does not spread to the North with the advent of cold weather.

The Scare in 1897.

The next yellow fever scare was in the fall of 1897. The first official information of the existence of yellow fever in the south, reached the State Board of Health on the morning of September 7. Under the circumstances it was deemed urgently necessary to establish immediately an inspection service at Cairo. Upon reporting the matter to Governor Tanner, he advised: "Secure services of as many competent medical men as may be necessary and use every endeavor to keep yellow fever out of the State, and to control its spread should a case appear in the State. Payment of all expense incurred will be approved by me."

On September 9, Dr. Phillip S. Doane, Chicago; A. H. Mann, Springfield; and Dr. W. F. Grinstead, Cairo, were appointed as inspectors to co-operate with Dr. John B. Neely of Chicago, surgeon in charge of inspections, stationed at Cairo.

A rigid system of inspection was inaugurated by these officials. All boats and trains coming into Cairo day and night were met and every passenger from infected districts inspected. During the period of Cairo's quarantine, train inspection was carried out in Chicago chiefly as related to thorough disinfection of trains from the South, with chief attention to those of the Illinois Central Railroad.

Quarantine and inspection service in Cairo was maintained from September 9 to September 30, 1897, to prevent the spread of and danger from infection of yellow fever, which was at this time very prevalent at the various southern points, chiefly New Orleans, Mobile, and Atlanta. From September 7 to 30, 147 trains, 12,707 passengers on trains; 12 steamboats, and 576 passengers on steamboats, were inspected. On September 19, Dr. C. S. Nelson, Springfield, and Dr. J. C. Fults, Waterloo, were appointed as sanitary inspectors to assist Dr. Neely in enforcement of quarantine against yellow fever.

On September 19 two cases of yellow fever were reported at Cairo, and two more on the following day. The diagnosis of yellow fever in these cases was disputed by the people of Cairo, and by a majority of the local physicians. Many citizens and a few physicians also, declared that yellow fever could not exist in Cairo at that time of year. That there was no analogy between the appearance of this disease and the season of the year did not occur to those taking exception to the diagnosis. A case of yellow fever can occur in any part of the State of Illinois at any period of the year. The disease will not spread, however, at certain temperatures, and parenthetically, it will not spread under the climatic conditions most favorable to its propagation if proper sanitary conditions are found and the patients are kept isolated.

The following statement seems to remove all doubt that true cases of yellow fever existed in Cairo in 1897:

"Dr. John Guiteras, of the Marine Hospital Service, arrived in Cairo from Mobile on Sunday, September 19th. After an examination of the patients, P. J. Reynolds and Michael Ryan, he pronounced the disease yellow fever. Dr. Guiteras stated that the disease prevailed in a mild form, and as the patients were convalescing and all precautions to prevent the spread of the malady had been taken, he was of the opinion that there would be little danger of infection. He advised a continuance of the quarantine effected until the patients were entirely well."

It is of more than passing interest to note that high temperatures existed in 1897 as well as in 1878, as proven by the following telegram dated October 2 sent to the Secretary by ex-Surgeon of the Marine Hospital Service, Dr. John B. Hamilton, of Chicago:

"I advise sticking to present regulations until lower temperature. Cairo is still the danger point, and refugees from infected districts cannot with safety be allowed to enter the city."

The following comment would indicate a yellow fever scare in 1898:

"The appearance of yellow fever in Ocean Springs, and its rapid spread to other cities of the south gave rise to well grounded apprehensions that the disease might reach Illinois, and notwithstanding the lateness of the season, prevail in epidemic form in the cities of the southern part of the State, Cairo especially. * * *"

"The danger to which the state was exposed in September, 1878, was not fully realized until too late. Even the distinguished President of the State Board of Health, apparently saw little reason to apprehend danger at this time and confident that the lateness of the season also precluded the possibility of an outbreak of yellow fever in Illinois, he counseled against the very quarantine restrictions which one year later during the same month of the year he strongly advised. Even while the disease was at its height in Cairo early in September, 1878, he pronounced 'the panic unwarranted' and expressed the opinion that 'the end must be near.'"

Sanitary inspector, Dr. James de Courcy, was detailed for duty at Cairo on October 4, to enforce quarantine regulations against passengers and railroads in the vicinity of Cairo. The quarantine restrictions were raised and inspection service was terminated on October 18, 1898.

The Scare of 1905.

From 1898 to 1905, the Illinois State Board of Health records are free of any scare of yellow fever until 1905. Late in July, 1905, yellow fever was reported in more or less epidemic form at New Orleans. The secretary, Dr. James A. Egan, left at once for Cairo, where he investigated the sanitary condition of the city and proceeded to Memphis where he ascertained that a quarantine against New Orleans had already been established and that the situation was far more dangerous than commonly supposed.

The secretary determined to establish a train inspection service, and from the first of August every train and steamboat coming from the south was boarded, and every passenger inspected, and only those permitted to land in the southern part of Illinois who could present proper credentials from health authorities and evidence as to his recent whereabouts. Competent medical men were employed for this service.

Within a short time after the establishment of train inspection, the conditions in the south grew so much more serious, that the City Council declared a rigid quarantine against the south and admitted travelers only upon the presentation of permits issued at Cairo. Anticipating the invasion of the city by yellow fever patients, a well-equipped isolation hospital was established in a houseboat, and under the care of a competent attendant, the boat was ready to be taken to a point of safety in midstream. It was not necessary to use this boat.

Rigid quarantine was maintained from August 3 until October 17. Nine inspectors were employed and several watchmen. During this time hundreds of persons coming from infected points were diverted in other directions, and in this manner, the State was saved from an invasion of fever.

It is gratifying to report that regardless of the inconvenience and consequent depression of trade, the people of Cairo were in sympathy with the efforts of the State Board and expressed approval of the work and the manner in which it was conducted.

Dr. George Thomas Palmer, sanitary assistant of the Board, was placed in charge of the quarantine service at Cairo, during the enforced absence of

Dr. Egan and his staff of yellow fever inspectors at Cairo in 1905. Dr. Egan is the man in the center of the first row.

the secretary. In response to the very evident need of such an officer who could relieve the secretary of some of the details of the work of the office, the General Assembly had made an appropriation for an assistant secretary, which went into effect on July 1, 1905. In order that Dr. Palmer might have greater authority in the performance of his duties at Cairo, the secretary appointed him as assistant secretary to the State Board of Health and asked for the approval of the Board, which was granted.

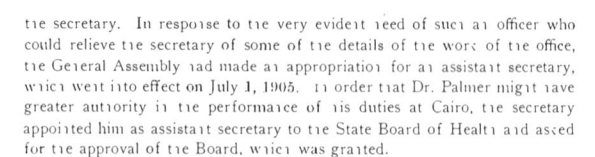

Typhoid Fever.

In following the history of the rise and fall of typhoid fever in Illinois, the theories prevailing at various times in regard to its cause must be kept in mind.

The views as to the origin of the disease, and the early theories in regard to its cause, are set forth in the preceding part of this volume. For an understanding of the preventive measures taken to control typhoid fever since the establishment of the State Board of Health in 1877, reference is here made only to the theories and facts in regard to its course and transmission of the disease, generally accepted for varying periods since that time.

When the Board was first established, typhoid fever was universally looked upon as a filth disease. The typhoid bacillus was not discovered until 1880, when it was first found in the tissues by Ebert, and was not isolated until four years later, when Gaffky grew it in pure culture. Although this and the other great discoveries in bacteriology were made in the early eighties, they were not generally accepted, nor did they modify the prevailing views in regard to the control of communicable diseases to any great extent, until the middle nineties.

What the prevailing views of practicing physicians were during the first 15 years of the Board's existence is shown from the following statement in regard to typhoid fever by Dr. N. S. Davis in his *Lectures on the Principles and Practice of Medicine*, published in 1884:

"A careful adherence to well ascertained facts concerning the etiology of typhoid fever will require us to accept the three following propositions:

"'First, that cases of typhoid originate in dwellings or buildings of any kind in which, from either overcrowding the number of occupants, or the neglect of ventilation and cleanliness, the air, furniture, and walls, become strongly impregnated with the organic matter exhaled from the skin and lungs of the occupants. * * * *

"'Second, that the more the soil of any given locality becomes impregnated with the intestinal and urinary excretions by progressive increase of the density of the population provided the two conditions of drainage and water supply remain the same, the more frequent and severe will be the cases of typhoid among the inhabitants of such locality. * *

"'Third, cases of genuine typhoid have occurred and are still occurring occasionally in every civilized community, in persons who have had no traceable communication with previous cases of that disease, or with any of the recognized or suspected sources of infection. * * * *

"'Probably no fact is better established than that the disease under consideration generally originates from the use of air or water impregnated with some one or more of the products derived from the decomposition of organic matter. It does not follow, however, that such product of organic change must necessarily be formed outside of the human body.'"

Dr. Davis was a leader of the local medical profession at the time, and had been active in many movements for sanitary reform in the city of Chicago and the State, consequently it may be presumed that his views are representative of the time.

The views held were doubtless based on those expressed by Dr. Charles Murchison in 1860, as enunciated in his famous theory of the pytrogenic origin of typhoid, which held that it is "generated and probably propagated by certain forms of decomposing matter." In the succeeding 25 years the facts were tortured in every conceivable manner to fit this theory. Sometimes the incubative period of the disease was shortened to a few hours when it "immediately followed" exposure to certain fetid contaminations. A favorite way of accounting for an epidemic was the finding of defective drains or nearby privy vaults, cess pools or decaying matter of any kind.

Some, who had been impressed with Pettenkofer's observations on cholera, leaned strongly towards ground water and defective drainage of the soil as a factor in the production of typhoid. An example of such a view is that expressed by Health Commissioner Ware of Chicago in explaining the cause of the greatest typhoid epidemic in the history of the city, namely that of 1891 and 1892. In his annual report to the mayor for the year 1892, he says: "We have typhoid fever, and always will have so long as there remains so much undrained property."

In the *Sanitarian*, a leading British publication on sanitary science, appeared the following statement in 1880: "Typhoid fever is traceable to filth with as much certainty as smoke is to fire."

Imbued with these ideas, Rauch, as secretary and executive officer of the State Board of Health doubtless believed that in prosecuting his great scheme of a general sanitary survey of the State, started after the threatened invasion of cholera in 1883, that he was killing a whole flock of birds with one stone.

Public sentiment favored, and in fact, demanded that something be done to prevent the invasion of cholera. Appropriations were ungrudgingly given by the State and local authorities for such work, and thus Rauch had the opportunity of his lifetime to do what to him must have seemed an effective drive to rid the State, not only of cholera, but of all filth diseases.

The following comment of the *New York Medical Board* is pertinent to this question:

"There is no doubt that the extra cleanliness produced by the cholera scare (1878) will effect a saving of life from other filth diseases, far in excess of the mortality from cholera itself, unless it should be spread beyond all expectation."

Typhoid Handled as a Filth Disease.

The time during which typhoid fever was considered a filth disease and measures for its control were conducted with this end in view, includes the period of activities of the State Board of Health from its establishment in 1877 to approximately the time of the World's Fair in Chicago, in 1893.

The official records of the Board prior to 1890, show that no special attention was given to the control of typhoid fever, outside of the extensive general campaign waged to clean up the State.

Table 28.

CASES OF TYPHOID FEVER REPORTED IN ILLINOIS.

Year.	Jan.	Feb.	Mar.	Apr.	May.	June.	July.	Aug.	Sept.	Oct.	Nov.	Dec.	Total.
1917	115	132	109	233	91	73	186	405	637	193	94	55	2,342
1918	89	82	55	52	51	64	212	241	286	102	24	86	1,344
1919	33	33	39	47	32	64	265	294	306	346	251	183	1,893
1920	124	80	88	115	103	138	162	211	284	257	198	109	1,869
1921	96	74	83	89	72	152	336	443	419	392	185	82	2,423
1922	79	73	81	74	135	116	182	255	254	273	173	103	1,798
1923	65	31	89	52	54	68	99	233	320	259	315	277	1,862
1924	139	72	43	59	63	63	124	168	191	176	125	231	1,474
1925	119	71	62	58	71	124	217	298	297	310	206	297	2,130
1926	111	50	44	44	34	65	106	214	305	386	203	115	1,677
1927	52	62	39	40	32	70	141						

Table 29.

DEATHS FROM TYPHOID FEVER IN ILLINOIS.

Year.	Jan.	Feb.	Mar.	Apr.	May.	June.	July.	Aug.	Sept.	Oct.	Nov.	Dec.	Total.
1918	26	37	24	21	33	27	37	84	75	86	44	39	533
1919	29	18	19	9	22	15	35	57	52	41	45	41	383
1920	35	24	22	12	15	18	38	34	53	58	47	24	380
1921	23	19	17	10	15	32	43	53	56	65	40	23	396
1922	18	15	16	12	25	10	21	33	33	38	32	29	282
1923	17	12	13	12	14	8	28	45	48	43	31	46	317
1924	33	9	13	5	10	6	22	23	17	37	23	43	241
1925	24	5	11	7	11	19	32	60	55	43	31	29	327
1926	9	4	5	9	7	6	24	30	37	44	41	14	230

The mortality records that were collected from 1880 to 1886, incomplete as they admittedly are, show an annual average of 1,335 deaths from typhoid in the entire State. When from this number are deducted 413, which is the average annual number of typhoid deaths recorded in Chicago, it is found that 922 deaths were recorded for the other sections of the State, a figure so small as to be hardly probable, in view of the fact that other evidence shows that typhoid fever was quite prevalent in Chicago as well as downstate during this time.

HEALTH CONDITIONS AFTER 1877   341

In 1887 conditions during the summer caused the Board to express grave solicitude in regard to the health outlook for the State. Intensely hot weather in July and the prolonged drought were among the more important causes of this fear. The great prevalence of diarrheal diseases and numerous outbreaks of typhoid fever, the former directly due to high temperature, and the latter intensified by water supplies affected by the drought, were noted during the summer.

An outbreak of typhoid occurred in February and March, 1889, at Concordia College, Springfield, resulting in 24 cases and two deaths among students. The cause of the outbreak was attributed to the use of drinking water taken from a well located near a privy.

Twenty cases of the disease with four deaths occurred in 1890 among students of Augustana College, Rock Island. The outbreak was reported due to defective drainage and plumbing. An especially virulent typhoid infection in a family of eleven near Urbana, with nine deaths, was reported. Also another instance in the same locality of seven cases in one family of nine children, with two deaths.

Bacteriologic Period.

Bacteriology was pretty well established in the early nineties. From this time on typhoid fever was no longer considered as a necessary evil. Attention was given to gross pollution of water supplies in the handling of epidemics. The disease was also made reportable. A more accurate means of diagnosis was offered by the Widal test.

These illustrations indicate very well how widely prevalent typhoid fever was prior to 1900 in Illinois. Neither cities nor rural districts escaped although the cities suffered worse because of common water supplies through which the disease was transmitted. In Chicago, for instance, a long drawn-out epidemic stretching over three years began in 1890, resulting in no less than 4,494 deaths. It attracted particular attention because of the World's Fair scheduled for 1893. Very exhaustive investigation of the water supply followed, bringing about such efforts at purification as was possible at the time.

Situations like these were common and prevailed continuously until sanitarians and the public came to recognize and appreciate the bacteriological character of typhoid fever. As soon as clear conception of these facts became established typhoid fever started to decline in Illinois.

These activities were reflected at once in substantial declines in typhoid fever rates. How rapid the rates fell is illustrated in Figure 19.

From about 1900 on outbreaks of typhoid fever drew attention first to local water supplies. Municipalities delayed the installation of adequate public water supply safeguards, as a rule, until an epidemic fell upon them and then, after the conditions were pointed out by a sanitarian, permanent improvements were made. This is about the history of typhoid fever until about 1910. Up to that time polluted water had grown to be regarded as the chief offending agent in the spread of typhoid. One city after another went through disastrous or very serious experiences and came out with improved water supplies that prevented recurrence on a large scale.

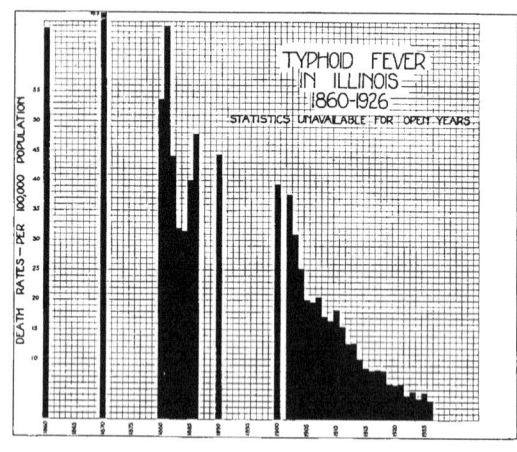

FIG. 19.

Period of Systematic Control.

With the increasing knowledge of typhoid fever and the study of many outbreaks in all parts of the world, the time arrived around 1910 when serious efforts were made to control all of the factors which played a role in the transmission of the disease.

The spread by milk was found to be frequent, and pasteurization was inaugurated to check it. Flies were given a great deal of attention, and were found to play an important part especially in rural communities.

Human carriers were detected as causes of certain outbreaks, and when the importance was fully recognized, steps were taken to prevent this source of infection by the examination of stools and urine of convalescent cases. Contact infection was also controlled, especially by immunization and more general hospitalization of cases.

One of the most outstanding features of typhoid control during this period was the development and application of epidemiologic methods for the detection of epidemics, and tracing them to their sources. Thus this period is characterized by a chronicle of one small local outbreak after another, discovered, traced to its source, and stopped, with the result that the typhoid mortality was low, yes, 15 or 20 times lower than in the previous periods, during which such occurrences were much less frequently heeded, or correctly traced to their origin.

Table 30.

DEATHS AND DEATH RATES FROM TYPHOID FEVER IN ILLINOIS.

Year	No. deaths	Rate per 100,000 population	Year	No. deaths	Rate per 100,000 population
1860	1,183	65.7	1909	917	16.5
1870	1,758	70.3	1910	1,039	18.4
1880	1,652	53.6	1911	893	15.5
1881	2,082	66.	1912	744	12.7
1882	1,424	44.1	1913	758	12.8
1883	1,054	31.9	1914	6,090	10.1
1884	1,066	31.5	1915	538	8.6
1885	1,379	39.9	1916	512	8.3
1886	1,689	47.8	1917	520	8.3
1890	1,700	44.4	1918	533	8.2
1900	1,897	39.3	1919	383	5.9
1902	1,882	37.7	1920	380	5.8
1903	1,578	31.	1921	396	5.9
1904	1,300	25.2	1922	282	4.
1905	1,047	20.	1923	317	.7
1906	1,061	19.7	1924	241	.5
1886	1,119	20.5	1925	327	4.5
1908	944	17.2	1926	230	3.2

Water supplies came under close bacteriologic scrutiny, and were only too often found showing evidences of fecal pollution. A great step was taken in the purification of such water supplies around 1915 and after, by the use of chlorine in minute quantities as a disinfecting agent.

Stepwise declivities in the rate are noted following the adoption of the various measures. These are noted especially in the death rate from this disease in Chicago, where the effects are more striking because the measures were effective in the whole area, while in the State, they were adopted at various times in different localities

Antityphoid inoculation was advocated by the Secretary of the State Board of Health in 1911 and the columns of the *Bulletin* were devoted to explaining its merits.

Another investigation which reflected credit upon the Board and its organization was that of the 1913 typhoid fever epidemic at Rockford. When in the previous year, hundreds of cases of the disease suddenly developed in that city, an investigation independent of the State Board of Health was made by the city authorities aided by outside experts, and at an expense of several thousand dollars. Impure water was assigned as the cause of the outbreak. When, however, in the late summer of 1913 another epidemic of typhoid threatened, the service of the Board was requested for the purpose of determining the cause of its recurrence. Almost all the cases were traced to milk and bread from dairies and bakeries in which cases of typhoid fever had existed. The sale of milk and bread from these dairies and bakeries was stopped and the epidemic ceased.

Experiences of this kind attracted attention to milk supplies. This might have been anticipated. As water supplies came to be more and more sanitary there remained considerable typhoid fever and investigators began to look for other media of transmission. Milk was next to water in importance so that it was logically the next in line to be sanitated. From 1915 onward a considerable number of typhoid fever outbreaks were traced to milk on the one hand while the sanitary quality of municipal milk supplies improved through the increasing use of pasteurization on the other.

After 1915 refinement in control technique was the dominating feature in efforts directed toward the eradication of typhoid fever. Free distribution of anti-typhoid vaccine was started in 1914 but it was after the World War, during which emergency the efficacy of this prophylactic was admirably demonstrated by the military, before it was used to any significant extent. Its use was promoted successfully after that time and it was generally appreciated and utilized subsequent to emergencies like the devastating tornado that swept southern Illinois in 1925 and the many floods that inundated considerable populated areas almost annually.

An emergency sterilizing outfit serviceable for temporary use in connection with local public water supplies was made available by the State Department of Public Health in 1917. It was used from time to time.

A field laboratory outfit serviceable for the examination of specimens helpful in the diagnosis of cases and in the location of carriers was made available about this time.

About 1921 two other important refinements took place. One was a determined campaign to locate and supervise carriers. The other was a revision in the quarantine rules which along other things required negative laboratory examinations of specimens taken from typhoid patients before raising quarantine. The prosecution of these procedures had a very pronounced favorable influence over the trend of typhoid prevalence in Illinois.

The two following tables include most of the important outbreaks that occurred during the period covered. It is noteworthy to observe that the number of cases involved in epidemics grows smaller as the date becomes more recent.

Some Water-Borne Typhoid Fever Epidemics in Illinois.

County	Locality	Year	Months	Cases	Deaths	Remarks
Winnebago	Rockford	1912	Jan.-Feb.	185	15	Cross-connections and polluted public supply well.
Menard	Old Salem	1915	Sept.-Oct.	100	20	Flooding of public water supply wells and no sterilization.
Kane	Elgin	1916	August	200	20	Leaky valve in cross connection in Elgin Watch Factory between safe and polluted supplies.
Douglas	Tuscola	1916	May-June	130	?	Privy vault to well.
Rock Island	Joliet	1918	July-Aug.	125	24	Pumping of raw river water through a bypass.
Cook	Maywood	1920	October	75		Severe dysentery due to leaky valve in cross-connection.
McLean	Bloomington	1920	Jan.-Feb.	300	21	Leaky cross-connection between industrial supply and the drinking water supply.
Clark	Marshall	1922	Apr.-May	10	3	Flood of wells during high water.
Cook	Chicago	1923	Nov.-Dec.	200	20	Excessive pollution at the 68th St. pumping stations minus sufficient increase in chlorination.
Whiteside	Sterling	1924 1925	Dec.-Jan.	12	2	Leaky valve in factory cross-connection between safe and polluted water supplies.
Bond	Greenville	1925	January	3,000		Severe dysentery and paratyphoid due to tile water main absorbing sewage from leaky sewer main.
—	Winona (Ind.)	1925	June	13*	3*	Spread into eight states from polluted water supply used by convention delegates.
LaSalle	Lockport	1925	Aug.-Sept.	14	3	Polluted public water supply.

* Illinois cases and deaths.

Outbreaks of Milk-Borne Typhoid Fever in Illinois.

County	Locality	Year	Months	No. cases	Remarks
Winnebago	Rockford	1913		16-31	Bottle
Cook	Park Ridge	1915	Jan.-Feb.	28	Polluted water at dairy
Macon	Decatur	1917	May, June, July	100	Milk bottle
DuPage	Wheaton	1918	August	18	Source unknown
Rock Island	Joliet	1918	December	55	Carrier
Morgan	Jacksonville	1919	Feb., March	12-14	Carrier
Douglas	Tuscola	1920	Aug., Sept.	30	Carrier
Madison	WoodRiver Twp.	1919	Sept.-Oct.	6	Dairy
Coles	Mattoon	1920	June, July	30	Carrier
Hancock	Fountain Green	1920	July, Aug.	84	Carrier or Convalescent
Carroll	Mt. Carroll	1921	December	5	Carrier
Macon	Decatur	1921	June, July	10	Carrier or Convalescent
Kane	Compton, St. Charles Twp.	1911	August	10	Carrier or Convalescent
Bond	Greenville	1921	January	8	?
Morgan	Jacksonville	1921	Aug., Sept.	8	Convalescent
Bond	Greenville	1922	July-Aug.	20	Carrier
Henry	Kewanee	1922	May-June	35	Carrier
Douglas	Newman	1923	April, May	10	Carrier
Montgomery	Litchfield	1924	August	25	Carrier

As water and milk supplies in recent years became more and more generally of good sanitary quality other factors in the spread of typhoid fever began to take prominence.

Thus in 1924 an outbreak, confined principally to Chicago and environs, was traced to the eating of raw oysters. This discovery ultimately led to drastic action in relation to shell fish. The State Director of Public Health issued an order in the early part of 1925, forbidding the sale of oysters for any except cooking purposes. This action in turn resulted in a general sanitary reform of the oyster industry, referred to elsewhere in this volume.

Little of significant importance concerning typhoid fever in Illinois has transpired since the sanitary reform of the oyster industry. Automobiles have become a larger and larger factor in the spread of the disease. This was demonstrated in 1925 when touring parties brought typhoid back from an Indiana town and caused mild outbreaks at Freeport and Polo. It is also indicated by the fact that foci of the disease are more and more widely distributed and a growing diminution in the average number of cases involved in any one epidemic.

With increased facilities for managing the disease mortality has tended downward although it has fluctuated from year to year as it always will so long as typhoid remains upon the earth.

Indeed severe outbreaks will occur from time to time where preventive sanitary precautions are neglected for any reason. This was demonstrated in 1927 when Montreal. Canada. experienced one of the worst epidemics ever reported on the North American continent. It involved more than 5,000 cases and nearly 500 deaths and extended over a period of more than six months.

In Illinois the mortality and sickness from typhoid fever in 1926 was the most favorable ever recorded. Only 230 deaths were reported.

The favorable record in 1926 was simply another step forward in the improvement that has been going on fairly constantly since the opening of the century. As ultimate extinction of the disease approaches, the degree of annual decline grows smaller, but no less significant and valuable. Since 1918 the decline in the mortality rate has amounted to slightly more than 60 per cent.

MORTALITY FROM TYPHOID FEVER IN ILLINOIS.

Year.	1918.	1919.	1920.	1921.	1922.	1923.	1924.	1925.	1926.
Number Deaths	519	383	380	396	282	317	239	327	230
Rate per 100,000	8.2	5.9	5.8	5.8	4.0	4.7	3.5	4.7	3.2

The fly in the ointment of the splendid 1926 experience is the bad record of the 34 counties which make up the extreme southern third of the State.

These 34 counties, with but little more than one million people, lost 116 inhabitants to typhoid fever, whereas the other 68 counties with a population of fully six million, lost only 114. There is some evidence that warm climatic conditions favor the propagation of typhoid. The fact that mild

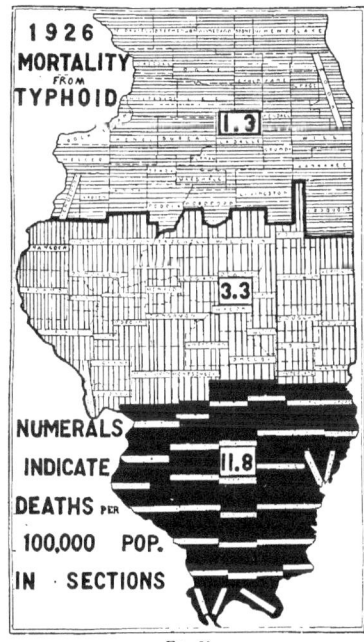

FIG. 20.

weather prevails much longer in southern than in northern Illinois may be a factor in the unfavorable typhoid rate in the southern section.

The rate per 100,000 was only 1.3 in the 33 counties that make up the extreme northern third of the State. Here nearly five million people are concentrated.

in the central third, the rate was 3.3. A little less than one and one quarter million people dwell in the 35 counties here concerned.

The very favorable record in Cook County influenced the good showing in the north. In that county where the estimated population is 3,486,600, there were only 26 deaths recorded from typhoid. That gives a rate of 0.7. The rate for the other 32 northern counties was 2.7, considerably more favorable than either the central or southern sections.

There were 20 cities of 10,000 or more population, and 27 counties from which no deaths at all from typhoid fever were reported. Indeed the mortality was confined largely to the small communities and rural areas.

These data point directly to the wholesome influence of public health activities. Typhoid fever death rates decline as volume of public health service increases

Scarlet Fever.

When the State Board of Health came into existence in 1877, Chicago was passing through the greatest epidemic of scarlet fever in its history. The death rate from the disease in that city was 190.5 per 100,000 population that year.

Doubtless the disease also spread into the neighboring territory and was more or less prevalent throughout the State, yet this situation received practically no attention from the Board. The reason for this is not difficult to apprehend if the problems and resources of the Board at that time are considered. Furthermore there is the fact that no special precautions were taken against the disease by health authorities in the seventies.

Even in a city the size of Chicago, which had a population of about 500,000, the reporting and placarding of scarlet fever cases was not enforced until 1877, and then it brought forth violent protests from the people. Physicians referred to it as the "Yellow Card Nuisance."

In 1880, a census year, 1,364 deaths from scarlet fever were reported for the State, which is a rate of a little over 44 per 100,000 population. Never since that year has the reported mortality rate exceeded 32 per 100,000.

The course of scarlet fever from 1860 to date, is shown in Figure 21, by the decennial and annual records, as far as these are available.

This chart shows that mortality from scarlet fever declined rapidly after the big epidemics of 1877 and 1880. The reason appears to be found in the activities of health officers. No noteworthy advancement was made prior to 1915 in medical knowledge concerning scarlet fever. A great deal was undertaken by the public health agencies, however, and particularly in Chicago where the best local organization in the State was at work.

The control measures employed included public education, the requirement of case reports, the isolation of patients and the quarantine of premises, the medical inspection of school children and, to a less extent, the hospitalization of patients. None of these things developed uniformly in the State nor were all of them begun simultaneously. The educational propaganda started first, about 1880, when the State Board published and distributed literature freely. The Board also made the disease reportable but few notifications were received except in Chicago where local ordinances were employed.

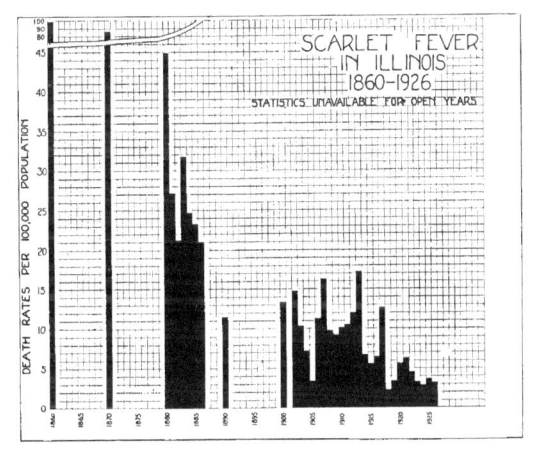

Fig. 21.

Shortly before 1900 it became the practice of the State Board of Health to send medical inspectors to epidemic foci. These men promoted isolation of patients as their chief control measure and this appears to have been accompanied by favorable results in reference to the spread of the disease. Scores of communities suffered from outbreaks during the first decade of the twentieth century so that the reports of the State Board are filled with accounts of investigations and resultant control measures, usually in the form of quarantine.

Another very important factor in controlling scarlet fever began to assume importance about 1908. This was the promotion of milk pasteurization. During the previous year Chicago went through a serious epidemic of scarlet fever and evidence gathered by the epidemiological investigators indicated the milk supply as the means through which the disease was spread.

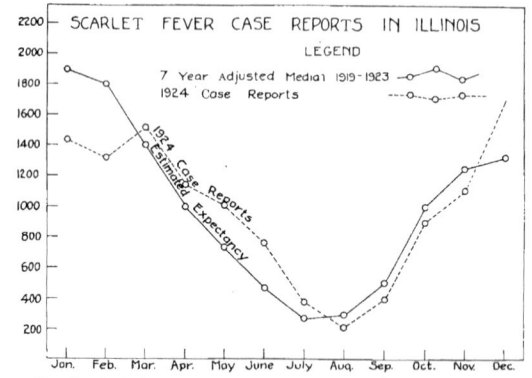

Fig. 22. Note the sharp upward swing of the 1924 line for December.

Table 31.

CASES OF SCARLET FEVER REPORTED BY MONTHS IN ILLINOIS.

Year	Jan.	Feb.	Mar.	Apr.	May.	June.	July.	Aug.	Sept.	Oct.	Nov.	Dec.	Total.
1916	1,878	1,891	2,281	1,564	1,547	893	416	239	488	933	1,264	1,682	15,076
1917	2,284	2,625	3,403	2,488	2,230	1,329	699	351	528	401	232	648	17,220
1918	758	611	561	505	362	148	150	101	231	189	201	208	4,025
1919	440	588	662	586	495	289	99	97	304	656	893	1,101	6,210
1920	2,449	2,235	2,335	1,708	1,456	862	429	293	715	1,385	1,972	2,637	18,478
1921	3,116	2,525	2,241	2,113	1,629	710	330	412	857	1,569	1,778	1,743	19,023
1922	1,987	1,817	1,388	936	671	465	240	370	526	1,143	1,419	1,314	12,256
1923	1,556	1,071	1,066	816	739	475	241	227	444	768	1,003	1,123	9,474
1924	1,435	1,317	1,508	1,148	1,003	780	383	208	396	891	1,105	1,516	11,690
1925	2,064	2,103	2,384	1,772	1,682	909	351	261	377	753	1,279	1,725	15,692
1926	1,847	2,129	2,051	1,507	1,397	947	486	297	376	816	1,124	1,265	14,244

This disclosure led the health commissioner of Chicago to require the pasteurization of milk supplies offered for sale in that city. The order became effective in 1908 but it was 1915 before facilities were available to make the entire supply of the city completely pasteurized except two percent which was certified.

Observation of the improvement brought about in Chicago as an apparent result of pasteurization led to the gradual extension of this procedure throughout the State. It was promoted with vigor by the State Department of Public Health subsequent to 1921, a fact referred to elsewhere in this volume.

The medical inspection of school children doubtless was an important factor in controlling scarlet fever and other diseases as well. It has never

Table 32.

DEATHS FROM SCARLET FEVER IN ILLINOIS BY MONTHS.

Year.	Jan.	Feb.	Mar.	Apr.	May.	June.	July.	Aug.	Sept.	Oct.	Nov.	Dec.	Total.
1918	28	17	22	23	11	8	5	4	2	10	13	6	149
1919	19	27	29	23	18	13	8	6	4	18	29	33	225
1920	50	55	55	29	33	22	8	4	13	24	41	36	370
1921	45	49	51	47	34	32	11	12	17	30	38	47	413
1922	57	48	37	31	16	13	7	15	9	18	24	30	305
1923	36	28	42	15	23	13	7	7	10	11	10	27	229
1924	27	27	25	27	18	10	8	4	6	9	15	36	206
1925	34	28	59	34	32	11	6	9	5	10	20	20	268
1926	34	23	38	31	26	21	10	10	5	11	14	9	233

Table 33.

DEATHS AND DEATH RATES FROM SCARLET FEVER IN ILLINOIS.

Year.	No. deaths.	Rate per 100,000 population.	Year.	No. deaths.	Rate per 100,000 population.
1860	1,698	98.7	1909	516	9.2
1870	2,162	85.1	1910	575	10.1
1880	1,369	44.4	1911	608	10.5
1881	856	27.1	1912	694	11.9
1882	687	21.2	1913	1,022	17.2
1883	1,048	31.7	1914	405	6.7
1884	832	24.6	1915	346	5.6
1885	802	23.2	1916	403	6.5
1886	743	21.	1917	791	12.7
1890	442	11.5	1918	149	2.3
1900	643	13.3	1919	225	3.4
1902	735	14.7	1920	370	5.6
1903	519	10.2	1921	413	6.2
1904	368	7.1	1922	305	4.5
1905	177	3.3	1923	229	3.3
1906	602	11.3	1924	206	2.9
1907	880	16.3	1925	288	3.7
1908	533	9.7	1926	233	3.2

been practiced with a large degree of systematic regularity except in Chicago but influence on communicable diseases there always has a pronounced effect on the prevalence rates in the State. Many other places employed public health nurses for work in the schools, especially after the World War, and their work produced marked improvement in the communicable disease incidence in the communities which they served.

The year of 1917 marks the beginning of the period when statistics of a reliable character became available for the State generally. In that year means for securing fairly complete reports of cases of scarlet fever, along with other diseases, were employed. This enabled State health officials to keep informed about the situation at all times and to be in a position to exercise control measures.

The most important step forward toward the control and ultimate elimination of scarlet fever came from bacteriological research in 1921. It is of especial interest here because two Illinois physicians, George F. and Gladys H. Dick, working together in the McCormick research laboratories in Chicago, discovered that a certain strain of streptococcus is responsible for scarlet fever and that toxin from these organisms may be used to determine through skin tests susceptibility to the disease. Prophylactic and therapeutic agents were also developed from the toxins.

The fundamental scientific facts in regard to the etiology of scarlet fever had been known for some time. The first was that some one or more of the streptococci were concerned in its symptomatology. As to the causative relations of the streptococcus there were two schools. One held that the streptococcus was the cause of the disease. The other held that streptococci were so nearly ubiquitous and caused so many diseases that they could not be the specific cause of scarlet fever. This school held that the specific cause was some unknown organism, but that the streptococci contributed materially to the symptoms. The theory upheld by Bristol that the rash of scarlet fever was an anaphylactic phenomenon for which streptococci was the bacterial cause, lent more support to this side of the question than it did to others.

Dr. A. R. Dochez, by the use of certain culture methods, demonstrated the one variety of streptococcus which he claimed could produce the disease, and in that way seemed to establish the primacy of the streptococcus as the etiologic agent and, at the same time, to answer the point made by Jochmann that an organism which was so wide-spread and caused so many diseases could not be the specific cause of scarlet fever.

It remained for the Dicks in 1921 to prove experimentally that a certain strain of streptococcus grown from throats of persons having scarlet fever, when injected into susceptible human beings, produced the disease. The Dicks extracted a toxin from this streptococcus which is now being used to make a skin test for determining the susceptibility of persons to scarlet fever. This procedure, called the Dick test, is done the same as the Schick test in reference to diphtheria. A toxin for preventing scarlet fever has also been developed. It is given in much the same way as toxin-antitoxin for the prevention of diphtheria. Not only that but there is now available an antitoxin for the curative treatment of scarlet fever.

The outlook for ridding the country of scarlet fever is therefore promising.

The greatest prevalence of scarlet fever is almost always experienced in mid-winter, usually in January or early February. Greatest freedom from it is enjoyed in August. The disease runs almost as true to this course as vegetation does to the seasonal changes which govern floral life.

For some reason which is not altogether clear, scarlet fever lost a good deal of its virulency during the second and third decades of the twentieth century. In 1926, for instance, there were 14,244 cases reported with only 233 deaths whereas 19,825 cases in 1917 left 791 dead. Fatalities mounting to 1,000 or more per year were evidently common in Illinois prior to 1900 but it seems improbable that the number of cases was correspondingly large.

The trend of the disease both as a cause of death and sickness may be observed from tables 31, 32 and 33. Its seasonal behavior is illustrated in Figure 22. A graphical illustration of the mortality record from scarlet fever is given in Figure 21.

Diphtheria.

The State Board of Health, in the years immediately after its organization in 1877, was especially concerned with the regulation of the practice of medicine, and the suppression of epidemics of yellow fever, cholera and smallpox. The other contagious diseases, including diphtheria, which were then attributed to filth and bad sanitation, were left largely under the control of local health organizations or practicing physicians.

There are no statistics available showing the prevalence of diphtheria or the death rate from the disease in Illinois for the years 1877, 1878 and 1879.

In 1880, the United States census shows that in Illinois, with a population of a little over three million, there were 3,783 deaths from diphtheria, or 123 for each 100,000 inhabitants. Chicago, too, in this year recorded a rate of 290 per 100,000 population, the highest diphtheria death rate ever recorded for the city. The diphtheria death rate continued high in 1881, 1882 and 1883.

In 1883 the State Board of Health distributed an educational circular on the prevention and control of diphtheria from which the following paragraph is quoted:

"Diphtheria has so often appeared where uncleanly conditions have prevailed, when it could not be traced to continuous propagation by contagion that its relation to filth as a cause may be assumed for sanitary purposes. It is immaterial whether this filth exists in visible and disgusting form such as the garbage heap, the cess-pool or the privy vault or in the invisible and possibly inodorous gases from an illy constructed sewer; from decaying vegetables in the cellar or in the poisonous exhalations from the human breath and body in unventilated rooms. All these undoubted causes of ill health should be at once abated."

This same circular also stated that diphtheria frequently caused more deaths than typhoid fever, smallpox, scarlet fever, and measles combined. During the first 10 years of the State Board of Health, from 1877 to 1886, Chicago annually averaged 168 deaths from diphtheria for each 100,000 of population.

Diphtheria was indeed a terrible disease, and today it can readily be appreciated how futile were the efforts, made at great expense, in trying to combat its spread by re-laying sewer pipes and drains, on the theory that it was a filth disease.

In 1887 the health department of the city of Chicago declared that diphtheria was not a filth but a contagious disease like smallpox.

Table 34.

DIPHTHERIA INCLUDING CROUP, CHICAGO CASES AND DEATHS, 1893-1899.

Year.	Reported.	Deaths.
1893	2,604	1,481
1894	1,921	1,406
1895	No data	1,652
1896	2,708	1,098
1897	No data	776
1898	No data	680
1899	No data	917

Another step away from the filth theory took place in 1891 when the State Board of Health ordered that bodies dead from diphtheria could no longer be transported by common carriers because of danger of spreading the disease.

In Chicago, diphtheria was made a reportable contagious disease in 1892

Although there were many cases of diphtheria and many deaths, and talk of closing some of the public schools because of epidemic conditions, yet not a single vial of the serum was called for at any station until October 5, 1895. This was true in spite of wide publicity given through the public press and illustrates the sceptical attitude of physicians toward the new treatment for diphtheria.

Because physicians were slow to use the new remedy, and especially because of the many deaths, the health department used all available members of its medical staff in administering antitoxin, and in teaching the medical profession the methods of using it. This practice soon made necessary 36 additional supply stations while 434 drug stores were authorized to act as agents for the distribution of diphtheria culture outfits.

Between October 5, 1895, and April 1, 1896, there were 1,468 true cases (bacteriologically verified) of diphtheria treated with antitoxin of which number 1,374 recovered and 94 died, a fatality of 6.4 per cent.

An analysis of 805 of the true cases referred to above shows

Treated on.	Total.	Recovered.	Died.	Death rate (Per cent)
1st day	61	61	0	0.00
2nd day	187	184	3	1.60
3rd day	372	362	10	2.68
4th day	109	92	17	15.60
Over 4 days	76	54	22	28.94
	805	753	52	6.46

By November, 1895, antitoxin administrations were being used to such an extent that it was spoken of as *generally adopted*.

The use of antitoxin as a preventive of diphtheria in Illinois began during the autumn of 1895. It was argued that a drug which could cause so prompt and complete recovery from diphtheria ought to be helpful in its prevention. This proved to be the case so that the practice of injecting antitoxin into susceptible persons exposed to diphtheria expanded coextensively with the use of this product as a curative.

Collecting Case Reports a Problem.

Once started the use of antitoxin became routine practice and caused far less trouble for health officers than the matter of case reports. In the State at large very little pressure was brought upon the local doctor to get reports because there were no local health organizations of consequence but in Chicago first one expediency and then another was employed to promote reporting. The medical profession was more or less recalcitrant on the whole so that Chicago was one of the last of the large cities in the country to reach the point where diphtheria quarantine was handled in an efficient way from a public health standpoint. Table 35 indicates by the relatively small difference between case and death reports that notification was by no means complete during the period.

After 1907 improvement in case reports began to be noticeable first in Chicago and later throughout the State. This was stimulated by the activity of health officers, local and state, and the completeness of registration increased in direct ratio to the increase in public health facilities for enforc-

Table 35.

DIPHTHERIA AND CROUP—ILLINOIS AND CHICAGO.

NUMBER OF CASES AND DEATHS 1900-1907 AND DEATH RATES PER 100,000 POPULATION.

Year	Entire State Deaths	Entire State Rate	Chicago Cases reported	Chicago Deaths	Chicago Rate
1900			3,033	840	49.5
1901			2,237	515	29.4
1902	1,079	21.6	2,760	627	34.8
1903	1,175	23.1	3,300	637	34.4
1904	884	17.1	2,607	409	21.5
1905	825	15.7	2,901	433	22.2
1906	1,022	19.2	4,457	554	27.7
1907	1,015	18.9	5,338	555	27.1

Table 36.
MORTALITY FROM DIPHTHERIA IN ILLINOIS.

Year	1921	1922	1923	1924	1925	1926
Number Deaths	1,478	1,181	811	470	409	411
Rate per 100,000	22.3	17.6	11.9	6.8	5.7	5.7

ing the notification requirements of health officers. Fairly satisfactory case registration dates from 1907 in Chicago and from 1917 for down-state. For all practical purposes the case reports were complete subsequent to these years.

Free Antitoxin.

Chicago introduced a system for supplying antitoxin at reasonable prices from convenient stations in 1895. A similar system was created for the State in 1905 by a legislative enactment. In 1907 the State Board of Health began the free distribution of antitoxin to all citizens. For this purpose an appropriation of $15,000 was made in that year. Distribution was effected

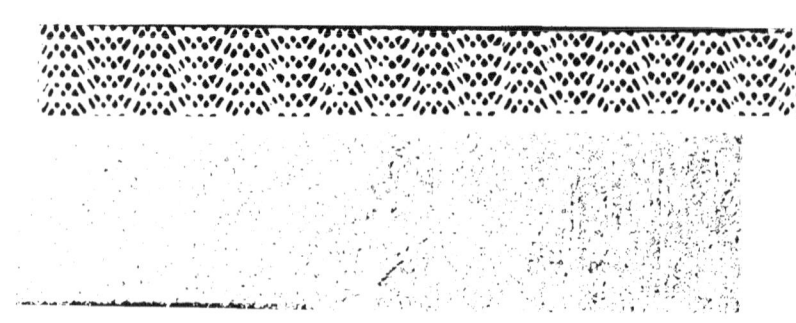

HEALTH CONDITIONS AFTER 1877

through a system of agents, usually local druggists, one of whom was located in every county seat with two or more in all of the larger communities.

This practice prevailed continuously and is still in vogue. It was satisfactory except that unforeseen epidemic conditions from time to time prior to 1921 exhausted the funds appropriated and created a shortage in the antitoxin supply. This resulted in hardships the character of which may be readily surmised. An emergency appropriation was made by the General

Table 37.

CASES OF DIPHTHERIA IN ILLINOIS.

Year.	Jan.	Feb.	Mar.	Apr.	May.	June.	July.	Aug.	Sept.	Oct.	Nov.	Dec.	Total.
1916	973	810	736	529	640	643	471	525	797	1,364	1,627	1,337	10,682
1917	1,263	1,072	1,312	1,124	1,141	930	890	722	1,212	814	2,046	1,161	13,687
1918	1,028	649	751	863	565	566	487	362	604	990	703	705	8,075
1919	731	769	665	635	668	470	541	528	992	1,898	2,050	1,505	11,452
1920	1,139	938	1,058	778	793	686	624	454	904	1,907	2,700	2,243	14,294
1921	1,874	1,364	1,350	1,215	1,085	944	744	848	1,613	3,667	3,505	2,384	20,793
1922	1,918	1,361	1,211	863	820	703	576	654	880	1,844	2,297	1,945	15,162
1923	1,697	1,090	1,032	727	678	532	392	411	607	1,114	1,318	1,118	10,716
1924	1,007	790	671	577	464	378	367	269	416	557	693	664	6,853
1925	584	458	439	391	370	323	287	266	273	490	584	541	5,066
1926	486	392	357	327	300	367	232	204	273	493	581	519	4,531

Table 38.

DIPHTHERIA—MORBIDITY, MORTALITY AND FATALITY RATES.

Fiscal Year.	Population.	Cases.	Deaths.	Per 100,000 people. Cases.	Per 100,000 people. Deaths.	Deaths per 100 cases.
1917–18	6,310,556	11,000	1,527	174.3	24.1	13.8
1918–19	6,398,068	8,060	979	125.9	15.3	12.1
1919–20	6,485,280	12,876	1,061	198.5	16.3	8.2
1920–21	6,572,492	16,764	1,243	255.1	18.8	7.4
1921–22	6,659,704	19,931	1,258	298.9	19.2	6.3
1922–23	6,746,916	13,883	989	205.8	13.3	7.1
1923–24	6,834,126	8,853	647	129.5	9.5	7.3
1924–25	6,921,344	5,530	400	79.9	5.8	7.2
1925–26	7,092,000	4,666	410	65.7	5.7	8.7

Assembly early in 1921 to cover immediate needs and subsequent to that time the biennial grants were ample to meet all requirements.

With the discovery and use of diphtheria antitoxin the death rate throughout Illinois declined very rapidly. The rate of 85 per 100,000 population in 1886 was cut to only 17 by 1902. This marvelous drop in the death rate caused many of the enthusiastic special workers in the field of preventive medicine and public health to prophesy that the year of 1925 would find diphtheria wiped off the face of the earth. They based this forecast on the facts that complete information existed in regard to the causative agent of diphtheria, that antitoxin would cure it and that antitoxin would give temporary immunity to exposed persons.

A study of the Chicago figures and also the State figures (see Fig. 23) show that from 1902 to 1922 the reduction in diphtheria mortality was very small. The failure to lower the diphtheria death rates during the two decades may be explained in part by the following factors:

1. Ignorance during part of this time of the role played by diphtheria carriers in spreading the disease.

Table 39.

DIPHTHERIA CARRIERS.

Year.	Jan.	Feb.	Mar.	Apr.	May.	June.	July.	Aug.	Sept.	Oct.	Nov.	Dec.
1921							179	174	292	480	316	420
1922	270	239	235	165	139	214	136	117	257	429	678	477
1923	455	306	255	249	353	288	346	227	286	432	522	577
1924	527	383	327	285	284	227	340	289	262	337	417	292
1925	327	207	259	188	287	244	242	181	167	259	310	137
1926	148	119	134	122	126	89	118	67	92	145	164	242

Table 40.

DEATHS FROM DIPHTHERIA IN ILLINOIS BY MONTHS.

Year.	Jan.	Feb.	Mar.	Apr.	May.	June.	July.	Aug.	Sept.	Oct.	Nov.	Dec.	Total.
1918	146	105	100	94	83	66	66	53	77	159	102	91	1,142
1919	100	92	91	63	69	44	60	48	89	135	141	112	1,044
1920	121	106	68	83	76	47	44	47	64	126	181	165	1,128
1921	137	122	93	88	92	84	56	81	92	231	223	179	1,478
1922	181	108	120	74	88	45	43	46	75	132	130	139	1,181
1923	133	88	74	59	36	27	26	36	45	89	107	91	811
1924	83	34	41	38	36	32	33	16	31	37	44	55	480
1925	47	23	29	33	29	27	23	25	24	46	51	52	409
1926	38	37	35	32	26	24	32	14	24	53	52	44	411

2. Self-medication of illnesses regarded as nothing more serious than severe sore throat.

of these procedures came to be part of the routine practice in fighting diphtheria in Illinois and it is to the promotion and practical application of these two things that credit is given for the remarkable decline in diphtheria since 1921.

Popularizing Toxin-Antitoxin.

Like antitoxin at first toxin-antitoxin was regarded with distinct skepticism on the part of doctors and the public so that it came into more or less general use quite gradually. The Schick test required time and considerable skill but its employment before administering toxin-antitoxin was advocated. This was another difficulty in the way of generalizing immunization against diphtheria.

Table 41.

DEATHS AND DEATH RATES FROM DIPHTHERIA IN ILLINOIS.

Year	No. deaths.	Rate per 100,000 population.	Year.	No. deaths	Rate per 100,000 population
1860	1,199	70.0	1909	1,001	18.
1870	1,489	59.0	1910	1,332	23.8
1880	3,783	122.9	1911	1,302	22.7
1881	2,924	92.7	1912	1,414	23.4
1882	2,172	67.2	1913	1,347	22.8
1883	2,201	66.6	1914	1,092	18.2
1884	2,219	68.6	1915	1,120	18.5
1885	2,755	79.8	1916	1,356	21.8
1886	3,997	113.3	1917	1,725	27.7
1890	3,561	93.	1918	1,142	17.9
1900	2,067	42.8	1919	1,044	16.2
1902	1,076	21.6	1920	1,128	17.2
1903	1,175	23.1	1921	1,478	22.2
1904	884	17.1	1922	1,181	17.4
1905	825	15.7	1923	811	11.9
1906	1,022	19.2	1924	480	6.8
1907	1,015	18.9	1925	409	5.7
1908	979	17.8	1926	411	5.7

Experience came to the rescue. A few pioneers all over the country began giving toxin-antitoxin to all children under their protection without reference to the Schick susceptibility test. One of these was the medical officer of the fraternity school at Mooseheart, Illinois, where more than 1,000 children are constantly enrolled. Beginning with 1920 all children in the institution have been immunized with toxin-antitoxin, newcomers getting the immunizing doses upon arrival. No case of diphtheria developed there to date subsequent to 1920 although the previous history showed 16 to 50 cases annually.

Statistics also came in with helpful suggestions. They pointed out that by far the heaviest losses of life from diphtheria were among children less than six years old.

360   HEALTH CONDITIONS AFTER 1877

Thus about 1922 the State Department of Public Health began to advocate the use of toxin-antitoxin in children under eight without regard to the Schick test. A number of voluntary and professional organizations elected to lend their influence to the cause of diphtheria eradication and some, like the federation of women's clubs and the parent-teacher associations became quite active in the campaign.

In the meantime the State had begun to distribute material for making the Schick test and toxin-antitoxin without local cost to any citizens who desired to use either or both. Previously a field laboratory equipment had

[Figure 23: Diphtheria in Illinois 1860-1926. Death rates per 100,000 population. Statistics unavailable for open years.]

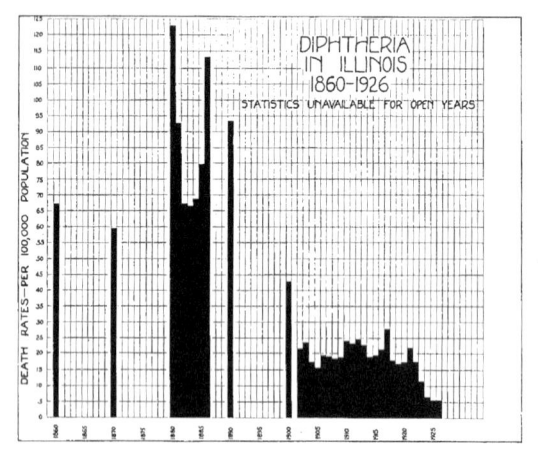

FIG. 23.

been purchased and the State employed bacteriologists who were prepared to go at once to the scene of outbreaks which had got beyond local control. Not only so but branch laboratory service had been developed by the State for the purpose of expediting the diagnosis of diphtheria.

All of these factors counted in the manifest success toward ridding the State of diphtheria. The first step was the realization that diphtheria is contagious and is spread from person to person. That took place about 1890.

Then came antitoxin, placed on the market in 1895. The next important measure was the laboratory diagnosis of diphtheria. This began as an official function of the State in 1904 when the laboratory was started. It developed until five branch laboratories located at convenient points offered prompt service in diphtheria cases to all parts of the State without local cost. In 1917 a field diagnostic laboratory outfit was put into service also.

Following the introduction of free laboratory service came the free distribution of antitoxin, undertaken by the State in 1907 and continued. Then came the Schick test and toxin-antitoxin in 1913 and the adoption of both by the State about 1920.

The downward trend of diphtheria was due to the organized use of these factors. As each came into prominence a new advantage over the disease was gained and a new declevity in mortality from diphtheria dated from its use on a considerable scale.

Reference to Figure 23 and the various tables accompanying this article tell the story of how rapid the progress against diphtheria has been. Not only has the prevalence and mortality declined but the percentage of fatal cases has gone down.

After 1921 improvement in the mortality rate from diphtheria was phenomenal. The number of deaths reported for 1926 in Illinois was less than one-third of the number reported in 1921. Figures for the intervening years are shown in Table 36.

Tuberculosis.

Tuberculosis in Illinois subsequent to 1877, may be viewed in two periods, the one prior to 1910, during which time not much was accomplished in lowering the death rate, and the other from 1910 to date, during which the trend of mortality was definitely downward as a result of the systematic control measures instituted.

The period prior to 1910 may be considered in two phases, the one before and the other after the time, in the early nineties, when the tubercle bacillus became generally accepted as the causative agent. Although the tubercle bacillus was discovered in 1882, it took approximately another decade for this fact to become accepted generally enough to affect the manner of handling the malady and in curative and preventive medicine.

The course of tuberculosis in Illinois, as shown by the annual death rates, as far as these are available, is illustrated in Figure 24.

This chart shows that in the first period, the rate remained practically stationary for 10 years. Then for another decade it manifested a tendency to increase. Toward the end of the period there was a slight fall.

The second period is marked by a pronounced initial decline that continued until about 1917 when the mortality rate jumped up again to the level which characterized the diseases during the first decade of the twentieth century. This increase probably had some relation to the World War. The strain of that emergency together with deprivations in food, high pressure working conditions and new kinds of exposures probably caused a rekindling of tuberculosis in many people in whom it had been arrested or quiescent.

At any rate 1918 was the peak mortality year in the second period. After that date a steady decline marked the mortality from tuberculosis. Not only had the time arrived when results from control measures were to be expected but a new zeal and added momentum characterized anti-tuberculosis campaigns in the State. Good economic conditions also prevailed,

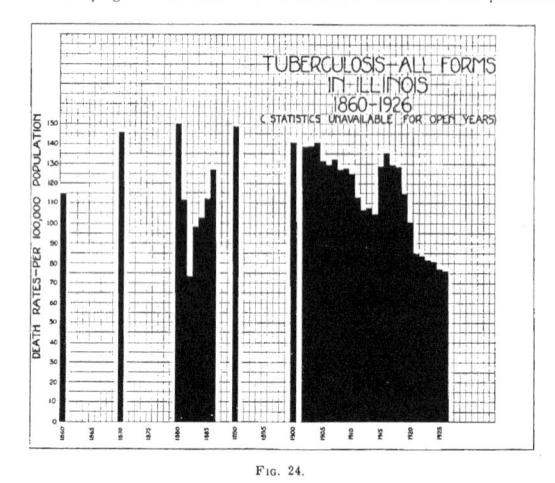

[Figure: TUBERCULOSIS—ALL FORMS IN ILLINOIS 1860-1926 (STATISTICS UNAVAILABLE FOR OPEN YEARS). Death rates per 100,000 population.]

FIG. 24.

making possible the extension of preventive work on a larger scale than would otherwise have been the case.

Early Attitude.

The early volumes of the annual reports of the State Board of Health

of such pestilential diseases as cholera, yellow fever, and smallpox, and licensing of practitioners of medicine.

Furthermore, the fact that the infectious nature of tuberculosis had not been definitely proven, while the sanitary precaution to prevent the spread of cholera and similar diseases had apparently been effective where they had been carried out, gave every cause for the Board to proceed along these established lines at the time.

Table 53.

CASES OF TUBERCULOSIS REPORTED BY MONTHS IN ILLINOIS.

Year.	Jan.	Feb.	Mar.	Apr.	May.	June.	July.	Aug.	Sept.	Oct.	Nov.	Dec.	Total.
1916													
1917	172	2,485	2,415	1,976	1,720	2,249	2,619	2,495	2,484	892	311	4,111	23,929
1918	1,840	1,142	1,722	1,446	1,602	1,353	1,563	1,182	973	891	1,208	637	15,559
1919	1,390	1,397	1,430	1,923	1,586	1,723	1,720	1,447	1,627	1,719	1,693	1,580	19,241
1920	1,433	1,164	1,820	1,320	1,295	1,468	1,065	729	1,209	1,012	938	1,114	14,563
1921	989	1,103	1,366	1,253	1,208	1,283	1,508	1,063	937	1,100	1,147	1,374	14,197
1922	1,153	1,111	1,685	1,229	1,640	1,417	1,464	1,171	1,164	1,429	1,634	1,386	16,483
1923	1,775	1,161	2,489	1,463	1,610	1,351	1,151	1,122	1,096	1,355	1,083	865	16,512
1924	1,328	1,077	1,111	1,482	1,239	1,223	1,582	1,709	1,175	1,277	999	904	18,015
1925	901	1,182	1,143	1,101	1,151	1,190	1,051	825	1,166	1,015	1,332	1,941	14,904
1926	934	1,132	1,359	1,755	1,853	1,793	1,463	1,738	1,291	1,399	1,131	1,129	16,997
1927	1,518	1,175	1,329	1,414	1,157	1,362	1,040						

Table 54.

DEATHS FROM TUBERCULOSIS IN ILLINOIS BY MONTHS.

Year.	Jan.	Feb.	Mar.	Apr.	May.	June.	July.	Aug.	Sept.	Oct.	Nov.	Dec.	Total.
1916													
1917													
1918	724	677	876	939	818	671	596	585	581	742	720	630	8,559
1919	728	721	756	768	712	612	610	553	454	509	459	513	7,395
1920	639	737	631	626	628	563	524	468	450	423	431	448	6,568
1921	506	455	571	505	545	428	447	444	449	435	375	456	5,617
1922	492	477	576	551	547	468	445	440	384	408	395	437	5,620
1923	489	506	559	542	527	474	448	421	410	410	408	378	5,572
1924	544	469	560	505	543	482	446	416	409	420	424	424	5,642
1925	505	433	555	504	502	511	470	386	415	407	408	441	5,537
1926	454	407	579	531	556	486	441	410	408	438	347	438	5,495
1927													

At the beginning of the semi-centennial period in the year 1877, little was known about the cause and prevention of tuberculosis. However, as early as 1861, France had established hospitals for the poor tuberculous children of Paris. In 1865 it was demonstrated that tuberculosis could be transmitted to the lower animals by inoculating them with diseased tissue from tuberculous human lungs.

The attention of the people of Illinois was first attracted to the seriousness of this disease by the high death rate at State institutions. As early as 1870, the death rate from tuberculosis at the State penitentiary began to concern the management of that institution. A report made in 1899 showed a 10-year average mortality of 16.3 per thousand inmates; the average age of inmates being 35 years and the average term of commitment being two years. Warden Murphy's report in 1895 showed 70 cases of tuberculosis, 29 deaths. and 26 discharges; and of those suffering from tuberculosis as high as 78 per cent had died from this disease in this institution.

Unfortunately there are no accurate records available during this early period showing the prevalence of tuberculosis in the State as a whole, except the United States decennial census reports of deaths. These give the

Table 55.

ANNUAL DEATHS AND DEATH RATES FROM TUBERCULOSIS IN ILLINOIS.
—ALL FORMS.

Year.	No. deaths.	Rate per 100,000 population.	Year.	No. deaths.	Rate per 100,000 population.
1860		118.7	1906	6,899	129.8
			1907	7,142	132.4
1870		145.6	1908	6,944	126.8
			1909	7,078	127.3
1880	4,645	150.9	1910	7,049	125.
1881	3,624	111.7	1911	6,509	113.3
1882	2,385	73.8	1912	6,212	106.5
1883	3,285	98.5	1913	6,371	107.6
1884	3,492	102.5	1914	6,521	104.8
1885	3,866	111.9	1915	7,816	128.1
1886	4,472	126.7	1916	8,408	135.6
			1917	8,065	129.4
1890	5,698	148.9	1918	8,579	128.7
			1919	7,395	114.7
1900	6,786	140.7	1920	6,568	100.5
			1921	5,617	84.9
1902	6,895	138.3	1922	5,620	83.8
1903	7,032	138.7	1923	5,572	82.
1904	7,234	140.5	1924	5,642	81.1
1905	6,891	131.7	1925	5,537	77.9
			1926	5,493	76.2

deaths from tuberculosis as follows: 4,645, in 1880, and 5,698, in 1890 representing a rate of 150.9 and 148.9, per 100,000 respectively.

Since Discovery of Cause.

Thereupon Dr. Scott, Secretary of the State Board of Health offered a resolution as follows: "Resolved that a committee be appointed by the State Board of Health and the Sanitary Association to confer with the State Superintendent of Public Instruction and the county superintendents of schools to draft such needed amendments to the school laws of the State as will render it necessary that teachers qualify physically as well as mentally before receiving certificates to teach, and that a thorough knowledge of school hygiene be included in the recommendations of all teachers; also to formulate such other amendments as will place all public schools directly under medical supervision and inspection."

In accordance with a joint resolution by the General Assembly the State Board of Health made an investigation of tuberculosis in the State in 1900. The report to the Governor recommended the establishment and maintenance of a State tuberculosis sanatorium. This report after reviewing the tuberculosis situation and citing figures to show its economic importance, presented the following as part of arguments for a sanatorium:

"Sanatoria are institutions designed for the open air treatment of consumptives under medical direction, embodying ideal hygienic and educational methods, viz: the isolation of the patient, the destruction of sputa and morbid excretations which contain bacilli, thus removing from him the danger of infecting others or of reinfecting himself. Under the constant supervision of a medical officer, he is educated in hygienic principles, there is a strict regulation of his daily life and such measures are enforced as may be indicated by the needs of the patient. There is a systematic regulation of rest and exercise according to the varying condition of the patient, a carefully chosen dietary, an abundance of wholesome food, and constant exposure to fresh, pure air and sunshine, promoting oxygenation of the tissues, together with special remedies administered for symptoms as they may arise.

"To quote a prominent clinician: 'A patient outside the sanatorium is disinclined to accept the yoke of a rigid and severe discipline. In the sanatorium nothing is left to his caprice, he never receives recommendations more or less vague, but rest, exercise and alimentation are measured and even the cough is disciplined. This almost military education creates an influence very favorable to the evolution of recovery and assures success of therapeutic means, and the patients rapidly acquire habits of hygienic discipline which they continue in their homes.'

"At the International Medical Congress for the consideration of tuberculosis, which met in Berlin in May, 1899, the world's most prominent investigators of the disease were present. It was the unanimous conclusion of this notable assemblage that all means of controlling tuberculosis, preventive and curative, were combined in the conception of the sanatorium.

"As far back as can be remembered, consumptives have sought localities where they could have the benefit of a mild sunny climate possessing either a high altitude or a marine atmosphere. The cure of consumption by climate has become traditional, but experience in sanatorium work has proven that the value of any special climate or altitude or atmosphere has been exaggerated. Weber, who can speak with higher authority on this subject than any other writer, says: 'The blind confidence that has existed in climate influence has caused neglect of other necessary hygienic measures and has frequently caused an aggravation of the disease.' It is now conceded that there is no climate possessing immunity from consumption. Climatic conditions are far from exercising the salutary influence attributed to them, and excepting in the extreme zones of the earth, the cure can be effected wherever the air is pure without extreme changes of temperature."

366 HEALTH CONDITIONS AFTER 1877

The State Board of Health first declared tuberculosis to be a contagious disease in 1901.

A second report was submitted to the Governor in 1902, recommending the establishment of a State sanatorium. Attention was called to the fact that the records of the State showed from 7,000 to 8,000 deaths per year from tuberculosis and that there were more deaths from tuberculosis than from typhoid fever, whooping cough, measles, scarlet fever, and smallpox combined.

Numerous attempts were made to get public appropriations for a State sanatorium but these efforts failed.

Tuberculosis was the subject of a symposium on the occasion of the annual meeting of the Illinois State Medical Society held at Bloomington, Illinois, in 1904. This was participated in by members of the State Board of Health. Following this a circular was printed by the Board entitled "Cause, Prevention and Cure of Tuberculosis." This was distributed in July, and during the year it was necessary to turn out four editions, the last consisting of 100,000 copies. This circular was distributed freely during the following year. It was in 1904 also that Dr. T. B. Sachs published the report of his intensive studies on the incidence of tuberculosis in the Jewish district on the west side of Chicago. The cases found in a house-to-house survey and through dispensary records were shown on a spot map, and were so numerous that the study attracted a great deal of attention.

The report and charts appealed especially to State Senator Edward J. Glackin, himself a resident of the district, and his interest later found expression in the drafting of bills for sanatoria which he introduced in the legislature. The first of these was for a State sanatorium, in 1905, which failed to pass. The next one provided for the establishment of municipal sanatoria which will be referred to later.

Anti-tuberculosis Efforts Organized.

A meeting was held at Chicago on December 15, 1904, for the purpose of bringing together all of the organizations actively engaged in the prevention of tuberculosis in Illinois. This meeting was attended by represent-

educational work. The State Medical Society had been active as far as its facilities permitted.

At the preliminary meeting of the conference, a committee on organization was appointed with instructions to prepare the necessary by-laws for a new society, and to nominate a board of directors to report to a general meeting to be called later.

The committee met on December 16, 1904, and proceeded to effect an organization to be known as the Illinois Association for the Prevention of Tuberculosis, in which all of the groups interested would be represented. A constitution and by-laws were drawn up, to be submitted at the first annual meeting scheduled for January 19, 1905, at the Public Library Building, Chicago.

From that time on this Association, under various titles, was a dominating factor in anti-tuberculosis work in the State. Due largely to its efforts every county felt the influence of organized effort referred to at greater length in the chapter on auxiliary health organization. Its best work was done after 1910, however.

Organized efforts from the outset was directed toward legislation and education. The voluntary agencies and the State Board of Health joined forces in both directions. At each meeting the General Assembly was besieged with lobbyists and appealed to with bills, the first of which usually asked for a state sanatorium. Exhibits graphically portraying the ravages of tuberculosis were displayed upon every opportunity. They were shown before medical meetings, teachers' conventions, farmers' institutes and even the General Assembly.

Having been agitated the subject of tuberculosis among prisoners would not down. The situation at Joliet attracted especial attention because of interest manifested by the warden and because of the paucity of medical service in the institution.

The agitation about tuberculous prisoners was important chiefly because of its bearing upon the general situation. It brought the subject into the press. It made the law makers take notice. It helped to create a public opinion about tuberculosis. The reforms in prison construction and prison management that resulted were good measures for application everywhere, so far as the principles involved were concerned. The publicity brought on by the involvement of the penitentiary carried these relations home to large blocks of the population in an easy, quick way.

Another definite step was taken by the State Board of Health in 1906. Laboratory facilities for the examination of sputum specimens were put into operation. This offered a means for the accurate diagnosis of tuberculosis in many cases, and led to the treatment at a more opportune time in the course of the disease.

It was in 1906 also that the movement against tuberculosis in the schools began. This started in Chicago where nursing services, medical examination and ventilating facilities were promoted.

The Chicago Tuberculosis Institute secured the consent of the commissioners of Cook County in the summer of 1906, for the establishment of an open-air camp for consumptives at the Dunning institution. The camp was designed for poor consumptives and particularly for those living in the congested poorer quarters of the city. A great deal of interest attached to the results attained, as the project was undertaken to prove that out-of-door treatment was therapeutically and economically sound.

The developments mentioned thus far had their effects. One community after another began to pass ordinances requiring case reports and movements resulting in the establishment of sanatoria, preventoria, open-air school rooms and dispensary service began to take on momentum.

Thus in 1906, Peoria passed an ordinance requiring case reports. The same year Sangamon County appropriated $200 for providing tents in which local hospitals could isolate tuberculous patients. About the same time the Illinois Homeopathic Medical Association established an open-air sanatorium at Buffalo Rock in LaSalle County. A little later, about 1908, the State Board of Health attempted to stimulate reporting by requiring the names of persons from whom sputum was collected for examination at the State diagnostic laboratory.

Legislation Secured.

All of these things brought pressure enough on the General Assembly to result in a law enabling cities to build and maintain sanatoria. This took place in 1908 after failure had pursued all efforts to secure a State tuberculosis sanatorium.

The act, known as the "Glackin Law", provided that upon the adoption of the propositon by a referendum vote by any city a tax of not to exceed one mill on every dollar of the assessed valuation might be levied to defray the cost of establishing and maintaining such sanatoria, and for the care and treatment of persons suffering from tuberculosis.

The city of Chicago took advantage of the law in 1909, proceeding at once to build a sanatorium. The same year Lake County established a tuberculosis sanatorium, to be maintained by the county, which meant that indigent persons only could be admitted without charge. The Chicago Fresh Air Hospital, a private institution conducted by Dr. Ethan A. Gray, was opened this year.

In 1909 and 1911, bills were again introduced in the legislature providing for the establishment of a State sanatorium, but were not enacted. Thus the establishment of municipal sanatoria had to be relied upon until 1915, when the legislature passed a law providing for the establishment of such institutions by counties.

The movement against tuberculosis gathered considerable momentum by the work done in Chicago between 1907 and 1911. Under Health Commissioner Evans an ordinance prohibiting the sale of milk from tuberculous cattle was passed, the requirements of case reports was rigidly enforced, dispensaries for diagnosis and treatment were established, and a specialized nursing service was inaugurated, an anti-spit crusade was conducted and withal a general public sentiment against the disease was created and

Will You Become a Crusader?

In the interests of **Health, Cleanliness** and **The Law**, you are earnestly requested to co-operate in enforcing the reasonable and sanitary regulation embraced in the City Ordinance, Number 1493:

"Spitting is prohibited upon sidewalks, in public conveyances, theatres, halls, assembly rooms, public buildings, or buildings where any considerable number of people gather or assemble together, and in similar places"

W. A. Evans
Commissioner of Health.

Chicago Anti-Spitting League

Reproduced from a circular used in Chicago's anti-spitting campaign.

put to work. Mortality began to decline and this made other folks take notice.

The Association for the Prevention of Tuberculosis took on new life and reorganized in 1910 with Dr. W. A. Evans as president. From that time forward a close cooperation between voluntary and official agencies was observed with telling results. The law enabling counties to erect and maintain sanatoria came in 1915. After that the story is one of increasing facilities for fighting tuberculosis and ultimately a long anticipated and welcomed decline in mortality which gave evidence of permanent advantage.

Following a well-established rule, the rate of progress in tuberculosis control did not conform to a straight line, but was interrupted by a break or step backward in 1911. That year the milk ordinance, under which Chicago was making such headway in its fight against tuberculosis, was invalidated, by an act of the legislature which prohibited any municipality in the State from requiring a tuberculin test for the cattle from which its milk supply was derived; the so-called "Shurtleff Law."

After a year's delay, another ordinance was passed which provided that milk sold must be of a grade defined as "inspected," or else be pasteurized according to methods set forth in the ordinance. No tuberculin test could be required for cows used for the production of inspected milk, but the standard for this class of milk was so high, that the real effect of the ordinance was general pasteurization.

But the effect of the State law as a whole was that delay and procrastination occurred in the purification of the milk supply of the largest city in the State; in fact complete pasteurization of the milk supply was not obtained until nearly five years later when Dr. John Dill Robertson, on July 22, 1916, issued an order during an epidemic of infantile paralysis, definitely requiring the pasteurization of all milk except certified.

Upon the recommendation of Dr. John Dill Robertson, Commissioner of Health of Chicago, the Municipal Tuberculosis Sanitarium in 1916 made a house-to-house survey for tuberculosis, in the central district of Chicago. A total of 165,700 persons were examined, of which number 8.6 per cent were found to be tuberculous. A total of 14,282 unregistered cases were found and listed for supervision.

In 1916 the sanitarium augmented the school inspection service of the health department by adding 50 doctors and 50 nurses to the force, with the understanding that a part of the work of the entire force would be devoted to the diagnosis and prevention of tuberculosis among pupils in the schools.

A comprehensive program for the finding and reporting of all cases of tuberculosis; and the segregation of all open cases not under the care of family physicians; and the prevention of the exposure of open cases of tuber

A health survey of White County was made in 1915, under the auspices of the Illinois State Association for the Prevention of Tuberculosis, and the Illinois State Board of Health. The work was done by Dr. I. H. Foster, inspector for the Board of Health, and Miss Harriet Fulmer, R. N., extension secretary of the Association for the Prevention of Tuberculosis.

The tuberculosis cases and deaths from the disease in White County in 1915 are shown by the spot map, reproduced in Figure 25.

Three progressive steps were taken by the State in the campaign against tuberculosis in 1915. The one was an order making tuberculosis a reportable disease, the second the promulgation of rules and regulations for the control of pulmonary tuberculosis, and the third was an enactment of the county sanitarium law, also introduced by Senator Glackin of Chicago.

In the November election of 1916, Adams, Champaign, Morgan, McLean, Ogle, Livingston and LaSalle Counties, voted to build sanatoria. At the next regular election the counties of Boone, Bureau, Christian, Clark, Clay, DeWitt, Coles, Crawford, DeKalb, Douglas, Fulton, Grundy, Henry Jackson, Jefferson, Kane, Lee, Logan McDonough, Macon, Madison, Marion, Piatt, Pike, Randolph, Scott, Stephenson, Tazewell, Vermilion, White side, Will, Winnebago, and Woodford took advantage of the tuberculosis sanitarium law.

Since the Organization of the State Department of Public Health.

When the State Civil Administrative Code was passed in 1917, and the State Board of Health was abolished and the State Department of Public Health created, in the Department a division of tuberculosis was established as a special unit. The assistant director of the Department, Dr. George T. Palmer, was assigned as acting chief of the division, a clerk and stenographer were employed and the division of tuberculosis began to take an active part in the state-wide anti-tuberculosis campaign.

On account of shortage of nurses for tuberculosis and other health work, the State Department of Public Health, the State Department of Welfare, and the Illinois Tuberculosis Association as it was now called, established a school for public health nurses, giving brief but comprehensive courses several times a year.

To secure a more definite idea of the extent of the tuberculosis problem in Illinois the division of tuberculosis outlined a plan of survey to be employed by nurses and others engaged in this work. Through this plan a large number of tuberculosis surveys were made in various localities in the State.

Shortly after the United States engaged in the World War, there was created a subcommittee of the State Council of Defense, devoted to tubercu-

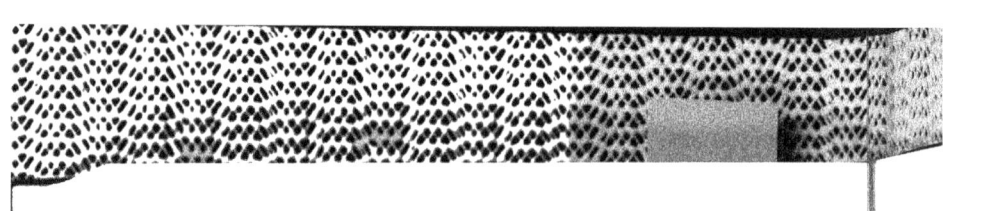

WHITE COUNTY, ILLINOIS.
Pop. 23052 - 1910 Census.

128 ● Living Cases of Tuberculosis - 1915
64 ■ Deaths from Tuberculosis - 1914-15

N.B. To obtain exact number of living cases multiply <u>known deaths</u> by 10.

FIG. 25.

losis, of which the assistant director of the State Department of Public Health was made chairman. This subcommittee was coordinated with the division of tuberculosis of the State Department of Public Health, and with the Illinois Tuberculosis Association. It ceased to function after the Armistice was signed.

On account of the importance of excluding tuberculous individuals from military service and the necessity for greater medical knowledge in the care of returned tuberculous soldiers, the State Department of Public Health, in conjunction with the Illinois Tuberculosis Association, conducted clinical conferences on the diagnosis and treatment of tuberculosis, utilizing the best known teachers of this subject in the Middle West. Conferences were attended by physicians from all parts of the State. Special tuberculosis clinics were also given before county medical societies.

To meet the needs of returned tuberculous soldiers, who on account of inadequate facilities for care of the tuberculous in Illinois, were subjected to neglect, a working agreement was entered into between the State Department of Public Health, the American Red Cross, and the Illinois Tuberculosis Association, whereby the Department and the Association provided for scientific examination and medical direction of returned soldiers.

At the beginning of 1918, the War Department advised the State Department of Public Health of the return of about 1,700 tuberculous soldiers. This number was increased to 1,800 at the time of signing the Armistice.

It was fortunate that the establishment of county and municipal tuberculosis sanatoria was continued through the war period, for these sanatoria served a useful purpose in hospitalizing the service men who returned afflicted with tuberculosis.

Early in 1919, the LaSalle and McLean county sanitariums were opened. In addition to Chicago, the cities of Rock Island, Peoria and Rockford were maintaining tuberculosis sanatoria at that time.

The Adams County tuberculosis sanatorium began operation after the end of the year. A small sanatorium was in operation in DeKalb County, and plans were being made for more extensive buildings. Tazewell, McDonough, Woodford, and Kane tuberculosis sanatoria were under process of construction.

The tuberculosis death rate in the State in 1923 was 81.8 per 100,000 population, and tuberculosis stood fifth from the top of the list of causes of death.

Questionnaires were sent in 1925 to all private, county and municipal tuberculosis sanatoria in the State to obtain up-to-date data for a revised directory. Surveys were made of tuberculosis cases on record in the counties of the State with the object of providing better home care and to protect others from infection. The surveys showed that regular and periodic tuberculosis clinics were in operation in 48 counties and that 15 county sanatoria with 1,375 beds were in operation.

The McDonough and Madison county tuberculosis sanatoria were opened in 1926.

Three important bills relating to the control of tuberculosis were enacted by the legislature in 1925.

One made the maximum tax for municipal tuberculosis sanatoria two instead of one and one-third mills on the dollar of assessed valuation.

The second was a law regulating the pasteurization of milk and requiring a permit from the State Department of Public Health.

The third law appropriated $2,000,000 for the purpose of indemnifying owners of tuberculous cattle destroyed under the provisions of the law of 1919, which authorizes the slaughter of domestic cattle found to be infected with tuberculosis. This had been practiced before but never before had so much been appropriated at one time.

The latter was the so-called "Tice Bill" which provided for the tuberculin testing of cattle, the establishment of accredited herds, and for the enrollment of counties under the county-accredited plan, under which it is obligatory for the remaining herd owners to test, whenever more than seventy-five per cent of the cattle in any county have been tested, and proper certification of this fact has been made to the county authorities, in accordance with the provisions of the law.

Tuberculosis eradication among dairy cattle had progressed very rapidly, and by the end of 1926, the situation was approximately as follows: Sixty-five counties were under federal and State supervision for the eradication of bovine tuberculosis; 21 counties had herds 75 per cent free from bovine tuberculosis; and one county was 100 per cent free from bovine tuberculosis.

Miscellaneous Communicable Diseases.

The comprehensive sanitary surveys made in approximately four hundred cities and villages during the years 1882-1885 indicate in a general way that very little attention was given by local authorities in these municipalities at that period to control, suppress or prevent the so-called minor contagious diseases such as measles, whooping cough, chickenpox, etc.

The statistical data available for that early period are given in the special comments under each of these diseases or in the chart accompanying each.

In fact the data on these so-called minor diseases are very fragmentary until about 1902. In all sections of the State except Chicago they were far from complete until very recent years. Only since 1920 have the statistical data by months been made accessible in tabular form by counties.

Table 56.

CASES OF CEREBROSPINAL FEVER REPORTED IN ILLINOIS.

Year.	Jan.	Feb.	Mar.	Apr.	May.	June.	July.	Aug.	Sept.	Oct.	Nov.	Dec.	Total.
1917	12	14	28	42	65	57	61	36	37	36	29	33	450
1918	48	58	69	62	53	19	26	11	16	8	4	12	389
1919	16	15	14	12	18	12	14	11	16	27	22	9	186
1920	31	33	28	12	14	13	7	12	13	16	20	9	210
1921	20	25	25	11	18	15	19	12	16	27	18	19	219
1922	19	22	25	27	15	6	11	11	11	6	6	14	176
1923	15	8	25	17	9	6	11	11	3	11	11	4	131
1924	11	2	9	7	7	4	5	11	8	9	6	2	81
1925	9	9	8	3	4	5	.....	.....	5	8	4	24	60
1926	7	8	7	11	13	5	13	3	11	8	12	14	117
1927	15	11	17	31	32	41	20	.....	.....	.....	.....	.....	.....

Table 57.

DEATHS FROM CEREBROSPINAL FEVER IN ILLINOIS.

Year.	Jan.	Feb.	Mar.	Apr.	May.	June.	July.	Aug.	Sept.	Oct.	Nov.	Dec.	Total.
1918	51	47	67	59	46	31	35	37	24	39	27	33	500
1919	30	27	36	22	23	16	30	22	16	23	18	26	289
1920	29	29	23	22	17	19	21	21	18	18	18	13	248
1921	3	15	9	4	3	6	7	6	4	7	7	5	76
1922	4	3	6	10	6	6	4	2	2	2	2	2	49
1923	8	5	9	10	6	4	2	7	.....	4	4	3	62
1924	3	2	5	8	6	3	4	2	3	2	4	1	43
1925	3	5	9	2	9	3	1	4	4	5	4	7	56
1926	7	1	6	5	9	6	6	3	3	3	6	3	58

Table 58.*

DEATHS AND DEATH RATES FROM MENINGITIS, CEPHALITIS, CEREBROSPINAL FEVER AND ENCEPHALITIS IN ILLINOIS.

Year.	No. deaths.	Rate per 100,000 population.	Year.	No. deaths.	Rate per 100,000 population.
1860	701	41.2	1910	734	13.
1870	1,975	77.8	1911	688	11.9
1880	872	28.3	1912	632	10.8
1881	2,863	90.8	1913	658	11.1
1882	2,310	71.5	1918	541	8.56
1883	1,535	46.4	1919	386	5.99
1884	1,971	58.3	1920	371	5.68
1885	2,106	60.9	1921	306	4.62
1886	2,276	64.5	1922	249	3.71
1900	1,485	31.0	1923	250	3.68
1907	968	17.94	1924	204	2.96
1908	782	14.28	1925	215	3.03
1909	744	13.38			

* A group of diseases has been included because of the nomenclature that confused the identity of any in the earlier part of the period covered.

How prevalent most of these diseases were in Illinois prior to about 1917 can only be guessed at from circumstantial evidence. They were first made reportable to the State Board of Health in 1915. Machinery for collecting reports with any satisfactory degree of completeness was not established until 1917. Case reports from 1920 on give a fair conception of prevalence trends. From mortality records one may gather some idea of epidemic cycles but the ratio of deaths to cases has doubtless declined in reference to several diseases so that the actual number of deaths is not always a reliable index to prevalence.

There follows a brief mention of these various diseases so far as any interesting facts are obtainable.

Cerebrospinal Fever.

Long before 1927 cerebrospinal fever had ceased to be an important cause of death in Illinois. By that year mortality had dropped to less than 1 per 100,000 while evidence pointed toward total disappearance. Fifty years earlier, as shown by the graph in Figure 25, this disease was one to be greatly dreaded and a frequent cause of death.

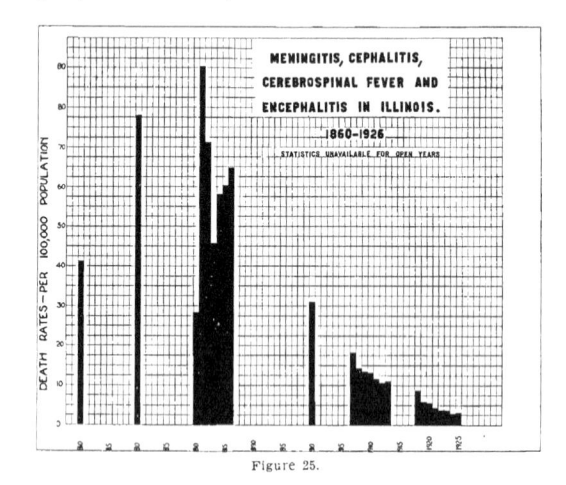

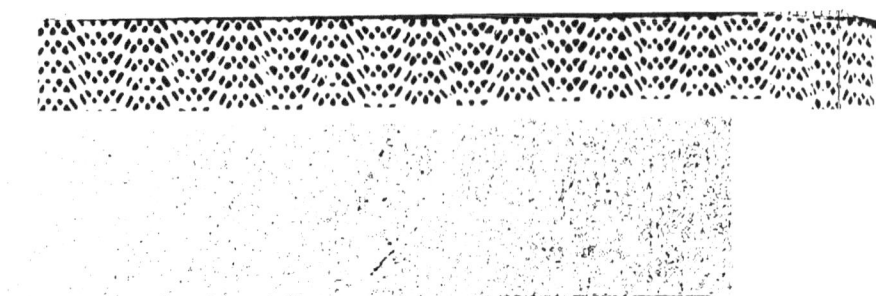

Figure 25.

Prior to 1880, especially in the census returns, many acute diseases of the brain and meninges, were classed under such indefinite headings as inflammation of the brain, dropsy of the brain, convulsions, meningitis, both nonspecific and tubercular, and many other brain affections such as abscess and tumor; also a certain number of cases of anemia and intoxications with convulsions or coma were included under meningitis and similar brain affections.

Tubercular meningitis was first recognized as an etiologic entity in the years just prior to the first great epidemic of cerebrospinal meningitis, which began in 1872. During this epidemic cerebrospinal fever began to be recognized as a distinct disease.

The next great epidemic occurred in 1881-1883. It was this outbreak that was largely responsible for the high death rate recorded from this disease in Illinois during the early eighties, although it cannot be assumed that all of the deaths recorded under this rubric at that time were true cases of this disease. The same confusion and uncertainty in diagnosis still existed due in part only to unqualified practitioners of medicine but largely to the fact that the finer and later bacteriologic methods of diagnosis had not been developed.

Knowing that cerebrospinal fever, prevailed extensively over the whole United States during the epidemic of 1881-83, it may be assumed that a large per cent of deaths attributed to this cause in the early eighties as shown on the chart, were really due to the true form of this disease.

The next nation-wide epidemic occurred in 1898-1900. This manifested itself in Illinois by a death rate of a little over 3 per 100,000 population. By this time the disease was well established as a clinical and etiologic entity. The rate recorded is one obtained from the census returns and is therefore probably not very accurate. Nevertheless, it shows that Illinois was swept by the epidemic at that time.

Another outbreak was recorded in 1912 and an increased incidence was shown beginning about 1925, but insignificant in comparison to the prevalence of the disease in the first decade of this 50 year period.

DIARRHEAL DISEASES.

Nomenclature for diseases of the intestinal tract was so thoroughly abused that it is difficult to arrive at any satisfactory conclusions concerning the prevalence of what are usually referred to as diarrheal disorders. In the mortality returns for 1880, for example, there were listed cholera infantum, cholera morbus, diarrhea, dysentery, enteritis and bowels as the responsible agents for 4,600 out of 45,017 fatalities registered from all causes. This corresponded to a rate of about 148 deaths per 100,000 population.

Another clue to what may have been the case is found in the high fatality rates among children. It is common knowledge that intestinal difficulties constitute one of the greatest hazards to child life. It is easy to believe therefore, that an excessively high mortality among children is evidence of a high prevalence of diarrheal diseases. There were 10,968 deaths among children less than one year old and 19,667 less than five, reported in 1880. These figures amounted to twenty-four and forty-three percent respectively of all registered mortality in that year

Using mortality figures found under the same nomenclature referred to above it is found that the incomplete returns for the years 1881 to 1886 inclusive give an average mortality rate of 155.9 per 100,000 population. Statistics for the five years ended with 1925 give an average mortality rate of

Table 59.

DEATHS AND DEATH RATES FROM DIARRHEAL DISEASES IN ILLINOIS.

Year.	No. deaths.	Rate per 100,000 population.	Year.	No. deaths.	Rate per 100,000 population.
1860	2,320	128.8	1905	4,552	87.
			1906	4,612	86.8
1870	4,420	188.3	1907	4,857	90.
			1908	5,224	95.4
1880	4,600	148.	1909	5,686	102.3
1881	5,723	181.5	1910	6,309	111.8
1882	3,478	107.7	1911	4,973	86.5
1883	3,624	109.7	1912	4,970	85.2
1884	3,716	110.	1913	5,520	93.2
1885	3,677	106.5			
1886	4,229	119.9	1918	4,284	67.4
			1919	2,993	46.4
1890	....	....	1920	3,532	54.
			1921	3,250	49.1
1900	....	....	1922	2,241	33.4
			1923	2,369	34.8
1902	3,967	79.5	1924	1,938	28.1
1903	4,298	84.7	1925	2,208	31.1
1904	4,320	93.9			

35.3 from diarrhea and enteritis. This classification includes practically all mortality of the period that might be called "diarrheal" in character.

Still another evidence that diarrheal diseases were highly prevalent during the last quarter of the nineteenth century is the fact that summer was the most unhealthful season of the year then. Year after year the great-

economic conditions have all been important factors in bringing about more favorable mortality rates from diarrheal disorders. The substitution of the

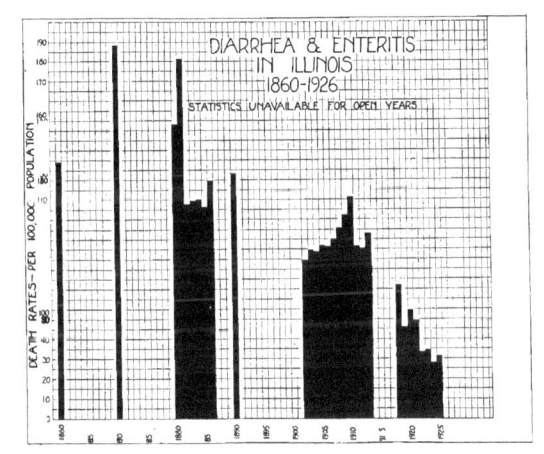

FIG. 26. Deaths due to diarrhea, dysentery, cholera infantum, cholera morbus, enteritis, teething and bowel complaint are included in the statistics illustrated in this figure.

automobile for the horse, a change that robbed the house fly of his most prolific breeding place, doubtless was an important factor in preventing the spread of diarrhea.

INFANTILE PARALYSIS.

Infantile paralysis first appeared on the vital statistic records of Illinois in 1912. In that year 58 deaths were charged against it. This does not imply that the infection never existed or that it never proved fatal in the State prior to that time. Public attention however had never been specifically called to the fact that it was an infectious disease and doubtless its presence in the early acute stage was often overlooked by physicians. It is altogether likely that cases developed from time to time without ever assuming alarming epidemic proportions for the crippling after effects of this disease were frequently seen.

After 1913 poliomyelitis went down into recorded oblivion with the confusion that prevailed in Illinois vital statistics until 1916. In that year over

12,000 cases were reported in New York and about 1,000 in Illinois. A general panic prevailed. In 1917 a recurrence of the epidemic occurred resulting in 236 deaths. Since that time mortality from infantile paralysis has varied from 25 in 1926, the lowest to 150 in 1921.

The crippling effects of the disease created a grave problem in curative medicine that required the services of specially trained physicians. So great was public demand for this type of work that the State Board of Health, later the State Department of Public Health, established clinics at various points in the State in 1916 for the benefit of victims of poliomyelitis. New and old patients continued to demand this type of service so that it remained a function of the State Department of Public Health until 1925 when the

Table 60.

DEATHS AND DEATH RATES FROM POLIOMYELITIS IN ILLINOIS.

Year.	No. deaths.	Rate per 100,000 population.	Year.	No. deaths.	Rate per 100,000 population.
1912	58	.99	1922	52	0.8
1917	236	3.8	1923	48	0.7
1918	115	1.8	1924	26	0.4
1919	75	1.2	1925	41	57
1920	57	.9	1926	25	34
1921	150	2.3			

curative clinical work was taken over by the Illinois Society for Crippled Children.

In the meantime poliomyelitis continued to occur from year to year in cyclic waves that characterize almost every communicable infection. Subsequent to 1916 and 1917 the outbreaks were less extensive in magnitude and the disease appeared to be generally milder in character, the percentage of fatal cases being lower.

Poliomyelitis is another of the warm weather infections. Case reports for September are usually greater in number than for any other month. It rises quickly to its maximum incidence once it begins to spread. Indeed the

Even before Ross discovered in 1897 that malaria is spread from one person to another only through the anopheles mosquito the prevalence of and mortality from malaria was on the wane in Illinois. Very early people recognized that drainage was important as a preventive of malaria but drainage was promoted more for agricultural than for health reasons. Thus the decline of malaria was incidental to the building up of cities and the development of agricultural pursuits rather than the result of a conscious attack on the disease.

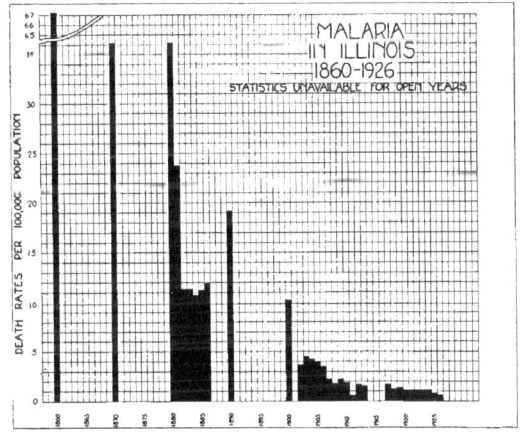

Figure 27.

After it became known that mosquitoes are the carriers of malaria, preventive work was directed against that insect. Undertakings of this kind have been confined largely to the extreme southern counties of the State. There alone does malaria still exist to any significant extent. Elsewhere drainage destroyed the breeding places of the malaria-bearing mosquito and with his disappearance the disease vanished.

In 1916 the chief sanitary engineer of the State Department of Public Health called attention in an article in *Health News* to the heavy economic losses caused by malaria in southern Illinois. No systematic malaria-preven-

Table 61.

Cases of Malaria Reported in Illinois.

Year.	Jan.	Feb.	Mar.	Apr.	May.	June.	July.	Aug.	Sept.	Oct.	Nov.	Dec.	Total.
1917	60	81	30	40	53	121	162	102	121	11	89	1,510	2,389
1918	1	....	....	....	....	....	2	1	3	....	....	....	....
1919	18	20	55	97	2	1	417	294	265	170	97	63	1,499
1920	59	112	84	114	142	194	171	279	117	132	87	123	1,614
1921	80	44	82	44	68	138	257	148	129	66	63	37	1,156
1922	50	60	22	30	60	54	43	78	61	11	22	9	500
1923	3	3	26	6	4	5	11		10	2	4	3	91
1924	1	2	....	1	1	4	12	14	13	3	4	6	58
1925	5	18	....	2	12	8	20	6	6	2	1	34	114
1926	7	5	4	....	8	6	8	7	15	10	5	11	86
1927	5	1	1	9	16	4	11	....	....	....	....	....	....

Table 62.

Deaths from Malaria in Illinois.

Year.	Jan.	Feb.	Mar.	Apr.	May.	June.	July.	Aug.	Sept.	Oct.	Nov.	Dec.	Total
1918	3	4	3	6	8	7	12	14	11	8	2	3	81
1919	4	2	8	4	2	6	15	10	9	17	6	6	89
1920	6	2	8	3	4	8	14	7	8	11	8	2	76
1921	4	5	3	3	1	5	12	14	10	15	3	3	78
1922	3	1	2	3	1	5	8	7	9	9	8	4	60
1923	7	4	3	4	5	3	9	4	9	5	2	4	59
1924	4	1	4	5	6	6	3	16	11	6	2	3	67
1925	2	2	1	2	3	10	9	9	10	4	4	6	62
1926	1	1	2	2	4	1	8	7	6	7	3	0	42

Table 63.

Deaths and Death Rates from Malaria in Illinois.

Year.	No. deaths.	Rate per 100,000 population.	Year.	No. deaths.	Rate per 100,000 population.
1860	1,146	66.9	1906	188	3.5
			1907	120	2.2
1870	9,030	35.5	1908	102	1.8
			1909	125	2.2
1880	1,114	36.1	1910	112	1.9
1881	753	23.8	1911	36	.62
1882	366	11.3	1912	101	1.7
1883	374	11.3	1913	94	1.5
1884	366	10.8			
1885	400	11.2	1917	108	1.7
1886	420	11.9	1918	81	1.3
			1919	89	1.4
1890	731	19.1	1920	76	1.2
			1921	78	1.2
1900	497	10.5	1922	60	0.9
			1923	59	0.9
1902	187	3.7	1924	67	1.0
1903	231	4.5	1925	62	.96
1904	218	4.2	1926	42	.58
1905	212	4.			

tion work by mosquito eradication was undertaken, however, until 1922, but in the meantime the matter was given consideration by the Southern Illinois Medical Society, and as the result of a resolution of that society, studies of mosquito-breeding places and the types of mosquitoes prevalent in some southern Illinois communities were made by entomologists of the State Natural History Survey.

Proposed and recommended by the State Department of Public Health, sponsored by the Lion's Club of Carbondale and receiving financial assistance from that club, the International Health Board and the Illinois Central Railroad, and directed by the sanitary engineering division of the State Department of Public Health, Carbondale carried on systematic mosquito control work for the season of 1922, and for the first time in history of the city enjoyed practically complete relief from the pestiferous insects. The results from the standpoint of reduction in malaria cases were equally gratifying. Vital statistics and house-to-house canvasses had shown that prior to 1922 the city suffered an average of over 250 cases of malaria a year (267 during 1921) Following the close of the mosquito-control work for 1922 it was found by a house-to-house canvass that only 10 cases of malaria had occurred during that year in the entire city.

This was the beginning of mosquito-malaria control work in southern Illinois which has continued at Carbondale and extended into half a dozen other counties with increasingly satisfactory results.

During the first fifty years of the existence of State public health service in Illinois medical research workers discovered the causative organism of malaria, found out how the disease is spread and prescribed very positive methods for its prevention. Thus so far as practical possibilities are concerned it may be said that malaria was completely conquered during this period.

MEASLES.

Measles was very generally ignored in reports concerning epidemic conditions in Illinois during the last quarter of the nineteenth century. It was included in a list of diseases for which epidemic information was requested in the sanitary surveys of 1882-1885 but practically none of the local reports mentioned it. Account was given of outbreaks of typhoid fever, cholera, diphtheria and scarlet fever but never a word about measles. Evidently it was regarded either as too common or too insignificant to mention. To be sure it appeared in the mortality tables where these were supplied but without comment.

In the general mortality statistics available for Illinois, measles is credited with 109 deaths in 1860 and 702 in 1870. These figures give rates of 6.3 and 27.6 per 100,000 population for the two years respectively. For the six years of 1880-1885 the average annual mortality rate, as reported in the statistics which were regarded at the time as about 40 per cent incomplete, was 13.5 per 100,000 people.

Measles is distinctly seasonal in character. More cases occur during the three months of March, April and May than during all the rest of the year. September is ordinarily the month of lightest prevalence in Illinois. The number of deaths per 100 cases, however, is greatest when the prevalence is least.

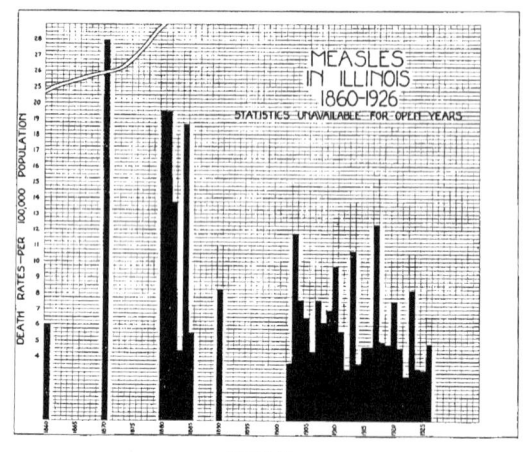

Figure 28.

Measles also travels in epidemic cycles. Thus every three or four years there are general outbreaks of major proportions. This experience is gen-

Table 64.

CASES OF MEASLES REPORTED IN ILLINOIS.

Year.	Jan.	Feb.	Mar.	Apr.	May.	June.	July.	Aug.	Sept.	Oct.	Nov.	Dec.	Total.
1917	4,959	6,483	11,106	10,534	9,415	4,255	1,331	312	189	122	389	417	49,512
1918	1,150	939	1,237	1,278	1,501	641	273	121	56	141	67	171	7,575
1919	711	1,072	2,453	5,754	5,204	3,142	1,110	255	118	342	706	1,727	22,594
1920	4,366	4,610	4,982	5,343	5,542	4,434	1,573	542	233	510	1,280	1,985	35,400
1921	3,932	4,527	5,911	5,894	4,854	2,435	531	129	85	164	271	560	29,293
1922	918	1,340	2,167	2,658	3,285	2,744	1,182	373	141	205	606	921	16,540
1923	2,154	4,011	5,604	10,345	12,055	6,320	1,420	306	125	363	1,053	1,953	46,709
1924	2,475	2,296	2,659	3,606	3,825	2,693	926	205	120	181	343	815	20,144
1925	1,575	2,664	4,615	5,985	6,237	4,010	982	169	151	273	682	868	28,211
1926	1,825	3,337	4,514	4,299	5,095	4,813	1,980	499	236	615	1,368	2,930	31,511
1927	6,041	8,469	11,126	7,622	4,562	2,084	592	....	....	....	....	....	....

Table 65.

DEATHS FROM MEASLES IN ILLINOIS.

Year.	Jan.	Feb.	Mar.	Apr.	May.	June.	July.	Aug.	Sept.	Oct.	Nov.	Dec.	Total.
1918	99	98	18	60	74	30	14	6	5	17	12	13	317
1919	12	29	30	49	70	37	27	14	5	5	6	22	306
1920	47	112	72	59	59	37	22	9	4	15	25	35	496
1921	33	47	80	49	50	20	12	3	3	2	4	6	309
1922	10	13	27	30	30	28	21	9	9	6	13	12	206
1923	24	29	79	116	165	87	31	20	3	9	2	11	576
1924	19	25	39	54	32	26	9	7	1	1	4	11	228
1925	11	19	36	28	52	25	13	7	4	7	3	12	217
1926	22	28	50	78	68	33	16	11	5	2	16	17	346

Table 66.

DEATHS AND DEATH RATES FROM MEASLES IN ILLINOIS.

Year.	No. deaths.	Rate per 100,000 population.	Year.	No. deaths.	Rate per 100,000 population.
1860	109	6.3	1907	413	7.6
			1908	336	6.1
1870	702	27.6	1909	385	6.9
			1910	549	9.7
1880	603	19.5	1911	325	5.6
1881	625	19.4	1912	191	3.2
1882	451	13.9	1913	638	10.7
1883	148	4.4	1914	217	3.6
1884	629	18.6	1915	286	4.6
1885	191	5.5	1916	285	4.6
			1917	766	12.3
1890	314	8.2	1918	317	5.6
			1919	306	4.8
1900	....	....	1920	496	7.6
1901	....	....	1921	309	4.7
1902	180	3.6	1922	206	3.1
1903	593	11.7	1923	576	8.5
1904	393	7.6	1924	228	3.3
1905	340	6.5	1925	217	3.0
1906	230	4.3	1926	346	4.8

1907. For the six years ended with 1926 a still more favorable rate, an average of 4.4, prevailed. Better medical care of patients coupled with better public health service are the only two factors to which the improvement may reasonably be attributed.

While nothing has transpired that provides mankind with means for preventing and controlling measles on a large scale, research work charged with hopeful promise has been done. In 1914 Hermann suggested the active immunization of infants by inoculating the nasal mucosa with the fresh swabbings of the nasal mucus of patients just coming down with measles. The purpose was to introduce the virus at a time when the infant was still carrying a certain degree of inherited immunity. Although he apparently had good success with the method on seventy-five children so treated, it has never been considered practical for general use.

In 1918 Nicolle and Conseil first reported favorable results with the blood serum of convalescent measles patients. Such serum given subcutaneously or intramuscularly in amounts of 5 cc to 10 cc as soon as possible after exposure is quite effective in preventing the disease. Passive immunity is established for three to six weeks. In some cities efforts have been made to collect a supply of convalescent serum taken usually five or more days after defervescence of the fever. Since at best such supplies are limited, some attempts have been made to use blood serum or whole blood of adults who have had the disease some years before. Much larger amounts must of course be used and the results have not been so uniform.

In 1924 Zingher recommended the production of active immunity by delaying administration of convalescent serum till the fifth to the eighth day from time of exposure. Symptoms of the disease are not prevented but the attack is very mild and the immunity established is permanent. When the serum is delayed till symptoms appear, no beneficial results are obtained even with large amounts.

In 1926 Tunnicliff and Hoyne produced a serum in goats by repeated inoculation of Tunnicliff's green producing diplococcus. The goat serum is apparently as efficacious as human convalescent serum in preventing measles and has the added advantage of unlimited supply. Degkwitz in Germany has used sheep instead of goats, injecting them with the Berkfeld filtrations of nasal secretions and sputum of measles patients.

The prevention of measles by immune serum or the production of permanent immunity by a mild attack have been demonstrated as important factors in measles control. For the treatment of the established disease no curative agent has been discovered.

Pneumonia.

Pneumonia was probably more prevalent fifty years ago than is indicated by the 1880 rate of 142.2 per 100,000 inhabitants. There was considerable confusion at that time in classification of deaths from the disease because of such nomenclature as typhoid-pneumonia and typhoid-malaria.

While the 1890 rate of 128.3 seems to indicate some progress, we note that ten years later (1900) the rate of 143.9 was higher than in either 1880 or 1890.

Again the pneumonia rate in 1910 was higher than ever before recorded as far as available records bear evidence. In fact, the 1910 rate is the highest ever recorded in Illinois with the exception of that for 1918, the great influenza year.

It is of passing interest to note that never in the history of Illinois was the recorded pneumonia death rate under 100 per 100,000 of population prior to 1921. Since 1920 the average annual death rate from pneumonia has been 87.5, and only once in the six years ended with 1926 did the rate reach 100. The exception was 1923 when the rate was 108.8. Whether we can say that we have finally reached the point when we are making permanent progress against this major agent of death, the future must determine. The rather elongated period of waning mortality at least lends encouragement to hope. New procedures employed against pneumonia only since 1913 and principally since 1920 include typing of the causative organism, the use of vaccines and sera and quarantine.

Typing.

For many years the problem of pneumonia was complicated by the fact that organisms indistinguishable from virulent pneumococci were found in the mouths of normal persons. In 1913 workers at the Rockefeller Institute for Medical Research in New York found that all pneumococci could be divided into four groups, types I, II, III and IV. This was of tremendous assistance not only in stimulating the use of specific antiserums in established cases of pneumonia, but of solving problems of epidemiology and control of the disease.

The determination of pneumococcus types was very popular during the period 1917 to 1920, but fell off so that it was almost unused in civil life after that. The reason for this was the fact that the physician could do only a very little more for the patient if the type was known and the process was considered a useless expense. In 1925 the State Department of Public Health promulgated rules and regulations for the control of pneumonia whereby all cases should be "typed" where facilities for such a procedure were available, and release from quarantine should be allowed only

Table 67.

CASES OF PNEUMONIA REPORTED IN ILLINOIS.

Year.	Jan.	Feb.	Mar.	Apr.	May.	June.	July.	Aug.	Sept.	Oct.	Nov.	Dec.	Total.
1918	602	560	1,242	1,409	612	163	142	68	223	10,373	2,274	2,876	20,798
1919	1,160	820	890	600	562	315	308	185	233	451	601	1,275	7,440
1920	7,012	4,019	1,855	1,066	936	485	282	215	266	335	604	980	17,885
1921	1,568	1,222	1,345	992	738	429	319	305	334	614	541	824	9,231
1922	1,250	2,629	2,942	1,621	1,113	548	433	830	448	736	989	1,659	15,189
1923	2,687	3,508	3,205	2,439	1,497	718	388	330	471	814	1,012	1,239	18,308
1924	1,713	1,798	2,048	1,643	1,217	738	815	822	559	677	747	1,440	14,217
1925	1,715	1,681	2,100	1,718	1,228	767	451	380	413	687	1,031	3,044	15,215
1926	1,819	2,028	4,208	1,961	1,470	1,223	897	531	477	684	987	1,344	17,629
1927	1,787	1,515	1,802	1,609	1,240	959	418						

Table 68.

DEATHS FROM PNEUMONIA IN ILLINOIS.

Year.	Jan.	Feb.	Mar.	Apr.	May.	June.	July.	Aug.	Sept.	Oct.	Nov.	Dec.	Total.
1918	984	902	1,181	1,348	683	232	185	171	453	5,197	1,571	1,548	14,455
1919	1,235	1,027	1,192	697	453	268	199	158	190	278	461	757	6,915
1920	2,218	2,169	893	678	583	267	179	171	177	273	479	643	8,730
1921	857	743	691	500	389	196	178	171	195	319	432	545	5,216
1922	758	782	1,053	712	482	242	179	171	195	357	471	740	6,142
1923	1,105	1,301	1,025	798	589	278	212	186	230	315	469	558	7,067
1924	764	748	812	690	459	322	182	150	231	323	385	655	5,730
1925	792	763	906	630	488	290	198	188	196	326	360	573	5,900
1926	780	742	1,473	824	540	295	194	161	206	295	460	657	6,627

Table 69.

DEATHS AND DEATH RATES FROM PNEUMONIA IN ILLINOIS.

Year.	No. deaths.	Rate per 100,000 population.	Year.	No. deaths.	Rate per 100,000 population.
1860	1,357	79.2	1905	5,877	112.3
			1906	6,136	115.5
1870	2,882	113.4	1907	7,386	136.9
			1908	6,008	109.7

upon the absence of pneumococci of that type from the throat of the patient. Standard laboratory methods were drawn up for the use of private laboratories, but little demand has come from the physicians for aid in this connection.

Vaccines.

The prevention of pneumonia by prophylactic vaccination with killed cultures of the organisms was placed upon a practical basis with the discovery of the various types of pneumococci. During the World War and

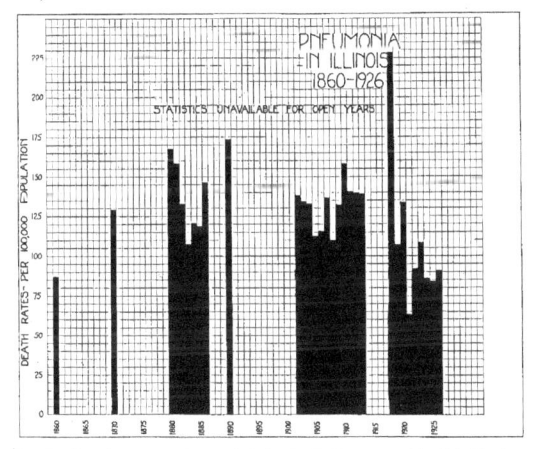

FIG. 29. For the years prior to 1900 the death figures used in this illustration included pneumonia, influenza, pleurisy and bronchitis.

immediately following the value of the process was definitely established. It is recommended for those people who are especially susceptible to pneumonia because of age, undue exposure or other causes. Since immunity will last only about eight months, the time of choice for administration is at the beginning of the pneumonia season each year. Under certain conditions, however, the State Department of Public Health has provided in its rules and regulations on pneumonia, for the compulsory immunization of individuals.

Serums.

Antiserum of Type I pneumococcus has yielded very encouraging results. This type causes more than a third of all cases of pneumonia with a mortality of 25 to 29 per cent without serum. The administration of specific antiserum has reduced the mortality to less than 5 per cent. Unfortunately many cases of pneumonia go untyped, hence do not get the benefit of serum. Probably 2,000 lives which are now lost annually in Illinois could be saved by this agent alone.

Antiserums for Types II and III have not been of service in treating pneumonia in man.

Isolation.

The transfer of the emphasis in pneumonia from the clinical aspect to the public health field has had a marked effect upon the problem of the control. Isolation and quarantine of the patient has been a factor of no little importance in preventing not only secondary cases among those in direct contact with the patient, but also pneumococcus "carriers" who in turn go out and infect others. The rules and regulations of the Illinois Department of Public Health (1925) called for isolation for a period of 14 days after the patient's temperature returned to normal, unless negative cultures were obtained before this.

WHOOPING COUGH.

Fifty years ago whooping cough was a disease which was apparently widely prevalent but one that received very little attention from the State Board of Health or the local health officers.

With the imperfectly classified and incompletely recorded statistics, we find an average death rate of 10.3 per 100,000 population for the years 1880-1886 inclusive.

The tendency to waves of whooping cough epidemics even then is indicated by a total of 954 deaths recorded for years 1880-1881 while but 541 were registered for 1884 and 1885. Then followed 1886 with another marked increase when 385 fatalities were recorded.

A more peculiar phenomenon than the epidemic waves of this disease is its unique seasonal character. Instead of reaching one prevalence peak during the year it climbs to a secondary high point in February, then recedes and rises again to the maximum high level of the year about July first. Whether the incidence is great or small the case reports follow this unusual seasonal course from year to year.

After twenty-five years of State health supervision, we find no improvement in the number of deaths from whooping cough. The average annual

Table 70.

CASES OF WHOOPING COUGH REPORTED IN ILLINOIS.

Year.	Jan.	Feb.	Mar.	Apr.	May.	June.	July.	Aug.	Sept.	Oct.	Nov.	Dec.	Total.
1919							618	802	723	554	818	1,206	4,721
1920	1,143	1,222	2,061	1,204	1,460	1,464	1,650	1,214	929	957	1,059	1,290	15,653
1921	1,530	1,327	1,482	1,440	1,466	1,821	1,928	899	606	341	378	343	13,561
1922	412	442	551	610	657	1,153	1,145	1,069	747	563	621	786	8,756
1923	1,103	973	1,214	1,095	947	892	953	694	490	488	494	501	9,844
1924	579	620	680	550	528	524	847	782	662	641	875	950	8,238
1925	1,191	1,048	1,121	1,352	1,184	1,172	1,149	767	547	478	453	612	11,074
1926	739	804	939	870	827	801	894	717	714	773	958	838	9,874
1927	779	896	1,015	850	906	1,089	1,224						

Table 71.

DEATHS FROM WHOOPING COUGH IN ILLINOIS BY MONTHS.

Year.	Jan.	Feb.	Mar.	Apr.	May.	June.	July.	Aug.	Sept.	Oct.	Nov.	Dec.	Total.
1918	48	65	76	83	68	58	53	44	41	71	58	31	696
1919	26	11	25	15	21	23	44	35	23	21	11	15	270
1920	44	83	50	43	56	29	47	47	22	35	41	56	553
1921	45	57	43	57	68	50	58	39	27	18	22	11	495
1922	15	20	22	22	23	13	18	29	15	24	16	22	239
1923	45	76	68	42	44	40	45	45	34	33	19	30	521
1924	32	43	48	48	24	19	31	26	25	15	19	23	353
1925	26	28	24	40	33	27	37	36	20	22	15	7	315
1926	30	36	52	58	27	19	23	29	21	14	35	23	367

Table 72.

DEATHS AND DEATH RATES FROM WHOOPING COUGH IN ILLINOIS.

Year.	No. deaths.	Rate per 100,000 population.	Year.	No. deaths.	Rate per 100,000 population.
1860	382	22.3	1905	692	13.2
			1906	496	9.3
1870	640	25.2	1907	530	9.8
			1908	491	8.9
1880	488	15.8	1909	448	8.
1881	466	14.7	1910	393	6.9
1882	252	7.8	1911	281	4.8
1883	238	7.2	1912	402	6.8
1884	280	8.2	1913	388	6.5
1885	261	7.5			
1886	385	10.8	1918	696	11.0
			1919	270	4.2
1890	359	9.3	1920	553	8.5
			1921	495	7.5
1900	497	10.3	1922	239	3.6
			1923	521	7.7
1902	544	10.9	1924	353	5.1
1903	720	14.2	1925	315	4.4
1904	348	6.7	1926	367	5.

rate for 1902-1907 was 10.7. The rate twenty-five years earlier was about the same.

Here again fluctuation in mortality is shown with 720 deaths in 1903 and but 348 in 1904. At this time public health authorities were busy with attempts at controlling diphtheria, smallpox, typhoid and even in a large city like Chicago did little or nothing towards isolation of whooping cough patients.

While it is generally considered that results are not yet satisfactory in our efforts at control of whooping cough, progress is apparently being

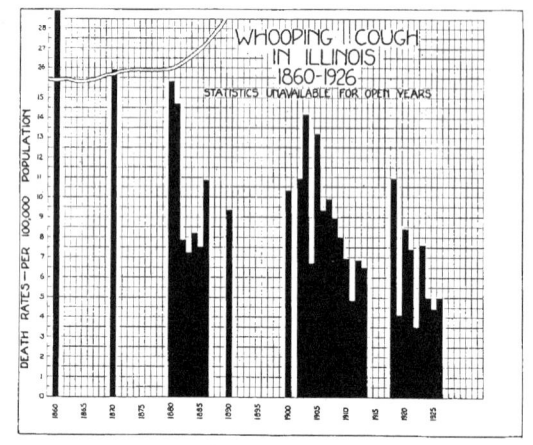

FIG. 30. (The 1860 line should indicate a rate of 22.3.)

made. Certainly the death rate has declined. Control measures have included isolation of cases, control of contacts, exclusion of cases from

At this writing we are still relying on early quarantine and isolation as chief means of control. How much, if any, credit should be given to vaccine treatment for the improved death rate or as a prophylactic measure is uncertain. The results of the use of vaccine are conflicting. Workers are agreed that the product should be freshly prepared,—preferably not more than two or three weeks old. As a prophylactic measure, vaccination has shown considerable promise in the hands of several investigators. Less can be said of it as a cure, once the disease has become established.

In 1922 Orgel reported a method of intracutaneous injection of vaccine by which the disease could be diagnosed in its early stages and thus preventive measures taken before the appearance of the characteristic whoop. Hull and Nauss and others, however, had no success with the method.

Infant Mortality.

A considerable number of sanitarians regard infant mortality rates as indexes to general health conditions. Some go further expressing the opinion that infant death rates reflect the character and efficiency of public health service. The facts fit the requirements in either case so far as Illinois is concerned.

Fifty years ago infant mortality in Illinois was fully twice what it is now. At that time public health service had scarcely survived the labors of birth and it remained an infantile organization for twenty-five years.

Neither birth nor death registration was complete fifty years ago but there is abundant evidence that infant mortality was high. In 1881 there were 218.8 deaths among infants under one year of age for every 1,000 births reported. Birth reports were estimated to be from 40 to 50 per cent incomplete and death reports from 30 to 40. In 1926 there were 69.3 infant deaths registered for each 1000 births recorded. Statistics for births and deaths were complete for all practical purposes.

In 1881 a trifle more than 24 per cent of all deaths recorded were among infants less than one year old. In 1926 a trifle less than 11 per cent of all deaths were among persons of the same age group. This is positive evidence of substantial improvement in infant mortality.

Then there is the evidence of actual numbers. For the six years ended with 1886, when the population of Illinois was about half what it was in 1927, there were 67,811 infant deaths reported. For the six years ended with 1926 there were only 60,525 infant deaths reported. The ratio to population in the more recent years is less than one-half of that for the earlier period.

Probably the greatest single factor in the saving of infant life was the improvement that took place in the sanitary quality of municipal milk supplies during the fifty year period. Up until 1921 there is no record of less than 11,000 infant deaths per annum except in the years prior to 1884. Since 1921 the period during which the safe milk campaign has been stressed, the total number of infant deaths has never reached 11,000 in any one year while for each of the three years ended with 1926 it was less than 10,000.

The period during which the most improvement in infant mortality occurred is the same period in which the greatest improvement in the sanitary quality of municipal milk supplies took place.

The danger to infants and children of using a poor milk supply is well known. There are two factors concerned—the presence of disease producing bacteria and the presence of enormous numbers of other bacteria, not necessarily pathogenic, but which overwhelm the digestive tract of the infant

Table 73.

DEATHS OF INFANTS* AND RATES PER 1,000 BIRTHS REPORTED IN ILLINOIS.

Year.	Infant deaths.	Rate per 100,000 population.	Year.	Infant deaths.	Rate per 100,000 population.
1880	10,968	.....	1911	11,113	124.
1881	11,826	218.8	1912	11,155	108.
1882	10,772	229.2	1913	11,607	109.8
1883	10,382	224.8			
1884	11,305	246.4	1916	14,518	119.9
1885	11,277	237.3	1917	14,029	118.9
1886	12,749	215.3	1918	13,109	105.7
			1919	11,148	91.4
1890	.....	.....	1920	11,641	87.5
			1921	10,644	76.
1900	.....	.....	1922	10,187	74.9
			1923	10,810	78.9
1907	11,947	140.	1924	9,743	69.
1908	11,774	154.3	1925	9,844	71.8
1909	11,491	144.7	1926	9,297	69.3
1910	12,281	149.4			

*Less than one year of age.

by mere numbers. In the summer time, especially when the weather is hot and ice difficult to obtain in sufficient quantities, infant diarrhea due to bad

order pasteurization was extended to all milk in Chicago and since then it has been strictly enforced. Other cities in the State likewise have gradually been supplied with more and more pasteurized milk.

In 1922 the State Department of Public Health initiated a pasteurization program with so-called model milk ordinance intended for the improvement of milk supplies in the State. During the next five years 60 cities adopted this ordinance. An outgrowth of the campaign was the pasteurization law of 1925 which required all plants selling pasteurized milk in Illinois to ob-

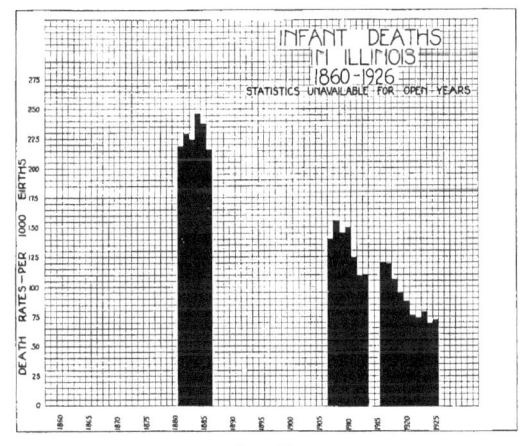

![Figure 31. Infant Deaths in Illinois 1860-1926. Statistics unavailable for open years.]

Figure 31.

tain a license from the State Department of Public Health. Not only was the quality of pasteurized milk improved but there was a large increase in amount. In 1927 there were 352 such plants in the State (not counting the plants supplying milk to Chicago) pasteurizing 390,702 gallons, an increase of 59,000 gallons over the previous year. It is estimated that 50 per cent of the people downstate drink pasteurized milk, while all of Chicago receives it, or a total of more than four and half million of the seven million people in the State.

SUMMARY AND CONCLUSION.

Since the year 1927 ends a fifty year period in the life of the Board and Department of Public Health of the State of Illinois, it is proper that the Department should use the occasion to gather together some of the outstanding events in the health history of the State to make them easily available for those interested. To those who have an interest in studying the subject more exhaustively, this history may stimulate inquiry and offer suggestions as to sources of material. The narrative and appraisal of what has been done was written in consultation with a few of the men who have had something to do with the effort. It is to be regretted that it was not possible to have had the advice of many who did not participate but time and tide do not wait. How valuable the appraisal would have been had it been possible to summon to the Board men like Rauch, Reilly, Johnson and Chambers, the men who planned the earlier health work in the State. But they are gone, except Johnson who is advanced in years, and the best that can be done is to judge of their plans by the effects those plans wrought, immediate and remote.

It is also an appropriate time to speculate somewhat as to what the future holds. In this, however, what is said must be regarded as general and indicative rather than specific.

The Director has a rather definite program for the Department of Health for a ten year period. There is no uncertainty in his mind as to what should be done nor as to his intention to accomplish this program to the limit of his strength, influence and opportunity. Such uncertainty as he has relates to the vicissitudes of place and position and the uncertainties of the public mind. It is not deemed advisable to state that program in this place.

Sources of Material.

Those who wrote about conditions in the upper Mississippi Valley prior

that war the medical department of the United States army was poorly organized. Surgeon General Forry was the first of the army medical officers to grasp the possibility of evaluating the healtifulness of different sections of the country through the opportunities of the military posts. The lay writers who told of health conditions in the territory and state when they lectured and wrote books, magazine articles, newspaper articles and letters back home supplied a considerable part of the record prior to 1850. Soon after the beginning of the century, Dr. Daniel Drake established the Medical and Physical Journal in Cincinnati. Before long the physicians of Illinois began writing for this Journal. A little later Dr. Drake made the first of at least two voyages of discovery in health matters in Illinois, reporting at length and in detail in his Journal.

A little later other medical journals were established, in St. Louis, Louisville, Buffalo and Chicago, and Illinois physicians began writing for these Journals and occasionally for the American Journal of the Medical Sciences in Philadelphia and in other eastern journals. In 1816 the formation of medical societies was begun at Lawrenceville, Illinois. In 1848 the American Medical Association was formed with the cooperation of Illinois physicians. In 1850 the Illinois Medical Society was formed. The Chicago Medical came in the same year. Much of such record as there is of health conditions in Illinois is found in the pages of these journals and the transactions of these societies. However, all of this record, including that of the physicians is opinion, on evidence and subject to the limitations of such.

The Federal Government began making its decennial census reports in 1790. Prior to 1850 these reports contained no demographic material except number of population, increase in numbers during the previous decade, distribution of population geographically and as to sex, age, color, racial stock and special classes. In 1850 a little vital statistics was given. In 1860 still more. But these incursions into vital statistics were timid and halting and oftentimes inaccurate and misleading. The introduction to the report of 1850 said: "The tables of the census which undertake to give the total number of births, marriages and deaths in the year preceding the first of June 1850 can be said to have very little value". Nevertheless the policy was continued. Each census year the reports were increasingly accurate and detailed. In 1900 the policy of reporting vital statistics annually was adopted. Chicago began reporting vital statistics in a very limited way in 1843. These were inaccurate as well as incomplete. In the 1870 report Dr. Rauch gave an estimate of the degree of incompleteness and applied a corrective factor for all of the earlier reports.

Nevertheless the record from somewhere about 1843 to 1850 on is a statistical record as well as one based on testimony of opinion. In all probability between 1843 and 1863 the testimony of opinion was better and more dependable than the statistical. Since about the latter date the statistical source of material has been the more dependable.

Since the French-Canadians and the Indians left few descendants in the State, they can be eliminated from an estimate of the physical vigor of the stock. Likewise since they made no outstanding contribution of a disease they can be eliminated from this limited study of the diseases of the State. When malaria became so prevalent and deadly soon after 1780 it made a smoke screen beyond which it is not easy to see any important disease in the preceding period. Therefore, it must be assumed that there were none of outstanding importance though rheumatism, pneumonia and the diarrhoeas must have been much in evidence.

Health 1780 to 1877.

There is no record for the State of Illinois prior to 1877 as to the physical vigor of the people, the birth rate, the size of families the average length of life, the endurance, presence and absence of physical and mental defects, average stature, physical prowess, positive health so-called and prevalence of non-reportable diseases either fatal or non-fatal. This statement is only partially true as to such items as physical vigor, birth rates, size of families, length of life, endurance and physical prowess, as to each of these items there is a limited amount of evidence of opinion, most of which is very general and but little circumstantial. In collecting material for this narrative it seemed best to base the presentation on those items as to which the evidence was best. That almost limited it to the major forms of communicable diseases commonly known as the reportable diseases.

When the period prior to 1877 is compared with that since, the record shows an almost unbelievable gain. In brief statements relative to each of several diseases and as to general unhealthfulness and general death rates opinion will be given as to what in a general way has been the contribution of the state and local health departments to that end.

statistically. However the contrast between then and now is so great that minor variations do not obscure it. In less than one hundred years a most unhealthy region has become one where health is of the best. In effecting this change several factors have operated. One has been the change in the country itself especially improvements which have resulted from clearing the land and draining it. Another has been the change in the people such as growth in intelligence and knowledge, elevation of the standards of living, increase in earning power measured in purchasing power of the dollar and learning how to live among their neighbors as well as with their families and the individual with himself. Another has been the improved service rendered by the medical profession in its various divisions of doctors, dentists, nurses, druggists and hospitals. And a fourth is the preventive medicine agencies principally the state and local health departments and also in some measure the cooperating agencies for prevention of disease. For the general improvement in health and the reduction in the death rate between the period prior to 1877 health agencies are entitled to half the credit. In order to establish that claim they credit themselves with the generalship, strategy and leadership in the health campaign, with their activities in education of the public in health, their propaganda to interest as well as to inform the public as well as with their more direct and specific activities in health promotion and disease control. They claim, moreover, that even after crediting other factors with their half of the accomplishment the health agencies show a return of improvement and benefit of and to the people which can not be approximated by any other arm of government. This is because they have made prevention their field and prevention is economically sound.

Malaria.

Malaria was the great menace to Illinois in the period when its very existence was in the balance. It was everywhere in the State. It was said to be endemic and periodically became so prevalent that it was said to be epidemic.

The last great epidemic wave was in 1872. The territory in which it is endemic has gradually been lessened until now some of the mosquitoes and some of the people are infective in only about fifty foci located in about twelve counties. Shortly there will be no endemic malaria in the State. In making this transformation the largest single factor has been drainage. The health department using the term in its inclusive sense can only claim a minor part in this great achievement; yet they have contributed and are continuing to do so.

Typhoid Fever.

In all probability there was some typhoid fever in the state from its early settlement. As the fog of malaria was lifted typhoid came to be recognized. The disease increased as did the density of population. For this increase progressive pollution of water supplies was the principal factor. The prevalence of the disease was at its peak in the first half of the nineties.

It has now become a disease of minor importance. For this improvement the health agencies can claim the larger part of the credit. To do so however they must absorb the water and sewage departments claiming them as parts of the health machine.

Yellow Fever.

This disease is scarcely a memory in this State. Nevertheless, the health machinery did its full duty in the few epidemics that occurred and it has functioned in throwing a wall of protection around the State whenever danger threatened. They can claim credit for whatever of security was added to that which the location and relative freedom from yellow fever mosquitoes supplied.

Cholera.

This disease has not reached within five hundred miles of Illinois since 1877. The only credit the State Board of Health can claim is that they have added to the security of the people when the disease has threatened on a few occasions. The local health departments are entitled to more credit. They were active in every epidemic wave which swept over the state after 1835.

At times cholera caused conditions to be very bad but just how bad they might have been had the local health departments and the individual doctors failed to function is beyond the imagination.

Snakebite.

This form of animal poisoning once ranked with milk sickness, a form of vegetable poisoning, in importance. It is now trivial causing no deaths and almost no sickness. Clearing the country is entitled to credit for the improvement

Smallpox.

This disease was a very great menace prior to 1877 and for at least ten years thereafter. It was fairly prevalent during the following ten years. For thirty years it has been a potential rather than a present danger most of the time. Its relative control is one of the sanitary achievements of the century. However, the record of the United States as regards the control of smallpox when compared with that of the countries of northwestern Europe is disgraceful. It is commonly cited as proof that something more than the gradual growth of public intelligence is necessary to prevent epidemies of this disease. For the achievement in lessening the prevalence of smallpox the health agencies can claim much the largest part of the credit.

Scarlet Fever.

Scarlet fever has become a disease of secondary importance. In spite of the increased density of population and the increased frequency and intimacy of contact of people the disease has declined in prevalence. The theory is that the greatest decline in prevalence was that which occurred prior to 1897 and that the principal decline since then has been in the virulence of the disease—the case fatality rate. This is in great measure true. For this latter improvement the better service of the medical profession and the elevation of the general standards of cleanliness have been the principal contributing factors. For the lessened prevalence of the disease. the health departments can claim most of the credit. Taking the field in its entirety the health agencies are entitled to somewhere near half of the credit.

Diphtheria.

The very great decrease in the prevalence and in the fatality of diphtheria is one of the achievements of which society can be proud. Prior to the discovery and general use of antitoxin the treatment of diphtheria was symptomatic. Health departments can claim the credit for having popularized the use of this remedy. The medical profession are entitled to the credit for using it intelligently. Following its introduction and use the death rates from diphtheria fell markedly. Due to the fairly generalized and increasing use of vaccination against the disease, diphtheria is rapidly shrinking in importance. Within a decade diphtheria will be of secondary importance. The health agencies are entitled to much more than half the credit for this improvement particularly if they admit to membership the research workers.

Whooping Cough.

The decrease in this disease has been marked though in it there has been nothing spectacular or dramatic. The health agencies claim some of the credit though much of it belongs to the gradual growth of public intelligence.

Measles.

The best that can be said for the measles fight is that the disease has been held in check. That the people from the cities are now in a better position as regards measles when emergencies develop is somewhat to the credit of health agencies. Within the last ten or fifteen years it has been discovered that the secondary infections in measles are of more importance than the primary disease, that something can be done to prevent these secondary infections and that the bacteriology of these secondary infections is liable. The credit for these discoveries belongs to the medical profession and to the research men. It seems that the bacterial cause of measles, an antitoxin, and a vaccine have been discovered or are about to be discovered. Should these supposed discoveries be established the stage will be set for the control of measles. It will then be up to the health agencies acting as boards of strategy to lay and to execute plans for the control of measles. For what has been accomplished the health agencies can not claim a major credit.

Erysipelas.

This disease once prevailing always as endemic and occasionally breaking out into epidemics, at least one of which was almost if not quite pandemic, has become a fairly unimportant disease. The recent discovery of an antitoxin for it promises still further improvement. A part of the importance of erysipelas in the past was due to its close relationship to puerperal fever and scarlet fever and its relationship albeit less close to meningitis and pneumonia. The principal factor in the decrease in erysipelas is the elevation of the general standards of cleanliness and other general standards in some measure. The medical profession are doing their work better and that is contributing to the end. The health agencies claim some of the credit though they are not in the first rank.

Puerperal Fever.

It is customary to say that the mortality rate of mothers in childbirth has not improved. This may be true when comparison is made between present day conditions and those of the recent past. It is not true if comparison is made between the period before 1877 and that after 1877. There is less puerperal fever than there was; principally because of the elevation of standards of general cleanliness and application of the discovery by Oliver Wendell Holmes that puerperal fever is contagious. Better medical service is a factor. The Chicago Health Department under Dr. A. R. Reynolds inaugurated a midwife and obstetric service in the early part of the present century.

Meningitis.

Meningitis was once a periodically epidemic disease causing a heavy death rate. It is rarely epidemic now. In fact, very rarely—almost never. This improvement is partly due to health department work and partly due to knowledge of the danger of crowding, particularly in sleeping quarters.

Infant Mortality and Mortality of Children Under Five.

In no other division is the improvement in health more definitely indicated than in that which relates to young children. The statistical proof of decrease in the death rate of babies under one year of age from all causes is not so easily arrived at in Illinois as elsewhere because the State has not been long in the Birth Registration Area and births are not yet all registered. In other states the registering of births is better incorporated in the *mores*. Nevertheless, there is proof enough to establish the fact that the insecurity of baby life and child life which was accepted as inevitable three quarters of a century ago would provoke remonstrance if not rebellion today. Little of this improvement came before 1877. The great era of betterment began about 1910. The health agencies can justly claim credit for half of the gain, the other part being divisible between better medical service, elevations of standards and improvement in environment. The largest single factor in bringing about the improvement was the improvement in the milk supply which stimulated improvement in other foods and a decrease in the prevalence of flies. The health agencies fought the battle for better milk.

Diarrhoeas and Dysenteries in Adults.

These disorders were responsible for heavy death rates and sickness rates among the Indians, the French Canadians and the American settlers living in Illinois. This continued up to and after 1877 but not very long thereafter as an important ailment. They have virtually disappeared. Improvement in standards of living and in food and water supplies and better medical service are the principal factors which have brought about this improvement. The contribution of health activities consisted in improving water and food supplies, in educating the people and contributing indirectly to the elevation of standards.

Decrease in the Summer Sickness Rates.

Summer time was formerly four to six times as unhealthful as it now is. The prevailing illnesses of the period were malaria, typhoid and the diarrhoeas. For this improvement the health agencies are largely due the credit. Their campaigns against flies and filth generally, their milk fights and baby saving campaigns are directed principally against those disorders which prevail in summer. Better medical service, improved sanitation and higher service have contributed to the end.

Consumption

In the early days Illinois enjoyed but one good reputation for health. That related to consumption. When the figures became available soon after 1850 it was found that at least at that date the reputation was not deserved though it may possibly have been earlier. Between 1850 and 1900 there was a considerable reduction in the prevalence of consumption. This was the result of elevation of standards more than any other single cause. Recognition of the contagiousness of the disease was a related cause that was helpful in effecting the improvement. The Chicago figures show that just prior to 1907 there was a slight increase in the disease. Between 1907 and 1922 there was a second great decrease. For this decrease the activities of health agencies are entitled to most of the credit. The decrease has come to a stand still since 1922 just as it did soon after 1900.

Influenza.

There has been no success in combating influenza.

The Pneumonias.

The pneumonia rate was comparatively low prior to 1877. It rose intermittently until about 1920, although the intercurrent influenza pandemics and endemics made interpretation of the pneumonia figures difficult and even impossible at times. For some reason the disease or group of diseases

tation enjoyed by the Chicago Health Department made friends for the proposal. The Chicago Health Department owed its existence to the Chicago Medical Society and to the individual efforts of strong medical men who belonged to that society. The same general statement applies to other local health departments. The Municipal Tuberculosis Sanitarium in Chicago owes its existence to the Chicago Health Department aided by the Chicago Tuberculosis Institute.

Regulation of the Practice of Medicine.

No part of this narrative has more peculiar angles than that which relates to the proposals to regulate the practice of medicine and to promote medical societies as post-graduate medical schools than the reference to acts of the territorial legislature and several legislatures thereafter.

The proposals to establish a State Health Department which came from the Aesculapian Society and later from the State Medical Society provided for two objectives. One of these was regulation of the practice of medicine. In 1877 and for nearly forty years thereafter this was the chief objective of the Board of Health.

Between 1900 and 1905 the State Medical Society became greatly interested in separating this objective from the other objective, the promotion of health. However, it was not until 1917 that this was accomplished. The society was right in its judgment as experience soon demonstrated. Under the old order too much of the Department's energy and time was taken up with regulating the practice of medicine and too little of resource remained for promoting health. There was some advantage in consolidating the great professional army engaged in curing disease with the small but compact army engaged in fighting it. But in practice it has been found that the practice of medicine is better regulated in the Department of Registration and the Department of Public Health is left some energy and enthusiasm for planning to promote health.

Platform.

This chapter and narrative is brought to a close by turning from the past to the future and giving some objectives for the next ten years and also projecting aspirations and possibly hopes for a fifty-year period. In doing this it is advisable to state a platform reciting the basic principles upon which the Department stands and hopes to stand.

The State Department of Public Health is the centralized agency for health promotion and disease prevention in the State. It is not an agency for the cure of disease or for the custodial, remedial or reparative care of the sick or convalescents. When perchance it becomes necessary to care for the sick as a measure for protecting others against contagion it will give the most humane and scientific care it can. But such assumption of duty as the care of the sick implies is merely a temporary expedient and one from which it is seeking always to escape.

The various schemes for health insurance so called are really plans for the economic care of the sick. Some of them have some excellent features for the prevention of disease. However, curative care is their chief objective and such being the case they are beyond the domain of this Department. If this Department should be called on to cooperate with such a scheme it would hold that it was its duty to do so in so far as the prevention part of the program is concerned. A few years ago the Department found itself giving reparative or after care to persons who had recovered from infantile paralysis. Since these persons were not infective the problem of giving them reparative care was beyond the field of the Department. Fortunately, the State Rotary Clubs and the Shriners were found willing to assume the duty of giving this after care.

The Department stands on the same platform with relation to supplying drugs free. It is its duty to supply vaccines and nitrate of silver solution and other drugs for prevention. It should not supply any drug for cure. The State Department of Public Welfare maintains a line of hospitals and other institutions for the care of those who are mentally or physically sick.

The Department of Public Health has no duty that calls it to intrude into the field of the Department of Public Welfare. When questions of prevention arise in that field the Department of Health is willing and anxious to assume its full measure of responsibility. The law establishes education of the public and propaganda for health as among the duties of the Department of Public Health. This is a proper provision above all in a democracy. It is a fundamental factor in prevention. The State Department of Public Health is an advisor of the legislature in matters of health promotion. This is a recognized function of a Department and is the basis of the relations between it and the legislative branch of government.

Since the meaning and force of laws are determined by the judiciary, the Department carries some responsibility for keeping that body informed as to what is common information on health subjects and giving it information more directly when called on to do so.

The State Department of Public Health considers that the duty of planning campaigns against disease and promoting health rests on its shoulders. Much of the attack and defense is commanded and executed by local health departments. The State Department of Public Health promotes the interests of local health departments wherever it can do so. It lends them all the aid it can. It has the right to interfere locally only when the local department is so derelict that the people of other communities are endangered. A breakdown in local administration that has local effect only is a local matter calling for no State intervention. The people progress fastest when they reap their own rewards and suffer their own punishments. But if the local department is inefficient to such a degree as to imperil the State generally the State Department has the right to intervene. If the enemy is pouring through a certain gap and over the State generally the State has the right to stop the gap regardless of where it may be.

The same principles apply to the relation of the Department to the practitioners of medicine. In the battle line against disease the individual is in the outermost skirmish line. Next comes the home and then the school. Then comes the first professional line of defense, the doctors and the hospitals. Still further back are the first line of Health Department workers. The service rendered by physicians and hospitals is constant— never ending and valuable. The State Department of Public Health never interferes in the domain of any practising physician or hospital except where it becomes necessary for the protection of society. In almost all cases a satisfactory adjustment between these cooperating agencies is made and it is of a kind that works efficiently, economically and satisfactorily.

The Future.

This narrative may give the impression that the ultimate in attainment has been reached and that health can not be further improved. It is largely to correct any such tendency that this venture in forecasting the future is made.

Some problems have been met and solved. Some diseases have been eradicated and more are on the way toward eradication. Some diseases are satisfactorily under control and some are certainly headed that way. But there will be new diseases to take the place of some old ones. Some diseases not now under control must be brought to heel; some diseases now disregarded must be tackled; the span of human life and efficiency must be increased; the solution of new problems and old problems long neglected must be undertaken.

The effect which should follow the reviewing of the battles of the past is to gird us for those of the future. It is hoped that the Director of Public Health in 1937 can promote the health of the people and the development of health departments, his own and the local departments, with even greater satisfaction, than now prevails in the mind of present Director.

The further development of every division now in the Department and the inauguration of several new divisions can be foreseen within the next few years. There must be a division to promote what is sometimes erroneously called positive health. Such a division would begin operation by promoting periodic physical examinations at first in large groups of industrial workers which is called closed groups; later in more open groups and finally among the general population. In time this division would take on such activities as the promotion of winter sports, the promotion of all sports regardless of season; the planning of vacations for the renewal of bodily vigor; the promotion of play for adults as well as for children, the promotion of some movement such as the *Turner and verein* of Germany and the Swedish societies for cooperative physical development and finally, the advancement of the knowledge and practice of the rules of health. Such a division would have for its motto "Keep the Adult Well"—parodying "Keep the Well Baby Well"—the slogan of infant-welfare work.

Somewhere in the Department, genetics will be undertaken before many years.

Genetics.

The next step will be an increase in the amount and variety of information given on the birth certificate. That document now gives some information that is valuable from the legal standpoint. For the health department it serves to locate the babies for purpose of education and training of mothers and for statistical purposes. It will be enlarged so as to give information that is comparable in scope with that given on the death certificate. Such registration would contribute to a solution of the problems of prenatal care of the parturient and of the baby during the first thirty days of life. The certificate will contain some information which can serve for studies in genetics.

Respiratory Diseases.

The diseases not now engaging the attention of the Department which

Some Consideration of Death Rates

At the present time the crude or uncorrected death rate is unnaturally low. When the calculated death rate based on the average age at death is compared with the death rate as calculated on the basis of reported population, the two are found in marked disaccord. This is principally because of the instability of the population, migration back and forth between counties, between the states and between the urban and rural districts. Industrial changes have come to be large factors in this. Within the life-time of men now living a good part of this instability will have ended. There will be a better accord between the death rate indicated by the average age at death, the average age of the population and the death rate calculated on population. This will not mean a death rate materially lower than the present one. It will mean the prevalence of one that is nearer an index of sanitation, hygiene, health work, freedom from disease, bodily vigor and good heredity than the present one is or can be corrected to be.

Old Age as a Cause of Death.

In the earlier vital statistics old age was given as a cause of death with great frequency. As employed in that period the term was loosely used and it served as a catch bag for deaths in people fifty years of age and older from a multitude of causes. Because its use prompted loose diagnosis vital statisticians and health officers brought enough pressure to cause its partial abandonment. Before many years, old age as a cause of death will be used with the approval of health officers because it will then have a scientific meaning.

Deaths from heart disease, apoplexy, Bright's disease and such occurring among old people will be properly recorded. The disorders due to bacterial and other causes likewise. There will remain a large number of people who will die because of senility and they will be properly classified under that head.

By that time the direct and the ultimate effects of bacterial infections will be so well understood and so many of these infections will be wiped out or will be avoidable that the problems of senectitude can be studied.

Many of the bacterial disorders which now threaten men will have been brought under control. This does not mean, however, that there will be none such. Even then disorders which are endemic and mild in certain regions will periodically break out and sweep over the world. Yellow fever once existed on this basis in Cuba and periodically broke away to sweep as a highly fatal disease over parts of the United States. Influenza made a great sweep over the world as late as 1918. Periodic waves of disorders of the same type may still be expected.

There will be changes in virulence of the existing bacteria in the territory which they normally inhabit. And there will be new bacterial diseases evolved to fit new conditions. All in all there is no reason for thinking that we shall soon see an end of the age-long strife between man and germs.

Increasing Span of Life.

The average age at death is said to be about 58 years now. This is interpreted as the average span of human life. In the pioneer days in Illinois few men were over 40 years of age. Men 50 years of age were regarded as old. It is said that somewhere in that early period, the average span of life was about 33 years. If men were occupied with preparation for work for twenty years only thirteen years were left for productive work. When the average span of life is 58 there are about thirty eight years for productive work. Before long the average span of life should be at least seventy. This would mean fifty years for productive work. When the average span of life reaches seventy years there will be large numbers of men and women working profitably at eighty years of age and of centenarians there will be many.

The State Department of Public Health has no thought that the future will be free from health problems. Such problems will always be present. They will not be those of yesteryear, nor those of today. They will be new in many of their aspects but they will be important to the happiness of the individual and the welfare of the State. When the Department began in 1877 health standards were low. An individual was satisfied with rather poor health because neither he nor his neighbor knew of the possibilities of a better standard. The same was true in even greater measure of collective health called the health of the State. Today, the standards of individual and community health are far higher. It has been one function of the De-

EXECUTIVE OFFICERS AND MEMBERS OF STATE BOARD OF HEALTH.

Presidents.		Date.[1]
John H. Rauch, M. D.	1877-1879	1877
H. Wardner, M. D.	1879-1881	1877
J. M. Gregory, LL. D.	1881-1884	1877
Newton Bateman, LL. D.	1884-1887	1877
W. A. Haskell, M. D.	1887-1893	1881
John A. Vincent, M. D.	1893-1894	1893
Wm. E. Quine, M. D.	1894-1896	1893
B. M. Griffith, M. D.	1896-1897	1890
L. Adelsberger, M. D.	1897-1898	1897
A. C. Corr, M. D.	1898-1899	1898
C. B. Johnson, M. D.	1899-1902	1897
Geo. W. Webster, M. D.	1902-1914	1900
J. A. Robison, M. D.	1914-1917	1913

Secretarys.		
E. W. Gray*, M. D., (from July to Dec.)	1877-1877	1877
John H. Rauch, M. D., Act. Sec.—Dec. to May	1877-1878	1877
Anson L. Clark, M. D.	1878-1879	1877
John R. Rauch, M. D.	1879-1891	1877
Wm. R. MacKenzie, M. D. Aug. 4 to Sept. 24,	1891-1891	1883
F. W. Reilly, M. D.	1891-1893	1891
J. W. Scott*, M. D.	1893-1897	1893
J. A. Egan, M. D.	1897-1913	1897
Amos Sawyer*, Act. Sec.	1913-1914	1901
C. St. Clair Drake, M. D.	1914-1917	1914

* Not members of the Board. Dr. Egan became a member of the Board in 1901.

Board Members	Date.[1]	Board Members.	Date.[1]
R. Ludlam, M. D.	1877	G. R. Schafer, M. D.	1896
W. M. Chambers, M. D.	1877	E. P. Cook, M. D.	1896
John McLean, M. D.	1881	Z. D. French, M. D.	1897
R. L. McCain, M. D.	1882	C. H. Starkel, M. D.	1896
Wm. R. MacKenzie, M. D., Sec., August-September, 1891	1883	R. F. Bennett, M. D.	1898
Geo. N. Kreider, M. D.	1884	J. C. Sullivan, M. D.	1901
A. W. H. Reen, M. D.	1884	W. Harrison Hipp, M. D.	1901
H. V. Ferrell, M. D.	1887	Wm. O. Forbes, M. D.	1901
D. H. Williams, M. D.	1888	Henry Richings, M. D.	1902
Geo. Thilo, M. D.	1893	R. E. Niedringhaus, M. D.	1905
Sarah Hackett Stevenson, M. D.	1893	W. R. Schussler, M. D.	1907
J. B. McFatrich, M. D.	1893	C. J. Boswell, M. D.	1909
Julius Kohl, M. D.	1893	Adam Szwajkart, M. D.	1913
Oscar O. Baines, M. D.	1895	P. Luster, M. D.	1913
D. R. Brower, M. D.	1896	T. B. Lewis, M. D.	1913
Florence W. Hunt, M. D.	1897	Thos. O. Freeman, M. D.	1914
P. H. Wessel, M. D.	1897	J. J. Hassett, M. D.	1914
M. Meyerovitz, M. D.	1897	Enos S. Spindel, M. D.	1914
		Felix Kalacinski, M. D.	1916

[1] Year of appointment.

ILLUSTRATIONS

	PAGE
Adult physical examination, State fair	206
Annual appropriation, 1879-1927	207
Cerebro-spinal fever, meningitis	376
Chicago mortality rate, acute respiratory diseases, 1870-1910	93
course of the total mortality in Chicago, 1867, 1868	90
decennial mortality rates—all causes—Chicago, 1870-1910	94
mortality rates—Chicago—1871-1879, 1922	91, 92
Diarrhoea and Enteritis in Illinois	379
Diphtheria rates in Illinois	360
Field laboratory equipment	259
Dr. George Fisher's neglected grave in Randolph County	275
Health exhibit at fair	227
Malaria in Illinois	381
Map—typhoid mortality in Illinois	347
Map—White County, Illinois, on tuberculosis	372
Map—Yellow fever districts in Cairo	330
Number inspections all sanitary purposes	224
Number investigations proposed sewerage installations	223
Number investigations public water supplies	223
Number water analyses	224
Organization State Board of Health, 1877	138
Organization State Board of Health, 1901	165
Organization State Board of Health, 1915	177
Organization State Board of Health, 1927	199
Population served from public water supplies	229
Prevalence of venereal disease in Illinois	272
Public water supplies installed	229
Scarlet fever case reports	350
Scarlet fever deaths in Illinois	349
Seasonal distribution of deaths, 1843-1925	95
Section of main laboratory at Springfield	255
Smallpox in Illinois	308
State fair better baby conference in action	237
Tuberculosis deaths in Illinois	362
Typhoid fever deaths in Illinois	342

PHOTOGRAPHS.

Adelsberger, Dr. Louis, Waterloo	175
Bain, Dr. Walter G., Springfield	245
Bateman, Newton, LL. D., Galesburg	124, 146
Black, Dr. Carl E., Jacksonville	10, 118
Brainard, Dr. Daniel	48

PHOTOGRAPHS

	PAGE
Dilly, Orrin, Springfield	231
Doan, Dr. Thomas D., Palmyra	203
Drake, Dr. C. St. Clair, Chicago	162, 190
Drake, Dr. Daniel	37
East, Dr. C. W., Springfield	222
Egan, Dr. James A., Chicago	162
Esper, Gloria June, first 100 per cent girl	239
Evans, Dr. William A., Chicago	197, 203
Ferguson, Harry F., Springfield	222
Goodbrake, Dr. C., Clinton	40
Gregory, John Milton, LL. D., Champaign	124, 146
Griffith, Dr. B. M., Springfield	155
Haller, Dr. F. B., Vandalia	61
Hamill, Dr. Robert C., Chicago	66
Hansen, Paul, Chicago	221
Haskell, Dr. W. A.	155
Hemenway, Dr. Henry B., Springfield	266
Howard, Sheldon L., Springfield	232
Hoyt, W. H., Chicago	230
Hrdlicka, Dr. Ales, (Washington, D. C.)	17
Hull, Dr. Thomas G., Springfield	247
Jewell, Dr. J. S., Evanston	41
Johnson, Dr. C. B., Champaign	175
Kessinger, Samuel W., Litchfield	267
Leonard, Dr. Thomas H., Springfield	220
Lillie, Dr. Charles W., East St. Louis	197
Lowden, Governor Frank O., Oregon	183
Ludlam, Dr. Reuben, Chicago	124
MacKenzie, Dr. William R., Chester	140
Mannheimer, Dr. Michael, Chicago	89
Marquette, Father	117
Massie, Dr. William, Edgar County	53
McShane, Dr. J. J., Springfield	210
Monroe, Mrs. E. N., Quincy	197, 203
Palmer, Dr. George Thomas, Springfield	220
Prince, Dr. David, Jacksonville	75
Quine, Dr. William E., Chicago	155
Rauch, Dr. John H., Chicago	124, 140, 146
Rawlings, Dr. Isaac D., Chicago	190
Reilly, Dr. Frank W., Chicago	162
Reynolds, Dr. Arthur R., Chicago	313
Richardson, Baxter K., Springfield	267
Robertson, Dr. John Dill, Chicago	197
Robison, Dr. John Albert, Chicago	175
Ryan, Charles, Springfield	210
Sawyer, Amos, Hillsboro	162
Scott, Dr. John W., Springfield	162
Searcy, Earl B., Springfield	266
Skoog, Paul L., (California)	243
Sloan, Dr. Edwin P., Bloomington	197, 203
Small, Governor Len, Kankakee	4
Taylor, Dr. G. G., Chicago	268
Vincent, Dr. John A., Springfield	155
Wardner, Dr. Horace, Cairo	124, 146
Webster, Dr. George W., Chicago	175
Woodward, Dr. J. J., (Washington, D. C.)	79
Wright, Dr. John, Clinton	75

INDEX.

—A—

Abel, Dr. Theodore C., Chicago..
Adelsberger, Dr. Louis, Waterloo..
Advisory Board, members of..192
Ague ....
Allen, Dr. J., ..., debate on cholera......................................
American Bottoms...19, 23, 24.
American colonists ....
American Regime, The..
Amoebic dysentery, see Dysentery.
Anders, Dr. ...., Chicago, on typhoid fever.................................
Andrews, Dr. C. N., Rockford..
Andrews, Dr. Edmund, Chicago..
Anemia ....
Anthrax ....
Antitoxin distributed and Pasteur treatments....................................
   see Vaccines.
Appropriations.....133, 135, 137, 139, 143, 166, 169, 171, 181, 185, 206,
   division child hygiene and public health nursing...............
      communicable diseases ....
      lodging house inspection..................................
      sanitary engineering ....
      tuberculosis ....
      vital statistics ....
   for State Board of Health.................................133,
   for State Department of Public Health........................
      graph on ....
   for Vaccine farm, University of Illinois.....................
   for water laboratory, University of Illinois.................
   for yellow fever epidemic....................................
Arnold, Dr. Lloyd, Chicago..
Asthma ....
Atwater, Dr. R. M.,...
Autumnal fever ....
Auxiliary health agencies...14, 171,

—B—

Baily, Dr. F. K., Joliet..
Bain, Dr. Walter G., Springfield..
Baines, Dr. Oscar O., Chicago...
Barbee, Dr. Thomas, Marshall..
Bartlett, Dr. Elisha, ..., on typhoid fever................................
Bateman, Newton, LL. D., Galesburg.....................................124, 125,
Beaumont, Dr. ....
Bemiss, Dr. S. M., (La.)..
Bennett, Dr. R. F., Litchfield..
Berg, Elin, Springfield...
Better baby conferences..137,
Bilious fevers..
Births ....
   and infant deaths..
   rates ....
   registration drive in Illinois...............................
Black, Dr. Carl E., Jacksonville..
Black, Dr. Luther A., Chicago...
Black fly ....
Black Hawk War..
Black tongue ....
Blane, William ....

(414)

INDEX 415

	PAGE
Blankenmeyer, Dr. H. C., Springfield	254
Board of Health, see State Board of Health.	
Boggess	30
Bondurant, Dr. Flint	254
Borendel, Dr. F., Peoria County	41
Boswell, Dr. Chas. J., Mounds	411
Boudin, Dr. ...., on typhoid fever and malaria	78
Bovine tuberculosis	369, 374
Bowen, Dr. ...., Joliet	39
Brainard, Dr. Daniel	47, 48
Breast feeding demonstration	240
Breed, Dr. ...., Princeton	80
Breen, Clara, Springfield	2, 10
Brennan, Dr. Earl, East St. Louis	258
Bridges, Dr. T. B., Chicago	104
British Regime, The	13, 26, 28
Bronchitis	85, 30, 100, 408
Brower, Dr. Daniel R., Chicago	411
Buhlig, Mrs. Blanche, Chicago, committee on child hygiene	342
Bundesen, Dr. Herman N., Chicago	203, 272
Burns, Dr. ...., Mackinaw	38
Burrill, Prof. Thomas J., Urbana	244, 249
Butler, Major, (Washington, D. C.) on dental hygiene	242

C

Cadwell, Dr. George, Kaskaskia	126, 130
Cahokia	23, 32, 34
Cairo	32, 144, 145, 412, 611, 668
Cancer	17, 298, 305, 408
Carr, Clark E., (1850)	43
Carroll, Dr. ...., on typhoid fever	76
Cassiday, Hugh, Springfield	252
Catlin, Dr. George,	38, 49
Cerebrospinal fever	64, 375
graph on	376
Chamberlain, Dr. ...., Kane County	42
Chambers, Dr. William M., Charleston	124, 125, 137, 279, 396, 411
biography of	125
Chancroid, see Venereal diseases.	
Chapman, Dr. H. W., Whitehall	85
Cheneoweth, Dr. W. J., Decatur	86
Chicago, chronicle health and sanitation in	101-114
fire (1871)	106
DeWolf, Dr. Oscar C.	105, 323
drainage canal, sewage from	168, 245
Evans, Dr. W. A.	2, 196, 197, 203, 272, 291, 294, 302, 369
health department	43, 44, 47, 50, 89, 247, 250, 261, 405
annual reports of	87, 105
Health history prior to 1877	101-114
Mannheimer, Dr. Michael, charts by	89
milk	300, 301
prohibiting sale of from tuberculous cattle	369
Rauch, Dr. John H., appointed sanitary superintendent	105, 106, 107
Reynolds, Dr. Arthur R.	105, 166, 313
Statistics	50, 51, 83, 87, 89, 90, 99, 102, 103, 104, 106, 107-114, 313, 320, 397
annual death rates (1843-1877)	107
Consumption	111
diphtheria	109, 354, 356
erysipelas	114
malaria	113
measles	112
pneumonia	110
respiratory diseases	110

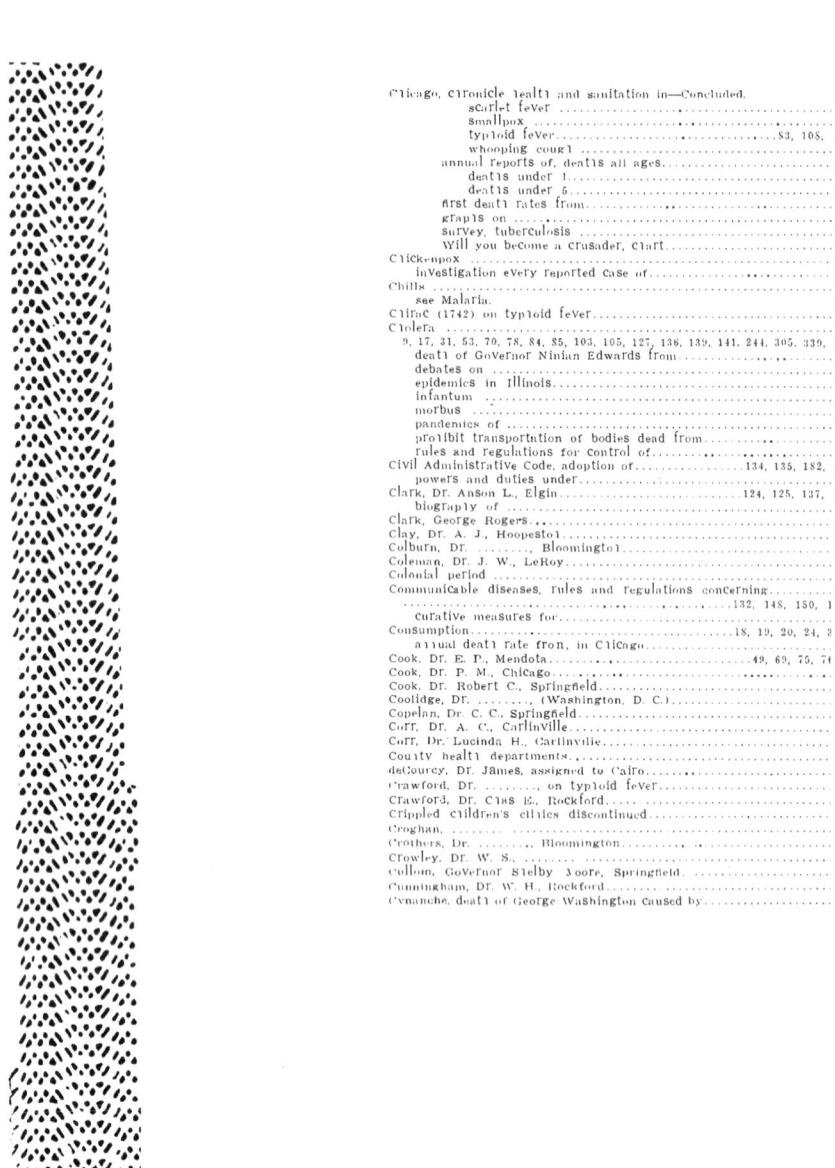

Chicago, chronicle health and sanitation in—Concluded.
    scarlet fever ....
    smallpox ....
    typhoid fever...83, 105,
    whooping cough ....
  annual reports of, deaths all ages................................
    deaths under 1..
    deaths under 5..
  first death rates from..
  graphs on ....
  survey, tuberculosis ....
  Will you become a crusader, chart................................
Chickenpox
  investigation every reported case of.............................
Chills
  see Malaria.
Chirac (1742) on typhoid fever..
Cholera ....
  9, 17, 31, 53, 70, 78, 84, 85, 103, 105, 127, 136, 139, 141, 244, 305, 339,
  death of Governor Ninian Edwards from..........................
  debates on ....
  epidemics in Illinois..
  infantum ....
  morbus ....
  pandemics of ....
  prohibit transportation of bodies dead from......................
  rules and regulations for control of..............................
Civil Administrative Code, adoption of....................134, 135, 182,
  powers and duties under..
Clark, Dr. Anson L., Elgin..............................124, 125, 137,
  biography of ....
Clark, George Rogers...
Clay, Dr. A. J., Hoopeston..
Colburn, Dr. ...., Bloomington...................................
Coleman, Dr. J. W., LeRoy..
Colonial period ....
Communicable diseases, rules and regulations concerning..........
....132, 148, 150, 1
  curative measures for...
Consumption...18, 19, 20, 24, 3
  annual death rate from, in Chicago.............................
Cook, Dr. E. P., Mendota..............................49, 69, 75, 76
Cook, Dr. P. M., Chicago..
Cook, Dr. Robert C., Springfield.....................................
Coolidge, Dr. ...., (Washington, D. C.).........................
Copelan, Dr. C. C., Springfield.......................................
Corr, Dr. A. C., Carlinville...
Corr, Dr. Lucinda H., Carlinville....................................
County health departments..
deCourcy, Dr. James, assigned to Cairo..............................
Crawford, Dr. ...., on typhoid fever...........................
Crawford, Dr. Chas E., Rockford....................................
Crippled children's clinics discontinued.............................
Croghan, ...
Crothers, Dr. ...., Bloomington.................................
Crowley, Dr. W. S...
Cullom, Governor Shelby Moore, Springfield........................
Cunningham, Dr. W. H., Rockford...................................
Cynanche, death of George Washington caused by..................

INDEX 417

PAGE

—D—

Dappert, A. F., Springfield... 2
Davis, Dr. N. S., ... 40, 45, 52, 57, 70, 74, 76, 85, 88, 338
    debate on cholera 45
Dawson, Dr. ...., on typhoid fever... 70
Deaths, see Mortality
deLesseps, ... 25
Deneen, Governor Charles S., Chicago 169
Dengue, pandemic of.. 46
Dental demonstrations 200, 242
Development of State health service.. 133
    three periods 132, 138, 165, 177, 199
    four personalities 134
DeWolf, Dr. Oscar C., Chicago..105, 323
Diarrheal infections 14, 18, 20, 21, 25, 30, 41, 72, 81, 85, 90, 305, 377, 398, 403
    among Indians 83
    annual death rates, Chicago..104, 108, 354
    in adults 84, 86
    infant mortality due especially to.. 377
    mortality from 377
        graph on 379
Dickinson, Dr. ...., Peoria... 39
Dickson, Dr. S. H., .. on typhoid fever... 79
Diehl, Dr. C. H., Effingham.. 296
Dilly, Orrin, Springfield..231, 233
Diphtheria 9, 96, 136, 168, 244, 250, 353, 364, 382
    among Indians 55
    annual death rates, Chicago..104, 108, 354
    cases of 357
    carriers 358
    distribution of antitoxin for..............................216, 217, 244, 353, 361
    mortality from 353, 357, 360
        graph on 360
    outbreak at Rock Island 259, 260
    phenomenal progress in eradication of... 366
    prohibit transportation bodies dead from... 150
    rules and regulations for control of... 150
Directors, State Department of Public Health....................................182, 190
Division of child hygiene and public health nursing................... 189, 199, 231
    committee on child health needs in Illinois................................200, 242
    of communicable diseases 185, 210
    of general office 185, 209
    of laboratories, biological and research...................................189, 247
        diagnostic 181, 186, 193, 245, 246
    of lodging house inspection..............................164, 171, 173, 186, 265
    of public health instruction..189, 192, 236
    of sanitation 185, 221, 243, 247, 381
    of social hygiene 188, 247, 268
    of surveys and rural hygiene...189, 206, 243
    of tuberculosis 185, 220
    of vital statistics 186, 230, 254
Doan, Dr. Thomas D., Palmyra... 203
Doane, Dr. Philip S., Chicago... 334
Drainage, see American Bottoms
Drake, Dr. C. St. Clair, Chicago...135, 162, 225, 411
    appropriations under 194
    biography of 190
    regime 135, 174–194
Drake, Dr. Daniel.....19, 36, 37, 38, 39, 43, 47, 52, 54, 57, 60, 64, 67, 68, 73, 78, 84, 397

Dropsy ....
Drude, Dr. Francis, Quincy..................
Dunne, Governor Edward F., Chicago.....................
Dufray, Martin ....
Dysentery 9, 14, 18, 20, 21, 25, 28, 30, 7
   annual deaths and rates in Chicago............................
   mortality from ....
Dyspepsia ....

—E—

East, Dr. C. W., Springfield....................
Edgar, Capt. I. D., (Washington, D. C.)..........
Edgar, Dr. W. S., ..., debate on cholera...................
Educational propaganda ....
Edwards, Governor Ninian, death from cholera..............
Egan, Dr. James A., Chicago............... ....78, 177, 232,
   appropriations under
   regime ....
Egyptian mummies ....
Ellis, Dr. C. C., Joliet.......................
Embalmers, law passed regulating practice..................
English, Dr. . . . ., Jacksonville.......................
Epizootic, horses died from in Chicago..................
Erasmus, scientist, on typhoid fever.................
Ergot paralysis ....
Erysipelas 50, 52, 54,
   annual death rates in Chicago............................
Evans, Dr. Wm. A., Chicago..................2, 196, 197, 203, 272,
Exhibits 135,
Eye troubles ....

—F—

Faucher, Homer C., Chicago...................
Faught, Eva E., Carbondale...................
Felder, Dr. W. L., ..., on fevers........................
Ferguson, Harry F., Springfield...................
Ferrell, Dr. H. V., Carterville.......................
Fisher, Dr. George, Kaskaskia.......................
Fitch, Dr. .... (Ind.) ....
Flagg, Dr. ...., Edwardsville........................
Flint, Dr. Austin, ..., on typhoid fever and malaria............
Fluxes ....
Food poisoning ....
Forbes, Dr. Wm. O., Chicago...................
Fordham, Dr. .... (England).......................
Forry, Dr. ..... (Washington, D. C.)...................
Fort Chartres ....
Foreword ....
Foster, Dr. I. H., Chicago...................
Freeman, Dr. Thomas O., Mattoon...................
French-Canadian Regime, The.......................,13, 15, 22, 28, 2
French, Dr. A. W., Springfield...................
French, Dr. Z. D., Lawrenceville..................
Fruterrer, Dr. Gustav, Chicago...................
Fry, Luella, Springfield...................
Frye, Dr. J. C., Peoria...................
Fults, Dr. J. C., Waterloo...................

—G—

Callbrieth, Dr.   on puerperal fever.................
Gardolphe, Dr. Michel,   on origin of syphilis..

INDEX 419

	PAGE
Garrott, D.. Erasmus, Chicago	315
Gates, D.. Joseph, Maine	88
Gehrmann, D.. Adolph, Chicago	247
General health history prior to 1877	15
Genesis of public health law	127
Genetics	408
Gerhard, D.......... (Penn.) on typhoid fever	71, 73
Gerhard, D.. Frederick, Chicago	41, 61
Gilchrist, D.. (1735) on typhoid fever	71
Gilmore, D.. W. H., Mt. Vernon	257
Glackin, Senator Edward J., Chicago	179, 220, 291, 366
law for tuberculosis sanatoria	163, 172, 179, 365, 368, 371
Godfrey, D.. E. S., (New York)	211
Goitre survey	242
Gonorrhea	22, 24, 60, 254, 270, 298
Goodbrake, D.. C., Clinton	40, 85
Goodell, D.. W. L., Effingham	86
Gorgas, General William Crawford	25
Gout	18
Graphs, see Illustrations	
Graves, D.. N. A., Chicago	293
Gray, D........., Jefferson County	57
Gray, D.. Elias W., Bloomington	130, 131, 132, 137, 139, 140, 411
Gray, D.. Ethan A., Chicago	363
Gregory, D.. John Milton, Champaign	124, 125, 137, 146, 411
biography of	125
Griffiths, D.. B. M., Springfield	153, 155, 411
Griffitts, D.. T. H. D.	233
Grinstead, D.. W. F., Cairo	334
Guiteras, D.. John (Ala.)	335
Gumston, D.. C. G. ...., on typhoid fever	70

—H—

Haines, James	31, 43
Hale, on unity of fevers	73
Hall, D.. L., Kane County	40
Hall, D.. Thomas, Toulon	64, 84, 85
Haller, D.. F. B., Vandalia	40, 61, 118
Hamill, D.. Robert C., Chicago	33, 53, 61, 66, 89
Hamilton, D.. John B., Chicago	335
Hamtranmck, Major	26
Hanson, General J.	26
Hansen, Paul, Chicago	221
Harris, D.. J. O., Ottawa	87
Haskell, D.. W. A., Alton	153, 155, 411
Hassett, D.. J. J., McLeansboro	411
Hauff, D........., on puerperal fever	66
Health conditions in Illinois after 1877	304
promotion week	135, 179, 294
Heart disease	305, 408, 409
Hemenway, D.. H. B., Springfield	266
Henkes, Kilby, Springfield	252
Hennepin, D. ...., on milk sickness	67
Henry, D......., Springfield	38
Henry, D.. Alexander	18, 19
Henry, D.. J. F., Bloomington	36, 52
Hepatites, chronic	57
Hewins, D.. L. T., Loda	46, 86
Hildreth, D.. S. P., (Ohio)	33, 65
Hipp, D.. W. Harrison, Chicago	411

                                                                                    PAGE
Hirsch, Dr. 43, 44, 47, 49, 50, 55, 56, 57, 63, 64, 65, 71, 78
History of certain diseases prior to 1877.. 35
    after 1877 304
    steps in establishment of typhoid fever as a specific disease................ 70
Hoffman, (1728) on typhoid fever.. 71
Hoffman, Dr. T. A., Beardstown.. 41
Holden, A. B., ... 19
Holliste, D., J. H., on nursing sore mouth...................................... 69
Holmes, D., Olive Wendell..43, 66, 73, 74
Holmes, D., W. H., ...254
Holsten, D., ..., on puerperal fever....................................... 65
Howard, Sheldon L, Springfield...232
Howland, D., ..., Ottawa... 39
Hoyt, W. H., Chicago...208, 232, 233, 253
Hrdlicka, D., Ales, (Washington, D. C.).................17, 18, 19, 20, 49, 53, 55, 58, 60
Hubbard, Gordon S., Chicago...22, 23, 102
Hull, Thomas G. Springfield..247, 252
Hunter, D., I. W., on origin of syphilis.. 60
Hunt, D., Florence W., Chicago...411
Hulbert, D.   ...., Ottawa... 39
Huxham (1784) on typhoid fever..71, 72

—I—

Ilkemire, Dr. J. A., Palestine..258
Illinois and Michigan Canal...40, 42, 101, 106
Illinois Medical Society formed... 39
    debates on cholera... 45
Immigrants 29, 35, 47, 66, 101, 136, 142, 147, 154, 172
    measles brought in by.. 54
    smallpox carried by.. 50
Indians 13, 15, 17, 19, 21, 39, 53, 398
    diarrhoeal diseases among.. 83
    high death and low birth rates... 29
    smallpox, disease of... 49
    syphilis among... 58
Indigestion 18
Infantile paralysis 187, 234, 370, 379
    clinics for..199, 235, 380, 406
    table on 380
Infant mortality 19, 30, 86-88, 242, 393, 403
    among Indians 19
    annual death rates in Chicago..113
    detailed rates on 201
Infants, diseases among 14
Influenza 90, 96, 191, 404, 408
    and pneumonia, epidemics of.. 63
    mortality for in Chicago...109
Ingals, D., E., ..., debate on cholera..................................... 45
Intermittent fever 26, 35, 36, 40, 72, 78
    annual death rates, Chicago..113
Intra-departmental organization..208-272
Introduction 13
Isthmus of Panama 25

—J—

Jackson, ..., on unity of fevers... 73
Jayne, D., ..., Springfield.. 38
Jenner, D., Edward, (England)..320
Jenner, Si. U., (1849) (England), on unity of fevers............................ 72
Jesuits 24, 32, 42
Jewell, D., J. S., Evanston..41, 70

INDEX

	PAGE
Johnson, D., C. B., Champaign	42, 55, 64, 80, 82, 175, 396, 411
Johnson, D., Hosmer A., Chicago	105, 143
debate on cholera	45
Jonas, N. M., Chicago	164
Jones, D., Jacksonville	38
Jones, D., H. W., Chicago	66
Jones, D., Joseph, (Ohio Valley)	58

—K

Kalacinski, D., Felix, Chicago	411
Kaskaskia	23, 26, 32, 34, 273, 274
bottoms	115, 118
removal of capital from	118
survey of Ohio to 1877	116
Kessinger, Samuel W., Litchfield	267
Klebs, D., A. C., Chicago	290, 293
Koch, ..., discovery of anthrax and tuberculosis bacillus by	244, 364
Koenle, D., Gottfried, Chicago	2, 102
Kohl, D., Julius, Belleville	411
Krafft, ..., on origin of syphilis	59
Kreider, D., George N., Springfield	411

L

Laboratories, Branch	258
certificates of approval for	262
diagnostic biological and research	186, 189, 193, 247, 248, 254
examination of water supplies	244
equipped for making diagnostic examinations	166, 173, 181
investigations conducted by	252
total examinations, table on	256
LaFevre, ..., French trade	39
Lakes and ponds, stagnant	34
Lancise (1718) on typhoid fever	71
Laub, Wm. G., Chicago	265
Leasure, D., ... (Penn.) on puerperal fever	65
LeBlanc, on malaria	25
Legislation	129, 130, 132, 133, 198, 215, 248, 311, 404
important health laws enacted	179, 214, 216, 271, 272, 374
medical practice acts	273–286
organization of State Board of Health	127, 137, 404
regulating practice osteopathy	284
requiring pasteurization of milk	204
Leonard, D., Thomas H., Springfield	229
Lewis, Archie, Chicago	265
Lewis, D., T. B., Hammond	411
Lillie, D., J. G., Woodford County	41
Lillie, D., Charles W., East St. Louis	196, 197
Lincoln, Abraham	67, 115, 137
Lincoln, Nancy Hanks, death from milk sickness	67
Lister, Lord, (England)	131, 244
Local boards of health, creation of	172, 189
attempts to improve	196
Local health district and law providing for establishment of	179, 215
Lodging house inspection	171, 173, 208
act creating	164
chart on	165
Long, Dr. Esmond R., ..., on consumption among Puritan families	20
Long, Prof. John H., Chicago	245
Lortet, ..., on origin of syphilis	59
Lottery, see American Bottoms	
Louis (1829), treatise on typhoid fever	20, 70, 71, 73, 75

422   INDEX

	PAGE
Lowden, Governor Frank O., Oregon	135, 179, 182, 183
Lowry, Dr. Edith B., St. Charles	235
Ludlam, Dr. Reuben, Chicago	124, 137, 153, 411
biography of	125
Luster, Dr. R. D., Granite City	411

—M—

MacCulloch, John (1829)	35
MacKenzie, Dr. Wm. R., Chester	140, 152, 153, 411
Malaria	
9, 13, 19, 20, 21, 24, 25, 26, 28, 30, 33, 39, 42, 47, 73, 74, 77, 78, 84, 90, 118, 168, 254, 399	
and typhoid fever	69–83
annual death rates in Chicago	104, 113
cases of	382
French no immunity to	25
history of prior to 1877	35
mortality and rates	382
graph on	381
noticeable decline in	304
Mann, A. H., Springfield, inspector at Cairo	334
Mannheimer, Dr. Michael, Chicago, concerning charts by	89, 105
Manse, Dr. Hiram, Lafayette	87
Marquette, Father	18, 23, 42, 83, 117
Marriages	13, 23, 26, 397
Massie, Dr. Wm., Grand View	53
Maternity and child hygiene	199, 238
advisory committee on	200
Sheppard-Towner Act	200, 238
Matthews, Dr. J. P., Carlinville	85
McCain, Dr. R. L.,	411
McClanahan, Dr. B. V., Galesburg, committee on child hygiene	242
McCulloch, W. W., Chicago	265
McFatrich, Dr. J. B., Chicago	411
McGarragh, Dr. .... on milk sickness	68
McIlvaine, Dr. T. M., Peoria	150
McIntosh, Dr. Donal, Urbana	249
McLaughlin, Dr. R. G., Heyworth	85
McLean, Dr. John, Pullman	411
McShane, Dr. John J., Springfield	210–219
McVey, Dr. ...., Morgan County	53, 57
Measles	33, 96, 366, 374, 383, 402
annual death rates in Chicago	104, 112
brought in by immigrants	54
cases of	385
Medical examination of school children	238
Practice Act, The	127, 130, 132, 156, 159, 273
acts of 1817, 1819, 1877	273–286
divorced public health service and regulation of	182
minimum requirements	282
standards for medical education	281
Meeker, Dr. ...., Chicago	52
Members, State Board of Health	124, 137, 411
biographies	125, 137, 190
Menard, Pierre, Kaskaskia	273, 276
Meningeal fever	57
Meningitis	56, 64, 375, 403
graph on	376
Merriman, Dr. ...., Springfield	38
Mettaurer, Dr. ...., (Va.) on fevers	78
Meyerovitz, Dr. M., Chicago	411
Midwives, certificates to practice required	285

INDEX 423

PAGE
Milk..........................164, 181, 202, 204, 227, 252, 257, 260, 301, 342, 350, 369
  model ordinance for...202, 204
  pasteurization of 202, 226, 260, 395
  sickness 66, 84, 400
    mortality from 67
    prevalence of 66
Miller, Dr. Ben S., Chicago, appointed sanitary superintendent.................. 106
Missionaries 13, 22
Mitchell, Dr. R. W., (Tenn.)... 143
Model milk ordinance adopted...202, 204
Modern health crusade...290, 294
Modified quarantine 213
Monette, Dr. J. W., (Miss.)... 73
Monroe, Mrs. E. J., Quincy..196, 197, 203
Morbidity, decrease in summer sickness rates...................................... 404
  general unhealthfulness 29, 398
  see various diseases.
Morgan, (1768), on ague and fever... 26
Morgagini (1761) on typhoid fever.. 71
Mortality 25, 62, 202, 230, 234
  all causes..96, 97
  certain causes, Illinois and Chicago, tables on..................................96, 304
  children under 5 years, table on...88, 89
  cholera 43-46
  diarrhoeal infections 377, 378
  diphtheria..55, 108, 353
  increasing span of life... 410
  infant..19, 30, 86, 113, 201, 242, 393, 394, 395, 403
  measles 43, 385
  milk sickness... 67
  pneumonia and influenza...62, 388
  population and number deaths, tables on..98-100
  rates 29, 304, 398, 409
    all causes..96, 343, 351, 354, 364
    annual, certain diseases.. 107
    infant.. 394
    Springfield 116
    tuberculosis 364
    typhoid fever 108
    see Chicago statistics
  scarlet fever.. 351
  smallpox 310
  tuberculosis 364
  typhoid fever...82, 108, 338
  see illustrations, Chicago statistics
Mosquitoes..19, 25, 35, 36, 46, 101, 381, 400
Mound builders 13, 15, 58
Murchison, Dr. Chas. (1862) on typhoid fever....................................71, 339
Murphy, Dr. J., Peoria..39, 87

—N—

Nance, Dr. ...., Lafayette... 53
Nauss, Dr. Ralph W., ... 252
Neely, Dr. John B., Chicago.. 334
Nelson, Dr. C. S., Springfield...211, 336
Neuralgias 57
Niedringhaus, Dr. R. E., Granite City.. 411
Noble, Dr. Harrison, Bloomington..61, 70
Notthaft, ... (Germany) on origin of syphilis................................. 59
Nursing service.. 246
Nursing sore mouth... 69

INDEX

PAGE

—O—

Olson, Dr. C. W., Lombard.. 364
Ophthalmia neonatorum..33, 289
    epidemic 57
Osborne, Governor Chase (Mich.).. 67
Osler, Dr. Wm.. 74
Outbreak of yellow fever starts machinery for control of epidemics........ 141
Owen, Dr. Dale, (Ind.).. 68
Oysters, typhoid fever attributed to.......................204, 214, 257, 346

—P—

Palmer, Prof. Arthur Wm., Urbana......................................221, 246
Palmer, Dr. George Thomas, Springfield..................185, 220, 336, 371
Panama Canal, deaths in... 25
Paralysis, ergot... 64
Parkman, ...18, 23
Parran, Dr. Thomas, Jr., (Washington, D. C.).............................. 198
Parrish, Randall... 44
Pasteurization, law passed requiring....................................... 202
    milk supplies.............................164, 181, 260, 361, 342, 350, 395
Pasteur, ... (France)...131, 169, 244
Payne, Dr. H. R., Marshall.. 40
"Petechial fever" (typhoid)... 70
Petit (1814) on typhoid fever... 71
von Pettenkofer, Max, (Germany)...................105, 114, 131, 137, 339
Pettit, Dr. J. W., Ottawa.. 293
Pettit, Dr. Roswell T., Ottawa... 258
Phillips, Dr. G. W., Dixon.. 61
Physical examinations, annual..................................206, 242, 298
    scientific examination of returned soldiers.......................... 373
Pickett, ... (Ala.).. 13
Pierce, Dr. C. C., (Washington, D. C.).................................... 272
Plague 400
Pleurisy 33, 109
Pneumonia.......................12, 20, 25, 30, 33, 62, 96, 387, 398, 404
    and influenza... 62
    annual death rates in Chicago.. 109
    cases of... 388
    graph on... 389
Poles, in Illinois.. 28
Poliomyelitis, see infantile paralysis
Ponds and lakes, stagnant... 34
Population of Illinois, increase in... 100
    and number of deaths, tables on....................................... 98
Powers and duties, under State Board of Health Act........................ 184
    under ophthalmia neonatorum act...................................... 185
    under vital statistics act.. 184
    under miscellaneous acts... 185
Preface 7
Presidents, State Board of Health.........................146, 155, 175, 411
Prince, Dr. David, Jacksonville... 75
    debate on cholera... 45
Prosser, Dr. ...., Jacksonville.. 38
Prost, (1804), on typhoid fever... 71
Public health administration in Illinois..............................127–272
    intra-departmental organization.................................208–272
Puerperal fever...50, 51, 53, 54, 74, 202, 402
    epidemic of... 65
Puritan fathers, suffered from consumption................................. 70
"Putrid fever".. 53

INDEX

—Q—

Quaife	31, 102
Quarantine, during yellow fever epidemic	142, 327, 330
modified	213
rules and regulations pertaining to	132, 150, 180, 210, 212
yellow fever committee appointed	143, 334
Quine, Dr. W. E., Chicago	56, 150, 411
Quinine	42, 77

—R—

Rabies	215, 251, 253, 256
vaccine for	219
Rauch, Dr. John H., Chicago	
	102, 105, 106, 107, 124, 125, 131, 251, 266, 280, 303, 339, 396, 411
appropriations under	137, 139, 141
biography of	125
general State sanitary survey	147, 198, 339
regime	134, 139-159
resignation of	153
yellow fever outbreak at Cairo	141, 327
Rawlings, Dr. Isaac D., Chicago	2, 161, 190, 312, 407
advisory board appointed	196, 197, 203
appropriations under	206
biography of	190
regime	135, 194
Raymond, (1911) scientist, on origin of syphilis	59
Reed, Dr. Silas	63, 86
Reen, Dr. A. W. H., Peoria	411
Reeves, Dr. J. E., (Va.)	70
Regime, American, The	27
British, The	26, 28
Drake, The	135, 174-194
Egan, The	134, 159-174
French-Canadian, The	13, 15, 22, 28, 29, 53
Rauch, The	134, 139-159
Rawlings, The	135, 194
Reilly, Dr. Frank W., Chicago	105, 152, 156, 162, 315, 332, 396, 411
Respiratory diseases	110, 408
Reyburn, (1856) on fevers	75
Reynolds, Dr. Arthur R., Chicago	105, 166
article by	313
Reynolds, Governor John, Belleville	32, 67
Rheumatism	21, 25, 33, 50, 398, 408
Richardson, B. K., Springfield	2, 243, 267
Richings, Dr. Henry, Rockford	411
Ridley, Dr. ...., on puerperal fever	65
Ringland, Dr. Geo. ...., on epidemic of dysentery	86
Robertson, Dr. John Dill, Chicago	196, 197, 370
Robison, Dr. John Albert, Chicago	175, 411
Robson, Dr. R., (Ind.)	59
Roe, Dr. Edward, Bloomington	70
Ross, Alexander	18, 59, 381
Rouse, Dr. ...., Peoria	39
Rowe, John (1838) on milk sickness	68
Rush, Dr. Benjamin, Chicago	71, 72, 73, 74
Ryan, Charles, Springfield	210

—S—

Sachs, Dr. T. B., Chicago	366
Sadler, Dr. Lena K., Chicago, committee on child hygiene	242
Sandburg, Carl	36
Sanitation, provisions relating to	132, 139, 221
stream pollution, investigations of	163, 172

426 INDEX

	PAGE
Sawyer, Amos, Hillsboro	162, 174, 210, 411
Scarlet fever	17, 33, 50, 55, 96, 136, 253, 348, 366, 383, 401
among Indians	53
annual death rates in Chicago	109
case reports	350
epidemic of in Chicago	103, 106
mortality from	351
graph on	349
Scrofula	19, 60
Scurvy	69
Searcy, Earl B., Springfield	266
Seasonal distribution of disease	89
Secretaries, State Board of Health	140, 162, 411
Senility, as a cause of death	409
Serres (1814) on typhoid fever	71
Sewerage in City of Chicago, prior to 1877	101
Schafer, Dr. G. R., Morton	411
Schackford, Dr. B. S., Decatur	258
Schermerhorn, Dr. ...., Ottawa	39
Schmidt, Dr. Louis, Chicago	272, 299
Schoolcraft	21, 22, 31
Schoolfield, Dr. ...., Joliet	39
Schussler, Dr. W. R., Orland	411
Scott, General ...., troops enroute to Black Hawk War	102
Scott, Dr. John W., Springfield	156, 162, 365, 411
Shattuck, Dr. Lemuel, (Mass.)	131
Shawneetown, survey of prior to 1877	118
Sheppard-Towner Act	200, 238
Shoemaker, Dr. S. H., Monroe County	85
Silver nitrate, distribution of vaccine	218
Singleton, Dr. ...., (Va.)	63
Skoog, Paul (Calif.)	243
Sloan, Dr. E. P., Bloomington	196, 197, 203
Small, Governor Len, Kankakee	4, 7
Smallpox	9, 21, 22, 24, 25, 26, 33, 39, 78, 105, 136, 141, 167, 194, 253, 306, 353, 363, 366, 401
and Vaccination	307
annual death rates in Chicago	111
cases of	309
deaths from	49, 50, 61
disease of Indians	49
free vaccination against	49, 156, 248, 250, 307, 401
of school children required	148
vaccine for, distributed	219
general epidemics of	156
history of epidemics in Chicago, article	313
investigation of every reported case of	202, 312
pay for field work undecided	161
prohibiting transportation of bodies dead from	150
troops immunized against	182, 188, 311
Smart, Dr. Charles ...., on typhoid fever	79
Smejkal, Dr. Edward J., Chicago	164, 265
Smith, Dr. ...., Jacksonville	38
Smith, Dr. C. R., Decatur	258
Smith, Prof. George W., Carbondale	34
Smith, Dr. Harold, Chicago, committee on child hygiene	242
Smith, Dr. Nathan, ..., on unity of fevers	73
Smith, Dr. Stephen, (New York)	105
Smith, Dr. W. R., Cairo	332
Snakebite	47, 401
Snuck, Dr. ...., Darwin	39
Social hygiene, see Venereal disease	
Sorgatz, Dr. George F.,	254

INDEX 427

PAGE

Spalding, Dr. ...., Galesburg... 64
Spalding Dr. Heman, Chicago... 315
Spanish fever (dengue).. 46
Spanish Influence, The... 27
    expedition 14
Spindel, Dr. Enos S., Springfield.. 411
Springfield, survey of prior to 1877... 115
Stahl, Dr. Daniel, Quincy...41, 86
Starkel, Dr. C. H., Belleville... 411
Standard railway sanitary code.. 226
State Board of Health, future of.. 407
    machinery 133, 136
    members of...124, 137, 411
    organized 127, 137, 404
    presidents of...146, 155, 175, 411
    secretaries of..140, 162, 411
State water survey, Urbana, to make investigations.............170, 173, 221, 246
Statistics, see mortality, vital statistics, Chicago statistics
Stearate of Zinc toilet powder...205, 214
Stermont, Dr. D. W., ...,... 279
Stevenson, Dr. Sarah Hackett, Chicago... 411
Stewart, Dr. J. T., Peoria... 85
St. Martin, Alexis... 23
Strothers (1729) on typhoid fever...71, 72
Summary and conclusion..396-411
Summer complaint... 86
Sullivan, Dr. J. C., Cairo.. 411
Survey of certain Illinois cities, prior to 1877............................101-119
    fifteen cities in Illinois.. 198
    State sanitary..147, 187, 243, 322, 370, 374
Sydenham (1661) on typhoid fever...71, 72
Syphilis...17, 21, 22, 24, 252, 256, 270, 298
    origin of... 58
Synochia (malaria) 78
Szwajkart, Dr. Adam, Chicago.. 411

—T—

Tanner, Governor John R., Springfield... 284
Tanner, Dr. F. W., Urbana... 258
Taylor, Dr. G. G., Chicago.. 268
Taylor, Dr. L. C., Springfield...63, 247, 261
Ten Brook, Dr. John, ...,... 270
Tetanus infections..65, 168, 244
Texas tick fever.. 105
Thilo, Dr. George, Oak Park..249, 411
Thompson, Dr. Samuel, Edwards County.................................40, 52, 84
Thornhill, Verna (Washington, D. C.) on dental hygiene.......................... 242
Thwaite, ...,... 32
Tillson, ...31, 35
Todd, Dr. ...., Springfield.. 38
Tornado zone, relief work in...243, 260, 263
Trachoma surveys.. 289
Traders 22
Trappers 13, 22, 24
Treacy, F. A., ...,.. 210
Trembles, Indian... 67
Tuberculosis.......................................17, 20, 36, 60, 168, 244, 252, 294
    annual death rates in Chicago... 111
    cases of, table on.. 360
    mortality from..89, 362
        graph on.. 362
    in White County, map on...371, 372

INDEX

Tuberculosis—Concluded.
  phenomenal progress in eradication of.......
  sanatoria, establishment of............ 163, 172, 179, 220, 28
Tuberculin testing of herds.................................16
Typhoid fever...
    ....5, 18, 20, 21, 31, 33, 35, 40, 44, 47, 69, 90, 118, 136, 168, 244, 2:
  and malaria ....
  attributed to contaminated oysters........................
  carriers ....
  cases and deaths from.....................................
  epidemics of..
    milk-borne and water-borne..............................
    food poisoning as a source of confusion.................
  graph on ....
  history of steps in establishment of as a specific disease.....
  investigation every reported case of......................
  phenomenal progress in eradication of.....................
  prevalence of after 1850..................................
  rules and regulations for control of......................
  troops immunized against..................................
  vaccine distributed.......................................
  see Chicago statistics
Typhus fever.................................17, 33, 35, 73, 74
  in Illinois...
  mortality in Chicago......................................

—U—

United States Public Health Service, Marine Hospital Service crea
University of Illinois, appropriations to equip and maintain water l
  State Water Survey to make investigations water supplies...
  vaccine farm established at...............................
Utesch, John W., Chicago.....................................

—V—

Vaccination against smallpox.................................
  history of epidemics of smallpox in Chicago, article......
  required of school children...............................
Vaccines, distribution of.....................148, 182, 188, 218, 2:
  farm established for propagation of.......................
Vandalia, survey of prior to 1877............................
  removal of capital from...................................
Vaughan, Dr. Victor C., (Mich.)..............................
Veatch, Dr. W. P., Roodhouse.................................
Venereal disease..   .....17, 21, 22, 24, 58, 60, 186, 253, 257, 2:
  chart on ....
  establishment of clinics..................................
Vincent, Dr. John A., Springfield............................
Vital statistics and mortality rates, all causes.............
  collection of..   ....130, 135, 1:
  decennial census reports..................................
  in Chicago................56, 51, 83, 87, 89, 90, 99, 102, 1
Vollmer, Dr. Maude, Moline...................................
Voluntary health agencies................................14, 1

—W—

Wardner, Dr. Horace, Cairo..........................124, 125, 12
  biography of..
Ware, Dr. John S., Chicago, on typhoid fever.................

INDEX

	PAGE
Wells, Dr. Walter A., (Washington, D. C.)	56
Wentworth, John, Chicago	101
Wenzel, Dr. F., Belleville	41
Wessel, Dr. P. H., Moline	411
Whistler, Dr. ...., Chicago	102
Whitehead, Dr. ...., LaSalle	39
Whitmore, Dr. J. S., Metamora	53
Whooping cough	25, 33, 252, 366, 374, 390, 402
annual death rates in Chicago	112
cases of	391
mortality and rates	391
graph on	392
Wightman, Dr. Grace Sa, Chicago	235
Wilkins, Colonel, ..., (1768)	26
Will, Dr. Conrad, Jackson County	150
Williams, Dr. Daniel H., Chicago	153, 411
Williamson, Dr. T. S., (Ohio)	21
Winter, S. G., Galesburg	258
Wolcott, Dr. Alexander, ..., on malignant fevers	102
Woodward, Dr. J. J., (Washington, D. C.)	79, 84
World war activities	182, 186, 373
social hygiene a problem	186
troops immunized against typhoid fever and smallpox	182, 188, 311
Worrell, Dr. T. F., debate on cholera	45
Worthington, Mrs. Sarah M., Sterling	31
Wright, Dr. ...., Warren County	45
Wright, Dr. John, Clinton	75

—Y—

Yates, Governor Richard, Jacksonville	167
Yellow fever	9, 46, 72, 73, 136, 157, 168, 244, 353, 363, 400
appropriation for	143, 333
epidemics of	46
inspectors at Cairo, cut of	337
map of Cairo	330
outbreak of at Cairo	32, 141, 172, 212, 327, 338
prohibiting transportation of bodies dead from	150
rules and regulations for control of	150
Young, Dr. D. W., Aurora	87
debate on cholera	45

—Z—

| Zeit, Dr. F. Robert, Chicago | 245 |
| Zeuch, Dr. Lucius H., Chicago | 15, 24, 26, 27, 32, 42, 44, 50, 53, 54, 55, 57, 68, 84, 88, 278 |

AUXILIARY HEALTH AGENCIES.

	PAGE
American Child Health Association	287
American Dental Association	288
Aesculapian Society of Wabash Valley	74, 130, 279, 404
American Medical Association	262, 397
American Public Health Association	130, 131, 171, 287
American Red Cross	291, 313
American Society for Control of Cancer	298
Carnegie Foundation	251
Chicago Dental Society	200, 243
Chicago Heart Association	296
Chicago Infant Welfare Society	301
Chicago League for Hard of Hearing	296
Chicago Medical Society	40, 103, 288, 301, 366, 405
Chicago Tuberculosis Institute	290, 368, 405
Children's Bureau	287
Children's Hospital and Milk Commission	300
Conference of State and Provincial Health Authorities	171
Illinois Council Parent-Teacher Associations	200, 242
Illinois Dental Society	200, 240, 242
Illinois Federation of Women's Clubs	200, 201, 240, 242, 288, 289
Illinois Health Society	303
Illinois Medical Society, Transactions	39, 44, 47, 54, 55, 57, 63, 65, 69, 74, 76, 81, 85, 87, 130, 159, 200, 240, 242, 279, 280, 283, 287, 288, 289, 293, 397, 404
Illinois Social Hygiene League	298
Illinois Society for Crippled Children	235, 380
Illinois Society for Mental Hygiene	297
Illinois Society for Prevention of Blindness	289
Illinois Tuberculosis and Health Association	220, 293, 303, 373
Industrial and practicing physicians	297
International Health Board	287
Jersey County Medical Society	130, 132, 280
Laboratories and Universities	296
Lawrenceville Aesculapian Society	130, 397
Elizabeth McCormick Memorial Foundation	302
National Board of Health	139, 143
National Educational Association	287
National Health Board	383
National Safety Council	295
National Tuberculosis Association	287
Parent-Teacher Associations	295
State and local dental societies	296
State Board of Health Auxiliary Sanitary Association	245, 247, 249
State Health Society	296

REFERENCES AND BIBLIOGRAPHY

	PAGE
Army Statistical Reports	64
Bloomington Intelligencer	45
British Research Council, Savage and White	81
Bulletin Society Medical History of Chicago, 1912	105
Buffalo Medical Journal, Flint	78
Bureau of Ethnology, Bulletins 30, 34, Hrdlicka	17, 18, 19, 26, 49, 53, 55, 58, 60
Cairo Bulletin	46
Centennial Survey of the State of Public Hygiene in America	244
Chicago and the Old North West, Quaife	102
Chicago Health Department Report	43, 49, 50, 54, 56, 87
Chicago Inter-Ocean	280
Chicago Medical Examiner, Veatch	79
Classical Work on Fevers, Bartlett	43
Committee on Practical Medicine	40, 44, 46, 47, 52, 57, 61, 63, 66, 67, 70, 76, 84, 85, 86
Continued Fevers, Murchison	71
Epidemiology and Public Health, Vaughan	79
Egyptian Republican	45, 50
Handbook of Geographic and Historical Pathology, Hirsch	43, 50, 55, 56, 63, 71
Health News (State Medicine) (Bulletin)	169, 177, 192, 266, 267
Historic Illinois, Parrish	44, 53
History of Alabama, Pickett	13
History of Continued Fevers, Bartlett	73, 77
History of Illinois and Her People, Smith	34
History of Indian Tribes of United States, 1857, Schoolcraft	22
History of Morgan County, Short	45
History of Practice of Medicine, Zeuch	15, 24, 26, 32, 42, 44, 50, 53, 54, 61, 67, 68, 84, 88, 278
Illini, A Story of the Prairies, Carr	43
Illinois & Indiana Medical & Surgical Journal	52, 75, 78, 279
Illinois as It Is, Gerhard	61
Illinois Historical Collection, Alvord Carter	26
Illinois Historical Library Publications	31, 43, 118
Lectures on the Principles and Practice of Medicine, Davis	338
Life of Lincoln, Sanburg	36
London Lancet	78, 153
Lyon Medical, 1912, Gandolphe	59
Medical and Surgical History of the War of the Rebellion, Smart	79, 84
Medical Repository of Original Essays	63
Military Surgeon	84
Military Tract Medical Society, Egan	78
Monmouth Atlas	46
Morgan's Journal	26
My Own Times, Reynolds	32
New Orleans Medical & Surgical Journal	58
New York Journal of Medicine	64
New York Medical Board	339
New York Medical Journal and Record	19, 70
New York Medical & Surgical Journal	58
North American Indians, Catlin	49
Northwestern Medical & Surgical Journal	74
Philadelphia Medical & Surgical Reports	57
Pictures of Illinois, 100 years ago	118
Pioneer Health Conditions	36
Pioneer History of Illinois, Reynolds	67
Pioneer Mothers in Illinois, Worthington	31
Practice of Medicine, Anders	76
Practical Treatise on Enteric Fever	70
Reminiscences of a Pioneer Woman, Tillson	31, 35
Report on Practical Medicine	40, 44, 46, 47, 52, 57, 61, 63, 66, 69, 70, 76, 84, 85, 86
Sanitarian (1880)	339
Sanitary History of Chicago, Rauch	102
Sanitary Investigations of the Illinois River and Tributaries	222

	PAGE
Settlement of Illinois, The	30
Sixty Years in Medical Harness. Johnson	42, 55, 80, 82
Springfield Journal (1852)	45
St. Louis Medical and Surgical Journal (1849)	40, 85
Systematic Treatise on Diseases of the Interior Valley of North America, Drake	38, 47, 49, 52, 53, 54, 60, 64, 84
Transactions, American Medical Association	75, 78, 79
Transactions, Illinois Medical Society	39, 44, 47, 54, 55, 57, 63, 65, 67, 74, 76, 81, 85, 87
Western Medical and Physicians Journal	39, 52, 63, 64, 70, 73, 76, 86, 397

CPSIA information can be obtained
at www.ICGtesting.com
Printed in the USA
BVHW04s1037080718
521071BV00014B/147/P